A Year in the Life of Bottle the Curmudgeon, Bottle of Beef Book 1, by Paul Tompkins

What you are about to read is the book of the blog of the Facebook project I started when my dad died in 2019. It also happens to be many more things: a diary, a commentary on contemporaneous events, a series of stories, lectures, and diatribes on politics, religion, art, business, philosophy, and pop culture, all in the mostly daily publishing of 365 essays, ostensibly about an album, but really just what spewed from my brain while listening to an album. I finished the last essay on June 19, 2020 and began putting it into book from. The hyperlinked but typo rich version of these essays is available at:

https://albumsforeternity.blogspot.com/

Thank you for reading, I hope you find it enjoyable, possibly even entertaining.
Warning, if you find something in this book offensive or insulting, please remember that these are my merely my thoughts. You aren't required to agree or do anything just because I wrote them down. It'd be a scary old world if we actually did all the things our brains dream up, wouldn't it?

Typeset using 11pt Palatino, in case you wanted to know.

© Paul Tompkins 2020, All rights reserved.

Welcome to my record collection.

This is a book about my love of listening to albums. It started off as a nightly perusal of my dad's record collection (which sadly became mine) on my personal Facebook page. Over the ensuing months it became quite an enjoyable process of simply ranting about what I think is a real art form, the album. It exists in three forms: nightly posts on Facebook, a chronologically maintained blog that is still ongoing (though less frequent), and now this book.

Some of my reviews are positive, some negative, some have barely anything to do with the album at hand. They might not be what you expect from album reviews, but I hope you at least find the good ones entertaining. They tend to be train of thought reactions rather than calculated essays; some are heavily researched, some are completely off the top of my head. If nothing else, know that I'm really listening to them and whether they are amazing or abysmal I want you to go listen to them too if you ever get the chance. There are no photos of the covers, but presumably you can find them online. They are meant to be read one day at a time with the actual album, but I won't tell if you just enjoy a good binge read (wink, wink).

P.S. I call myself Bottle, because it's funny.

1) Spirit – Twelve Dreams of Dr. Sardonicus

    I debated heavily how to start our journey. Should we go right for the good stuff? Or, should we kick it off with pure shock? Nah, let's start with the mildly obscure 4th album by my favorite psych-rock band, Spirit. Hey, if Hendrix gave you the nickname "Randy California" you can't be too bad. Give it a listen, I think you'll be pleasantly surprised. Interesting fact, the track list on the back of the jacket is completely out of order.

2) Plastic Ono Band - Live Peace in Toronto, 1969

    That fourth album by Spirit (a band we'll hear at least a couple more times) was such a treat that we must unfortunately suffer today. Side A is pretty much a bunch of talented musicians playing for fun with no real rehearsal time. Side B however, is a special treat. Remember, the only rule on this bus is: listen to the whole album. Hating it is just as good as loving it, and if you want Lennon and Clapton jamming together, you're gonna get Ono bleating like a goat having an epileptic seizure "all over you" for an encore. Why? Because Johnny Boy didn't give a damn whether you liked it or not.

    Now sit down, shut up, and listen to the first ever performance by The Plastic Ono Band - Live Peace in Toronto 1969. If those poor unsuspecting Canadians could handle it and clap, so can you.

    I promise the next one will be less mentally taxing.

3) The Beach Boys - Surfin' Safari

I just couldn't send you off to beddy-bye with plastic Ono nightmares (I'm not a complete monster), so here's a palette cleanser: the first Beach Boys album, Surfin' Safari. Tomorrow we'll head back to prog-rock town, but no hints or spoilers.

I'll also tell you that I'm using a very cheap, plastic USB turntable called the ion iTTUSB. The turntable may be cheap, but it has an adjustable counterweight and the phono preamp and DAC on it are pretty decent. It really is running straight from USB into my computer and out to my headphones with perfect RIAA EQ, and no artifacts or strangely distorted effects. It's almost certainly discontinued by now.

4) Procol Harum - A Salty Dog

Tonight, we're listening to A Salty Dog, by Procol Harum. It's got Folk, Blues, strings, horns, and one of the most red-velvet cake lead guitar tones I've ever heard. I mean it, you can practically taste the cream cheese frosting on Robin Trower's guitar doodles. I'm partial to Side B, but it's an enjoyable listen from start to finish. Go check it out while I decide what to throw at you tomorrow night.

5) Emerson, Lake, & Palmer - Tarkus

So, I know *about* Emerson, Lake, & Palmer, but I've only ever heard a handful of tracks. Let's change that.

Here's Tarkus, the sophomore album that nearly drove them apart, and took a long time to win over its audience. But, look at that album art! Side A is a 7-part suite about semi-mythical creatures portrayed in the titles and artwork, the protagonist gets stabbed in the eye and runs off into the water; it's everything I've ever tried to construct, and I haven't even heard it before tonight. It is Prog personified, with wacky organs and synths, badass guitar solos, and occasional singing.

Side B is "some other stuff," and that's cool too. I generally sneer when people say things like "why didn't I find this sooner?", but for me it's because I listen to anything all the time. I'll never get to hear everything, but I try to make a dent.

This is a great album, and it's earned a spot on my "listen to this 300 more times shelf" next to Spirit and Procal Harum. Definitely go check it out when you get a chance.

6) Fever Tree – Creation

My original plan was to just do one album each night (unless the first one was somehow unsatisfying), but tonight's choice of Tarkus was based on cool cover art for an album I've never heard before, and since there's 2 rum and coke's for every can, I'm more than happy to say this is an awesome cover for a band I never even knew existed (which for me is saying something). I hope I'm not disappointed...

... and the answer is "yes and no." The band is quite good and I want to hear their other 3 albums, but this album shows some definite disadvantages holding them back.

In no particular order:

- They can't seem to decide if they are pop-folk or blues-rock, which wouldn't be bad if they were recognizably the same band in both genres.

- The band is primarily a front for the producers/songwriters, and you can tell. There's a little something that just comes across as manufactured in every track. Like, a lyric that doesn't sound right, or a clearly contrived string arrangement. It genuinely sounds like Scott and Vivian Holtzman were workhorsedly imitating a particular band or song that was already popular, but they weren't creative enough to really do it right.

- There's no stylistic coherence to this album at all. One moment they sound like real contemporary rockers Steppenwolf or Iron Butterfly (both bands we'll hear a lot in the near future), the next they are singing a faux Neil Diamond ballad, then there's Spanish guitar and trumpet, and tempo/meter shifts for no musically relevant reason.

So, to recap, if I just randomly picked any track from this album I'd say "that's really interesting," but when you smash them all together, I think "is this a compilation album of the singer's session work?"

Oh well, it's certainly not the first time a cool cover left me feeling underwhelmed, but I definitely wouldn't call any particular track terrible. We'll give it a good solid "meh." At the very least, I had a lot to say about it, and that should count for something.

7) Steppenwolf - Monster

Speaking of Steppenwolf, let's listen to Monster (a good version of the negative comments I had about Fever Tree). I dare you to find a more relevant statement about our present-day country than the title track suite of 3 connected songs, AND THAT WAS 50 YEARS AGO!

I love this album, and it's one that I constantly listened to on my dad's gigantic record cabinet (it's got the skips to prove it). That guitar solo on Draft Resister, the spastic piano/guitar duet that is Fag, and real female background singers!

Every track is an anthem for the people, a reminder that whatever narrative you've been fed is simply untrue, a plea for basic human compassion and consideration, and the cover art is sideways!!!

This is an album worth having in your head while going to sleep. Goodnight everybody.

8) Joni Mitchell - Ladies of the Canyon

Let's go in a completely different direction and listen to Joni Mitchell's Ladies Of The Canyon (that's the one with "Big Yellow Taxi" and "Woodstock").

I don't really have anything specific to say about her. Maybe that's because she is an expert songwriter; her songs are perfectly constructed pop-folk. You might not like certain aspects of her vocal stylings, her tendency to blatantly ignore important punctuation in her vocal phrasing, or the way she avoids resolving leading tones directly, but it's impossible to pretend that she does it by accident: she knows exactly what she's doing, and you either like it or you don't.

This album also has some of the coolest sounding vocal overdubs. I'm not a fan of alternating guitar and piano accompaniment (similar to my criticism of Fever Tree), because it makes the song order sound perfunctory and directionless, but since this album is clearly a collection of vignettes rather than a story, that argument is moot. I do, however, agree with most critics that Side B is much stronger (dare I say better?) than Side A.

Did I mention "Big Yellow Taxi"? Yeah, that's from this album. It might be the only song in existence that uses triangle as the primary accompaniment for the chorus, and it's one of the best songs ever written (lyrically, thematically, structurally, etc.).

Non-sequiter: I never cared before now, but it really is true that the last song on each side is garbage as far as audio quality is concerned. 17-18 minutes seems to be a good stopping point. Anywho, enjoy.

9) Pharoah Sanders - Jewels of Thought

There are so many ways I could go about choosing the next record in a collection this big and varied, so many paths I could travel, but I've never heard Pharoah Sanders.

This is essentially African free jazz (lots of traditional African instruments), and I love that the album notes tell you which musicians are playing on the left and right channels.

And let me tell you, that central solo on Hum-Allah... is the craziest thing I've heard by anyone who isn't John Zorn (who incidentally was only 13 at the time of this recording). Sun in Aquarius Part 1 is a beautiful chaos that gives way to some equally beautiful nonsense inside a piano, then builds back to a relentless cacophony of everything before the break (no surprise I love it).

Part 2 picks back up just before another wicked banshee tirade and somehow seamlessly morphs back to straight jazz.

I really love the use of voice as an ululating instrument, full solo halfway through Side B, with an imitative bass duet right after, before all hell breaks loose again. Really cool stuff.

10) John Mayall - Blues from Laurel Canyon

It occurred to me today that it would be interesting to compare Joni Mitchell's Ladies of the Canyon with John Mayall's Blues from Laurel Canyon. They are both about the same part of LA at pretty much the same time. Mitchell is of course the local, speaking about characters from a folk perspective, while Mayall is the outsider on vacation singing the blues.

Her songs are about relationships, his is the real result of a breakup (disbanding the Bluesbreakers). Her's are minimal, voice and self accompaniment, his is a newly formed 4-piece band. Her's is happening in the present, his is a recollection.

Both however share a sense of loneliness in a place so full of people. A feeling that something is missing, that people walk in and out of your life because we *are* essentially alone.

My dad loved John Mayall (he told me so, and there's a whole fistful of records here to prove it), and well into Side B I'm starting to get why. There's nothing stale, reworked, or trite about the tracks as they unfold; it's all blues, but of infinite variety and nuance. He never recycles or rehashes an idea, he just keeps moving steadily forward and deals with whatever life throws in his path.

Whether I want to or not, I have to listen to Canned Heat next, because the lyric in "The Bear" is too important to ignore:

"All the men of Canned Heat are part of my family. I'm gonna remember the things that they did for me." Tomorrow.

10) Canned Heat - Hallelujah

I promised you Canned Heat, and I never renege. Here's Hallelujah, the album they released just before Woodstock. They were the wacky, wily, white boys playing blues every night on Sunset Boulevard.

Somebody narced on us and we wound up in jail? Sell some song rights for bail money. Zappa kicked you out for smoking pot? Ok, come play with us! Lease our own club and invite everybody to play? That's a great idea!

Mayall wasn't lying, "The Bear" and crew were pretty much the center of attention, and hanging out with them was seemingly an instant career boost in the late 60s. Bob Hite and Alan Wilson trade off vocal duties, and they couldn't be more different: Hite is pure rowdy roadhouse, but Wilson lives over in Grateful Dead territory. This is not a concept album, it's just good old-fashioned workhorse blues-rock of its day. There's some really raunchy guitar work, screaming harmonica, studio experimentation, and even some upright bass. They can be goofy, or play it dead straight, but it's fun either way. I think this is the only album I have by them on vinyl, but I'd love to find a few more. I'll probably listen to more albums tonight, but I haven't decided which yet. 'Til then, cheers.

11) 3 More Albums from the 28th of September

Ok, I've decided. It's Blood, Sweat & Tears (with Satie, without an oxford comma). Why? Because Jim Fielder was a Mother of Invention before he bled, sweat, and cried through the constant cycle of lead singer auditions the band went through until he quit to do session work.

BS&T is their sophomore album, mostly written by Al Kooper, but realized by David Clayton-Thomas (and you know the first 2 songs of Side B even if you didn't know it was them). BS&T is a lot like Joni Mitchell, in that you either like them or you don't because they are exactly what they want to be: a rock solid band (pun intended) with a brass/wind section that didn't really care about genres or image or any of that stuff. They made whatever music came out of their instruments and it was pretty enjoyable.

If you're a real Grammy buff, you'll know exactly what record I'm going to listen to next. Go ahead, try to guess without looking it up...

Yes, BS&T won album of the year over Abbey Road (and the seemingly random choice of album I'll listen to after it).

The Beatles were basically done at this point. They had one more album already mostly recorded, but John was off playing with Ono, and Paul was about to be imaginarily dead.

People didn't really like this album, then slowly realized they were wrong, then pretended like they weren't dumb and said "I always thought it was great."

So now, as I bring us around to the close of one Markov chain of musical associations and consider where I'll go next, I want to make a couple points.

First, I'd like to think that my seemingly random perusal of my dad's record collection is starting to show you that everything is actually connected in multiple ways. The way I talk about one album points to the others in various ways that I didn't actually predict, and is so completely autobiographical that you could never fully understand it. I had the idea that this process might make an interesting book (and you're not gonna believe me, but you're reading it right now).

Second, this is obviously a personal and sentimental journey that I'm sharing with you, but we can't ignore the octopus in the room. These are 30/40/50 year old pieces of plastic that were a big part of my dad's life, and an equally big part of my childhood and my identity. Considering I'm listening to first or second runs of most of this music in its original form, the replacement value is incalculable, they are irreplaceable, and I don't mind telling you I'm getting a little teary at how relevant this album is turning out to be at this exact moment.

Third, I've only scratched the surface in the last week, and this cleverly concealed listen to Abbey Road as the penultimate record of the week closes the "loss" portion of our journey.

One more record to go. You already know it's connected to the others by losing its nomination for a Grammy to BS&T, but I think you'll be pleasantly surprised at how non sequitur it really is.

I told you it would be off the wall, but at the risk of sounding cheesy, it is time for me to "let the sunshine in." It's The Age of Aquarius, by the 5th Dimension.

I know I appear to be spastic, unpredictable, occasionally crass and moody (there I go using words that I know will be meaningful, but you don't), but that's because you aren't inside my head. The connections are there if you look and listen hard enough (like that iconic bass line from Cream), I'm just not very good at cataloging or explaining all of them.

You can't be sad listening to this album. It's simply not possible. The 5th Dimension are awesome, and just when you least expect it, I'll bring them back again and you'll smile because now you're in on it. Unless you forget. Don't forget.

12) Men At Work - Business As Usual

I'm just beginning to sort the stacks into crates, and there's only one New Wave album in the collection. All creatures great and small, of course it is. Men at Work's debut album was the first Australian album to really get popular in America, and how could it not? You can be mad at me for saying it, but it's a better album than a few by The Cars or The Police. Colin Hay is definitely on par with Ric Ocasek in both the songwriting and quirky personality departments. And don't be fooled, he's got some Andy Summers level guitar chops to boot. Go give it a listen. You'll feel pretty good afterward.

13) Beacon Street Union - The clown died in Marvin Gardens

I could play anything from the numerous bands and artists I've mentioned already, but I'm having more fun exploring things I've never heard.

I think it's completely fair to call Beacon Street Union obscure. They only made 3 albums and this is the second. I don't pretend to know why they reused the same dead clown as The Doors did a year before, or why they do an Elvis impersonation in the middle of Side A, but I do know that everything else is pretty great. The guitar doodles on "a not very august afternoon" are really enjoyable, and they use their orchestral backing in creative ways.

I don't have anything to suggest for comparison, they are pretty unique like most of the psychedelic bands of the time. I wouldn't call them groundbreaking or essential, but they make some pretty good music for zoning out and wobbling your head back and forth. I was a little apprehensive about the 16-minute "baby please don't go," and while it's no Inna-Gadda-Da-Vita it does have some great jam sections broken up by the vocal refrain (which you may or may not find quite annoying).

All in all, it's a pretty good album except for the cover of "Blue Suede Shoes." Whatever reason they had for including it is completely lost on me.

14) Lighthouse - One Fine Morning

Stop whatever you're doing and go listen to this album. The whole thing. Don't argue, just do it. If you haven't noticed, my dad liked *full* bands (strings, horns, winds, keyboards, guitars, drums/percussion), and there's plenty more in our future.

Sure, this is straight up 70s Canadian pop/jazz-rock, but it's soooo good! How are they not better known? Every arrangement was done by the band themselves, instead of by some becubicled "producer." They list their "road crew" with the band members for crying out loud. Top notch.

15) Mothers of Invention - We're Only In It for the Money

I've postponed it as long as possible, but you were going to find out about the original Mothers of Invention albums in my collection eventually, so let's listen to "We're only in it for the money."

I must admit my special love of this particular album, because the whole reason it exists is to say "what's going on [in the world right now] is really stupid." The cover and gatefold photos are switched, because record labels are dumb (mine most definitely included). Zappa even called McCartney to ask permission, but lawyers and stuff.

Zappa didn't like either end of the socio-political spectrum, and as I mentioned a few albums ago, today isn't any different than the late 60s (because we basically just ignored those actual problems for 50 years). Go ahead, try to not find it relevant....

16) Julie Driscoll with Brian Auger & The Trinity - Streetnoise

It's Streetnoise by Julie Driscoll/Brian Auger and the Trinity. 4 sides of 4 tracks from 4 people doing whatever they felt like doing. Driscoll's voice doesn't have a "timid" setting and it's hard to not notice the sheer badassery of Auger's organ playing. It's a complete fusion of rock, jazz, neo-modality, and a hint of gospel/funk, so much so that it's almost impossible to categorize what you're hearing, or predict where it will go next.

I've got more records from both artists, and now I won't hesitate to give them a spin as soon as they rise to the top of the stack.

17) Original Cast Recording of Hair

So many musicals. Let's listen to the original cast recording of Hair. Diane Keaton was in it. I know, I know, it's no secret that I've been sneaking in cover versions of its most well-known songs, so we might as well go back to the source.

This musical was pretty radical for its time, and given our continued state of societal hypersensitivity you might find it equally uncomfortable. It's also not really a musical that works well in album form, but that's a silly thing to get hung up on.

18) Rotary Connection

So, this one time in 1968, some record execs thought "wouldn't it be great if we could find a way to make money off Muddy Waters and Howlin' Wolf again?" Obviously, they would need some hip youngsters as the backup band, because the psychedelic scene was the thing....

Here's the debut album that won Rotary Connection those gigs. I think technically it's Psychedelic Soul, but I'd file it under the "what the hell am I listening to" section (a compliment in my book). Strings, brass, sitar, harp, choir, pretty sure there's both an actual theremin and a vocal imitation of a theremin in there, alongside the normal guitar/bass/drums. There's a spectacularly bizarre cover of just the chorus from "Like a Rolling Stone," and had Isaac Hayes considered the unique contributions an electric harpsichord could make when helping to write the eternal classic "Soul

Man," well let's just say the world would be a completely different place.

Rotary Connection's material was lost in the 2008 Universal fire, but I have 2 of their records, so we'll hear from them again at some point. Most bands from the psychedelic era sound like they are sympathetic to the experience while remaining in full control of their mental and physical faculties. Not so here. These people sound completely out of their minds, and if you need proof listen to their insane Gregorian chant/Partridge Family rendition of Jagger and Richards' "Ruby Tuesday."

The whole album is concluded by sporadically sampling itself, and I'm half tempted to listen to the whole thing again just to make sure I didn't fall asleep and imagine it.

P.S. for the record, I like Electric Mud, but I haven't heard that Howlin' Wolf album so no comment.

19) Iron Butterfly - Inna-Gadda-Da-Vita

I've teased it enough, tonight it's Iron Butterfly. Obviously Side B is the main attraction, but despite their somewhat lightweight lyrics the songs on Side A are pretty awesome. Nasty fuzz, overdriven organ, and some of the best bass lines ever, they flat out rock. Heavy, indeed. I haven't listened to the full Inna-Gadda-Da-Vita in ages, but 17 minutes goes by *snap* like that. We'll hear Iron Butterfly again and again and again whenever I finally get around to repeating bands (it'll be a while), but for now all you need to do is close your eyes, bang your head, and enjoy.

20) Jefferson Starship - Blows Against the Empire

Tonight, we're listening to Blows Against the Empire. If you're at all familiar with the complicated Jefferson [flying ship] history, this is the first mention of "Starship" but not actually the official band. It's various combinations of Jefferson Airplane, The Grateful Dead, Santana, and Crosby, Stills, & Nash all playing Paul Kantner's concept album about stealing a spaceship and getting the hell off this jerk of a planet.

Lyrically it's a multi-layered autobiographical science fiction metaphor about the band breaking up, Paul and Grace having a baby, and 60s/70s US politics. Musically, it's a free form psychedelic folk-rock extravaganza that quite frankly makes Radiohead's Ok Computer sound like fan art (there's either some definite influence or magical coincidence going on is all I'm saying).

The mash up of folk, blues, and noise rock is pretty enjoyable in my book and there is some really nice instrumental noodling scattered throughout. It's not obnoxious or cheesy like Starship eventually became in the 80s. Definitely check it out if you've never heard it before.

21) Vanilla Fudge - Near the Beginning

What do Styx, Yes, Deep Purple, and Led Zeppelin all have in common? They share a common influence, of course. It might boggle your mind a little to think that Led Zeppelin had to "open" for another headliner before people really started to like them, but they paid their dues in the states by warming up the crowd for Vanilla Fudge.

Known for taking popular songs and jamming/soloing all over them, and generally assumed to be managed by the mob, these guys don't suck. Don't get me wrong, they are weird and they won't hesitate to just stop mid-song for some nightmare inspired noise foolery, but they do objectively rock.

Near the Beginning is actually their 4th album (so they're not exactly telling the truth, capiche?), but it continues my current infatuation with organ-based rock, and contains yet another full-side piece called "Break Song" on Side B (recorded live in concert). If you like serious blues inspired guitar mangling, bassists who use fuzz pedals, and self-indulgent organ solos, you will not be at all disappointed.

22) The Moody Blues - Every Good Boy Deserves Favour

Speaking of strange noises, let's listen to Every Good Boy Deserves Five Hundred Thousand Dollars, I mean Favour. Hello, Mellotron. I don't have any particular reason for choosing this album over the others in the collection, but it has some nice music on it.

For me, the Moody Blues have always been ignorably good; they aren't as flashy as their contemporaries, but they don't really qualify as soft rock either. They aren't afraid to chase whatever proggy neo-classical daydream any band member had that day, but they never go completely free form and every song sounds well structured, however SQUIRREL! its sections or transitions appear.

Did I mention the Mellotron? You know what it is? They're moody and they're blue, and I guess that's the kind of truth in advertising you don't get from most bands. Every song sounds like it's playing during the closing credits of a film you don't actually remember watching, but here you are in a theater thinking "yeah, I guess that sums it up pretty well." I literally just listened to it, and it's already evaporated into my brain like an eerily calm nostalgic fog. That could just be me, but I suspect a lot of people have a similar experience with their music, and walk away not knowing for sure which character on the cover they are (old man or child).

23) Seals & Crofts - I & II

I went and opened my big mouth and said "soft rock." No, no, I said it. I'm a big boy. I can handle the first two Seals & Crofts albums back-to-back.

Actually, this Warner Brothers repressing was a good thing. Those albums were both out of print, but the duo was mid-career. If you're really investing in a group it makes sense to acquire their back catalog and make it available to new fans. It's also interesting because the first album is 90% Seals, while the second album is about 50/50, 60/40 at the worst.

Obviously, I'm a fan of the harder stuff, but you know me well enough by now to realize that I find immense pleasure in simply understanding something, making connections no one else has noticed, playing with ideas, and saying "I like it" to a group of people who thought I would hate it.

If you thought The Moody Blues were squirrely, then James Seals is about to take you to school for show and tell. His songs are abstractly "folk rock" but he writes whatever music he wants to write. I hear all sorts of other bands like the Beatles and Meat Puppets and faint whiffs of Supertramp on the second album (chronological time isn't important), and he certainly wasn't at all afraid to experiment with vocal effects and delivery. I also can't neglect to mention the strange effect produced by juxtaposing the baroque flavor of Crofts' melodic mandolin playing with the decidedly romantic orchestrations by Bill Holman.

After which Dash Crofts said "ok, that was fine, but it's just not groovy enough. No, no, we won't go full funk, but let's crank it up two or three notches at least. A little bit of electric blues isn't gonna kill you. You might even sound like you're having fun, wink wink. Sure, obviously, you write all the lyrics and we'll have a couple slow tunes; I just need a little more swing and rhythm, you know?"

That's the real difference. The first album is a serious songwriter making his occasionally strange "art," but for the second album his friend said "take the stick out of your ass," and it totally worked. The second album is not necessarily happier, but it's definitely more fun.

And a "1, 2, 3, country!"

Actually, I'm surprised the last song on the second album isn't a bigger hit today. "Leave" is pretty awesome with a couple great guitar solos. It's the best mash up of classic soft rock and blues I've ever heard.

24) Creedence Clearwater Revival - Green River

If you don't like CCR then I can't help you. John Fogerty and friends are the blues-rock standard, and Green River is their best album. You're allowed to like other things, but you can't legitimately deny that every single song on this 9-track record is a hit. There isn't a single filler track on the whole album. It is its own "best of CCR" album.

There's always been a lot of negative press about Fogerty's "writing" and ego, but there's a fundamental difference between "composing music" and "writing a song." Writing a song has very little to do with the specific notes a musician plays, and every great song is technically an improvised orchestration. You can play pretty much whatever you want so long as you are "playing the song." That's what jazz as a genre is, and that's what Creedence Clearwater Revival does with John Fogerty's songs. A different group of people would have played their parts differently, but the songs would still be the same. This group of people just happened to do it perfect.

25) The Band

After a couple false starts (albums I just wasn't in the mood to enjoy), I settled on the self titled sophomore album by The Band (their first album was born in Dylan's Basement Tapes) because I giggle a little when I think about "the brown album."

Some people make the argument that this is actually a concept album, and I think I agree. It's quite a bit like Ladies of the Valley and Blues from Laurel Canyon in that the songs are about actual characters, but they are fictional. Mayall and

Mitchell were writing about their impressions of real people and a real place. The Band though, is imagining a whole world, much the same way Fogerty was pretending that his native California was actually a swamp. Before the band became The Band they were literally "the band" that supported big name artists (and actually changed Bob Dylan's writing style by simply touring with and living near him), and I would argue that simply acknowledging that persona *is* the actual concept of the "Americana" genre.

The Brown Album (tee hee) is itself a melting pot of the characters, landscapes, and nostalgia that define our memories and sense of home. The mash of blues, country, boogie, and ballad on this album don't seem as squirrelly as the last few because that kind of "everything influences everything" is the core of the world they live in.

It would be easy to compare them to the Grateful Dead (because the sonic similarities are obvious), but I think there's also a real difference you can hear. The Grateful Dead sound this way because they live inside the world that The Band is describing.

The concept of this album is "American Nostalgia." I think that's what affected Dylan the most; up until this point he had been the champion of whatever people he focused his attention on, but after his tour with The Band he started to see the value of describing why they simultaneously acknowledge the benefits of progress yet long to return to the lives and experiences that that progress takes away. It's also the album with "Up on Cripple Creek" on it, and I don't know why but I fucking love that song.

26) Michael Jackson - Thriller

This might be the most complicated album review I've done so far because this is a complicated album. Let me get a few unorganized thoughts out there before I try to stitch them back together into some sort of coherent perspective.

I hate this album as an album. Whether you agree with me or not, this is a terrible album. That's strange, because the majority of the songs are great. I completely separate an artist's personal life from their art: great people can make terrible music and terrible people can make amazing music and I don't think you necessarily have to be consistent in what you do or don't like. Music doesn't have morality or ethics or embarrassment or any of that stuff. People are the way they are because the world they live in forces them to behave in particular ways and "civilized society" is a compromise between individual desires and the general good. Ok, enough vagueness.

There is an EP appropriately called "Thriller" hiding in this hyperbolic dog turd of an album, but it's so squashed and manipulated by the big business of raking in billions of dollars on the juggernaut that was Michael Jackson that it's hard to hear properly.

Every album is actually a concept album (that's the difference between an album and a generic set list), and it's super frustrating when someone ruins it.

Thriller proper is Wanna Be Startin' Something, Thriller, Beat It, and Billie Jean (not necessarily in that order). It's a suitably complicated narrative about fictional Michael courting Billie Jean. That's it, and it's a work of genius, regardless of whether or not you like Michael Jackson or any of his music.

The other songs on this album ruin it. If they were a separate album I wouldn't mind at all, but here they are making me nauseous and detracting from a real masterpiece of recorded music.

You have to remember, this is one of the most ludicrously expensive records ever produced. This isn't just Quincy Jones or Epic looking to make a few hits, this is CBS saying Michael Jackson will now be the King of Pop, because we own him and we aren't going to let anyone else even come close. That's why those other songs are there and noticeably cringe worthy. That's why there's a childishly misogynistic duet with Paul McCartney, and boring old breathy Michael singing "girl, I love you" in various ways.

The relationship in Bottle presents Michael Jackson's actual Thriller is complex and realistic. Michael puts on his bravado jacket and tries to woo Billie Jean, not realizing she's actually highly manipulative and about to make his life an ironic nightmare. That's a damned good EP in my opinion.

But instead, this album becomes an entirely different story as a whole. It's now the struggle between the artist and his corporate overlords, and it makes me feel so sorry for the real-life tragedy of Michael Jackson. His job was to be alone in his imaginary childhood amusement park going noticeably insane because the people who managed his life knew how to make a shitload of money off of it (dog turd, remember). That wasn't enjoyable to watch on TV, now was it?

Anyway, sorry to ruin your Saturday morning cartoons and cereal. If I had four hundred billion dollars I'd have Bottle of Beef publish the real 4-song genius masterpiece that is Thriller, but I don't so you'll just have to collect and arrange them for yourself. Have a good weekend, or try to at least.

27) Michael Brown - Alarums & Excursions

This evening, for your entertainment, I present a truly obscure album.

Michael Brown was a pretty interesting dude. He's categorized as folk (what else can you call it I guess), but he was a cabaret composer through and through. He spent a year writing songs and music for every show put on by the first real American impresario, Julius Monk. He also produced in-house musicals for major corporations, and wrote children's books, and all sorts of other stuff. He and his wife Joy were the ones who gave Harper Lee a full year's salary to write whatever she wanted (To Kill A Mockingbird) as a Christmas present 'cause he happened to also be friends with Truman Capote.

He's the kind of silly and saucy I like, and he had a genuine fascination with infamous historical figures. This album is heavily banjo oriented, but it matches his persona perfectly. If nothing else, it's an interesting diversion from the dreary pre-winter Saturday happening outside right now.

28) Supertramp - Breakfast in America

I somewhat casually threw out the idea that all albums are concept albums, and I think I need to flesh out what I'm really talking about. I'll use a record from my own collection (obviously I'm slowly adding all of these albums to "my" collection, but I assume you know the difference).

The phrase "concept album" is popularly used to describe an album that intentionally tells a story or grapples with a main theme; like a novel, or an explicit series of paintings, or a film. I argue that every album has a concept, but that concept isn't necessarily the title, or artwork, or even the songs. The concept is what created the album in the first place, the collective idea that changed the internal desire to make and record music into a real physical object. All of my reviews try to get at that underlying concept in some way.

The most basic and boring is obviously "here are some songs we recorded recently." Next would be live albums that try to capture a moment in time, showcase the living band at what we think is their peak, or are themselves an intended spectacle. Quite often, we don't connect with this concept; we don't "get it" because it is too wrapped up in real life.

Sometimes, the album you thought you were making turns out to be completely different, and tells a much more complicated story. I think that's what happened with Thriller and the band Fever Tree.

The original concept for Supertramp's Breakfast in America was the diametrically opposed life philosophies of Rick Davies and Roger Hodgeson, but it morphed into their common concepts of what is and is not fun. Home life is not fun, but touring around foreign countries playing music sure is. They didn't plan it, the making of the album did it all on its own. That same magical melding of coincidences is what I try to aim for whenever I motivate myself to slap another p(nmi)t album together.

Lots of people confuse this album for an American satire, which it certainly is not. The caricature of the US that we receive isn't about us at all. It's the notion of going off on an adventure to a place we only know about in our imagination, and it's no different than CCR, or The Band, or George Harrison's excursions to India, or Mayall's version of LA.

Through the magic of making music, the limited intentions of two songwriters evolved into a much bigger, magical experience. It's also what made the publishing of Seals & Crofts I & II so fascinating (a humorous review if I do say so myself). It's what makes Breakfast in America an eternally great album (and Thriller too, in spite of my hating it).

I hope at least one of these crazy-person essays inspires you to carve out an hour to really sit down and listen to what I consider the greatest human achievement of the 20th century: the album.

29) Simon & Garfunkel - Bridge Over Troubled Water

... and so, completely unintentionally, we round out week three with the last Simon and Garfunkel album: Like a Bridge Over Troubled Water.

I honestly didn't notice it until I had actually decided to write about this album, but there's a Paul on days 7, 14, and 21. My subconscious works overtime, and the fact that my dad passed away on a Monday (Labor Day) never even crossed my mind. Morbid, but completely coincidental.

It's also the last Simon and Garfunkel album, even though they didn't actually know it while it was happening. Coincidences.

It's an album about Simon and Garfunkel, even though Paul Simon didn't necessarily intend it that way. It's all over the place, musically speaking. It's an album about absence, and friendship, and breaking away and coming home, and two people creating something much bigger than themselves. All those things are coincidental as well.

It has the first 16-track recording, made by manually synching two 8-track machines. It's been misinterpreted, and certain aspects of its making led Simon on his world music path. More and more coincidences. The more I ramble on, the tighter the tapestry weaves itself.

One last coincidence: my friend Steven Stark 's singing voice sounds identical to Art Garfunkel's (not to single him out or anything, it's just fascinating to hear considering his penchant for Artie's later music).

Tomorrow is a new week and who knows what interesting things will happen. Cheers.

30) Jimmy Hendrix and Buddy Miles

Let's hear the exact opposite of last night's album. Two friends who lived separate lives and careers, but met as young side men for different projects, and came together for brief moments of awesome. The last of these moments is Jimmy Hendrix and Buddy Miles as 2/3 of Band of Gypsies. It's a double feature, and the encore is Buddy Miles' Them Changes, his first solo album right after.

Band of Gypsies wasn't actually planned. The Experience had broken up, and 3 failed bands tried to record Hendrix's new material. All sorts of legal, contractual, and personal problems were affecting Jimi, and 2 nights at the Fillmore East with his actual friends Buddy Miles and Billy Cox being voluntary paid employees solved more than a couple of them. They rehearsed for a few months, but the concert itself was unplanned, improvised, and a little bit like 3 people winging it. In the end, 4 tracks credited to Hendrix and 2 credited to Miles became the live album Band of Gypsies.

As far as live albums go, it's pretty good. Hendrix gets fairly out there as far as noise making, and in my opinion, Miles gets listed up near the top of the best singing drummers roster. A lot of critics really didn't like Miles' drumming, but that's because they were brain dead idiots. I don't like the mix of his kit and the off-center panning is a little annoying, but he's dead solid, chaotic when he should be, and it brings out the idiosyncrasies of Hendrix's playing in a new, exciting way.

Buddy Miles was an interesting dude in his own right. He was the lead singer of the California Raisins for crying out loud. "Them Changes" also ended up being re-recorded by every major band he played in, and he got to hear Clapton play it live via cell phone on his death bed (and it became a permanent part of Clapton's live performances).

In a weird way, I think Them Changes (the album) is Miles' vindication of Hendrix and the project that coincidentally brought them together. Where Jimmy couldn't quite make it happen with new band mates, Buddy brought everyone he could find to just do their thing.

Again, critics either love him or say really shitty things about him, but the latter are complete idiots. Is he Marvin Gaye or Stevie Wonder? No, but he doesn't need to be. Is he John Bonham or Ginger Baker. Again no, but again that's not what he's trying to be. I've said it before, and I'm sure I'll say it again: when the people you think are amazing say "no man, this guy, right here," you should take a step back and consider what it is you don't, or can't, understand.

31) The Doors and Morrison Hotel

I feel crummy today. It's probably just the combination of stress, and allergies, and cold weather. Let's do another pair of records.

The Doors are explicitly "the doors of perception," so it's no surprise they are a radical, countercultural, philosophical behemoth of psychedelic blues rock. They are also one of the very few completely consistent bands I can think of: their entire discography is one gigantic album in my head. They are a lot like Creedence Clearwater Revival in that way; there's no question about whether it's The Doors or not, it is.

Even if you wanted to argue that their debut album and their 5th album are stylistically/sonically different, you can't really say the band "evolved." It's all there from the start, and what you're really noticing is the evolution of recording techniques/equipment/personnel, and the inevitable smoothing out of everything by the chronological passage of time. Any particular song could have been on any particular album.

But since we can't really break free from the chronology of time, we're stuck with thinking that they morphed from a self-indulgent psych-rock cadre into moderately unstable rock 'n roll royalty. Yet, no matter which album you're listening to, it's a fact that it sounds better with your eyes closed and your head tilted slightly backward.

32) Guess Who

Guess who got their name from a radio publicity stunt that became such commonplace shtick among DJs that the band eventually gave up and actually changed their name. Yes, no not Yes, The Guess Who, that's who. Holy hell, even I'm getting confused now.

Anywho, they made a lot of music. Since I'm on a roll with this twofer thing, let's listen to The Guess Who's year of classic rock radio station fodder, 1970. That's the year they put out both American Woman and Share the Land, and Canada has every reason to be understatedly modest about them. A bit like Vanilla Fudge, they objectively rock, just not in a balls to your face kind of way (sorry, I might have mixed my metaphors a little too strong tonight).

Up to this point they sort of struggled to keep members or tour properly, and after this Randy Bachman said "I really am going home" and did his own thing (but I don't have any BTO albums, so this is as randy as it gets, tee hee).

Did you know the Nixon administration had the ironic gall to suggest that actually performing the first Canadian single to go number 1 in the US at a White House concert would be "in bad taste." They literally had to go home because they couldn't get work visas for paying gigs. They aren't wrong, and Nixon was a jerk.

In a subtle way, these two albums are the chronological opposite of Seals & Crofts. You can tell that Bachman was the driving force behind their hard rock sound, and once he left, Burton Cummings was the softer songwriter of the pair. Not wimpier, but definitely more subdued and esoteric.

There are a few great moments of branching out into folk and jazz, but mostly The Guess Who are unapologetic rock, and I love it.

Totally random piece of information: these are by far the lightest, floppiest records I've ever held in my hand. Noticeably flimsy and it freaks me out a little.

33) Laura Nyro

I've got at least one more double-header in me, but after that I don't know. Let's listen to Laura Nyro.

"Who the hell is Laura Nyro?" you ask with an elevating tonal inflection. 50% of the reason she and David Geffen became millionaires in the first place, I answer deadpan. Besides selling a song to Peter, Paul, and Mary for

$5,000 out of nowhere, then being talked out of auditioning for lead singer of Blood, Sweat & Tears (the position our old friend David Clayton Thomas ended up getting, remember) to form and later sell her 50/50 publishing company with said Geffen for $4+ million, her songs became staples of tons of bands (just go back through the liner notes of albums we already listened to, and realize that's a mere sample), and she's in both the Songwriter and Rock and Roll halls of fame (though I suspect she had a few choice New York words for anyone who suggested she should be a celebrity). Jackson Browne was her boyfriend (not the other way around) for a while, but that's not really relevant. This isn't a like it or hate it kind of review, but there won't be any doubt exactly how I feel by the time you get to the end. She is a musical fact and we're going to give her the consideration she deserves as such.

I have both her acclaimed albums from 1968/69, Eli and the Thirteenth Confession and New York Tendaberry, so go already!

The only songwriter I can honestly compare her to is Harry Nilsson. That's not because they are similar at all, but professionally speaking they willingly made other people famous (and a whole lot of money in the process). I of course could be wrong, but they both seem genuinely most proud of creating their songs in the first place, and the fact that other people were able to leverage that foundation is icing on the cake. When you "go back to the source" you inevitably say "holy crap, yeah, I get it now." Whether you like her songs or not, you can't deny she's every bit as good a piano based singer/songwriter as fellow New Yorker Billy Joel; obviously not pop, but every bit the equal craftswoman.

These two albums are very, very different. Eli and the Thirteenth Confession is borderline Motown (and I wouldn't be surprised if the Supremes made an appearance in our future). New York Tendaberry, however, sounds like she locked herself in her apartment like the Collyer brothers.

I said in reference to Joni Mitchell that it's impossible to pretend that she didn't know what she was doing, but Laura Nyro takes that sentiment to a-whole-nother level. I said Julie Driscoll didn't have a timid setting, but Laura Nyro could probably hold her own in whatever dark alley she felt like visiting (even her whispery moments are razor sharp). If Patti Smith weren't busking in Paris at the time, you might think she learned that special brand of unhinged from Nyro.

All that said, I don't think these albums have the same punch in reverse order. They are, for better or worse, completely chrono-locked; you can't go backward from Tendaberry to Eli, it just doesn't make any sense. That difference is as much a product of the changing political/social climate as it is her obvious success, and personal drive.

To put things in perspective, I listened to New York Tendaberry two and a half weeks ago (when her name kept cropping up in the songwriter parentheses), but had no idea what I was actually hearing. Now in this coincidental two-albums-back-to-back format:

Holy crap. Yeah, I get it now.

34) The Bob Seger System

Even if you've only been reading these reviews with a wide toothed comb you'll know that 1) at some point I'll listen to a couple Motown artists, B) I'm still miles away from repeating a band, and Last) this coming Sunday will feature some sort of Paul. But, I bet you weren't expecting me to continue the baseball metaphor from yesterday and throw you a curve ball: a band that turned down Motown to sign with Capitol FOR LESS MONEY. I can't really decide if that was the right or wrong choice because there are persuasive arguments either way, but they definitely would have been a strange addition to the standard Motown roster....

You know Bob Seger, but if you only know his radio hits from the 70s and 80s you're in for a real treat/horrible time depending on your tolerance for anti-commercial, underground Detroit rock-n-roll.

I imagine that when the execs at Capitol heard the initial offering from The Bob Seger System they said "whaaaaa?" The gist of the story is that the first couple one-off singles were doing pretty well, but Capitol just couldn't let the debut album not include them. So, it's an album with a title track that doesn't match the cover (not the originally intended cover either), isn't listed on the back of the jacket, and clearly should have been left as the non-album single it was meant to be. Berry Gordy might have made the boys go through Maxine Powell's finishing school (a humorous picture in my mind), but there's no doubt he would have put every ounce of his energy into nurturing the newest members of his beloved Detroit's musically talented population. Berry Gordy was all about success for his artists being success for himself (not the other way around), and he wanted everybody on board. Not about Motown, not about Motown...where was I? Bob Seger. Ok. Focus.

Like I said, if you only know his later hits then this might be weird. This album is underground, drunk guys in a bar at 2AM type stuff. It's good, but more importantly it has some of that amateurish forcefulness that made all the great Detroit garage rock you might know. But, and it's a big but, it's Bob Seger. If you don't like Bob Seger, you won't like this at all. If, however, like me, you're kind of "meh" on him, then there's some real joy to be found in hearing him a little bit unpolished. So, maybe Berry Gordy would have made it worse. [shrug] I don't know.

I suppose I should clarify, the album is Ramblin' Gamblin' Man. I'm getting forgetful in my middle age...

35) Lord Sutch and Heavy Friends

Today's official album is really, really special. Screaming Lord Sutch might just be my spirit animal. He invented his own lordship, actively admitted to everyone that he sucked, specifically modeled his character after Screaming Jay Hawkins, and basically *was* Alice Cooper before Alice Cooper. In real life he created his own ridiculous political party and has the record for officially running for Parliament and losing over 40 times, just because he thought it was funny (eat your heart out Vermin Supreme). Sadly, he hanged himself in 1999, but 58 years of obviously untreated manic depression is a good run.

This, according to England, is officially considered one of the worst albums ever recorded (it's not). Everyone who participated thought it was funny right up until he actually published it, and that's the real tragedy. The hurtest butt, of course, was Jimmy Page. You can flush his opinion down the loo as far as I care.

I pointed this out in my diatribe about Michael Jackson, and here's another example of my separating the person from the music. Jimmy Page is a musical deity, but a garbage human being. I don't feel the least bit conflicted about listening to and enjoying his music, but I'd gladly say "shut your stupid face" if he ever said "hello" to me in a bizarro world where we were in the same room…but I digress.

Pure and simple, this is the sound of people having fun being obnoxious, and it's amazing. I guarantee he didn't trick a single person into participating, and the joy I mentioned in hearing raw Bob Seger is nothing compared to my indescribable ecstasy while listening to Lord Sutch and Heavy Friends. Raspberries to England, this is spectacular.

36) Butterfield Blues Band - Keep On Moving

Today's album is Keep On Moving by The Butterfield Blues Band. Paul Butterfield is genuinely regarded as one of the elite blues harmonica players, but beyond that everybody just kind of ignores his actual music the same way I personally ignore the Moody Blues. That's a shame, but it's a consistent reality for big band blues as a genre because most people find it too homogeneous a universe to visit for an extended period of time. It's the backdrop for the party in most people's minds.

This album certainly suffers that fate. Nobody has anything to say about it, but it's exquisite Chicago Electric Blues. Maybe that's it. It's too good. There's nobody to fight with about it; you'd be lying if you said they are terrible, and everybody would say "you're an idiot" if you had anything bad to say.

Butterfield isn't the "standout talent" because every single person making sound is amazing. Go really listen to it with proper headphones. Every single part is so naturally immaculate that it's easy to not notice how virtuosic it really is. The mixes and blending are astonishing as well. Seriously, go check it out.

37) The Rolling Stones

My earlier statements about the Butterfield Blues Band help crystallize an idea I've been struggling to explain for a long time: I don't like Rolling Stones' albums. I like the band, I like their songs, I like their variety and experimentation, but I would rather splatter house paint in my eyeballs than listen to an entire side, let alone two or three or any of the 30 full albums by them.

Up until tonight I couldn't really figure out why that would be true. I can listen to Yoko Ono, or 45 minutes of random train noises, I can enjoy the constantly changing rhythms of the clothes dryer for an entire cycle as though it were an improvisational percussion ensemble, I can tolerate screaming, and yodeling, and bad spoken word, but by the third Rolling Stones song in a row I'm ready to punch myself in the throat just so I can hear my own choking for air instead.

But, why? Because not a single person involved in recording this band at any point in their career gave a crap. With only 1 exception that I will talk about momentarily, it all sounds like the final mix down was done over the studio intercom by the coffee boy. Either the mics are 20 feet away from the amplifiers, or there was so much room noise that they had to use a dozen notch filters, or they set dials by rolling dice, or I don't even know what. Like I said, they wrote great songs, they played their instruments like normal people, but it all sounds wrong.

Now the exceptions, with some explanatory background. I love the sound of people playing their instruments and the tracks I'm about to talk about are pure ecstasy for me. Strangely though, I am not one of those people who lauds vinyl over digital in spite of my preference for the added sound of the mechanical playback equipment. The absence of crackles or tape hiss etc. doesn't actually bother me at all, what bothers me is deliberately removing the sound of playing for a quieter noise floor.

So, in that light, the first 3 tracks from Beggars Banquet are the most delicious sounds I've ever heard in my life. I know "Sympathy for the Devil" better than any analogy for really knowing things, but I have never in my life heard that lead guitar tone sound like an electrified pane of glass played with a glass pick by a ham-fisted angry child. That might not sound like a compliment, but it is raauuunchy in this form. At the complete other end of the spectrum, "No Expectations" has the most gorgeous slide acoustic guitar I've ever heard, so close you can imagine more than a few takes were ruined by actually bumping the microphone. Last, if every album sounded like "Dear Doctor," I wouldn't be writing this post at all. As it stands, though, that's it. 3/5 of the first side of Beggars Banquet is alls I can stands, and I can't stands no more.

38) The Incredible String Band - The Big Huge

Before I inherited this amazing collection of music, The Gorey End by The Tiger Lillies and Kronos Quartet was the strangest album in my collection. The two albums I have by Rotary Connection are at least as equally bizarre, but this next album blows them all out of the water. Tonight, we are listening to The Big Huge by The Incredible String Band.

First, some context. This is actually the second half of a double album. The original release was Wee Tam and the Big Huge, but the American form of humanity couldn't handle it all in one package, so it was released as two separate albums here. Their self professed influence upon some really big-name musicians might be a tad overstated, but it is a chronological fact that the Beatles, Rolling Stones, Bob Dylan, and Led Zeppelin knew The Incredible String Band, and attended their concerts before their own well know excursions into psychedelia.

"Psychedelic music" is a very on the nose family of genres. All of its various subgenres are explicitly "[musical genre] on drugs" (or for drugs, or about drugs, you get the idea). LSD, psilocybin, mescaline, DMT, the audio/visual "mind expanding" stuff. In general, though, you get the sense that the genre actually came first. Take Jefferson Airplane, for example. They are essentially a rock band that took a lot of drugs. Hendrix was a rock/blues guitarist who took admittedly way too much LSD. Even Syd Barret was a fully formed pop-folk singer before the methaqualone zombified him. I get the exact opposite impression from Robin Williamson and Mike Heron. I truly believe they were professional space cadets from the start, and they took up folk music because they just couldn't seem to burn out properly and got really bored. I also think people didn't really understand what they were actually hearing at the time. Let's be brutally honest, Bob Dylan liked "October Song" so much because he could hear himself mimicking it.

And Robin and Mike were super competitive with each other, maybe not Liam and Noel Gallagher fist-fight competitive, but not far behind either. As their career progressed, pretty much everyone felt like I feel right now: are they serious, or is this a joke? Yeah, that's the official critical response to this band, and we'll never get an actual answer to that question.

There's a popular theory that when a musical artist "jumps the shark," to borrow that clichéd Happy Days metaphor, it's because they actually took a leap of genius so big that no one else could possibly follow it for at least a couple generations. No. These guys rode in on a rainbow-colored unicorn, and everyone's brains shut down and all they could say was "would your magic horse like some of our apples?"

I imagine that had Ravi Shankar himself heard 4 seconds of this album, all he could do would be to pinch the bridge of his nose and say, "I *really* don't like it, but he's technically playing the sitar better than a couple of my own worst students." Yes, they are by definition multi-instrumentalists because they can do whatever you want to call that on any instruments you hand them.

Believe it or not, this is actually work for me to get through. I am a professional music listener, and this feels like a whole lot of unpaid overtime. Don't get me wrong, there are genuine moments of actual folk by Heron, but then Williamson prances in front of him in his jester's bells and the only possible response you can have is "what the hell?" because Mike just follows right along with him like it's completely normal. By the way, that's not hyperbole, it's literally Side B:

MH: What a lovely caterpillar.
RW: I was a dragon child.
MH: Well, I was born without a head, and the guard at the toll

bridge murdered me, and it was glorious.
RW: ... and we fall down as stardust to fertilize the earth.

[End scene]

I cannot picture any of you good people liking this. I can picture you laughing, but not saying "ooh! How intriguing. Let me hear more." I respect it, but it's right at the edge of my tolerance for weird. I don't want that to scare you off, though. This is just my reaction to it. Please, please, please go listen to it for yourself. You're more than welcome to disagree with me (I disagree with myself all the time, ha ha), assuming you do. The important thing is actually listening to it, or at the very least as much of it as you can stand.

39) Steve Miller Band - Number 5

Sometimes you just need to hear a rock star be a rock star without any pretension, or political spin, or scheming. A guy who can open an album with a psych rock adaptation of "God Rest Ye Merry Gentlemen," go straight into blues harmonica, and sincerely write songs about being nice to each other. A guy who by complete coincidence was Les Paul's godchild, decided to stay in San Francisco after spending his last $5 to see Butterfield Blues Band and Jefferson Airplane at the Filmore. A guy who knocked Chuck Berry's ego down to human size by threatening to send him packing. A guy who didn't even actually realize how big a deal it was playing with Muddy Waters, Howlin' Wolf, and Buddy Guy until after he himself achieved that level of fame. A guy who wanted to play guitar, and just did.

Steve Miller might be the most normal, level headed, guitar god ever created. He's said out loud that his only job is to make people glad they came to one of his concerts, and beyond that he's completely unimportant. He got a ridiculous reputation from being grumpy about his induction into the rock and roll hall of fame. Seriously, read my first paragraph. He was genuinely mad that they wouldn't *let* his friend induct him. That friend happened to be Elton John.

"Can my friend Elton present my induction?"

"Hell no, the Black Keys are going to announce you."

"Who? No, seriously. I don't know who those guys are."

  This album is Number 5. It might just be the nicest rock and roll album ever created. He dedicated it to NASA, Johnny Cash, Paul McCartney, and Richard Nixon, because Nixon "needed to be loved" as much as anyone else. I have two things in common with Steve Miller: I love playing guitar, and Donald Trump is way worse than Nixon (both jerks). I'm not as nice as Steve Miller.
  Actually, Number 5 is the Butterfield Blues Band of Steve Miller albums. It's a great album, but no one has anything to say about it. It's not bold or rebellious like the previous 4, but it's not the 70s/80s SMB that "classic rock" was created from either. It's a rock star and his friends making an album in Nashville about being nice to each other. To quote Kurt Vonnegut's Uncle Alex, "if this isn't nice, I don't know what is."

40) Spirit (4 albums for the price of 4)
  Let's get this out of the way first, copyright lawsuits are 90% garbage. You can't copyright a chromatic bass line, or a chord progression, or an idiomatic expression, or the use of falsetto, or any of the other nonsense record companies use to extort money from each other. Every single musician on earth "copies" what they like, what works, what they can expand on, add something to, what they care about. Taking a cool thing from another song, writing it down, and making it your own

is what makes Jimmy Page a great musician. What makes Jimmy Page a dog turd (or should I say Thriller?) of a human being (apart from the kidnapping thing) is that *after* he became an incredibly wealthy person he flipped all the people who inspired/influenced him the bird and pretended like he'd never had an unoriginal thought in his entire life. Oh yeah, by the way, Led Zeppelin also warmed up the crowd that hadn't yet arrived to see Spirit.

I'm always reluctant to name my favorite band (for many reasons), but my favorite band of all time is Spirit. There are literally thousands of bands I like just as much, but they aren't my favorite. Spirit is, and I'm not gonna fight you about it. Like, if you asked me who I'm going to vote for in 2020, my answer is Kamala Harris. We could have a 45-minute conversation about it where you call me bad names, but unless you shoot me in the face and kill me, or cause debilitating brain damage, I'm going to vote for or write down the name Kamala Harris, and my favorite band is Spirit. Facts. [Sadly, as I edit this, I'm being forced to choose between Trump and Biden. There's a dash of hope that he'll chose Harris as VP, but the murder hornets, and Confederates, and corona virus, and federalized secret police will probably kill us all before we get to make that pointless choice. Hey waddya know, I'm so slow at editing she IS Vice President now.]

Jimmy Hendrix gave their guitarist/leader the nickname "California" because there were two Randy's that he needed to differentiate, and this one said "my name is now Randy California because Jimmy Hendrix said so." Facts.

Every band has eras/epochs/whathaveyous. Number 5 was the end of Steve Miller Band's first era, and Spirit made it to 4 before temporarily imploding (the very first album I listened to, if you can remember that far back). I HAVE ALL FOUR. Now we binge.

Spirit's self titled debut album is everything you'd expect from a psych-rock band and more, plus some really stellar orchestral arrangements by Marty Paich (go read *his* wikipedia page if you want to feel like a lazy, useless human being). This album also leaves no doubt that Spirit could have been any kind of band they wanted to be. They play rock, folk, blues, and jazz like they aren't in any way different from each other. There's not a single bad song on this album, and I WILL fight you about that. Both sides of this album are equally good: there's no wasted energy or filler, and all 5 guys more than pull their weight.

That was February 1968. 10 months later they released The Family That Plays Together. This sophomore offering has been described as proto-prog-rock by people who didn't actually listen to the first album closely. This band could have been any type of band they wanted, and they rightly decided to be all of them. Oh hey, is that Marty Paich again as well. Call me crazy, but maybe just maybe the only limitation on their creative output in 1968 was someone willing to pay for studio time and distribution, and only 24 hours in a day. I imagine if someone fed them and paid their rent for a few months they could have written 12 albums worth of this insanely amazing stuff.

The second album is a little less fuzzy than the first (and that sets up a pun for their third album, as I am wont to do). By that I mean, it sounds more determined and solidified. They sound more comfortable in their diversity on this album, and I suspect that's as much a product of increased confidence in the band by the execs at Ode/CBS as it is another year's worth of simply being a band, and a better mix/master (sound engineers have a learning curve too, you know). Again, not one single second of fluff or mindless repetition. Nearly 40 minutes of top notch late 60s rock that flew in under the radar and still doesn't get the recognition it deserves.

And damned if 9 months later they didn't put out another one. It's clear that they were unstoppable. It's Clear. Get it? Ha.

But seriously, the band wasn't quite as happy with this album because they felt it was rushed. They wrote three albums, a film soundtrack and toured in two years. A little rushed indeed. It doesn't sound rushed it sounds muddy, and that's an engineering problem, not an "I'm feeling jetlagged" problem. It's not quite as experimental as the first two, but it still has some pretty sharp turns and tangents. Clear is also their last album with producer Lou Adler for Ode. They weren't quite about to fall apart yet, but they had started following advice from Neil Young so it was really only a matter of time. Neil Young seems like a great guy, but I wouldn't even eat at a restaurant he recommended. His official slogan should just be "your experience may vary; not responsible for lost or damaged property as a result of this experience." Nevertheless, they made an amazing fourth album before a series of unfortunate events sent various members in different directions, only to sporadically reunite with less than stellar rapport between various members. It didn't really matter though. Spirit was kind of like the Wu Tang Clan: Technically its members released solo albums that were stylistically different, but it's still recognizably the same group regardless of whose name gets the biggest letters on the cover. Should you happen to come across any of their later albums in your various travels, please don't hesitate to acquire them and send them to me for the love and adoration they so rightly deserve.

Sadly, we must bring the evening to a close with Twelve Dreams of Dr. Sardonicus, but what a great album. It's got folk and funk and hard rock, the horns and quirky guitar effects and vocal playfulness are back. Clear is clearly the weakest of the four albums, and I won't criticize you too much if you want to pretend it didn't happen. The first two albums and Sardonicus are a discography any band would be rightly proud to have created, and are pure joy to my ears.

They don't have to be your favorite band (I don't feel that lonely), they might not be for everyone, but I love them. Cheers.

41) Crosby, Stills, Nash, & Young - Déjà vu

Speaking of Neil Young, here he is with Crosby, Stills, Nash, Taylor, Reeves, Sebastian, Garcia (yes, the one they call Jerry), and Mitchell (even if she isn't credited as backup vocals, she's in there and so is "Woodstock"). I mentioned Wu Tang Clan last night, but the comparison works equally well for this group of omnipresent California hippies. They all played with each other in 12 or 20 different bands, and I think they just drew names out of a hat for instrumentation and songwriter credits. If you played in California in 1968-1971 one or more of them showed up to the gig and played whether you asked them to or not. Like in the pre-gig walk around they'd show you where the bathrooms and green room were, and point out where David Crosby had been camping that week so you could arrange your gear around him accordingly.

From an "album" standpoint it's actually kind of weird. Exactly like I described above, every track is from a recording session by the credited songwriter, and one or more of the group might not have been in the studio that day. It's more like a studio compilation than an actual album by a band. Even more bizarre, it's the best-selling album in every individual musician's discography. That's a little bit like saying "you know what would make this Buffalo Springfield album great? If we replaced Graham Nash and Neil Young with Bob Weir and Carlos Santana and had them play Joan Baez songs."

That sounds like I'm being negative. I'm not. One of the things that makes this album work so well is the intentional openness to interpretation that they created. Déjà Vu could refer to the similar situations all of these people keep finding themselves in, or the general notion of little people accomplishing big things, or even the actual fact that they all end up on each others' records anyway.

Amazing things happen when you just let people live their lives and stop trying to micro-manage who gets to go where, or who can be friends with whom. All of these amazing people were simply asking their government to stop waging war on the rest of the world in the name of "America." 50 years later, it feels like we've run out of creative ways to voice our opposition. That's why we scream at each other so much now, you know?

42) Simon the Magpie - Meow Meow

Tonight is Eman's Halloween dance, so I'm getting some quality headphone time in the car. I tried to figure out a way to bring the turntable and record crate, but sadly I failed.

That's ok. We'll just listen to the cat album Meow Meow by Simon The Magpie. This one's easy to find, and no annoying YouTube commercials. Just search for him on Bandcamp and hit play and enjoy, then give the funny Swedish guy a few dollars and carry it around on your phone everywhere you go, like I do.

Simon The Magpie is a Swedish DIY glitch-pop artist. He mangles and manipulates all sorts of instruments and electronic devices to make weird, interesting, even terrible sounds. His YouTube channel mostly documents his circuit bending projects, but he puts music up on Bandcamp. More importantly, he writes some of the catchiest tunes I've ever heard. Cats are a pretty common subject for his songs in general, and this is a whole album of songs about cats, thinking like a cat, and meowing. He's even uses a cat shaped toy keyboard.

Obviously, this is miles away from the "hippie rock" I've been listening to for the last month, but is it really? Sure, there's an ocean in between no matter which direction you go, and the subject matter is a little trivial, and he can swear as much as he wants, but musically speaking it's the same experimental attitude that prevailed in the late 60s and 70s. Really, is a song about getting stuck in an elevator because you were chasing a laser dot any more trivial than Steve Miller singing about spicy peppers? It's not rock, but it's nowhere near as bonkers as The Incredible String Band, in my opinion. It's the result of 50 years of tinkering with sound and technology and the craft of making large musical ideas come to life.

Forget about genres and labels and being angry about stuff and enjoy this lighthearted collection of catchy do-it-yourself glitch pop.

43) Soak - Omniphonic Globalnova

... and 22 years later we find my copy of the first album listed in the discography section of John Moyer's wikipedia page. Signed and dated in blue ballpoint pen under the CD tray in the parking lot of the Diamond Ballroom in OKC. He might be the bassist for Disturbed now, but I remember the confused look on his face when I told him they rocked that night and asked him to sign it. They did rock that night, but I remember this album sounding tragically underwhelming. Let's find out.

Actually, it's much better than I remember. Nothing earth shattering, but they've got some real personality. This just might call for another entry into the obscurity vault. It definitely doesn't show up in my YouTube search as an album (a later album and a couple live clips do, but not this one.) I wonder how many of these are actually out in the world in playable condition right now.

They belong to that weird in between world of alternative metal that incorporates funk. It's almost proto nu-metal, but it's really the kid brother of bands like Faith No More, Living Colour, and Primus with a healthy dose of noise rock thrown in. It won't change your life, but it's interesting.

44) Average White Band - Feel No Fret

Something really different for me: I don't know anything about Average White Band, and I haven't looked at their wikipedia page at all. All I know is this is a 50 cent "cut" album (meaning the label/distributor said "good god no, please don't send them back. Cut 'em, punch 'em, melt 'em, liquidate 'em, throw 'em like Frisbees, we don't care.") That doesn't mean it's going to be bad. It's also unopened. Let's open it and find out.

Not gonna lie, that band photo does not instill confidence. Let's check the back for some more clues. Way down at the bottom: 1979. That's not a good year at all. Moving up we get random thank yous (not important), produced by the band and a guy (not really meaningful), song titles are too vague to make any judgment. Strings, horns, and synthesizer "arrangements"? That's unnerving. Luther Vandross does backing vocals on the penultimate song on Side B? I don't recognize a single name anywhere? I'm worried. Not worried that it will suck. Terrible music is my bread and butter. I'm worried that it will be the worst combination of soft pop and softer jazz. Like Michael Bolton sings Toto, with special guest Kenny G. Please let me be wrong. Let it be cheesy blue-eyed soul, or funk with a tinge of generic rock. Ok, enough procrastinating.

Oh, thank goodness. It's funk. Sure, it's white guy funk with tinges of disco, but now I can look them up. They're Scottish? I mean, I saw the name Hamish, but he's a guitar player so I just ignored it. We're a dime a truckload in any country, us guitar players, but I totally missed his equally Scottish band mates.

This has a definite Bee Gees aftertaste, but it's got some real soul hiding in there too. The grooves are fantastic, and the aforementioned synths are actually quite tasteful. This is real 80s dance party on the 32nd floor type stuff. I can dig it.

45) Eric Burdon & The Animals

Love Is is the third album by Eric Burdon and the Animals, but it's not really Burdon's or the Animals' album at all. They'd been recording since the early 60s, and this was already the second incarnation of the band (hence the separation of names). Burdon was basically a floating lead vocalist and he'd hook up with War in a couple short years.

This is actually just 5 musicians giving some covers the old Vanilla Fudge treatment (there's only one original song on the whole double album). If you want to get fussy, it's Zoot Money and Andy Summers killing time before they go on to the famous parts of their respective careers; 25% of the whole thing is reworked material from their previous band, so "the Animals" is really just a convenient way for all of them to keep busy in the studio without having to go through the hassle of pitching a new band to the labels.

I expect you know exactly what you're going to get from Eric Burdon. 49% of the time he sounds like Mick Jagger, 49% of the time he sounds like Joe Cocker, and 2% of the time he's talking in his Eric Burdon voice. If you're ok with that then this is a pretty enjoyable hour of psych/blues rock jamming. It's not a hit singles kind of record, it's more a studio version of a gig they might have played: songs people know, played the way Eric, Zoot, and Andy want to play them. Nothing wrong with that at all, in my opinion.

46) Donna Summer - The Wanderer

You know what I'm gonna do? I'm going to open this factory sealed copy of Donna Summer's The Wanderer and listen to it.

Why? Well, remember when Laura Nyro helped David Geffen become a millionaire? He used that money to create Asylum Records, then wandered over to the world of film, then negotiated a deal with Warner Brothers and founded

Geffen Records. This is literally the first record Geffen Records published in 1980.

You know her as a disco superstar, but this is not disco. This is full on synth pop with some seriously hair-bandish guitar solos on the deep cuts (Tim May, Skunk Baxter, and Steve Lukather: at least two of those names should be familiar to you).

But Bottle, why should I care? Because before people started misspelling Donna Sommer's name, she was the lead singer of a super obscure psychedelic rock band called Crow. You can hem and haw all you want, but this is just as good as anything Pat Benatar did (and I love Pat Benatar).

Seriously, there's nothing cheesy about this album. It's peppy, but it's not vapid. It's got a little bit of soul, a little bit of new wave, and I honestly don't think any musician would feel silly playing any instrumental part from any of these songs. You can tell when a production team cares about the music they produce, and this is the real deal whether you like 80s dance pop or not.

47) Eddie Kendricks - Slick

A while ago I teased Motown, then gave you the old switcheroo. I'm sorry. I'll make it up to you by opening another 50-cent gem, Eddie Kendricks's Slick.

I thought about bringing out the Supremes, but Eddie Kendricks influenced their creation in the first place. I thought about doing another work-up and again thwarting expectations by looking at the stranger side of Motown, but I'm not in the right frame of mind. After Average White Band and Donna Summer, I just want to hear some real soul sung in falsetto by one of the founding members of the Temptations. I want to hear another producer's album with good songs (and let me tell you, Leonard Caston and friends can write some songs). Believe it or not, I even want a Seals & Crofts cover thrown in there.

This was Eddie's last record for Motown and it compliments Summer's The Wanderer quite nicely. Donna went in a new direction when she signed to Geffen, but Eddie left his group and label because he didn't want to change. You can't blame him; he's a Smoky Robinson protégé through and through. Eddie sticks to his shtick, but he's definitely not stale. Smooth, suave, sultry, sophisticated. Slick is an often over looked gem of late 70s soul.

48) Santana and Abraxas

I don't have to write a novel tonight because it's the first two Santana albums: Santana and Abraxas. Screaming guitars, organ solos, a full percussion ensemble, and unobtrusive vocals. Their goal was to be a jam band who played actual well-liked songs, and they more than succeeded. Every track could fill a whole side as far as I'm concerned. You can do as good as Santana, but you can't do any better.

Reviewers of the time thought this was vapid fast-as-hell garbage, but they hadn't heard even the simplest of modern-day sandal-core (180bpm is practically Largo at this point), so we can just laugh and ignore them.

49) Glass Ox - Draw Near

Here's something special that you'd probably never hear unless I share it with you. I've uploaded Draw Near, the sophomore album from Marshalltown's own Glass Ox, to YouTube, 'cause I'm cool. Statistically speaking, nobody owns this album. You might not like it, but I do, and at least now you can say you've heard it....

50) Happy Halloween, it's Classics IV and Steppenwolf

I didn't want to write about two albums tonight. I wanted to just surreptitiously move from a quote on the notes to Santana's Abraxas to bringing back one of my favorite bands (or at least as enjoyable as Spirit), but it's inconveniently

Halloween. Halloween happens to be the only context in which I can really talk about Classics IV. So now I have to try to fit Classics IV and Steppenwolf into the same universe. Luckily, we can just pretend that we're at a Halloween party where Classics IV opens for Steppenwolf, though I can't help feeling that everything would be infinitely easier if I had a couple Oingo Boingo albums on vinyl. Oh well, I'll try my best.

Classics IV is a cover band. I don't mean that in a bad way, but it is vital that we understand them in that context. Even the songs they were first to record are recognizably done in the style of more famous artists/bands. So much so that The Four Seasons actually threatened to withhold future exclusives to radio stations who played their first single, "Pollyanna."

Regardless, we really only invited them to sing their biggest hit, "Spooky," but their lead single/ title track is the last song on the whole album. Uuuuuuuuggghhhhh. It's cheesy I know, but it's a Halloween staple of classic rock DJ shtick, 'cause The Yost (that's what I call him) actually says "Halloween" (and if you definitely can't pretend you don't now know exactly what I'll play on next month's holiday). Actually, as soon as you associate "Spooky" with Halloween you realize that quite a few tracks on this album have that same haunting kind of vibe. Ok, ok, clap politely as they exit stage left, even.

Snaggle Pus, Steppenwolf, whatever. Let's see, gotta tie it back to Santana somehow, um, oh yeah, critics hated For Ladies Only. Some people thought Steppenwolf woke up in 1971 and decided to suck. No. Some people thought the band was being sexist. No. Some people thought heading in a more prog-rock direction was blasphemy. No. There's a two plus minute blues piano solo in the title track, for crying out loud.

This entire album is 1 rhetorical question and a definitive answer. "Why are stereotypical women angry at men? Because stereotypical men are misogynistic pigs." This is an album about hypocrisy on both sides. It's an album about intellectual laziness, and those barbs are surprisingly sharp. Artificial gender roles are simply the entry point.

Point: every single time John Kay says the title phrase "for ladies only" it connotes something different. That's because he's smarter than a 12-year-old. Point 2 point zero: did irony not exist before 1982? Steppenwolf is sexist the same way Ozzy is actually "the prince of darkness." Which is to say, neither are actually those things. I live in a full-on imaginary universe with bands and music and artwork I made up while I was sleeping, and that's more realistic than the actual words that come out of people's mouths when they talk about their own contemporary music. Did I miss the reverse psychology memo?

Simmer down, Bottle. Let's tackle this problem systematically. 1) women are mad because you treat them like crap. 2) are you coming at me from the high ground, or do we both agree that there are things we need to personally work on? 3) I love you, and it's not my intention to demean you, so let's actually talk about it. 4) oh shit, yeah, I didn't realize I was such a douche bag (so I dumped her instead of dealing with that problem, and fantasize about winning her back). [Flip record over] 5) whew, glad that's over. Now I can go back to chasing women. 6) chasing women. 7) Waaaah! please take me back. 8) there's literally nothing else I can say [instrumental]. 9) you'll be sorry without me. I mean I'm the one who's actually lost and confused and doesn't know where to go, but you know I'm right, and you should totally ride off with me. 10) [aside] we tell these stories about ourselves because we have no goddamned idea what it is we're actually supposed to be doing.

The moral of the story is yes women have every right to kick you to the curb if you treat them like that. That's an easy moral to miss if you're writing a forty-word newspaper blurb about a record you didn't actually listen to, but let's maybe give the multi-lingual war criticizing literary aficionado the benefit of the doubt. Maybe?

51) 5th Dimension - Up, Up, and Away

Surprise! I didn't write about an album last night, so we'll just kick off the weekend with the debut album by 5th Dimension, Up, Up, and Away.

I've said it before and I'll say it any chance I get: 5th Dimension are awesome. It's easy to just dismiss them as Sunshine Pop and move on, but this band is a seriously complex amalgam of everything happening around them. That's in large part due to Johnny Rivers, who handed them the title track by an unknown (but soon to be big) songwriter, Jimmy Webb. In my opinion, Rivers stands right along with Berry Gordy, Quincy Jones, Mutt Lange, and John Fogerty in the producer's pantheon.

Like The Wanderer by Donna Summer, this is obviously peppy and cheerful, good time background music, but it's not fluff. The songs are great, the musicianship is excellent, and the compositions/arrangements are like a masterclass in writing pop music for rock orchestra: dueling choirs, pop/rock/funk lines hiding inside croony ballads, tempo/meter shifts, complex harmonies under earworm worthy melodies. Yes it's pop, but with a special kind of inclusiveness, an everything can belong kind of attitude that only 5th Dimension can convincingly create. As good a start to the weekend as anyone could want. Cheers.

52) The Mothers of Invention - Freak Out!

Ready. Set. FREAK OUT! Imagine you're in a band and a few of you are getting bored with playing standard blues covers. Your leader is a whiny puke who doesn't want to lose gigs by playing original material, so you replace him with a guitarist who knows exactly what he wants to do: make fun of whiny pukes. Ok, Frank Zappa's in charge now.

It's Mother's Day (not in real life, it's rhetorical), so we're changing our name to The Mothers. Too edgy? Ok, we'll add "of Invention." Yeah, sure we're "a white blues band," but this country is pretty stupid, so we're gonna make fun of it as "a white blues band."

That's the real origin story. Zappa wanted to make fun of everything happening around him. Tom Wilson thought he was getting a generic white guy blues band so he was high the whole time, getting his mind blown in two completely different ways. He just kept indulging Zappa's crazy ideas until MGM said "holy shit, stop spending our money."

So, here's the irony. It's not the music Zappa's lampooning, it's the clash it creates with reality. The spoiled rich kids are sad and mopey, the drug addicts and losers are happy as can be, we're in here goofing around, and our producer is over there high as balls renting every percussion instrument within a 30-mile radius so we can bring in a bunch of homeless people to record a two-act ballet, public school is corporate citizenship training instead of library time spent actually learning something. None of it makes any sense!

For his entire life, Frank Zappa used his incredible innate musical imagination to say over and over and over again "what the hell are you talking about? Everything works the way it's supposed to work if you just let us figure it out for ourselves."

The moral of the story, in my humble opinion, is that we could have spent the last half a century rewarding the search for real intelligence, but instead we decided to be shiny, happy people driving to mind numbing endless factory line work for the benefit of the *already* wealthy. I didn't mean to insult REM, but I'm positive that's exactly the phrase Zappa would have used.

This album is so good, and so funny, and so sad at the same time. And, I'm sorry to disappoint you all, but Epstein boringly did hang himself, because he spent the last half a century ignoring Frank Zappa.

"Trouble Every Day" is *the* song that got The Mothers a record deal. Tom Wilson, one of the very, very few black producers with any interest in diversifying his roster, heard this song and said we have to have to have to sign them. He was surprised by what he actually got, but it's pretty obvious why this song made the light bulb go off inside his head.

The song was inspired by the Watts riots in LA, but it's an attack on society at large. The real heart of this song is Zappa standing there with the reality of the riot on one side, and the television coverage of it on the other. He's literally in the middle of it saying nobody will actually win this fight and the problem won't go away after the riot is over. So, what is the problem?

Segregation, nepotism, sensationalism, and abuse of power. If you tell people they're only allowed to live in a specific neighborhood, then this isn't a free country. If the only path to success is through inheritance, then shocker most of us will be poor. If you tell people stay inside because those black people are dangerous, then surprise we're all de facto racist. If you fence in a bunch of people, tell the world they are drunkards and criminals, and only come around to arrest/punish them, duh, they're going to get really angry. I'm not black, but I'm definitely not associated with the other half of this fight.

Zappa's point was that the economic elite, and thus the government, are racist, but everyday people are the ones who suffer. This is about believing that anyone is a lesser human. It's about creating a society where some people get to be wealthy without having to work for it while some people have to clean up their mess and pick up their garbage (and if you educate them, they might not pick up your garbage any more). But, we all suffer for it while they sit in their offices thinking up new ways to keep us fighting each other instead of calling bullshit.

He really is pointing at the TV and saying you weasley little pukes are telling me how scary the world I'm standing in right now is, then cut away to tell me you're safe and doing swell and you'll be first on the scene to give me all the gory details. Meanwhile, yeah I'm scared because I might get killed for this bizarro universe you created. News flash, I don't have the same skin color as the people I actually agree with on this particular issue.

That's my take on it. Your mileage may vary.

53) Woodhawk - Violent Nature

I've spent so much time in the 60s and 70s that I need a dose of today. I just stumbled on this album, and wowzers. Woodhawk is like a synthesis of everything good from the last 50 years of hard rock and British heavy metal without even a hint of schlock or self indulgence. It has a few softer moments, but it's pretty much straightforward heavy grooving guitar riffage with (I don't say this very often so you know I mean it) great vocals and not terrible lyrics. The solos are actual melodic solos, not pointless meandering etudes ("douchetudes" should be a real word), and their back catalogue is just as good as this latest release. I now own all three albums, and they're all fantastic. I'll shut up and tell you to go find them on Bandcamp, where the cool kids camp.

54) Maureen McGovern - Nice To Be Around

I like Woodhawk (the band I found yesterday) so much that it's a karmic necessity to listen to something I'm sure to dislike. So, I opened this 99-cent album from Target's "we're not going to chase you if you try to steal it" bin.

I don't think I'm being unfair when I say that Maureen McGovern was never famous. She had a few well-known soundtrack songs, but let's face it, she's not Anne Murray or

Cher. Don't get me wrong, she has a personality, but this record sounds like "Anne Murray sings songs rejected by Cher." Not surprisingly, Dionne Warwick and Barbra Streisand were her childhood idols.

I can't help but compare this to everything I've listened to in the last month, and it just never comes together: a good composition with frankly stupid lyrics, or a promising lyrical exposition with pure orchestrational hack work. It just doesn't work to my ears. She has a super forceful voice, which isn't a bad thing at all, and it's no wonder her main success came on Broadway, but she's not a pop star.

She is, however, a case study in which kind of record deal to never, ever sign. 40% is not an acceptable cut for any agent, ever. A full-salary back-up band is a lot like raising chickens and goats: you don't get to go on vacation.

I haven't heard anything else of hers (and I'm not going to), but the imaginary record executive inside me feels like they all just wasted her potential. Voice-wise, she has a real similarity to early to mid Grace Slick, and I feel like if they had led her more in the thought-provoking direction (as opposed to what I call the "mistress of toys" direction), she could have killed it. As it stands though, this might as well have been a Christmas album, because I just can't care. You are of course welcome to disagree.

55) Ten Years After - Cricklewood Green

Whether I intended to or not, I called Maureen McGovern a "wannabe." That idea didn't come out of thin air, though. I know how my brain works, and that entire frame of mind came from tonight's album.

It really shouldn't surprise you that I listen to so much more than I post about; I can't write about an album until I put it in a context box and shake it around a little (these posts are just as much about how I think/feel in the moment as they are the actual album). Sometimes it happens on first listen, sometimes a week or more later. Tonight's post about Ten Years After has been steeping in tepid water for about two weeks.

The cover of Cricklewood Green doesn't impart any knowledge to me. I stared at it for days and chose other things. Is it folk? Is it country? Blues? Pfffft, I don't know. Then I opened up the fold, and immediately thought "oh, they want to be the Doors." Keep in mind, I had no factual information about this band at all. I check wikipedia merely to verify that the information already in my head isn't completely back-assward. I still have very little biographical knowledge, because if I haven't even heard of a band then they weren't famous. That's immodest, I know, but I think I'm a pretty good litmus test on relative fame/obscurity (litmus test, acid rock, ya get it? Even I want to punch me in the face for that one.) Let's listen to it in real time:

Spacey electronic sounds...domo arigato Mr. Robot...very formulaic blues rock, but not terrible...ok guitar solo...is this a feminist anthem?... 50 years, that's another funny coincidence... wankery outro solo, ok next song... yeah, delay is a tough one without metronomes and digital sync...Skynyrd?...ooooh what a nasty weird note...definitely southern rock, next...whaaaa? Talking and hippy dippy nonsense and a harpsichord?...slight accelerando...still one more song on Side A, if this outro solo ever ends... I zoned out, why is he mentioning planets? End already!...NOOOOOOO! YOU DON'T FADE BACK IN...[swearing ahead] What the ever loving fuck?! It's really that important to highlight how fast he can play an acoustic guitar? [End of Side A].

Ok, a few things. They don't suck, but the process of assembling that side must have included more butt slapping and high fives than an entire MLB season. Someone, at some point, said the phrase "that'll really blow their minds." Doors wannabes is maybe too specific. I get the vibe that this is a "we're better than all of 'em" band. The songs aren't bad individually, but as a whole, to quote the horse from Ren and Stimpy, "no sir. I don't like it."

On to Side B, I guess. Actual rockabilly blues, ok that's totally pretentious, but fine...the longer this drags on, the more concerned I get...why does every riff give me déjà vu?...are the vocals from an overhead room mic?...the solo interlude is actually good on this one, though. I wish Side A had been more like this...please no, not a ballad...yes, I'm here to judge and it very much matters what you do...no, it's not a bad song, but it's definitely not what I want to hear. What god awful surprise does the last track hold in store? Time to find out...bass and organ, oh joy the bolero build...yes, yes, we're insignificant to the universe, how insightful...and electronic nonsense. Too little, too late, it just sounds self congratulatory at this point. Like, oh yeah we freaked your mind, huh?

Now let's do some fact checking. Fourth album, 1970, always wanted to record at Olympic (the London studio "as important" as Abbey Road), named after Elvis's 1956 explosion. You're not weakening my trash talk, wikipedia. You're supposed to tell me I'm being hypercritical and non-objective. This band made a bad first impression on me, and I'd prefer to apologize rather than feel smug and say "I told you so."

I felt bad for not liking Maureen, but I'm dangerously close to saying "puke" and "douche" again. That's not fair. I'm supposed to defend them in spite of their derivative bandwagoning, not wait until we're traveling beside a deep gorge to "accidentally" nudge them off the cart. No stars. A miserable experience. Hey everyone, smell *this*.

56) Cher - Dark Lady

If you've been paying attention, then you know I've accepted my own challenge Carey Elwes style (you know, Men in Tights metal gauntlet across the face) several times already. So, let's see if I can defend a Cher album that doesn't actually excite me much.

Now that's an album cover. Those of you in the know will be well aware that about a decade later, the gatefold photo of Thriller features Michael Jackson lying down with a tiger cub on his leg. Those songs I hated from Thriller? Pretend you're back in high school English and write an essay about how they are actually responses to the songs on this album. Does it really matter if that connection is real, or collectively subconscious, or completely coincidental? No, it doesn't.

This is a deep cut Cher album; not so much radio single material as character development. Cher is a "cult of the voice" singer, and I personally can't think of anyone else who could really sing these songs. Go right to the opener of Side B, it's overtly vaudville, right? So, this is the flip side of my critique of Maureen McGovern; Cher *is* a pop star who can also pull off the broadway schlock because her personality, accent, phrasing, etc. define her character.

The best part of this post is that as I write it, I like the album more than when I started. By the time you get to her version of "Rescue Me" you know full well she doesn't need you to rescue her. That's a dare. Then she makes a real aside, and you recognize the album for the imaginary musical it really is. And the album closes with a difficult sentiment for modern audiences to interpret: you're just like your mother, wink.

The hard part about this album is that it's actually a real song cycle (the kind Schubert and Beethoven and Brahms wrote). You have to hold the whole thing in your brain as a complete unending circle. You have to flip it over again and listen to Side A, and on and on and on until you see how all the songs connect to each other like the spokes of a wagon wheel (Cher's a "gypsy," duh.)

There, I think I accomplished my goal. I took this album from "meh" to "bravissimo" in like 45 minutes, and all I had to do was insult Michael Jackson and Ten Years After at the same time. See what you can accomplish when you put your mind to it?

57) Blood, Sweat & Tears 4

BS&T4 is the end of the first stage of the band (and the last one I have). They invited Al Kooper (the original front man) back to contribute. Ironically, they specifically stopped playing shows, assembled in San Francisco, dove right into new original material that would serve as the foundation for the future of the band, then 1/3 of them quit to work on solo projects.

The critics aren't wrong when they say this record sounds exactly like it was made by people who had to carve out time from performing to create it, and then decided to go do other stuff. Each song is exactly what you'd expect from Blood, Sweat & Tears, but they really don't interact with each other. It's just stuff. One or more of the songs might really speak to you, but I don't think anyone could really argue that the album is great. It has no direction, or story, or recognizable trajectory; songs for the sake of songs.

It is, however, the most weirdly constructed jacket: a tri-fold with the pocket on the outside spine. Maybe the redeeming quality is that there are some really unique sounds. Not crazy or funny like 2 and 3, but unique.

That's ok, though. Cher's Dark Lady was surprisingly complex, so it's a nice change to take a mental break. Don't think about it too hard, just enjoy the diverse sounds they were able to capture in a rare moment of collective calm.

58) Jefferson Airplane - Crown of Creation

Remember how I joked that David Crosby would show up at your gig and play any instrument not being held by a band member at the moment? Well, I honestly don't know why he wasn't considered an official member of Jefferson Airplane.

I've been bouncing albums off each other lately and coincidentally lacking a context to talk about Crown of Creation. Luckily, it's basically BS&T4 with much better results.

They're in San Fransisco, finding time between gigs to record a new 4th album. David Crosby tripped, fell through the west bay window, and spilled chocolate all over Grace's peanut butter, I mean handed them Exhibit F in his divorce proceedings with The Byrds, "Triad."

Anyone can be on the passenger list of whatever flying vehicle they're using that day, but if Grace Slick isn't giving us the safety briefing, I'm not really paying attention.

I tell you all that, to tell you this: I like a lot of female vocalists regardless of the genre. I don't think that's a sexual (or sexist) thing, I think it's a real acoustic phenomenon. My ears prefer the blend of assertive female vocals. Grace Slick, Cyndi Lauper, Cher, Donna Summer, Laura Nyro, Bjork, and on and on and on.

It's also a semiotic thing. For whatever reason, the incidental sounds of the vocal apparatus convey much more meaning and emotion from women. A stifled giggle, or warble, or breath, or belted note can drastically change the meaning of a phrase in a way that a male voice often doesn't.

I don't have much to say about the album, though. Like BS&T4, these are songs for the sake of songs, and one or several can be quite enjoyable. Blows Against the Empire is much better, and there're just too many other people singing lead here to really get me excited.

59) What kind of parade?

I read a thing about the guys from Slayer defending The Black Parade by My Chemical Romance. Why wouldn't they? As albums go, it's a great album.

I don't like genre labels. They have a use as entryways for expectation, but the idea that people are beholden to a particular genre (even their favorite) is just stupid.

MCR has 4 albums. I brought you my bullets... is borderline unlistenable for me (I suspect because of my personal kinds of hearing damage), Three Cheers... and Black Parade are amazing albums (which doesn't mean a couple songs on each are not garbage, it just means that their purpose for the album outweighs my negative opinion of them), and I lost interest in the band (because 2 and 3 are more than good enough for me) before their 4th album so I have no comment.

The statement says more about the decayed experience of listening to music than it does the music itself. My whole reason for dedicating my energy to say something about any album is centered on the notion that liking or not liking something is a useless opinion. Why you feel that way is important, and you can't define it until you've really listened to it.

All of my negative reviews have included a reason why I feel that way, and when possible, I challenge you to disagree with me, or force myself to change my opinion, or at least admit my bias. Either way, I'm still telling you to find it, buy it, digest it, and make use of any nutrients extracted in the process.

If I do "believe" anything, it's that the way you think about music is the way you think about life itself. I only play a hermit on TV.

60) My Chemical Romance - The Black Parade

Dear Bottle,
Please put up or shut up.
Sincerely,
Mayor Rev. U. B. Insightful

I assume you're challenging me to pull out my CD of The Black Parade and make some pertinent remarks about how it holds up in the context of the last 40-something albums from the 60s and 70s.

Ok, game on. I used to play songs from this album in actual university music theory classes for dictation and formal analysis. My CD collection is obviously not organized, but here it is. Press play.

The opening track, "The End," is the prologue to the concept, and the darkness proceeds. Call them Emo, or alternative hard rock, who cares? It's rock, it's loud, it's eclectic, it's jaw dropping. This album is almost 14 years old, but it's heavier than a couple legitimate contemporary death metal albums I've heard. That's a bold statement, but every single song is meant for you to scream along. When I say heavy, I mean it is all consuming. You feel every emotion double strength because the compositions are so detailed and precise. Every single twiddle, crescendo, whammy dip, chorus passage, sour harmony, abrupt caesura, everything serves the delivery of the lyrics and there is no empty space anywhere. To borrow a Mahler anectdote, every note proceeds as if it were completely inevitable, no other divergent unfolding could ever be possible.

There are a few albums that are emotionally precise enough to make me tear up, and this is one of them. To be clear, this is an exhausting album to listen to with the kind of focus and attention I bring to the table because I can't not actually perform it with my whole body (I'm physically affected by it).

I could spend paragraphs specifically connecting it to every other album I've talked about because it goes right down the checklist: borrowing from all sorts of genres, emphasizing strange vocal delivery to convey meaning, capturing that eclecticism in the theme and artwork, and never breaking the fourth wall ("now watch me shred" is anathema to this kind of sonic art). There are a couple ripping guitar solos, but they are literally "beyond words" moments that merely serve as a deep breath before the oncoming explosion.

"Teenagers" is the one garbage song. It fills a specific role for the album, but as a song by itself it's substandard popular drivel.

At heart, this is an album about how it felt to exist in the 16-25 demographic during the 2000s. That's when the generation gap became a crocodile moat just like it did in the late 60s. The difference, of course, was that there wasn't even a fight to fight. Everyone in a position of power just shut the door and said "nope, you don't get the opportunities to work your way up the business ladder. The job you take now is the rest of your life. Don't already have an advanced degree? Sorry, but you can take a number and if there's an opening for 'unpaid intern' we'll call you. Maybe you could go back to school to be a mechanic, or draw pretty pictures in my coffee or something. Your parent's will probably let you move back in with them."

Zappa constantly railed against the new breed of businessmen refusing to accept new ideas they didn't quite understand. And, as I said a little earlier in the day, music is a sandbox for life.

How'd I do, Mr. Mayor?

61) A different kind of art rock (Hapshash and the Colored Coat or Western Flier?)

What do you think of when you think of "art rock"? Lou Reed's Velvet Underground? David Bowie? Yoko Ono? Early KMFDM? Bauhaus? These are all artists/bands who brought ideas from the world of contemporary art into their music. What if we went the other way? What if I handed you an album assembled by an actual art collective who weren't specifically musicians; a real graphic design house very well known for their music related posterwork, but extending their output as producers/writers of two essentially compilation albums?

I'll let you ponder which name goes to the band and which to the album for a while (I didn't know until I looked it up). The only other albums I can really compare it to are by Rotary Connection and The Incredible String Band, and if you went and listened to either of them then you'll know that you're in for some weirdness. Yet, knowing this is art first, music second makes a big difference. I'm still not sure if the other two bands had any concept of reality to begin with, but this album has a clear intentionality to it. It's wacky because they are seeking out the wacky. The core of what they are going for here is a fusion of cajun/creole/zydeco with psychedelic folk and rock, and noise, a mash up of competing but ultimately opposite worlds, as the cover illustrates. These things can obviously coexist, but their differences are in fact integral to the experience. That's what a collective really is; a group of wildly different people working individually toward some larger communal goal.

So, they're British visual artists exploring American musical subcultures. Make your decision. Ok, time's up. The album is Western Flier, by Hapshash and the Coloured Coat, but I still can't figure out which of those fine gentlemen is Hapshash. My money's on the guitar player. Perhaps, if I can get them to answer the telephone right side up, I'll ask....

62) Jeannie C. Riley - Harper Valley P.T.A.

Sometimes, after the intangible suffering of work, I like to tangibly suffer. This may come as a real shock (he says oozing with sarcasm), but I'm not a fan of Country Music. Sure, I could ramble off a list of a couple dozen great songs that are country, and I like a lot of Willie Nelson, quite a bit of Jason Isbell, some Johnny Cash, and Nitty Gritty Dirt Band's "Fishing in the Dark" (who doesn't?), but songs about pickup trucks, rodeo, and religious redneck revelry just aren't my thing, you know? You're allowed to love it, but I'll keep it strictly professional if you don't mind, thank you.

Where was I going with this? Oh, yeah. 1968 wasn't all space cadets and political polemics. It's also the year that produced the absolute biggest country single and songstress in the pre Dolly Parton universe. I'm talking, of course, about Jeannie C. Riley's version of "Harper Valley P.T.A." (it wasn't the first version of that song, but it's the only one you've ever heard, I'll bet).

Did you know it's actually from an album? No, of course not. There isn't a wikipedia page for any of her 21 albums. Now that I think of it, I could pick a bunch of things to fill this slot (Kenny Rogers, John Denver, the crate of Christmas albums, and even more), but this is actually refreshing. There's no immediate back story for the album, so I guess I am fishing in the dark after all. Let's give it a whirl.

I have to know, what's the deal with listing the songs out of order? Do you know?

I don't need to rehash the story of the title track, if you really don't know it you can read all about it. "Widow Jones" is, to use a modern phrase, a cougar. That's two saucy songs, so we're in for some heart ache. "No Brass Band," not surprisingly is about her dad falling in with a bad crew and getting shot. "Mr. Harper" is, to use an old phrase, a lecher. 5 tracks in, I realize this is the same kind of album as Cher's Dark Lady. It's about Jeannie, the character: the girl next door in a small town dealing with the hardships of growing up with the ups and downs (mostly downs) of rural life. Life's hard, but "Shed Me No Tears."

You know what, that wasn't so bad. My only real criticism is that the compositions are perfunctory. It's a case of "the lyrics are over, just fade out. No, no, don't bother to actually end the song; no one cares anyway." I care. What about my needs? At least give the band a "shave and a haircut," or something. Oh well, what's Side B like?

That riff from "The Cotton Patch," could easily be the foundation of a Creedence song. Character wise, she's headed to Dallas for a wild time but she's clearly a country girl in the big city and barely gets a job in a dog food factory. "Sippin' Shirley Thompson" doesn't care and swears a lot (but secretly she does care). I know 'cause Jeannie told me so... I fought the law and the law won... sorry, where was I? Oh yeah, more small-town life stuff. Get to Louise and Satan already.

Ooooh. Louise got some soul, and she's gonna steal your man. Shoot her? I knew it! Nice. Oh, ok "Satan Place" is just a reworking of Harper Valley (a pun on Peyton Place). I'm sure it's supposed to be ironic, but it's not irony. Unless you didn't expect a town named Satan to be just like every other small town. Is it like Greenland/Iceland? With a name like Satan, it has to be good (Seriously, Bottle? Smuckers? Are you the Dennis Miller of music critics?).

Anyway, I think we need to take a moment to appreciate how little effort it took for me to actually enjoy this album. With the exception of the fade outs on Side A (somehow not as annoying on Side B), and the last song being a complete rip off of the first song, this album is pretty good. I'm actually curious about more of her albums. Really, they should be just as enjoyable; you wouldn't expect they'd keep paying for two albums a year for a decade if they weren't at least making their money back. Definitely go give this whole album a listen, it's really not bad at all.

63) Melanie - Gather Me

Speaking of interesting female voices, this is Melanie. I actually had no idea who she was, but it turns out I know a lot of her songs. You've heard at least one of her songs (unless you live under a rock and don't know what roller skates are), and it's on this album. She played at Woodstock. She's mainly a pop-folk singer/songwriter and wowzers she made a lot of albums. I have two of them and this is Gather Me. I also have Stoneground Words, which just topped BS&T4 for weirdest album jacket/packaging, but that's a different essay altogether.

Her voice is really interesting, and there's a contemporary singer who sounds a lot like her, but I can't quite think of who I'm thinking of; maybe you know? Maybe I'm just thinking of other Melanie songs I didn't know were Melanie (shrug).

There's not really a theme or shape to this album that I can describe, other than to say it's a diverse collection of folk styles. That's not entirely true, the album slowly morphs from country-ish songs to overtly Celtic songs, but that's not really a satisfying concept. Maybe she's saying these are all the various things that make her whole, the constellation of musics that is Melanie (Country, Celtic, Blues, and the slightest hint of old time Gospel). She's quite a good guitar player too.

The song that really intrigues me is "Some Say (I Got Devil)." It's very minor, but the accompaniment does some really weird stuff that I can't quite understand on first listen. I may have to transcribe it, just to figure out what I'm actually hearing.

It's a very singer/songwriter album, whatever that might mean to you, but there are some really interesting orchestrations/arrangements. If you detest Joan Baez, or Joni Mitchell, or Laura Nyro, then Melanie isn't going to win you over, but it's at least an interesting listen. I'll certainly check out the other album I have by her at some point....

64) Zager & Evans - 2525

Are you looking for something halfway between Simon & Garfunkel and Seals & Crofts? More rock oriented acoustic music, less neurosis? Well, I've got just the thing. It's Zager & Evans, 2525.

I don't like the phrase "one hit wonder," but 2525 is probably the only song you've ever heard by them. Wouldn't it be a hoot if Zager & Evans turned out to be the ones with an accurate doomsyear prediction? 505.083 years to go, fingers crossed.

I don't want to spoil it for you, but this is an album about how people suck and the world would be better if we actually loved each other. They attack that theme from pretty much every angle. It's subtle, but the message is that sex and emotions and nature are good, ideologies are bad, m'kay?

65) Seals & Crofts - Summer Breeze

If there's one thing I really like doing, it's hinting that Seals & Crofts might not be my cup of tea. I drink unadulterated coffee. The reason I don't like them is complicated (what isn't, coming from me?); I adore their music, but I don't care about their words. Honestly, if they had a boxed set of all their albums without vocals, I'd be completely happy. Karaoke/Muzak versions of their entire catalogue? Sign me up.

It's not a religious thing, or a thematic thing, or a hard vs. soft rock thing, or even the timbre their voices. I simply don't want to hear James Seals' poetry. I want to hear the combined compositional forces of Seals, Crofts, and Paich (Marty or his son David) make weird baroque folk with horns, strings, and anachronistically overdriven electric guitar. Rock orchestras are awesome.

I'm listening to the Summer Breeze album tonight, but the elephant in the room is always their later album Unborn Child. It's a sensitive subject, so I'll be neutrally hotelful.

Count: There is nothing offensive about that song, and the notion that their career took a nose dive for producing it is ludicrous. Pointercount: In the larger scheme of actual reality their viewpoint is idyllic and naive, but it's certainly not insulting or misogynistic like so many other arguments from that side of the debate. Let's agree that it's a Seals & Crofts song, and my argument is that none of their lovely compositions should have lyrics.

So, to sumo wrestle this idea. I don't hate Seals & Crofts, but I wish they didn't sing so much. Or, at all. Clear as mud?

66) Uriah Heep - The Magician's Birthday

I'm certain I'm supposed to hate tonight's album (not from my dad's collection). I'm supposed to call the band purveyors of 70s cheese rock drivel, overblown theatrical rock stars writing proggy pseudo sci-fi sillyness on top of a foundation of simple power chords. But, considering that that's exactly what Uriah Heep was trying to be in the first place, I have to love it. You have to love it. The Magician's Birthday is exactly what every concertgoer and record collector paid Uriah Heep to create.

I'm violently repulsed by Ten Years After because they took themselves very seriously. They thought they deserved to be rock stars, and everyone rightly said "no thanks." Uriah Heep told everyone "we're just guys who don't really know what we're doing, but you clearly want us to do more of it, so here."

Supposedly it's "loosely based on a short story," but if you can suss out the plot, I'll give you every penny of the 0.00 dollars I get paid to review albums. As far as I can tell, it's the same calendar date as it was when "the magician" was born, and girls are pretty awesome. Sunrise, sunset, presto-chango, it's my birthday (not MY birthday, you know what I mean).

I honestly think I love this album the same way Frank Zappa, Curt Cobain, and Lester Bangs loved The Shaggs' Philosophy of the World. It exists because they had to create it. They didn't have either the ability to argue with the impulsion, or any sense of embarrassment that might make them give up. They have every right to be proud of it, and they actually thank people for liking them enough to get to this point in the liner notes. Ten Years After literally wanted to copycat their heroes, but Uriah Heep said (just like Skid Row ten years after them), "we're glad this is working out, 'cause what the hell else are we gonna do otherwise?"

Same reason I adore The Chats right now. Same reason I can't truthfully say I hate Seals & Crofts. Rock isn't about talent or good looks or enlightenment, it's about being exactly who you are and getting your point of view far enough out into the world that people who couldn't possibly know you have to actually take a moment to consider whether or not they care.

67) Focus

I said I like The Magician's Birthday, but that Uriah Heep didn't really know what they were doing. I stand by that opinion, and today I'll show you an album by a much less famous band formed in the same year (1969) who did know exactly what they were doing. Sadly, most people only remember 2 things about Focus: the wacky first track from Moving Waves, and that Jan Akkerman was a completely underrated, bad-ass guitar slinger.

I don't own any of their albums, but I sure wish I did. These Dutch weirdos are all over the map, from classical to hard rock to easy listening, and they did it all without trying to force themselves to write pointless lyrics just so they could maybe have hit songs.

Focus is the reason I don't really like a lot of 70s glam or prog rock. They are way more enjoyable for me than Uriah

Heep, or Bowie, or Yes, or Slade, or Jethro Tull, or any other English art rock show group from the early 70s.

Moving Waves and Hamburger Concerto are great albums. Focus takes all the things that define 70s rock (from mindblowing jam sessions, to neo-classical, to the cheesiest of white funk and soft jazz), and unashamedly uses them to write actual compositions. Give them a try.

68) Rare Earth - One World

Remember a while back when I told you that weird story about Motown offering Bob Seger a whole lot of money to keep it in Detroit? Seger himself thought it was too weird, but Berry Gordy wasn't joking.

All sorts of true and false things have been said about the man, but he believed in two things: Detroit, and racial equality. They signed Rare Earth because they believed in them, and lacking an actual subsidiary for all the new white acts they were signing, they named the Rare Earth label after them (and it didn't hurt that they were the first white Motown group to gain some real notoriety).

One World is the album with "I Just Want to Celebrate," and the rest of the album is just as good. It's a serious funk rock album without any of the cheesy "look at us, we're white guys playing funk" garbage so common in the 70s. Rare Earth wasn't a gimmick, and that's why Motown took them seriously in competing with Atlantic and Capitol for a wider audience.

I think Bob Seger would have fit right it, but what do I know? At the end of the day, he probably felt being a small fish in a much bigger ocean was a step in the direction he wanted to go, while Motown might try to rein him in too much. I don't know, I'm not much of a Bob Seger fan anyway. Every once in a while, though, Rare Earth hits the spot.

69) The 4 Seasons - The Genuine Imitation Life Gazette

This might be my longest album review so far (don't worry they will get much longer in the future). But I swear a couple times, so it's worth the read.

How could I possibly mention Jefferson Airplane, The 4 Seasons, and Frank Zappa in the same context? Zappa said "this is rediculous" and a few years later The 4 Seasons said "you know what, Frank is right. This *is* ridiculous." To which Jefferson Airplane said, "Oh. Ok. Got it."

The real question is: which one is the most transgressive? Zappa said stop fighting, you look like idiots. Jefferson Airplane said I guess if love and community is a bad thing, then sure we're criminals and we'd be happy to move out into the fields and live peaceful lives without your garbage, let us go already. The 4 Seasons said hold my champagne for a moment.

In 1969, The 4 Seasons released the single most ironic, acidic, extravagant, and downright befuddling album ever created, The Genuine Imitation Life Gazette.

Zappa was accused of writing "shitty doo-wop" for satire (and his response was "well, duh"), and I'll argue any day of the week that Frankie Valli and friends said "you want to hear what it sounds like from the real deal? Ok, we'll tell you exactly how it feels to sympathize with nobody." Nobody understood this album, and that means they succeeded big time. I seriously don't know how it got released. The only possible explanation is that everbody said "it's The 4 Seasons, we aren't going to argue."

Well, let me tell you a secret. This isn't just a 4 Seasons album. This album literally influenced everyone, John Lennon, Jethro Tull, Jefferson Airplane, and even bands that don't start with "j." The statement this album makes isn't about "appealing to the psychedelic audience" like everyone thinks, it isn't an "experiment," it's straight up "we taught you everything we know, we raised you, of course we are a facade, go out and be who you know you should be and don't make us turn the car around."

Seriously, go listen to some early Mothers of Invention then really listen to The Genuine Imitation Life Gazette. The back of Jefferson Airplane's Volunteers doesn't look like that for no reason, and Paul and Grace didn't suddenly wake up with the urge to give Country/Folk Music a try only to have the band break up and eventually write Blows Against the Empire. They got backhanded across the face by The 4 Seasons and started being adults instead of the mewling children who made Crown of Creation. Lennon told Gaudio face to face it was one of his favorite albums, and to put it mildly the use of the "Hey Jude" outro and the cartoon of The Beatles and Ravi Shankar are anything but nice.

Whether or not you've even heard of this album, my statements might seem strange. 4 Seasons fans simply didn't understand it, didn't buy it, and the writers got a lot of grief for this album and the next (Frank Sinatra's Watertown). The band wasn't unhappy with the material, they were unhappy that it wasn't Top 40 material. Like I said, this wasn't a 4 Seasons album, it was a statement about the country in 1968, about where the money comes from, and how you take a bit of a hit (pun intended) when you forget which side of the entertainment line you stand on.

People do mention the lavish packaging, but they understate the sheer scope of detail, the inside jokes, the clear references to the bands and artists with whom their sympathies actually lie. And, they fail to appereciate the real gravity these songs had in the context of January, 1969.

In my little blurb about Classics IV, I hinted that The 4 Seasons as a business didn't take kindly to people imitating them, and this album drives that point home like a stake into a vampire. The 4 Seasons were a big deal before The Beatles, Stones, Hermits, etc. even bought a plane ticket, suffered no loss of popularity while said bands scampered around the country, got tired of zipping their lip and keeping up appearances for a brief 2 years, then went back to being The 4 Seasons.

Every track is pertinent. Yes, the opener is "about race relations," but that's not its actual meaning. The subtext of that song, and the album as a whole, is what I described above: we are The 4 Seasons; we tried to stay out of it, but you all clearly misunderstood; we don't like it any more than you do, but we live over here in the big house you're trying to light on fire. By all means, fight your fight, but don't pretend that we can fight it for you (we're one of those gaudy trinkets in the shop window on Main Street). Idaho is a lovely place, but musically speaking, fuck Idaho.

Contrary to what anybody says, no one made them do it. No one was sitting around saying "we have to appeal to the youth of today, get with the times, broaden our audience." When Gaudio says this album disappoints him but that it was something he "had to do," he's poilitely saying he shouldn't have needed to write this album, he shouldn't have needed to create an elaborate and expensive fake newspaper concept for everyone to latch onto, he shouldn't have needed to point out that everyone was acting like naive children coming of age in a mean old world, but clearly he did, and boy did he do it. He knew full well that the only way to firmly cement his band against the tsunami was to beat everyone to the punch.

The hard part about this album is that you have to really ask yourself how you feel about the subject matter, because Gaudio isn't spoonfeeding you any moral signposts. Do you like a world where parents get divorced and kids see their dads one day a week? Do you like a world where women find value in themselves only in terms of being the object of a man's affection? Do you actually think having money makes this charade more meaningful? Is it possible that you are just as much to blame for all the no fun we're having as your supposed enemy? Are you actually teaching your children to love, or are you just teaching them to hate each other the same way you do?

What this album really says is grow up, and actually do what you say you want to do. Want to drop out? Go right ahead. Want to play pretend? Fine. Wanna see us drop a ton of our own money just so you can feel validated? Bombs away. Now, if you don't mind, we'd like to go back to collecting our hard earned royalty checks from the head in the clouds pop we're known for making. Peace and love, don't touch my wallet.

My analysis may be contradictory to what you know or read, and that's because my analysis isn't newspaper critic/A&R blather. You can argue that Jake Holmes played a pivotal role in shaping the concept and story, but at the end of the day Gaudio hired him to help write it, Valli, DeVito, and Long helped make it good, and mild mannered don't rock the boat 'cause I'm secretly a shark Gaudio handed it to the execs at Philips and said "write the checks."

I'm glad he did, even if it didn't accomplish what he really wanted it to accomplish, which is secretly "GET OFF MY LAWN!"

70) Sonny Bono - Inner Views

I have a personal dislike for Sonny Bono, or more specifically Senator Sonny Bono. But, I don't want this to be about US Copyright law. I want it to be one of those reviews where I bring my admitted predjudices to the table and let the music speak its side of the argument. I want to hear Sonny without Cher. So, let's let the man speak. What are the Inner Views of Sonny Bono?

YOU HYPOCRITICAL LITTLE DWEEB! WHAT PERCENTAGE OF YOUR OWN ROYALTY CHECK DID YOU HAND OVER TO LENNON AND MCCARTNEY? IT'S CERTAINLY NOT PARODY OR ANY OTHER FAIR USE,

THE ENTIRE SIDE A IS A GODDAMNED DERIVATIVE WORK!

I sincerely apologize for my outburst, it was uncalled for and you have more to say. I will abstain from further comment until my official rebuttal. Please, go on….

…First, please excuse my umbrage at the phrase "All the songs on this LP were written and composed by Sonny Bono…." Though true in a legal sense, no one in this room today could in good faith argue that "I just sit there" and "I told my girl to go away" are not fully and intentionally derived from "A Day in the Life" by Lennon-McCartney. Hendrix learned "Sgt. Pepper" in a couple days because he was actually playing to the hometown crowd, and that's a level of respect you clearly cannot fathom. Therefore, I sincerely call into question your future career in politics. But, being as I am not a time lord, I will proceed to my real statements about this album. I assure you that I have genuinely positive things to say about your work, as well as a few very pointed criticisms.

You sir, have a very distinct and personally appealing style of vocal delivery, perhaps reminiscent of "Bob Dylan on Quaaluuds." Recognizing your role as producer of multiple successful solo albums for Cher, I understand wanting to "self direct" as I would call it. However, your wife had the benefit of a large group of people working together to create those albums in a way that played to her strengths of personality and showwomanship. You, however, are a dweeb. I mean no offense by that term, as there are a multitude of performers in all fields who make that persona work in their favor to unarguable success. Perhaps, in hindsight, it might have been more productive to bring in a neutral party who could have objectively said 1) these lyrics are garbage, 2) no human can realistically believe that all of the songs on this album exist in the same person. If these are in fact your "inner views," I might recommend a psychiatric evaluation for schizophrenia. 3) if they are in fact more general statements, the "inner views" of a variety of characters, then don't put yourself on the cover with the ghost of a woman trying to get you to turn around. Just don't.

I must reiterate my conflicted opinion of Seals & Crofts (obviously you don't know them, I am from the future), but like James Seals I do not care what you have to say. Whatever parts of this album you did or didn't compose are wonderful, but I would have enjoyed you scat singing like Ella Fitzgerald infinitely much more than what you have written here. You could have read a Waffle House menu with much better results.

Obviously, you have no idea what level of bizarrity will befall your future self and your family, but if I *were* a time lord, I could only implore you to take someone else's advice once in a while. You do not understand you, and the world would be a much better place if you let someone else be in charge.

I am Bottle, and I approve this message.

71) Three Dog Night - Live at the Forum

Tonight's album is going to be a little scattershot. I have thousands of things to say, but they trip all over each other in my brain.

In front of an audience of over 18,000 people on September 12, 1969 in Los Angeles, Three Dog Night was Captured Live at the Forum (I'll talk about that later). If you knew absolutely nothing about Three Dog Night and this was the first album you ever heard from them, you would probably say something like "wow these guys are fantastic! How come I haven't heard of them?"

Answer: because they literally became a band in 1968, the two albums they recorded in 1968/69 were practically still hot off the presses, and the fact that this album even exists at all is completely fortuitous.

It's a dirty little secret that live albums exist for basically 3 reasons: 1) they won't be together much longer and live albums count toward fulfilling your contract, 2) they ran out of ideas for their next real album, but they still have to generate new revenue to pay back the advance from the last album, or 3) both 1 and 2 at the same time and it's cheaper than real studio time.

Amazingly, none of those apply to this album. It's not actually a Three Dog Night recording. Obviously it's them, but the band is *opening* for Steppenwolf. They are recording Steppenwolf's tour, but since they are label mates and both bands are using the same production crew, why not? And, since the undercard is starting to kill it with their first couple singles on the airwaves, it certainly won't hurt to show everyone that it isn't an act; these guys really do rock that hard.

That wacky long title? Well, in subsequent retellings of the band's history, it's not exactly set in stone that this is that actual concert (memories get fuzzy, you know?). I personally adore the notion that they unintentionally created a live concept album about how famous the band would become in the next couple years. That's delicious and I don't care what the real truth is. I will point out, though, that after this first run they completely eliminated the date and crowd size from the cover (bummer).

Three Dog Night is pretty freakin' awesome. Unlike Sonny Oh-no, they knew the true value of buying their stuff from legit dealers (sorry, everything from the 60s was somehow about drugs, and I can't resist). Oh look, it's Harry Nilsson. Is that Laura Nyro in the big dark sunglasses? I swear, that guy looks just like Paul Williams.

These guys deserved every bit of fame and fortune they got, and they certainly weren't afraid to say "we couldn't have done it without these talented people you haven't heard of yet either."

To recap, this album is magic. It's one of the best live albums ever recorded, it's an unintentional greatest hits, it exists by pure coincidence, and if that doesn't make you feel warm and fuzzy inside then pour yourself another rum and coke and spin it again. You'll get there, I believe in you.

72) A Little Back Story and Metallica

I'm nearing the end of my 39th year on the planet, and I thought it might be interesting to explain where my love of albums began. I'm not going to begin the beguine, but I'll flash as far back as possible.

The first CD I ever got was Megadeth's Countdown to Extinction. I saw the video for "Symphony of Destruction" on MTV and my brain said "yes, more of that, please." I was 12 when that album came out and asked for a CD player and that CD for Christmas, but I had already been listening to albums on cassette for years. I remember sitting in the back seat of a car on vacation when I was 8 or 9, listening to Madonna's Like a Prayer on constant repeat (I still LOVE early to mid Madonna). Probably the oldest memory I have is listening to an actual record of the story of Gremlins. Point being, I was born at a time when cassette was king, vinyl still very much existed, and a CD player cost something ridiculous like $800. A portable CD player in 1992 was still a pretty substantial Christmas present, as far as I can remember. Nevermind, the Black Album, a friend named Donovan gave me his cassette of Use Your Illusion 1, another friend, Scott, gave me his cassettes of Master of Puppets and Ride the Lightning. I was on the same gymnastics team as Guard Young (if you know anything about gymnastics you've probably heard of him) and he loved AC/DC, but they didn't really click with me. That's what newly teenaged Bottle sounded like on the inside.

KATT used to play 7 at 7, seven full albums on Sunday night and I would record whichever albums I might like to tape for repeated listening.

Long story longer, what prompted me to say all that was I've been singing Metallica's "Don't Tread On Me" in my head since about 1:15 this afternoon, and I love The Black Album so much that I'm going to make this the longest stream of thoughts possible.

Every band has its die-hard fans, and Metallica's die-hard fans hated it because it sounded like sellout commercial toilet water, causing debilitating tinnitus in their ears. But, remember, those guys were bigger alcoholics than the band they themselves affectionately nicknamed "Alcoholica." (Alcoholism is not a joke, but pretending that Metallica "sold out" by writing the best songs ever recorded and going to extravagant lengths to record them perfectly while Bob Rock kept saying "you can play that riff better, and the EQ stays exactly where I put it" over the intercom every 10 minutes for 8 months *is*).

This is the album that made Metal an acceptable genre for anyone to like. I kid you not, I've met little old ladies who love Metallica (and Pantera). Not a gimmick, that good. Here we are 28 years later, and this is still considered as good an album as any humans could ever hope to produce.

Why? Because they sound like complete human beings. They are scared, they are depressed sometimes, they get angry, they tell ghost stories with relevant moral lessons, they say you have to keep trying even when you want to give up, and most importantly they say take a good look at yourself and be better.

73) Goodbye Cream

I am not at all a stranger to sitting on the floor in a collectibles shop and flipping through rows and rows and rows of records, debating what to actually buy, checking to make sure the actual record is in there, and walking out with a handful. As I was doing exactly that in the middle of running errands today, I came across Emerson, Lake, & Palmer's Pictures at an Exhibition and I thought "Tarkus is very lonely, and it is my civic duty to buy all three EL&P albums sitting here and reunite them.

    I'll write about them some other time. Today we're saying Goodbye Cream. That's not a non-sequiter. Cream is the encyclopedia example of a power trio. Goodbye Cream is their "we're not a band anymore" live/studio split. Nobody was really happy with it, but I think it's actually the perfect Cream album.

    Let's be honest, these three lunatics were more narcotics than human at this point. Critics thought the live tracks were poor imitations of their studio versions, and the studio tracks were amazing but completely unfulfilling. I like Cream as much as anybody, and I'm not at all disappointed. It sounds like Eric Clapton, Jack Bruce, and Ginger Baker smacking their instruments around they way they always did. Their intended multi-volume festivus would have been too much. As for the criticism that Clapton ruined everything by playing blues licks in tracks that weren't "the blues," that's the dumbest thing I've ever heard.

    Everyone rightly decided that a few good recordings from their final tour and 1 studio track from each member was exactly what a band that parted ways before the masters even arrived at the pressing plant should make. They were great, now they're done, let's all get on with it. As far as album concepts go, I find that quite satisfying.

    The standout track for me is Jack Bruce's "Doing That Scrapyard Thing." It sounds so infectiously, ridiculously British, and it puts me in mind of Supertramp, Syd Barret's Pink Floyd, and Robert Fripp's jovial silly music with Giles and Giles. I don't need any more than that.

74) Sagittarius - The Blue Marble

I would be truly impressed if you knew the name Gary Usher. The man did a lot of things, but none of them really ever panned out to much of anything. That's because nearly everything he did just seemed to miss the mark by a few inches. I've been trying to write about this album since mid October, but now a month later I finally know how to respond.

When Gary was a young man, he once played a song that he and his friend Brian wrote. When he was done, Brian's dad said "not bad, Gary, now usher yourself the hell out of my living room." That's about as good as it got for Gary.

On paper, the man did everything I should adore: he produced anything that seemed like fun, he made up band names for his studio projects, he helped write at least 9 more certified hits for the Wilson family singers (they lived near the seashore or something), but he made an album that got my hopes up way too high.

I looked at the cover of The Blue Marble by Sagittarius and thought "this is either the greatest concept album nobody talks about, or I'm going to be really disappointed. It's my fault, really. I flipped it over, took one look at the cartoon drawing of a man in a nightgown sitting on the moon and rubbed my hands like a bum at a trash can fire.

Damnit, Janet, I mean Gary. "In my room" is the perfect set up song. I was thinking, ok I know where Brian Wilson went with the stuff they wrote together, but now I'm going to get to hear the weird Gary Usher lucid dream about looking at earth from outer space. Yippee! Needless to say, I was really upset at having anything close to a similar opinion as Murray Wilson. Nevertheless, when it was over, I very much wanted Usher to get the hell out of my safe space.

The first 2 tracks are totally great, completely weird, but then he goes serious country, and where did the concept go? Who the hell is Gladys? Is she a serpent woman, why are you hissing? How much did you pay that trumpeter for one repeated note? Side A has so much wasted potential.

Side B opens with the title track. Again, it's perfect for the concept, but that concept has yet to materialize. In the cinematic adaptation of my writing these reviews I'm giving Gary a noogie like Biff in Back to the Future. Mcfly! Mcfly! This isn't an unrequited love album, Mcfly!

Usher has the most perfectly strange voice for what this album should have been; he sounds like the drawing of the dweeb in a nightgown on the back, his blend of Moog synths and traditional instruments is phenomenally bizarre, but his lyrics serve no discernable purpose.

Gary, dear. You created an amazing concept album, but forgot to actually include the concept. These are *your* songs, you're allowed to change the lyrics. Hell, you're allowed to pay someone else to write the lyrics but retain full copyright of that "work for hire" for the next century thanks to Bozo McChersexhusband. I mean, I can respect that this is what you wanted, but all I can say about it is "make like a tree and get out of here."

It is what it is. These songs are unique. It could have been amazing, but it isn't. It's worth a listen for the truly interesting things people made with Bob Moog's crazy electronic wizardry, but as an album it belongs buried way back in the miscellaneous crate so nobody unsuspectingly suspects it will be amazing.

75) Emerson, Lake, & Palmer - Pictures At An Exhibition

Once upon a time, Kieth Emerson bought a copy of Mussorgsky's Pictures at an Exhibition and said "how would you guys feel about turning this into a full showpiece for the band? We could take a few of the best parts, add some of our own, commission new paintings for it, the works." Greg Lake and Carl Palmer said "sure. Why not? That would make performing it pretty cool." Their label said "if you want to make a classical record it's gonna be distributed as a classical record" and they sadly put it in cold storage.

Fast forward a little, and somehow the trio made it through recording Tarkus without killing each other. At that point, they were grasping at straws to find anything they could agree on.

They had already recorded an actual performance of this piece, and it is amazing. They do the intro with the new pipe organ at Newcastle City Hall, and Palmer has to vamp on a drum roll while Emerson literally runs back down to the stage for the next piece. This is just an EL&P concert. Emerson's early Moog synthesizers are randomly detuning because the voltage controllers were affected by atmospheric conditions, they have to fade out between tracks because the applause breaks go on forever, they do their own wacky version of the Nutcracker Suite as an encore, and all the label could say was "we'll have to sell it as a bargain live album, but sorry we made you wait."

I told you I didn't really know the band because of my music specific ADD, but I'm a total fan-boy now. Their first 3 albums are spectacular, and I even secretly enjoy Love Beach because I have a morbid fascination with the last trainwreck of an album any band makes before their breakup (it's not really as bad as everyone says it is, but it does suck and you can't blame Lake and Palmer for voting themselves off the island, tax evasion charges be damned).

To summarize, I now adore Emerson, Lake & Palmer. They remind me of Gary Sandy's Andy Travis on WKRP. They look like dumb 70s jocks, but their music is pure madness.

76) REO Speedwagon - You Can Tune A Piano But You Can't Tuna Fish

You Can Tune a Piano, but You Can't Tuna Fish. In spite of it's all time classic cover and title, this is just one of REO Speedwagon's albums. It's got a couple real hits, some filler, and a couple tracks for which they didn't even bother to type up lyrics. They are a band who is great in small doses, they're funny, they can rock like nobody's business, a great show for sure, but they are not a compelling album band: two really good hit songs on each side and call it a day. All of their albums are like that: they would benefit immensely by removing all the stuffing and letting each one be a solid stand alone EP, double them up for a full length. It's not as if they "evolved." From beginning to now, REO Speedwagon is REO Speedwagon, you know exactly what you're going to get and you can literally pick any 7 of their songs and have an REO Speedwagon album.

The one standout jam, The Unidentified Flying Tuna Trot, is way too short for my 8 to 18 minute sweet spot (I want drum solos and bass abuse), and wimpily fizzles out before the harder rockin' but much less interesting "Say You Love Me...."

Their albums are specifically for their true fans who had no reason to care about a larger story or a cerebral adventure, they loved anything the band did because it was quality sing along rock and roll. Not particularly interesting, but high quality. Keep in mind, they only achieved real mainstream success with their 9th album, after 12 or 13 years of trucking back and forth across the country for a living, at which point everyone agreed that they'd always been that good.

Wait a minute. This is all really just a negative version of my comments about The Doors. Am I shallowly favoring Morrison's voice over Cronin's? No, I think it's that The Doors sound unpredictable even though they aren't, while REO sounds predictable because they are. The Doors are a metaphor band, REO is a breakup song band. You can bring whatever mood you feel to The Doors and be rewarded with some small (however vague) insight, but there's no negotiating with the Speedwagon; baby's gonna leave me, put the pedal down and shift through to cruising gear. For me, that's just not a rewarding headphone time with a tasty beverage experience. I'll gladly ride shotgun, but I'll probably take a nap in the middle.

I need something bigger. Something over the top insane. To be continued...

77) Guns N' Roses - Use Your Illusion I & II

...There's no shortage of stories and history about Guns n' Roses, so I don't really need to rehash it all, but I will point out things relevant to other albums I've talked about.

Use Your Illusion I & II (it's all one big work) are monumental. It had been 4 years since Appetite for Destruction, and rather than simply *an* album, they made a 2+ hour musicological documentary about being Guns n' Roses. That's what these albums are, the illusion is what you the listeners see, the reality is much more terrible and real.

The reality is that they sat around for 2 years because Steven Adler couldn't do Guns n' Roses levels of herion and still walk anymore. Fights with neighbors, getting arrested, they all ODed, died, and got resuscitated at various points, then decided to hire a new drummer, work up more of their early songs, a couple covers, write epic ballads, scathing tirades, divide the whole thing into exterior and interior points of view (color coded for your convenience), and just be the biggest, nastiest rock and roll band ever, presumably expecting to die in the process. It took a year and a half to record this glorious monstrosity. Obviously, their egos and addictions eventually got the better of all of them, but that's their future and we're living in the moment right now.

The red one is the fiery macho axl saying "you betcha, I am a dirtbag, but don't pretend I'm somehow the exception in this messed up world" as they speed their muscle cars out into the desert. The blue man group is Axl saying "here's how we actually feel about this stuff, we are human." Most people instantly gravitated to the second album (and it's still much more popular), but you can't have one without the other. To my mind, Use Your Illusion II is the adrenaline crash, the hangover, the depression to Use Your Illusion I's mania. The first album literally ends with a depiction of Slash and Axl's real overdoses, and the second album picks up with "none of this is good; the world, us, our relationships, none of it."

You can go scour the band's history for relevant details, but all of these songs are about themselves and the world they physically (if not quite mentally) inhabit.

As you may have noticed, my only criticisms of any of the people behind all of this music have come when they didn't do a good job of what I think they were trying to accomplish. These two monolithic statements are proof positive of how good the music can be. They certainly don't glorify that alien world in my mind, and it's hard for me to get on board with anything after (especially right now), but the Use Your Illusions are just spectacular.

78) Iron Butterfly - Heavy

If Steppenwolf is the motorcycles and attitude half of the equation, then solving for x gives us Iron Butterfly. Heavy is their first album, contact the William Morris Agency for booking.

They played shows and shows and shows, and their debut album reached 78 on the Billboard Charts without a single. By the numbers, they were the biggest group signed to Atlantic up to that point. They were booked to play Woodstock, but their management blew it. They also had to find new members almost every year, but that doesn't really matter.

Heavy is a pretty diverse album, but it's shrouded in an almost tunnel vision reverby low-mid blanket. In other words, it sounds stoned. So stoned you've lost peripheral processing...such pretty colors...no idea what he's singing about, but isn't it trippy?

Any other band and this would have stayed completely underground, but it's so obvious why everybody just instantly ate up this almost textural, but not actually intimidating weirdness. It's like you're at a house party, and you know you know who's house it is, but you can't remember her name at the moment, and half the people have passed out already, but the other half is spazzing out, and the band is singing something about trees being soldiers, and then the room starts spinning and the universe explodes and you flatline. Fun times.

79) Anthony Newley's Musical

Tomorrow is some sort of holiday, or something. Obviously, it has a song associated with it, and I'll talk about it somehow. But, I just stumbled upon what is surely the most obscure album in the collection: "… can Heironymous Merkin ever forget Mercy Humppe and find true happiness?" It's an x-rated British musical film (keep in mind x-rated for 1969 just means there's gratuitous nudity). It's not the most famous thing Anthony Newley ever did (somebody had to co-write "Goldfinger"), but it's definitely the most ambitious. Terrible, but ambitious.

I haven't seen this movie, but from just looking at the cover it had to be terrible. It had to be. Roger Ebert gave it a passive-aggressive complimentary review, Joan Collins filed it away as a reason to look for a third husband, Milton Berle was in it at all, this soundtrack never got republished once CDs were invented... I don't need to see it, but I have to listen to it. If Anthony Newley himself produced it, composed it, convinced his much more renowned wife to be in it, and tangibly suffered for it, it has to have some redeeming quality.

And it is a completely normal musical, as far as the songs are concerned. In spite of the cringeworthy plot outlined in the notes, a couple of the songs made me giggle because they were actually funny (musical funny, but nevertheless). The project as a whole surely deserved every raspberry it received, but it's no worse to listen to than South Pacific, or Brigadoon, or Damn Yankees. It's no Jesus Christ Superstar (which I totally also have), but the songs are actually servicable songs.

At the end of the day, the guy just wrote a musical and made it happen on an international scale. It earned 4 times its budget at the box office so I seriously doubt Universal actually lost much money. It's on youtube already, 'cause some people care about cheeky musicals that flopped. I don't want to meet those people, but at least it means I don't have to sit here and dub it so you can say you've actually heard it.

80) Arlo Guthrie - Alice's Restaraunt

There have been many great "I tell you that story to tell you this story..." stories. Ron White's was about calling himself 'Tater Salad.' Arlo Guthrie's was about the draft. There's a radio station in your town that will play the whole thing, Bob Dorr will play it in Iowa on one of his shows. I'm just going to listen to the actual record. Arlo did occasionally play a couple other songs. Now I want a pickle, for some reason.

81) Rotary Connection - Peace

"B-R-L-F-Q spells mom and dad." That *is* a non-sequiter. I'm procrastinating by listening to a Bobby Goldsboro 45, because we're about to go on an adventure.

I apologize in advance for what I'm going to do for the next two weeks. But, in celebration of today's truly riveting Macy's Thanksgiving Day Christmas Parade, and since everyone's life revolves around the next holiday, I'm going to let Bottle say mean things about every single Christmas album I have. I mean no personal offense, but I assume if you haven't thrown this book in the trash by now, you're complicit.

I have 13 of these things, and they are not the cream of the Christmas crop. If you love Christmas albums you might want to ignore me for the next dozen or so pages, but if you've taken a shine to the inventively playful insults my brain produces from time to time, we might bond a little more.

We'll start off as gentle as possible with what I assume is an intentional absurdity. I don't think they would be mad at all to hear me call them "wackadoodle." Do Christmas songs need sloppy acid-rock guitar solos? Is Christmas the holiday where we flip a coin to decide if a child or an old person dies, or is it the one where we pretend we aren't racist for a day? Does Santa get high from smoking mistletoe?

Rotary Connection says "YES," and it's hard to argue with their level of confidence. It's weird, is what I'm saying. You don't *have* to listen to the whole thing, but at the very least go find "Peace At Last." That song is unique.

82) The Kingston Trio - The Last Month of the Year

If I were going to be stuck in a department store elevator for 3 days with a Christmas album playing non-stop, The Kingston Trio's The Last Month of the Year might be survivable.

In general, it's thankfully ignorable. However, I cannot adequately express how mentally unsettling it is to pick seemingly random verses from a counting song. My OCD is generally mild, but it's definitely uncomfortable to skip from 3 to 5 to 8 to 10, when they count back down through *all* of them. A couple repeats of that and I'd probably punch the first person I saw after being rescued (don't worry, I'd apologize as I was doing it).

I also hope that reminding me that Christmas is the 25th of December (that's the last month of the year if you missed the memo) isn't a common trait. Both albums so far have done it, and I can't decide if it's a PSA, or sarcasm, or if there's just so little to say that no one even tries to avoid it.

83) Barbara Mandrell - Christmas At Our House

I thought I only had 13, but I just kept finding more. Luckily, I don't have a turntable that can play 78s. Unluckily, Barbara Mandrell is cued up and ready to play.

It burns! It burns! Make it stop! It's no secret I'm a godless heathen, but Jesus and I get along just fine. It's subtextually sexy Barbara Mandrell that gives me the heebie-jeebies. "Santa, Bring My Baby Home," "It Must Have Been the Misteltoe," bleurgh.

And then I got to "Born to Die." Pardon the pun, but sweet baby jesus, Shireen Salyor! "It must have broken god's heart/ For the future he could see./ Yet, he formed the hands and feet/ Knowing one day they'd be nailed to a tree." I thought the lyric "faces and numbers have rearranged" from Archie Jordan was unintentionally hilarious, but that's just hardcore.

I'm slightly concerned that Barbara thinks she's immortal because Jesus knew he was dying for her personally, but at least her final sermon (medley) is lyrically coherent.

I still can't get over that weird Reba-esque intrusion on Side A. Just, eww. Luckily, it's over, she didn't remind me what actual day Christmas is, and I've got another whole crate of music about drugs and motorcycles to wash away the aluminum aftertaste of this album's off-brand synthy gingerbread frosting.

84) Joyous Christmas

This one's supposed to be terrible, so it gets a bit of a pass. It's the 6th installment of Columbia's Joyous Christmas series. It's your standard live in Technicolor cavalcade of stars from the 40s/50s/60s being cheesy because they don't know any other way to be.

Highlights include Danny Kaye's ghastly Louis Armstrong impression, Doris Day's atrocious vibrato, a few has-beens and forget-me-soons, real working ensembles (an orchestra with an electric guitarist who isn't sure why he's there), Carey Grant sprechstimme-ing badly with Carlesbad Caverns levels of reverb, Bing Crosby being sappy and condescending at the same time.

Sure it's terrible, but it's the kind of terrible specifically designed to funnel money from the rich back down to actual people. All these celebrities were philanthropists in their own way, and they lived in a world where schlock and schmaltz was considered real show biz. I don't like it, but I can't really hate on it too much.

85) The Instrumental Christmas Favorites

I bet you thought there wasn't anything interesting you could learn by listening to old Christmas records. I bet you didn't know Jackie Gleason was a serious composer, arranger, and conductor. I bet you didn't know his music career was just as prolific as his tv/movie career. I bet you didn't know that to this very day, he has the longest running top 10 Billboard album at 153 weeks. No. You had no idea.

I...uh... I don't have that album, I just have this Christmas thing for which he arranged some music. But still. Knowledge, and stuff.

Here he is with other heavyweights Guy Lombardo...Eddie Dunstedter...the hollyridge strings... Ok, ok, it's not as impressive as I was trying to make it sound, but it has the definite advantage of very limited singing. And, as far as completely orchestral Christmas music goes, it's actually pretty good. Capitol bills it as "easy listening," but there's some really good stuff going on for the orchestrationally literate among us, despite it's overall JC Pennies/Sears & Roebuck naugahyde funiture department aura. It's campy and dated, no doubt about it, but there's some real charm to that as well. It's the kind of album you'd set playing low at your next dinner party so that I would chuckle and wink at you while everyone else just says "what the hell are we listening to?," every once in a while.

It's a double album, but it flies by pretty quick if you just have it on in the background. As for Ralph Kramden's contributions, they are indeed interesting. He's got the last three tracks, and they have a definite night-club aesthetic not heard on the previous 3 sides. Sophisticated, but with a couple of well-ginned tonics already down the hatch if you catch my drift. If you had to pick a Christmas album, you could easily do worse.

86) Barbra Streisand - A Christmas Album

Just when you think you've got me all figured out, I go and tell you I love Barbra Streisand's A Christmas Album. That's a half truth, I love Side A. Side B is meh.

Side B is Babs' first Christmas album. She was sick and pregnant in London, but the studio and personnel were already booked, so they just bashed it all together in 3 days or something and waited until the next year. It was worth it.

Side B is a boring christmas album by Barbra Streisand and Ray Ellis. Side A though, that's a Barbra Streisand and Marty Paich album that happens to contain Christmas songs.

Everybody put down their version of Jingle Bells, but gave no actual reason why it was supposedly so bad. That's because they simply didn't understand it. It's Barbra Streisand. Remember how I gave Joyous Christmas a pass? Remember how I gave Uriah Heep's pathetic attempt at prog rock a pass? These things are all exactly what they are supposed to be.

Sure, if you gave me the choice between a Babs album and field recordings of motocross races 80% of the time I'd choose the latter, but I've heard enough Broadway vocalists in training to recognize the real deal when I hear it. Barbra is phenomenal. You might hate her accent, or not find her attractive, but personality wise she's off the charts. You're supposed to experience the shock, then laugh and say "that was fantastic" just like with Blood, Sweat & Tears. This is theater, and the absurdity of a Jewish superstar making a secular Christmas album without actually insulting anyone is a big part of the appeal.

Her singing is immaculate, and Mr. Marty knew exactly how to arrange an orchestra behind her. The happy/sad tug-of-war that is Christmas is on full display, but she's so good at understatement that she doesn't need to nail a baby to a tree or put on moth-ball scented lingerie like some Barbaras with too many As in their name. She can just give a tinge of giggle or darken her tone to give you the exact emotional context of a lyric.

The secret ingredient, of course, is Marty Paich. As many times as I've mentioned him, it's obvious that everything he touched turned out pretty good in my book.

87) The Oak Ridge Boys - Christmas

And then there is this. This thing. I have so many questions. Who's apartment did they break into to shoot this cover? I'm pretty sure The Oak Ridge Boys live in a hollow log near a banjo playing opossum. Waaaiiiit... that's a mirror. That room is empty. They broke into an uninhabited apartment and just set up a christmas tree. Who abandoned all those children at this breaking and decorating fiasco? I'd take any package these weirdos gave me straight to the nearest bomb disposal robot.

"Christmas Carol"? A crazy lady who knows every song and thinks everyday is Christmas? Seriously? I hope for Bobbie Sue's sake they never find her. Even Santa Claus is over in the corner saying "please don't shoot! None of this was my idea, I swear!"

Look, I'm just a snarky imaginary music critic and you have every right to like The Oak Ridge Boys as much as you want, but let's not pretend that this is good for anybody. This is bad. My uncontrollable laughter is clearly a defense mechanism. I haven't even listened to Side B yet. I had to take a smoke break, and feed my dogs, and finish my rum and coke, and I'm still not mentally prepared to hear the rest of it. Well, here goes nothing.

Side B starts off better, wrong choice of word, it's more normalish Oak Ridge Boys. I spoke too soon, "Thank God for Kids" is creepy and confusing, but it's probably just bad songwriting. Silent night is fine. Damnit, as soon as I said that he started talking and it's like he's reading from cue cards while also trying to keep up with a metronome. Another song where you personify generic words? If I were Mary, I'd run as fast and far away as possible.

You know what I was saying about Barbra's personality being more important than just her singing Christmas songs? Well, it's exactly the opposite with these crazies. The more generic the better. Do not let them ad lib. Do not feed them after midnight. Lock your doors, hide your daughters and your sons, The Oak Ridge Boys are on the loose, and they will pet your dog until its head falls off.

88) Jefferson Airplane - Bless Its Pointed Little Head

I need a break from Christmas albums, how about you? Let's talk about Jefferson Airplane instead. You can disagree with me, but Bless Its Pointed Little Head is the last Jefferson Airplane album, in my opinion. I briefly mentioned Volunteers, and the remaining members kept the name going into the 70s, but it's not the same band for me.

It's not a strange opinion for me either. Syd Barret's Pink Floyd, Roger Waters' Pink Floyd, and David Gilmore's Pink Floyd are three different bands. Peter Gabriel's Genesis and Phil Collins' Genesis are different bands. There's Van Halen and Van Hagar. And so on.

Jefferson Airplane was a rock band, regardless of what other things they did on their studio albums. They were 20 something driftabouts who liked jamming in front of people, and that's exactly what they were doing in 1968 while the 4 Seasons were carefully calculating how best to express how silly and ineffectual that is.

Jefferson Airplane thought they were having fun. They recorded their shows at the Filmore East and West (New York and California), including new songs that weren't on their earlier albums, and went to bed. Then they woke up in actual real life 1969 feeling like moldy produce. "Oh no! We *are* just entertainment. We're not important at all." Thus ends Jefferson Airplane. I imagine it hurt.

I already told you I like what Paul Kantner and Grace Slick did with that hurt, I like it a lot, but I wouldn't call it fun. This album is fun.

You might be thinking "I don't get what you're saying Bottle, they were always politically motivated and skeptical." To which I respond "no." They knew something was wrong but they didn't have any proper way to express themselves, like children. Like children, they said "we're right and everybody else is dumb," put them down, said things like "bless its pointed little head," but the only thing they understood was the metaphor. They didn't understand the reality that makes that metaphor actually meaningful to the people in the audience. They didn't actually have an enemy, just a nebulous "them."

And, they weren't the only band growing up either. The Beatles released The White Album at pretty much the same time, and then fell apart. Don't blame Yoko, John Lennon didn't like the caricature of himself he was becoming. He didn't like having to explain to trespassing burnouts that he couldn't possibly be writing this nonsense for them personally (yes that's a very real thing he had to deal with). McCartney ran and hid on his farm and stayed a silly but famous musician, Harrison tripled down on the Indian spiritualism, and Ringo just sold his personal memorabilia whenever he needed some cash.

I feel like I lost my train of thought...Jefferson Airplane's live album Bless Its Pointed Little Head is awesome, just try not to think about its historical context too much.

89) Favorite Christmas Songs From Singer
The joke about this album isn't that it's generic orchestral/choral Christmas music. The music is not ridiculous at all. The joke is reading every word on the back cover. I'm admittedly too lazy to type it out myself, so you'll have to trust me when I say every 4th word is Singer. According to Singer, Singer Corporation had the brilliantly revolutionary idea that a record should have two sides, and they can be different from each other. I know I was getting pretty tired of those one-sided records with a big middle finger printed on the back (???). Thanks, Singer Corporation. And thanks for reminding me that you sponsor The Donna Reed Show. I heard she eats dollar bills (all my facts come from Rob Zombie). Did Singer Corporation invent the pyramid on the back? Singer, sewing machines and long play vinyl records, a match made in Heaven ("Heaven" is a registered trademark of the Singer Corporation. All sales final. Batteries not included. Known to cause cancer in the State of California. Parking not validated on Thursdays).

90) Merry Christmas from Masterseal Records
Singer's mid 60s Donna Reed commercial was a joke, but this is a Christmas album. "Historically, Christmas is a festive season, conveying great religious significance for those of the Christian faiths.... For those who do not subscribe to the Christian faiths, Christmas also has a meaning of more than passing significance."

It's from 1958 by Jacques Fontanna and His Orchestra and Choir from Masterseal Records. It sounds like it's from 1958. As hokey or nostalgic as it might sound to you, it's what people generally agreed sounded festive, celebratory, hopeful. Sleigh Ride is agonizingly too slow, but that's the only criticism I can conjure up. To bring back my favorite Vonnegut reference, this is the Uncle Alex of Christmas albums. If this isn't nice, then I don't know what is.

Not that you doubted me, but since I couldn't find it on youtube I dubbed my crackly poppy dirty 61 year old LP for your listening pleasure. You're welcome.

91) Oak Ridge Boys - Christmas Again

4 years have passed since that unspeakable winter night of 1982. All across the country, people slowly picked up the shattered remnants of their lives, villages rebuilt, children learned to laugh and play again. 4 years have softened our memories of the nightmares that await us should they ever return.

This snowy night, all is peaceful, all is quiet. Too quiet. Suddenly, far off in the distance, right on the edge of hearing, the faint sound of an electric piano floats on the wind like the scent of a thousand dead muskrats. The memories cascade, fear grabs you, and one terrible thought consumes your whole being. Oh no. Oh NO. OH NO! IT'S CHRISTMAS AGAIN, AND THE OAK RIDGE BOYS HAVE COME TO FEAST UPON OUR SOULS!!!

I'm joking. It's significantly better than their first Christmas album. This really is just an Oak Ridge Boys album that happens to be Christmas oriented. They aren't trying to be cute, or funny, they're just being a "country choir," and I don't really have anything bad to say about that.

Obviously, I hate it. I don't like the synth parts at all, and the songwriting is still awkward and emotionally incomprehensible at times, but this album is not for me. I am not their intended audience. I do legitimately like their chorale style intros, and if that were the album I'd be writing a completely different review. As a choir they sound really cool.

But that's not what this album is. "Santa Bring Your Elves" is a much better attempt at lighthearted sarcasm than anything on the first one, but I specifically warned you not to let them ad lib. You didn't listen, and they hit on Mrs. Claus. I hope your're happy.

Dear God, thanks for Jesus. Your friends, The Oak Ridge Boys. P.S. Tell Santa we're sorry for petting his reindeer too hard. We just get carried away sometimes.

92) Brian Auger & Julie Tippets - Encore

I shared Streetnoise with you what seems like ages ago. I have other things they did together, but I wanted to hear their 1977 collab without The Trinity, Encore.

Streetnoise was an unpredictable mish-mash of anything (and it was awesome), but this is a jazz album with some funky vibes (also pretty awesome). Julie Driscoll Tippets is really great, and Auger rivals Emerson when he wants to. I say that because sometimes he's perfectly happy to just hang back and keep her company. But when he does let loose, he's a keyboard maniac.

This is just a great all-around listen; insanely talented musicians making phenomenal music like it's what they do. Side B, starts with an interestingly strange Jack Bruce song (I definitely need to dig deeper into his writing). Gotta snark on something...um...er...nice lady mullet? Mull-ette? No joke, good stuff.

93) Steppenwolf - 7

In the grand tradition of counting all your recordings to produce ridiculous introductory sentences, Steppenwolf's 7 is their fifth album (because live albums are a separate category). It's the one with a song about John Kay and his mother fleeing East Germany as it was officially forming when he was 4, and also chicks, and drugs being bad. It's not a coherent story, is what I'm saying.

It is good old fashioned 60s/70s hard rock, and hard rock's version of country. It's an album for people who like Steppenwolf. None of the songs ever cracked the top 40, but since the band actually still exists, who cares? It's a lot like Steve Miller Band's Number 5 in that respect. No, it's not the stuff that made them famous, it's the stuff they made because that famous stuff made them professional rockers, or because their famous stuff hasn't happened yet and you live in a reverse time line.

If you like the band you like it (and I do), if you only like the three songs you know from their first album, you won't like it much and I assume the trumpets will confuse you...

...they confuse me too, but you're supposed to think that I know a secret you don't. Well, I do know lots of secrets that you don't know, but the reason why there are trumpets on Easrschplittenloudenboomer isn't one of them. What is the Hippo Stomp? No fucking clue, but that's because none of us know what it is. We're all just hippos sliding in water too deep to touch the ground. If you listed all of the possible metaphors for life, this would be one, I guess. We are fat, and we do like to swim. I told you this wasn't a thinking album. They don't have to be smart all the time. It's their 3rd fifth time in front of a tape recorder, and don't you forget it!

94) The Beatles - The White Album
[Insert White Album Cover Here]

So. What is it that makes the White Album an amazing mental kaleidoscope or a nonsensical mosaic of vacuity depending on which side of the bed you fell off that morning?

How can I even ask that question? It's blasphemy. The White Album is a masterpiece. How dare I! Shut up p(nmi)t, Bottle has the floor.

The White Album is Sgt. Pepper, the sequel. It exists at all because the fab four had to make another album, but they had to make that album as the band who created Sgt. Pepper's Lonely Hearts Club Band and The Magical Mystery Tour. They've sprained their epic imagination muscles, but the hallucinogenic residue is still blocking all their pain receptors.

This album can be whatever you want it to be (it is a blank canvas, after all) because it's just a string of empty metaphors. The boys brought their lego buckets to play time and dumped them all out on the floor. Sure, they made a sculpture, but it's the pieces rather than the finished shape that make it what it is (it's three EPs all smashed together, in my opinion, but I don't have the patience to write about that at the moment).

As I said a couple days ago, this is actually the end of the Beatles and what comes after is ironically their best work while they are learning to admit that the magic part is over. They all want different things, and they aren't willing to let the peanut butter and chocolate mix anymore. Like it or not, Zappa, The 4 Seasons, and Brian Wilson (even though he couldn't finish his until decades later) could make these kinds of modular monstrosities because they had a strong, personally meaningful reason to do it. The Beatles didn't, they were just making it up. The fact that they were the Beatles was omnipresent in their minds, and the ultimately hollow fame wasn't enjoyable for them. But they didn't know that at the time, they thought they were having fun.

Forget it's The Beatles for a moment, and it sounds like 4 uncompromising space cadets joined together by studio production and orchestral arrangement. This album isn't supposed to sound like that. It's not supposed to be a double album of random crap, and that's why Zappa wrote We're Only In It For The Money 6 months earlier (he was either psychic or right).

So, this album is literally bookended by Zappa saying The Beatles as you know them are finished, and The 4 Seasons turning up with a coffin, a bag of nails, and a hammer. We all know I'm making these relationships up, but it's a compelling narrative. I'm not creating that narrative to mess with you though. I'm simply bringing what I think are real subconscious consequences of the minuscule world that is big mainstream pop/rock. These people mingled, they went to the same parties, their friends told them stories about what happened after they left, and a lot of the weird stuff they did was the result of being petty little people in a tiny little gossip factory, using their illusions to make a dollar, or a statement, or just not be so lonely at the top.

95) Rammstein - Reise, Reise

My morning Markovian chain of looking up things on the internet somehow led me to Rammstein, and now I have to talk about Reise, Reise.

For those who don't remember or don't know them, Rammstein rose to prominence as one of the best industrial metal bands of the late 90s. Their success is predicated on two unrelated phenomena. First, they wrote super catchy, heavy dirty groove metal (hooray me for the 21 Pilots reference). Second, they perhaps unintentionally elevated human intelligence by being a specifically German band who intentionally paid attention to the collision of German and American culture. So much so that one of the primary appeals is actually translating their lyrics so that we can understand what they are saying. In other words, they say "you and I have fundamentally different outlooks on the world. I have been acculturated to yours, now you need to learn something about mine and I'm not going to spell it out, you have to get out your German to English dictionary and get to work." And we did, and they are awesome.

I've been talking a lot about the conceptual context of albums, and this one is a plane crash. This album takes place in an airplane that has malfunctioned, and nobody knows if we are going to survive. That's a pretty apt metaphor, in my opinion. All of the songs involve a literal or metaphorical journey, or an alternate perspective that you the listener have to meet halfway. It's not an accident, they highlight specifically German philosophical, linguistic, and cultural perspectives and place them in the context of singing to American audiences. The best part is that once you bite the hook, there is a real reward at the other end. You do actually learn something, and that is an obvious recipe for success.

Now I'm going to fight with a published music critic because his essay pretty much is the wikipedia article about the album, and because I can. I like the description "great black gaps in the fabric of human rationality," and his network of associations is ok, but the rest of Tim O'Neil's review in Entertainment Weekly is the standard misconception about how political oppression actually works. Their point is *never* that their East German upbringing is better, their point is that global Americanization is unstoppable and generalized American culture doesn't understand the difference between basic human values and political ideologies. Their opinion of Russia is just as condescending as their opinion of the US, but "Moskau" wasn't released as a single. Tim-o's notion that a socialist bias accounts for the poor decision to keep singing in German, thus not being superstars over here is laughable. Timmy didn't pull out his dictionary, and he probably didn't really listen to Sehnsucht, Mutter, and Reise Reise as a whole before pressing send.

They express their Germanity in the same way that Black Metal expresses its Scandinavian-ness, the same way any nationalistic identity expresses itself in the face of another intruding nationalistic identity. Like I said, being unapologetically German is the point, and they more than happily sing in other languages to specifically point out that simple translation doesn't work. You have to use the language of your subject matter, and Rammstein's subject matter is exactly the skewed perception that O'Neil demonstrates by telling them to "speak English" like a redneck at Taco Bell at 2AM.

Luckily, actual fans of Rammstein are more than happy to go back to school and learn about different points of view. You might not like that point of view, but at least 3 more brain cells are firing than before you made the effort.

Songwise, Rammstein approaches their inherently dark subject matter the same way Slayer, or Cannibal Corpse, or even Stone Temple Pilots approaches it. These things are so horrible, grotesque, and incomprehensible that they become fascinating and we have to conceptualize them in some way. Just like that Steppenwolf album where John Kay said right off the bat "I'm a despicable man and here's half an hour of songs from that perspective. For ladies only (wink, wink)."

96) - 'Twas the Night Before Christmas

Snuggle up kiddies, it's time for the last batch of Christmas albums. Fred Waring was a pretty interesting dude. He's most famous as a bandleader/radio personality, but his actual contribution to humanity is moderately important in its own right.

I told you the story about how vaudville composer Michael Brown coincidentally funded one of the classics of American literature. Fred Waring also funded a thing that turned out to be special. He funded the production and promotion of the first electric blender, called the Waring Blendor. It not surprisingly became a big deal in hospitals across the country for preparing special meals for patients. Thus, Jonas Salk used it while developing his vaccine for polio.

Yes, Fred Waring eradicated Polio for about $25,000 (a big sum in the 30s, but an inconsequential fraction of his fortune). Sure, someone would have invested in it eventually, and Salk would have succeeded regardless, but coincidence is the name of the game and this particular musician made the world objectively better by throwing a little bit of his fortune around.

The record? Oh yeah, it's good old 50s slap-happy radio music. My copy is so scratchy and skippy that it's pretty unlistenable even by physically holding the needle down, but I actually like Masterseal's Merry Christmas much more anyway. This is a classic though, so you can easily find the Pennsylvanians' enthusiastic versions of classic Christmas songs online, should you want to do so.

97) Andre Kostelanetz - Wishing You A Merry Christmas

All of my Christmas albums so far have come from the world of popular music. But the Classical world has no shortage of Christmas albums, and it's a nice change of pace. Andre Kostelanetz was a Russian conductor who did truly believe in melding the two worlds, and Phyllis Curtain was reasonably famous as far as American opera sopranos are concerned. This album really is a philharmonic concert with soprano and boy's choir, and there's not much funny or astonishing to say about it, other than it's like a thousand times better than most Christmas albums. The arrangements are quite complex, and it's not cheap or commercial in any way. Exactly what you'd expect from the New York Philharmonic.

98) The Beatles - Hey Jude

Super-duper Beatles geeks will understand why I say The White Album is the end of the band. It really was the last Beatles album. They hadn't actually been "a band" since Revolver. Harrison straight up said fuck touring, Lennon didn't like being a studio musician, Paul said seriously let's actually play together again, and Ringo showed up early every day because he was the only professional of the 4 at that point (it was his job, and he liked that job).

The last few years are a jumbled mess because Capitol wanted a mix of albums and compilations to distribute in America. I said this period ironically produced their best stuff, because they sucked at making albums. Their epic, iconic, best loved works are silly movie soundtracks, not Beatles albums. Lennon and McCartney were amazing songwriters, but they were flat out terrible at weaving a coherent narrative from their respective brain farts. That's why they smashed so many incomplete ideas together. When they went back to basics and just bashed their instruments in the same room for months on end, they wrote some amazing songs, figured out better versions of famous album tracks, and handed over the job of making it logical to someone else.

Let It Be, Abbey Road, and Hey Jude (that's the order in which they were created rather than published) contain the essence of what made the Beatles a great band. The concept behind all three was here's the amazing stuff these guys created but threw away while they were pretending to be superstars. That's a much better context to listen to them in, because you can't be disappointed. Oh, that's great! That song's great too! Oh, I forgot about that one! They aren't egomaniacs anymore; just 4 likable talented guys, like the old days. Obviously, they're bigger egomaniacs that ever, but that's the illusion working its magic the way it's supposed to.

The White Album sounds like they fell apart, but George Martin managed to salvage their image over the next two years. He probably didn't do it completely consciously, but he at least gave the audience what they would accept as the final chapter of their beloved band. People were sad when the Beatles broke up, but it's hard to argue that there was anything left for them to create as a group. It took reworking hundreds of songs to get the last 20 to be satisfying, and honestly who doesn't prefer the faster version of "Revolution" on Hey Jude over the original on The White Album?

Bottle says George Martin's compilation album Hey Jude is the best Beatles album and I suppose I see where he's coming from. "Christ, you know it ain't easy" is about as good a final send-off as anything.

99) Magical Mystery Tour
You might have the impression that I don't like The Beatles, but that's not true at all. I love The Beatles, but I get really worked up over the feeling that they just didn't care about the larger context of their music.

From the beginning they were a singles band, and there is absolutely nothing wrong with that. 90% of their output deserved to be top 10, and they deserved to be fabulously wealthy from it. The b-sides were just as good as the singles themselves. But, they specifically said they wanted to elevate "the album" to an art form, kept their singles off their albums (unlike other bands that built their albums around their singles), but I think they did a terrible job.

I realize that they were pioneers, and their influence is undeniable, but their idea of making an album never went further than simply picking the best songs they recorded that week. They weren't writing toward any coherent statement, they were just trying to make things sound like they existed in the same abstract framework. Yet, I would argue that a song's actual value comes from its ability to further contextualize the songs that come before and after it.

Go read anybody's reviews. They aren't about the albums. They are about the songs, the production, the characters, how long their hair in the photo is. The title on the cardboard box doesn't matter, and everyone fully recognizes these are songs for the sake of songs. See Crown of Creation, or BS&T4.

The albums in question are Rubber Soul, Revolver, Sgt. Pepper, Magical Mystery Tour, and The Beatles (White Album). Their output before and after are basically "best of what we've done in the last 6 months" collections, and they work within that context just fine. The 5 core albums work in that context too, but they told us that wasn't what they were doing.

Rubber Soul is a self depricating album. It's a group of songs that collectively says we are just an imitation of our heros. We serve a purpose, but we're not actually the real thing. Revolver says "drugs have taught us that none of this stuff is actually important." Sgt. Pepper is a fake band playing a concert and it isn't supposed to be meaningful. Ok, fine.

The best of the bunch is MMT. It's a soundtrack about a group of random people on a bus having unrelated, presumably drug induced experiences. That works. That's a great album. Or half an album. The US version is a large work on one side and unrelated stuff on the other. That's not any different from A Hard Day's Night, or Help!, or Tarkus, or Inna-Gadda-Da-Vita for that matter. It's a format issue, not a musical work issue.

I've already said that the blank covered "the beatles" is the worst of the lot. It's the worst because it doesn't even try. I get that they are subconsciously screaming that they can't actually do it. They can't create meaning from their meaninglessness, but then why even make them? Singles are good, singles are your thing, just write songs and play fewer shows and still be millionaires. Just make movies about being a famous band if that's what you want to do. Sequentially number them like everybody else did (you published VI, for crying out loud). Give each side a subtitle. I don't care, just make some effort to conceptualize what you're doing, because "none of this matters" can only stretch so far. "We're the biggest band in the world, and we're pointless [jazz hands]."

The songs are about random characters, relationships, spirituality v. mundanity, etc., but the albums are all about themselves. The resulting album isn't important, making it was what they cared about. Learning how the mixing board worked so they could change the eq was more important to them.

Maybe that's it. They say "none of this matters," and taking them at face value makes me angry because it does matter to me. Attempting to understand their work turns out to be insulting. I can't think of a single song I actually hate, but they really are just songs that don't add up to anything.

I love The Beatles, but except for Magical Mystery Tour (which they thought of as a stand-alone ep, and were mad that Capitol included 5 other fantastic songs with it), their albums are infuriating.

100) Bjork - Homogenic

My confusing (probably offputting) anger about the Beatles begs the question, what *is* a good album about creating a homogeneous collection of songs that actually add up to larger meaningful statements while being equally self reflective?

I'm glad you asked. Here's Bjork's 3rd album, Homogenic. All the songs take place in a character (call it Bjork) that has stepped back from the world to evaluate both it and her (?) relationship to it. This character has been hurt by love, doesn't really enjoy the pressures and responsibilities of daily life all alone, is for good or bad "very Scandinavian," and ultimately arrives at the intuition that existence is actually inherently positive and our struggle to embrace that love is the real matter of importance.

There are three songs I really don't like, but their purpose for the larger meaning makes that irrelevant (try to guess which ones).

She wanted it to sound homogeneous, and the pallet is a blend of electronics and real strings. Two opposite entities both vibrating in conjunction with each other. A lonely person connected to the world through technology, as a metaphor for life itself. That's beautiful.

101) Don Janse and 60 random children - Christmas Drummer Boy

If you are the type of person who genuinely enjoys your child's elementary school Christmas choir concert, then I have a real treat for you. This is not the St. Killian Boychoir at the Lincoln Center. These are 60 random kids being wrangled by Don Janse, who spent 30 years directing the U.S. Coast Guard Academy's Idlers. Don't get me wrong, it's not a trainwreck or anything, but these are untrained voices with an appropriately wide tonal focus.

My only criticism is that pesky problem of counting songs. They don't go the full Kingston by just skipping numbers, but their inventive approach to the 12 days of Christmas is pretty high up on the OCD scale of misery. Take special note of the coin toss approach to deciding whether the choir or the organ will perform "5 golden rings."

All in all, I think this album might be a unique addition to anyone's collection of confusing albums to play randomly at a dinner party. It's a real conversation starter. Invariably that conversation would start with "why are you playing this record in front of company?," or "please do not play that record for our guests," but last time I checked, those are real conversations.

My copy is the Hurrah Records H-X6, if you're weird enough to care.

102) Christmas - For Children Only

Christmas - For Children Only. You can't tell me what to do, Cricketone Chorus. I'm gonna drink my evening rum & coke while listening to your record, I'm gonna enjoy it, and your campy 50s orchestra and the Playhour Players can't stop me. How do you like them apples?

103) The Life Treasury of Christmas Music (1963)

We have finally reached the end of my Christmas records. I know you're all sad, so I saved the Life Treasury of Christmas Music for last. It's lovely music (mostly plainsong) with very little personality (it's the blandest reindeer of all), perfect for making you not exactly sad that it's over.

Oh. Still two more weeks of it in the real world. Oh well, look on the bright side. If nothing else, I've given you the gift of conversation. You could now say things like "if you think *this* is bad, then boy have I got a record for you," or "no no no, the best Christmas album by far is...." You can regale your friends with trivia, or frighten the hell out of your local used record store clerk. You're welcome, and merry future Christmas.

104) Iron Butterfly - Ball

It should be pretty obvious that I like Iron Butterfly quite a lot. For my money, I think they were truly one of the most innovative, experimental, and just plain enjoyably adventurous bands of the 60s, and their 3rd album Ball has everything. The opening minute is the most gloriously frightening thing I can think of (picking up right where Heavy left off in the explosive noisescape department), and even the admittedly ridiculous moments are still enjoyable (Lonely Boy makes me laugh every single time I listen to it). Doug Ingle is clearly not from the same reality that you and I inhabit, but he sure is fun. Erik Brann's psychotic guitar leads remind me of Robin Trower or Billy Gibbons, his tone is completely unhinged (like his amp is really about to explode), but somehow it doesn't sound obnoxious or out of place at all.

The songs are splattered all over the walls and ceiling like lunch time Spaggetios, but I think they are supposed to be. This band isn't so much an image as a juggernaut. They just walk into the room, crank everything up to 11, pummel you for half an hour, and you can't stop them or walk away. You're scared, then you're laughing, then you're really confused but headbanging. I have this weird urge to clap after every track.

Heavy might be a technically better album (and I like it a lot), but Ball is just a glorious collection of bizarre music that sounds like it came from a completely different universe.

105) Brown Bird - Salt for Salt

Today would have been David Lamb's 42nd birthday, so I'm listening to Salt for Salt by Brown Bird. I've pointed my facebook friends to it several times in the past, but this is just superb dark neo-folk.

They were once a full band, but scaled down to a husband/wife duo with Morgan playing violin/cello/bass and Dave playing everything else, one-man band style. It's surprising how full and energetic they can make such a small, intimate duo sound.

Songwise, the album focuses heavily on nature, the ocean, and the idea of meeting the oncoming storm (whatever form it may take) with the determination to embrace/accept the fight and persevere. The two sides are subtitled flesh and blood, and I can't think of a better analogy. It's a melancholic, at times angry sounding, album but it's so damned good that you end up feeling a real sense of catharsis in spite of knowing you'll lose the fight in the end.

MorganEve Swain is still out there performing as "The Huntress and Holder of Hands," as well as maintaining Brown Bird's discography, so I urge you to go check them out.

106) Dead Hot Workshop - 1001

You know Gin Blossoms, and The Refreshments, and I hope you know Meat Puppets, and you probably even know their younger depressed brother Jimmy Eat World, but I doubt you know the real hometown heroes of Tempe, AZ (unless you're like me and look up bands other bands say nice things about).

Rock is a generational form of popular music, and it's almost always paired with the other predominant genre of an area. In other words, whatever the 20-somethings are angry about blends with whatever they've been forced to listen to on the radio and produces the cocktail called "rock." The 60s were all about LA, the 70s were NY and Detroit, the 80s were LA and NY, the early 90s gave us Seattle, and the late 90s were straight out of Arizona. Yes, Arizona with it's incredibly distinctive country-tinged alternative rock. Amazingly enough, the really famous bands all looked up to one group of guys.

You know about Gin Blossoms because they drove their van all over the country for three years, until the major labels couldn't ignore the popularity they were generating and started buying up any AZ band they could find. Who did Gin Blossoms sell that van to? Who did the Refreshments name check on their big (and awesome) album? Whose singer did the East Valley Tribune call "the poet laureate of Mill Ave.?" Dead Hot Workshop.

Their major label debut, 1001, is exactly what you expect it will sound like, but history wants to annoyingly pretend that they were overshadowed by Gin Blossoms. The trouble is, as great as Gin Blossoms are (and yes, they are great), they were merely the commercial, marketable face of this particular scene. The Refreshments were closer to the real thing because they were sarcastic and a little rough, but Dead Hot Workshop is the real rock band of the group.

Keep in mind we are talking about alternative rock. The love songs are sad, the drugs do not make you happy, everyone thinks you are a loser because you're out in the dirt and rain working for a living instead of sitting in an office trying to sell people useless junk. Alternative rock says "reality bites" because it does.

Dead Hot Workshop sounds like you worked all day, have dirt in your teeth, and plan to wash it out with a beer or 3. They sound like if Gin Blossoms didn't care about radio hits. They sound like they are just trying to get their point of view out into the world, and it's fantastic. The real reason they didn't get super famous like their peers is because they aren't a sentimental or nostalgic sounding band. Brent Babb writes amazing songs but they aren't generic enough to appeal to everyone. You have to want to hear what he has to say.

If (like me) you have a real fondness for those few years when alternative rock *was* mainstream, then I implore you to go check out Dead Hot Workshop. It's a very familiar sound, but it still sounds fresh and genuine, and most importantly gritty.

107) Pharoah Sanders - Deaf Dumb Blind

Pharoah Sanders' next album after Jewels of Thought was Deaf Dumb Blind/Let Us Go Into The House Of The Lord. These two extended free jazz pieces are quite different from each other.

Deaf Dumb Blind features the over blowing and crazy extended techniques he's best know for, and is essentially a trio of soloists over a chaotic percussive ensemble. The soloists aren't really the focus though. The real power of the piece comes from how the ensemble as a whole builds and releases tension without ever actually coalescing. Each instrument sets up its own musical home base, so to speak, then extends out of it and returns. When two or more parts seem to return to their respective bases, it really does feel as though the chaos is retreating. To me at least, it sounds like a panning back and forth between the identifiably musical and a menagerie of animal sounds. Almost as if the ensemble itself is slowly breathing.

Into the house of the lord, on the other hand, is almost exclusively tonal, albeit non-metrical, jazz. The piece has a clear harmonic rather than rhythmic foundation, and the solo lines are much more soloistic in a traditional sense.

The two pieces really do sound earthly and spiritual, respectively. Sanders' works are overtly religious/spiritual in their conception, but I think they are also meant to be interpreted in the more abstract context of thought vs feeling, or physical vs philosophical. Humans can both explore/expand the physical limits of an idea AND psychologically operate beyond their own physical limitations.

Though I'm not specifically influenced by free jazz, I imagine that a lot of my own music stems from the same feeling of highly personal improvisation that this ensemble conveys.

Regardless, this is a fascinating listen just in terms of how different the same ensemble can sound depending on the nature of what the rhythm section is playing. I'm getting spoiled on vinyl and I really wish I had more of his albums.

108) Grofé - Grand Canyon Suite

I don't currently have any more actual Christmas albums to share with you, so I've decided to invoke the Die Hard Technicality and listen to Bernstein conduct Grofé's Grand Canyon Suite.

You'll probably hear the celeste solo from the third movement at some point in the next week, because it's used for the dream sequence in "a Christmas Story."

Tone-painting suites were Grofé's schtick. The desert, a big river, some waterfall, New York, you name it. If it's a region of our country, Grofé wrote a suite for it. Mostly no one cared too much, but Toscanini took a shine to this particular one. Disney did a short movie using it as well. It's unapologetically romantic orchestral writing, but you can tell that Grofé likes his orchestrational dissonance as much as Copland and Bernstein himself. It definitely has that same kind of American terroir, pairing the nostalgically idyllic

Hudson Valley School -esque landscapes with the violently impressive crash-bang weather our wide-open spaces are known for having. Quite a nice piece. Thumbs up.

109) Iron Butterfly - Metamorphosis

We all know I love Iron Butterfly, so this review of their 4th album, Metamorphosis, will obviously be positive. They have a couple new guitarists this time around, but I've already told you that doesn't matter. Iron Butterfly is Doug Ingle, and he simply doesn't know what the word "genre" means.

The real problem with Iron Butterfly is that everyone heard Inna-Gadda-Da-Vita and said "that's it. That's what we are going to remember you for, and you might as well not bother writing anything else. Ball? Sure, yeah, great album, put IGDV back on. Another version? No thanks, you got it right the first time. A fourth album? Okaaay. Nah, this just doesn't do it for me."

Well, I call shenanigans. The best part of IB is the weird parts, and this album has some of the weirdest. Obviously, the universe doesn't explode like on 1 & 3, and everyone but me hates the constipated grunting and early talk-box experiment in the middle of Butterfly Bleu, but that's because they thought IB was supposed to be a manufactured psychedelic Vegas production, or something. News flash, they were just weirdos doing weird stuff, and it's not their fault you don't like it anymore. Go back and listen to all four albums. There's nothing premeditated. They are clearly just doing whatever they thought of doing on every album without any indication that there was a staff meeting beforehand. Trust me, it's simply not possible that they felt any sense of embarrassment while they were doing it (remember Lord Sutch?), so why start questioning it now?

That's the thing about real unhindered creativity: you might only like one thing that creativity produced. I, on the other hand, like the unpredictable creative freedom in and of itself. IB is wackadoodle and I laugh as much as anyone at the most outrageous moments. Deadpan insanity is one of their most endearing qualities.

110) Simon & Garfunkel - Sounds of Silence

My wife and kids left to visit Oklahoma for the weekend. So slightly tongue-in-cheek, it's time to pull out my personal favorite Simon & Garfunkel album.

It's one of the albums I had the songbook for growing up, and I literally learned every song in my own way (I might have even rewrote the lyrics of "Kathy's Song" to be about my '77 van for a college class). I can still play most of them.

Shut up, p(nmi)t, this album has Bottle worthy trivia that's way more important.

This album (no sophomore slump at all) may have been produced by Bob Johnson, but he sure didn't produce this particular version of "The Sound of Silence." I'd give you a prize for guessing, but you'd cheat and I wouldn't be able to finish this essay, so tough.

The original version of "The Sound of Silence" was on their first album. They didn't create this version. Say whaaaat? Yeah, some dude with adamantium testicles was sitting at the booth and said "I need to hire studio musicians right now because the entire history of American pop-rock depends on it." A guy with balls so big and impervious to anything, that even Bob Dylan's ego had to admit that his vision had an impact. That man was Tom Wilson. Yes, the same Tom Wilson who brought you Zappa at all and produced Dylan's "Like A Rolling Stone" just decided to turn a random Paul Simon song into a hit rock single and thus create their 2nd album without them even knowing. The dude was a madmaniacle genius.

Paul Simon freely admits that he always felt like his songs were overly neurotic, but this is a fantastic album. It's a man alone with his thoughts. He's a consistent person, his world view and his self image come from the same sources of doubt. He sees the world for its false facade. These are the real inner views of a complex and conflicted individual. Sure, you might have a different outlook than Mr. Simon, but you can't pretend you don't understand that self doubt and confusion.

And "April Come She Will" is my favorite Art Garfunkel performance of his entire career (no offense to the Legion of Garf); I can't define it and it was probably pure coincidence, but he not Paul *had* to sing it.

This is one of the very few legitimately magical albums that could never have been planned out the way it actually ended up. Enjoy.

111) Psychic of Orange - A Very Psychic Christmas

Tonight's album review is very, very special for many reasons. 1) I ran out of Christmas albums to talk about/share with you, but 2) my friend Ken and Psychic of Orange released a Christmas album today, so 3) I get to talk about an interesting group of music genres and say nice things about a fellow music maker.

If you're not at all familiar with hypnagogic pop, or glofi, or ____wave, or any of their subgenres, they generally fall under the umbrella concept of technological nostalgia. More specifically, they play with your memories of developing computer/audio technologies and pop culture from the 1980s and 90s by elevating consumer level equipment and output to an artistic medium while refusing to make overt statements about any supposed value in doing so. It's a post-ironic artform, is what I'm saying.

Critics and social philosophers often describe it as "post-elevator" music, because we only know how to define things as derivative forms. To my mind, the real defining characteristic is the refusal to say what is good or bad, serious or funny. It's like the clinical detatchment of Brechtian Epic Theater, or looking at life through the eyes of anti-depressants (yay me I snuck a System of a Down reference in there). Like how I find such giddy joy in singing songs from a female protagonist perspective as a deadpan bearded dude. The real point is that you're not being told how to feel, you actually feel that way because you have a personal connection to/memory of the media itself: cheap synths, autotune, drum machines, distorted guitars, falsetto, what have you. It's more like recycling/repurposing than imitation and it can be all the permutations of happy/sad/cheesy/heartfelt at the same time.

Well, Psychic of Orange brings an R&B flavor (with some truly authentic autotune) to the party. The covers of Eartha Kitt's "Santa Baby" and Mariah Carey's "All I Want For Christmas Is You" are delicious.

And let's talk about track 9, "Presence." I don't know if it's on purpose or not (and don't tell me, Ken Fabian, because I don't want to know), but it's the doo-dooop-do-doo-doop part of "Hungry Like A Wolf" paired up with a metrically opposite version of the 3-note motive from "Boys of Summer" and the song is a pun on presence/present (which is basically the foundation of the universe this whole style exists inside). It's awesome. I love it. Thank you for making it.

112) Live - Throwing Copper

I miss my dad the most on Sunday, so I thought I'd share a very personal memory with you.

He bought this actual copy of Live's Throwing Copper for me as reward for doing my geometry homework. I don't know if he really had the formulas for the area and circumference of a circle switched in his mind (I doubt it), or if I was going though one of my not caring about school phases (I had a few), or if he just wanted to see if he could make me doubt myself (he couldn't). He bet me a CD, I won the bet, and I chose this gem of 90s social angst.

Coincidentally, it's an album about communication, or lack thereof. It's an album about death, and how we crumble under its inevitability, accepting the torture of mindless labors for a delusional feeling of belonging. The album starts with suicide, and ends with "I can't start 'til I'm dead," and we just keep on spinning. That's harsh.

The album itself is a semiotic masterpiece, because the overall meaning of each song is crystal clear, while leaving the details to the listener. You are not Ed, but you are a fellow human. You give the work meaning, and in doing so become the ego that the work is trying to tear down.

The songs themselves are not specifically related, but their collective identities under a nebulous title add up to a larger coherent meaning. At the uppermost analytical level, the only objective facts are life and death; the two cannot be separated or condensed, and our value as humans depends on how we travel from one to the other, mindful or not of our fellow passengers.

Go give it a listen from that perspective, and see if it makes more sense.

113) Claudine, l'album premier

Bonsoir, mes amis! Je suis Bouteille, et ce soir nous écoutons l'album premier de Claudine Longet. Luckily, she sings in English too, so I don't have to do this whole thing in French.

"Qui?," demandez-vous. You know, the French pop singer. She was married to Andy Williams. Bonjour? Bonjour? Cette chose est allumée? Pouvez-vous m'entendre?

Ok, I'll stop. She not surprisingly retreated from public life after her conviction for "negligent homicide." She shot her boyfriend, but it's not clear if it was premeditated (plus there was a bunch of procedural misconduct), and the jury had no evidence that she actually wanted him to die.

Anyway, would you like some of my tangerines? Sorry, I'm writing this while listening to the record, the silliest lyrics tend to creep in without warning and you know I'd never treat you mean.

It's definitely French-pop, accordions a-blazing. It's meant to be cute and bubbly, and it certainly is. Interesting fact, I live 30 something miles east of Andy Williams's hometown of Wall Lake, Iowa. Grab a glass of Champagne, and prendre plaisir.

114) Maurice Larcange - The French Touch

Speaking of l'accordéon, your Christmas Eve present is this delightful instrumental album from Maurice Larcange.

Larcange wanted to play professional soccer, but figured music was a more stable career to fall back on (why is my left eye squinting all of a sudden?) should his dreams not come to fruition. He firmly believed that "french song" was the pinnacle of musical achievements, not because he cared about singers, but because without cheesy songs he wouldn't be able to prove that accordions were better melodic instruments than human voices (or other instruments for that matter). I wouldn't go that far, but he does have a point. Accordion is a highly enjoyable melodic instrument, and it deserves a much bigger place in the serious music listener's library beyond Weird Al's greatest hits.

It's a very '60s mod album, meant to be listened to from your white futon, or egg-shaped chair with a dangerously perched glass of red wine at your fingertips. As always mes amis, enjoy.

115) Jesus Christ Superstar

I had two possible choices for my album on actual Christmas. I flipped a coin and it came up Woodstock. I was going to do a whole work up, a 12 days of Christmas joke with the punchline being "5 records of Woodstock!" (I have both the 3-record soundtrack and the double album Woodstock 2). Alas, it blows. It's not fun to listen to (unless CSN&Y singing to a nastily out of tune acoustic guitar while giving audible eq instructions to the sound guys is your idea of fun). Plus, there's 9 minutes of Ten Years After hiding in there, and that's 9 minutes too many.

Executive decision, plan 9 from outer space, we're listening to the original concept album, Jesus Christ Superstar. Murray Head sings Judas. I'll even do some real research for my snarky one-liners.

I have a tendency to be crass, but I assure you that's not my intention here. It's a fictional rock opera about Jesus and his apostles as actual people, and every religious group you can think of has a reason to hate it, but I love it. And, when some Peruvian prison inmates staged a full production as part of a rehabilitation program in 2014, even the Catholic Church gave it a thumbs up.

There aren't many true rock operas to begin with (tons of rock musicals, but I'm being picky about semantics today), and Andrew Lloyd Webber's is at least as good as Tommy; maybe not quite as good as The Wall, but what is?

You know who else liked it? Liked the whole idea of sticking a rock band inside an orchestra? Saw it in London near the end of his life, and wished he could have created something like it? Dimitri Shostakovich. Now there's a guy who knows a little something about writing operas certain people might get upset about. I bet Shosti would have adored Metallica's S&M as much as I do, too.

I have the original album with Ian Gillam and Murray Head, the former from Deep Purple, the latter a Chess afficianado enthralled by the nightlife of Thailand (that's a complicatedly obscure musical joke, if I do say so myself). I like the movie version too.

I like the story because the characters have real depth, they are motivated by their own sense of what is right and fight against what they perceive as calamitous. No one is inherently good or bad. There's no actual protagonist/antagonist structure, everyone gets swept along in the inevitable plot. It's really a much broader statement about the nature of political power itself. You take a mortal man, and put him in control... Shut up, Dave Mustaine, this is my puppet show.

Musically, this thing is phenomenal, and whole books could be written about how well it's composed and how deftly Webber handles aria/recitative/chorus in a rock context. The real power though, is that it's not an imitation of anything. He takes all the real compositional insights of late 60s psych-rock and seamlessly blends it with the crazier side of classical music. You can hear Bowie or Spirit or any of the other icons in it because Webber isn't faking anything. It's exactly what you could ever want an academically crafted rock opera to be.

... and with that, from my family to yours on this 4th day of the solar new year, have a Merry Christmas, and a Happy Gregorian Calendar New Year, and may our quest for more and interesting scratchy old platters of polyvinyl chloride bring us joy and comfort and amusement as we continue to argue about our current crop of potential political proselytizers. Peace on Earth, now let us feast.

116) The Best of Herman's Hermits

Tonight's review is a little bit all over the place. We all weight 5-15 more pounds than we did yesterday morning, and those of you who shared in my Christmas feast of Jesus Christ Superstar are undoubtedly anticipating my words for the dangerously delectable wafer-thin mint they are sure to be...and now for something completely different.

Let's listen to The Best of Herman's Hermits. It's not the best of Herman's Hermits, because that would be at least a four-record set, and half of those songs hadn't even been recorded at the time this record was pressed, that's why there are more greatest hits albums in their discography than regular ones (I didn't actually do the math, but there are many).

They are far and away my favorite of the British Invasion bands, but I'm more interested in the story they tell about the music business itself. When we think of a band that got "discovered" and turned into international superstars, we're thinking of these blokes. They were regular British teenagers with day jobs (though "herman's" acting career might stretch that description a little), who played in bands for fun. A guy heard them and thought "I can manage these kids." He called a guy who could handpick great songs for them to play, and thus a lot of people made money. They turned out to be way more popular over here than at home, so they came over here and made a lot more money. Sure, once they were actually famous everybody wanted their name included in the liner notes (like Jimmy Page and the other session musicians back home), but they weren't the kids hopping 6am flights to the next gig and eating cakes their fans brought to concerts for dinner. And let's not forget, these boys actually played their instruments.

I tried really hard to figure out who the June Harris that wrote the liner notes actually was, but I don't know for sure. Record collectors will know that the pre-Woodstock era of big music was all about the hard sell, and it's a very interesting essay if you can find it somewhere (I'm too tired and lazy to type it or take photos). You don't even have to search out this particular album (which took way too long to identify as the 1965 one because nobody bothered to put the year of publication on these things until some certain someone made it a vitally important tool for litigation), just listen to some really lovely British pop-rock made for Americans.

If you're really paying attention though, you'll notice that "Mrs. Brown..." is here, three years before their actual album of that name. That's because the album was actually a soundtrack to the movie. To quote the non-ursine Yogi, "Deja vu all over again...".

117) Tony Mattola - Roma Oggi

Speaking of hard sells: which alternate universe had Tony Mattola as America's Greatest Guitarist, and can I please apply for relocation? Even Google questioned whether I actually meant Tommy Mattola, when I clearly didn't. That makes me sad.

I mean, yeah, the cover is farcical, but I'm sure there's some truth to the notion that Italians like smoking and motorcycles and boobs. No, the music doesn't sound like that, but it does sound like continental Europe circa 1968. Larcange sounded like France, Mattola sounds like Italy, and they both sound like they are shaking martinis as they dad tango across the white shag carpeting in their knee-high socks and tennis shorts.

It's a lot like Larcange's album, only for guitar and with a little more improvisation. It's department store jazz guitar, and I actually really like it. He sounds like he's having fun, maybe not Django fun, but still.

The thing I hate about bad jazz guitar is the same thing I hate about bad metal: it's so stupid easy to just give up and be a douchebag, play 700 notes in the space of three, not care that the listener has to try to follow your nonsense. Mattola doesn't do that; he plays fast when the song is fast, and he plays some amazing, but still musically relevant runs when there's space to do so.

He doesn't steer too far in the other direction either (harmonic oatmeal with 27 different voicings of the same 2 dominant 11th chords like a lot of other jazz guitarists). He plays guitar like it's meant to be played, and though you might find the general style a little campy, I'd take this over Steve Vai, or Joe Satriani, or Paul Gilbert, or Pat Methany 24 days out of every month of the year.

If I made it sound like he was a nobody, then I apologize. He was highly successful, he played in The Tonight Show band for a while, played duets with Sinatra, hung out with Perry Como and Sid Caesar, even won an Emmy. Most of all though, he makes the guitar sound fun to play and he has a style that makes you think "I can learn to do that." That's much preferable to "smash my useless fingers with a sledgehammer 'cause Yngwie," but vacant amazement always seems to stick around longer than it should. Trust me, the world doesn't need 47 more Paganinis, it needs better music that doesn't require all that non-nutritious shredded lettuce to make it sound impressive.

118) Holy cow, I found a Throbbing Gristle LP in a crate today

I managed to get out of today's record collecting adventure with 5 albums for a little under $40. Believe me, if I had actual money to burn, I wouldn't anymore. It did, however, start me thinking about how I actually decide what to buy, and my weird criteria might be of interest to someone.

Some people collect records as an investment. I do not. Some people want audiophile mint rare import bootlegs. Not me. I want things that I like, or things that intrigue me. I'm going to listen to them, get fingerprints on them, and generally eliminate their resale value because I just like physically putting on records. The furthest I go into the real "collector" side of things is thinking I'd really like to say "I have that record."

When I go shopping, I'm going to spend $20-$50 and I'd prefer to have more than 2 frisbees when I get home. On the other end of the spectrum, I don't buy stuff I can find anywhere until I have a reason to buy it. I tend to favor things I'm simply not going to find again, assuming they don't cost enough to make me put something else back.

Today I got the first Steppenwolf album, ZZ Top's Eliminator, two Thomas Dolby albums, and something I never thought I'd stumble across in real life, D.o.A: The Third and Final Report of Throbbing Gristle (their 2nd album). They all deserve proper write ups, but Throbbing Gristle literally named their record label, and thus the parent genre, "industrial."

Most people would mistakenly call it "noise," but it's not just generic anti-music. It is the sounds of machinery, the metaphorical opposite of "agricultural" music, new, modern, metallic, if human rights violations had a soundtrack, the sick and depraved, the mass replication of force and enterprise. Think of it as ambient technological collage. "Nauseating" is the most common adjective thrown around, but I tend to find it quite pleasing (I'm weird, I know). I like that dark, impersonal, found-sounds on the tape recorder from hell's weekly staff meeting aesthetic.

If you've never heard of them, give these dead-beat dads of Industrial music a listen. You might like it, you might hate it. If nothing else it'll at least give you some sense of the lineage of bands like NIN, KMFDM, Front Line Assembly, Skinny Puppy, etc.

119) ZZ Top – Eliminator

We are Sex Bob-omb, and we're here to talk about ZZ Top and make you get confused and stuff!

I'm not interested in the pre ZZ Top story about Dusty Hill and Frank Beard pretending to be The Zombies. I'm not interested in their first 7 "boogie-woogie" albums, as critics like to call them. I'm interested in Billy Gibbons's drum-machine/bass-synth experiment that turned them from a solid and popular blues band into the iconic cultural megastars of the 1980s. You know the hot-rodded '33 Ford, you know the Legs, it's Eliminator.

I'm not making light of feminism, equal rights, or misogyny, and neither is Billy Gibbons. I've always been fascinated by how ZZ Top got away with it. On paper, they are dirty old men who sing songs about sex. Sex, sex, sex (and sometimes cars and drugs). They aren't beating around the bush either, the heart of their songs *is* the euphamism. How do they do it? Is it because they are generally humorous and their videos and fuzzy guitars made it obvious they were really goofballs? Is it because we're mansplaining away some inherently insidious sexism?

Nope. It's because they are the outsiders. These blues guys with 3-foot hermit beards and sunglasses don't actually belong to that world. They are chasing women who know exactly what they are doing (making the guys from ZZ Top want to have sex with them). That's the trick. The women are fast, but the boys are just trying to catch up. All of their songs (not just on this album) place the women in control of the situation. Even Dirty Dog (read "bitch") starts from the perspective that she led him on in the first place. It's fascinating.

And now we have to come back to the sound. It really is a drum machine, a bass synthesizer, and 3 Billy Gibbons overdubs. Dusty and Frank spent like 12 combined minutes in the studio adding finishing touches. You don't notice it so much because Billy's guitar sounds like it's about to spontaneously combust in his hands and engulf all of Memphis in its fiery inferno. I believe they might say it was "difficult to control" and "prone to feedback." It's fucking amazing is what it is.

We all tend to bash the "general public" when it comes to popular music trends, but this wasn't a fluke. Everyone took notice and bought 4 copies of this album to give to their friends who already gave their own 4 copies away. With a budget that amounts to a ham & cheese sandwich, 10 million sold in the states alone and they stopped bothering to count.

Critics had already written this off as "just another ZZ Top album" and then peed their pants when they realized they didn't have a clue. It wasn't their "8th album," it was the album that made us ashamed we didn't know about the previous 7 and demand as many more as they could possibly make forever (and we're still going to their shows 36 years later).

But, damnit if there isn't that "contested credits" problem again. Look, I'm not saying it's fair, and I'm not saying it's right, and I'm definitely not saying that it should happen at all in the first place, but if you aren't listed as a band member, Warner Bothers isn't gonna hand you any extra money. They don't even want to hand ZZ Top any more money than they have to, and that's why our friend Greg Graffin reminds us that "handshakes are nothing but a subtle 'fuck you,' and contracts determine the best friendships." Billy Gibbons and his imaginary electronic friends made a bad-ass ZZ Top album that somehow made dirty electric blues completely normal on 80s pop radio.

Sometimes truth is indeed stranger than fiction.

120) Thomas Dolby

I'll forgive you if you have the slightly skewed perception of Thomas Dolby as a "one hit wonder." It's certainly true that "She Blinded Me With Science" is his one massive hit, but he wasn't ever really trying to be an iconic superstar. By his own admission, he was a mediocre keyboard player who was most happy plinking out melodies on a monophonic synthesizer and bouncing tracks together to build wacky electronic doodles. He was a behind the scenes kind of guy, and one of the few people to really sit down and learn how to program the early models of computer based (rather than modular/analog) synthesizers. It's one thing to have access to a million dollars worth of brand new audio technology, but somebody has to know how make it do something other than fart out square waves. So, while you might only know one or two of his own songs, you've heard him collaborate with pretty much every famous artist of the 70s and 80s.

I'm not a super fanboy or anything, and I won't bore you with the intricate details of his convoluted discography (lots of remixes, rearranged republications, etc.), but any Thomas Dolby is worth obtaining should you randomly come across it.

I found his EP (excuse me, "Mini LP") Blinded by Science and the "May the Cube Be With You" single from another of his studio projects, Dolby's Cube. They are great fun. I think he's an amazingly unique and versatile vocalist, but he's surprisingly subtle about it. He probably didn't give it much thought, to be honest.

We take this kind of electronic wizardry for granted these days, so it's easy to overlook how groundbreaking his material really is. He didn't learn it from someone else, he didn't drag and drop prefab samples into a quantized grid, he sat at a $10,000 (in 1970s dollars) computer sequencer with a piano keyboard and floppy drive attached to it and figured out how to make pro-level crazy music with it.

I will side with the superfans though, and say I like "One of Our Submarines" better than "She Blinded Me With Science," but all of his output is pretty stellar. I don't think any of his solo work sounds dated at all, and you'd have a hard time convincing me that any big-name artist today is making purely synthesized music that competes at his level.

121) Steppenwolf

After a long day at work, microwaving my dinner back to an edible 3-digit temperature, feeding animals, playing ponies with the josinator, and changing bed sheets, it's time to pour myself a drink from that big bottle of turpentine, and listen to Steppenwolf.

Before you roll your eyes so hard your retinas detach, I know you know I love Steppenwolf. I don't have to defend it because I am one of those poor pathetic individuals who knows Hoyt Axton not for his great songs, but for his role as the dad in Gremlins. Maybe, just maybe, John Kay can make me forget that and instead teach me to appreciate good old - fashioned rock and roll again. The kind of rock and roll that sounds like a Canadian motorcycle gang crossed the border illegaly, slept on Chuck Berry's couch for a couple nights, borrowed a couple of Willie Dixon's old amps with busted speakers for their next gig, and beat up some Neil Young fans in the parking lot. That's not an insult, I'm pretty sure Neil Young beat up a couple of his own fans in a parking lot once or twice. What's that saying? I went to a fist fight and a hockey game broke out. They were born to be wild, after all.

It's the origin of the phrase "heavy metal," it's blues rock in all its variations with the gain cranked up, and goddamn the pusher man!

But on a serious note, not every debut album should be self titled, but every self titled album should be a band's first. It's specifically designed to say "this is who we are, where we come from, and what you should expect." Steppenwolf got that part right for sure.

I think I like them so much because they were proud to be a blues rock band, and they weren't afraid to play it as loud and brash as they felt. You don't have to like them as much as I do, so long as you admit that you're wrong.

122) Mastodon - Once More 'Round the Sun

What better album to enjoy on New Year's Eve than Once More 'Round the Sun? As a matter of fact, as far as I'm concerned, this was the decade of Mastodon. Some people claim they are the "saviours of metal," some people hate their proggy fusion of thrash, groove, and grunge with contemporary classical transitional material, some people get grumpy when they sing out of tune, but I think everybody forgets that they are one of the very few bands today who are actually doing whatever they want, making it up as they go, and actually making it work. 4 dudes from Atlanta being dudes from Atlanta, 3 of them take turns being lead vocalist, and the 4th screams in the background on occasion. I finally got to see them live back in June with Coheed and Cambria, and they were awesome.

The interesting thing to me is that they are fairly mainstream, but they sure don't act like it. They make gigantic concept albums, they take a definite "alternative" but literary stance on whatever they're writing about, and they sure aren't writing pop songs.

The subtext of this album is living like it's the last year of our lives, but I like the idea that we get one more turn before the space monster wakes up and devours us for breakfast.

Now, for any of you foolish enough to confuse counting for proper number theory, 9 is the 10th number of our decimal system, and our calendar is made up nonsense to begin with, so tomorrow does in fact start a new decade. Smartest of the dumb people still means you're dumb.

That was mean. I'm sorry, and I'll try to be nicer next year. Hopefully Mastodon doesn't resolve to do anything different than what they've been doing all along (being different), 'cause that would indeed suck.

123) Paul and Linda McCartney - Ram

Let's talk about Ram. It's the 2nd Paul McCartney album after John Lennon called them all into a staff meeting and quit the Beatles, and the first official Paul and Linda album before they named themselves Wings.

I mentioned that after the Beatles McCartney hid on his farm for a while and reemerged as a solo artist, but the story is actually much more complicated. Whole books could be written about what happened from 1969 to 1972, but I'll paraphrase. John and Paul were joint owners of 3 major corporations: a private publishing company, a publicly traded publishing company that eased the tax burden of the private corporation, and a record label that did all the actual work. John thought he could quit the band without losing his stake in Paul's future successes, and he turned out to be wrong.

The first solo album, McCartney, deserves its own write up so I'll simply describe it as what Paul did before the depression set in. Ram is what happened when Linda couldn't take living on their farm in Scotland with drunkenly depressed Paul McCartney and 3 kids anymore. She basically said "make another album, ya jackass. You aren't actually dead like Beatles fans pretend you are. I'll help you if that's what it takes."

That's where it got tricky. John and the corporate side of things thought they owned Paul McCartney the person's creative output. When Paul and Linda released "Another Day" as a single, they claimed it was Beatles property and that Paul was in breach of contract. To be fair, he had brought that song to the Let It Be sessions, and he was intentionally messing with Apple's release schedule out of spite. But, after they sued themselves, the legal verdict was that the corporation did not own the choice of who their songwriters wished to collaborate with, and they all agreed to a new 7 year contract with Paul and Linda rather than lose even more revenue.

So, Ram is an autobiographical album about headbutting your way forward, and it takes jabs at everything standing in Paul's way: the Beatles, John himself, Linda's ex-husband, Paul's own tendency to not finish songs, and so on. Sadly, the public and press didn't really understand what any of this stuff was about, so everybody said it was terrible and/or got offended. I can point you to some terrible crap written by McCartney, but this album isn't it. For starters, it's a real album. The songs about Linda aren't just romantic lip service, and the jabs at everybody else are legitimate things a hurt and depressed person might say about people who tried to ruin his life.

He wasn't going to let other people tell him what he could or couldn't do, and he succeeded. You're allowed to not like it, but it turns out I do. To quote my wife, "'Too Many People' is a very underrated song," and it leads off an equally underrated, as well as under-understood, album.

124) My Life With The Thrill Kill Kult - Hit & Run Holiday

I noticed today that the strange part of the world who actually knows about My Life With The Thrill Kill Kult has finally accepted that they are in fact "industrial disco." The history of Wax Trax and Chicago industrial music is a subject worthy of an entire library, but MLWTKK is my favorite band to emerge from those humble record store beginnings. They are an unpredictable band for sure, and I definitely don't like all of their albums, but Hit & Run Holiday is an album I think every human being on the planet should hear at least once.

This album is simply impossible to describe, because it doesn't actually belong to a musical genre as we understand them. It's actually a movie. I know that sounds weird, but the band is actually a movie. My Life With The Thrill Kill Kult was the name of the movie they were trying to make, but composing the soundtrack led them so far afield that they just shrugged and kept going as a band instead. All of their albums come from that perspective, it's the music for a trashy b-movie they would make if they were making movies instead of albums. If you're old enough to remember the "cult classics" section of your local video rental store, then you'll sort of understand what I'm talking about.

Well, Hit & Run Holiday is one of those Go-Go Dancer, pleasure cruise, Valley of the Dolls type cinematic experiences. Skewed funk, disco, rock 'n roll. The band describes themselves as "sleaze" the same way KMFDM calls themselves "ultra heavy beat." I told you "industrial" was a parent genre, and Thrill Kill Kult is your strange fourth cousin who dresses like Rob Halford but somehow convinces Great Aunt Gladys to do the Watusi with him at the family barbecue.

If it sounds like I'm struggling for words it's because I am. MLWTKK isn't a band you can describe, you really do have to hear them for yourself. I'm partial to this album, I See Good Spirits..., and Confessions of a Knife, but you might like others. They are all very different albums in their own right and you simply have to go check them out for yourself.

125) Carpenters - Offering

I've been avoiding Offering, the debut Carpenters album for quite a while. Now that I've heard it though, it's weird. As far as my unwritten standard evaluation of albums goes, it's actually a pretty good album, but Richard is weird. I wouldn't call it a speech impediment, but something about the way he forms words is a sound I've never heard before, and it sounds like he's double miced, or using a bizarre chorus effect or something. And his arrangements are strange too. The songs he wrote are fine, but the cover songs are wacky. Every track is somehow different, but they all elicit the same "why are you doing that?"

I gather most people had a similar reaction, because it was a flop until after their second album when they reissued it as "Ticket to Ride," with different cover art.

Now, I personally don't buy into the fallacy that music speaks about the psychological state of its composer/performer. Yes, they both had serious mental health issues, but that's not why this album sounds so strange. It sounds strange because you can hear the difference between the tracks that were "chaparoned" and the stuff they did because it was fun and probably made them giggle; the back and forth is what's confusing to me. Management obviously won out, because you've heard the famous Carpenters, but I can't help imagining how much more awesome it would have been (and probably healthier for them), if they'd just let these naive siblings play with all of the studio equipment instead of running them ragged as pop stars.

126) Chicago Transit Authority

So, Chicago Transit Authority. The band is pretty famous as the jazz rock standard, but their story starts at the bottom. Columbia didn't actually want them because they already had Blood, Sweat & Tears. But, since the producer of BS&T2 only did it so he could use the money to produce a band he actually liked, they didn't really have an argument to stop him.

Then, because the band had spent the previous two years writing 4-7 minute songs, they said we'll only publish a double album debut if we get to keep more of your future profits than normal. Yep, Chicago sold their future royalties to make the first album. At least it's good, in part because Peter Cetera didn't write any of the songs. Geez, 4 days in and I already broke my New Year's resolution to not be mean. Oh well, I'm sure Peter Cetera will get along just fine without my liking his songs. I like his bass playing, at least.

Hendrix was actually a big fan of Terry Kath, believe it or not. It's not hard to hear why if you actually listen to the album. He's a wizard. "Free Form Guitar" is generally regarded as the singularity that created "noise rock," and he was very vocal about the fact that it's just a guitar plugged into an amplifier and unabashedly abused for 7 minutes, no pedals or studio effects, just saturated vaccuum tubes.

Which brings me to my point. Like I said before, the self titled debut album is the "hello Cleveland" of concept albums. This time though, the band isn't just saying "hi," they're saying "we are the musical embodiment of using public transportation to see the city we come from." Of course, the actual Chicago Transit Authority had to send a cease and desist letter to retain control of their trademark (wait, you didn't know that legally enforcing your trademark/copyright was mandatory? Well, it is. If you don't actually threaten to sue people you pretty much forfeit your right to future claims against infringement).

Where was I? Jazz, blues, rock, violent noise, politics, live performance, a Beatles quote hiding in there, hard to argue that they don't represent their hometown. I'm from their future, and I don't like a fair bit of it, but this first album is a pretty great listen in my book.

127) The Mothers of Invention - Uncle Meat

It's time to listen to Uncle Meat. It's part of Zappa's much larger conceptual project No Commercial Potential. It was intended to be the soundtrack of a movie that never got finished. His larger vision was that it could all be cut up and spliced together in different ways but still be the same large scale experimental project.

I think we forget the most important part of Zappa's music, though. It's supposed to be funny. You're supposed to be in on the joke. He did all of this on purpose, to get you to think. He wanted you to question who exactly is telling you what's acceptable, normal, logical. He wanted you to see the humor in playing serious music on cheap toys and strange sounds on expensive technology. He wanted to read in depth sociological essays about his work so that he could respond by saying "no, I just put random crap together because it was funny." He wanted certain parts to be completely out of step with others so you couldn't actually tell which one was "right."

He wanted a bunch of talented, well practiced musicians making meticulous music that sounded like they were playing random garbage. He wanted to be ridiculous on purpose.

There are some really fantastic and inventive pieces of pure music on this double album. I think it's hilarious, and I highly recommend checking it out if/when you ever get the chance.

128) Paul McCartney - McCartney

Paul McCartney had a farm E-I-E-I-O. And on that farm he made an album, Oh-my-lo-fi-no!

That's not really true. Yes, he owned a farm, but only because buying property is what wealthy people do instead of paying taxes. They're called liquid assets because you can freely slosh them around when necessary. He let the neighboring shepherd graze the land so it didn't appear vacant, and eventually bought more of the surrounding property to further discourage sightseers. If you follow the documented timeline, they spent 2 or 3 months there after John said adios jerkos. They were back in London before Christmas, and that's where McCartney actually recorded his lo-fi self-titled solo album.

We ignore the fact that he's not some random schmuck, he is a corporate executive. When he walked into the New York offices of Apple Records even Allen Klein had to say "you're the boss." Go ahead, try postponing you're internationally renowned band's next album for your own anger fueled, clandestinely produced solo effort, see how well that works. The history of the Beatles' breakup is so convoluted at this point, that you have to take a step back and evaluate reality.

1) John Lennon quit. Straight up said "I'm not in this band anymore." Sure, George had quit before, but George didn't own any of it. There's only one hyphen and it's the one in Lennon-McCartney.

2) Paul had a full book of matches and his American lawyers were actual family. Bye bye bridge.

John broke up the Beatles, but Paul was the one who forced them to acknowledge it publicly. He bought new toys, made an album in his house, booked studio time under an alias to mix and master it, and pushed the release of Let It Be back because anger and viciousness is the first stage of depression. The actual bottom of the barrel didn't hit until everybody, and I do mean everybody, said "this is crap." That's what hurt, and that's why Ram turned out the way it did.

Nobody had any idea that the Beatles were over when McCartney was released, they thought it was going to be a normal old album of Paul McCartney songs, but they got the opposite of the Beatles instead.

So, what are the major criticisms of this album? 1) it's lo-fi, 2) the songs sound unfinished, and 3) "instrumental" music is a cop out. Are those criticisms fair? That depends.

1 - If you were expecting George Martin production on this solo effort, you would have been disappointed. If however, you want to hear an album 100% made by Paul McCartney, then that criticism makes no sense. This is the album he made, you can't argue that it isn't.

2 - Lennon and McCartney were a team, and they relied on each other to give their songs a final form, or at the very least act as a filter, more often than not. Any solo album by McCartney is going to noticeably lack the Lennon part of the equation.

3 - This is just a stupid criticism. 70% of Beatles songs have nonsense lyrics to begin with, and you're really just saying "this album of music has too much music on it." It might not be what you want it to be, but he's not playing fart sounds on a casio keyboard (it's not the 80s yet...).

At the risk of trying your patience, and straining your eyesight reading this monstrosity of a post, I'm going to go track by track.

The Lovely Linda - this is a song fragment (a test recording), and he giggles at the end. You've already heard The Ballad of John and Yoko, so either you make a connection, or we just keep going.

That Would Be Something - two tag lines and beat boxing. That's just experimental blues. Silly, but legitimate in its experimentality.

Valentine Day - It's an instrumental jam that could totally be a demo he might bring to a Beatles rehearsal.

Every Night - This is a great song. Short, but lovely.

Hot As Sun - Yes, it's a series of instrumental interludes. You know who might be able to write some good verses for it....?

Glasses - ok that was pointless. I like it, but I'll admit it serves no purpose.

Junk - perfectly fine song. Again, short, but it doesn't need to be any longer.

Man We Was Lonely - perfectly acceptable song. The most complete song so far, with interesting stereo effects, even.

Oo You - perfectly good blues song. I think you know where this review is going to end up...

Momma Miss America - really interesting instrumental piece. Not a "song" per se, but I've written 50+ eps full of stuff like this. Just saying, it doesn't suck as a piece of music.

Teddy Boy - I'm not going to pretend, this is a crummy song. Still a song, though.

Singalong Junk - an instrumental piece titled exactly how you'd expect the Beatles to actually feel about this song if they went ahead and made it an actual song.

Maybe I'm Amazed - the one track nobody could even begin to pretend was substandard in any way whatsoever. It also says something very specific about what you've been listening to this whole time. It's not absent-minded garbage. This song says "I can make this kind of thing whenever I feel like it, but I'm actually trying to do something different."

Kreen-Akrore - a piece named after a Brazilian tribe (now called the Panará) known for killing intruders. Hmmm.

So what's the verdict? You're all idiots. This is fantastic. This is what he would have brought to the next Beatles session if there were going to be one. They would flesh out the instrumentals, John would co-write some lyrics and tweak the music a little, George would play some interesting but subtle side riffs, Ringo would tastefully bang on the drums. Screw those guys.

Everybody gave Paul crap because he was the one who publicly said "the Beatles are over," but he's also the one who suggested they be an actual band again because John and George kept bickering and threatening to quit and being pissy about everything. Ringo was only mad because he sat in the lobby patiently waiting for everyone else to show up every day.

I side with Paul on this one. If the rest of his solo career was this good (it's not) I'd be a die-hard fan. "The Beatles" was a monstrous behemoth pop culture juggernaut, and it makes complete sense that each member had radically different interests outside of that world (I'll talk about George at some point, he just requires a lot more mental energy than I have right now).

I think this album should only be compared to other self-made major albums of the time, of which there are none. Paul McCartney is literally the first person rich, powerful, and talented enough to record, publish, and internationally distribute an album he made in his living room. That's insane for 1969, and it's equally insane today. Beck and Dave Grohl are the only people I can think of who've done something comparable, but they still had other people in a real recording studio with professional equipment helping them.

This, of course, is just my opinion: I think it's muchly much much more better than what everyone else says about it.

129) Moody Blues - To Our Children's Children's Children

So, what do the Moody Blues have to say to their great grandchildren?

Holy shit! I spilled my drink I was so startled by that opening. Oh yeah, going into space was a big crazy thing in 1969. This album was inspired by the moon landing (or the successful world wide medio-political hoax if you're the kind of person who believes a poor selling Moody Blues album was a vital step in the plot of our lizard overlords to brainwash us into believing that evil sciency stuff).

There are quite a few threads of a story here, but for whatever reason I can't seem to connect them. Hi kids, I hope everything doesn't suck for you in the future. Do space people get lonely? I'm long dead by now, but we bury ourselves underground, so I'm actually part of earth again if you want to come visit sometime. Sincerely, your hippy relatives from England (that was a country on Earth).

It also seems like it's meant to be one big multi-movement work, choruses reappear, they jump from a hundred years to a million years, but again it's just not vibing with me for some reason. It's much more folk oriented than I want it to be, and I'm kind of meh on it. It's not bad, I'm just not into it. Your milage may vary....

130) Moon Hooch - This Is Cave Music

I wasn't overly thrilled with last night's offering from the Moody Blues, so tonight I'm going to say now This Is Cave Music (Ha! Get it? 'Cause the cover was a cave painting. Oh, how droll I am).

I don't have the aptly self-titled debut album by Moon Hooch, but since this one starts off with No. 6 of their initial compositions, I'll take a moment to point out the first album was recorded in 24 hours in Brooklyn.

They spent some money and took a little more time with their second album. There's some synths and vocals on it, but they are pretty ok and it works with their persona. For those who don't know, Moon Hooch is saxophone-based dance/rave music. To put it in SAT terms, Electronic is to House as Acoustic is to Cave (again with the allusive humor: the band met in college. I'm on fire tonight).

They honed their style busking in the NYC Subway, which contrary to what you might have thought requires an actual audition and license, unless you want to go to jail instead of home at the end of your performance.

In real life they are modern day hippies. They spend their days volunteering at community gardens and self-sustaining communities near whatever city their gig is in that night. Some of the stuff they do is a little wacky, but they seem like genuinely cool guys. And, their music is awesome and super high energy.

The great thing about this trio is they don't sound forced, or gimmicky, or out of touch. It's legitimate club music (this album really does play out like a DJ set) made with saxophones and drums. It's got a beat, you can dance to it, and you literally can't frown while you listen to it because it's not dumbed down or formulaic either. They're awesome. Go check 'em out.

131) The Strokes - Is This It

Is This It? Probably not, but it's a valid question. Let's travel back to that strange old year of 2001 and talk about The Strokes. They didn't disappear or burn out, they still exist, you just don't care. It's not your fault, really. It's theirs. Not because they did anything wrong, but because they succeeded in changing the entire rock landscape with their debut album.

Their demo stirred up an actual bidding war, and when the dust finally settled, they knew exactly what they wanted their debut album to sound like. They wanted to sound like a garage band from the 60s/70s who travelled in time to make an album in a NYC basement in 2001 that sounded like it was made in the 60s/70s. They wanted to sound like they were playing these songs live, but also sound like it was made with drum machines and generally cheap equipment. They wanted it to sound the exact opposite of what everyone else was doing.

What they did was write catchy, peppy songs from the perspective of kids who don't have a future, or a way to profit from their talents. They don't even get to keep their original cover art, 'cause female butts are too provocative now for some reason.

The one nice aspect about the archaically complex and expensive technology used to carve grooves in a plastic disc is that the song "New York City Cops" is still on it. Their label removed that song from the CD because of 9/11. I hate censorship, and if you can't handle a story about his girlfriend that includes the phrase "New York City cops, they ain't too smart" because of a tragic event that has nothing to do with a song from before it happened, then you're taking the universe a little bit too personally in my opinion.

Is This It? I don't know, but it sure feels like it sometimes.

132) Neil Peart, my humble eulogy

It's been a very long day. It is also a sad day, as Neil Peart has died. I do not have any Rush albums in my collection, but I think the fact that there never have been and almost certainly never will be any Rush albums sitting in a used record shop is a better testament to their musical legacy than anything I could say. He was *the* iconic drummer of my adolescence, and I can only hope that he was in some way satisfied with his life's work (musicians never actually are, you know). Rest in peace, Neil.

133) Machines of Loving Grace - Gilt

As should be completely obvious by now, I have a deep and complex love of listening to recorded music. Even music I subjectively hate (like say, Country) has a right to exist, if only so that I can actively hate it while saying "you're more than welcome to love it." But, like everyone else, I have a favorite type of music and it's industrial rock from the early to mid 90s. You've all heard of NIN, Marilyn Manson, and Rob Zombie, but they are very much the Brad Pitt, or Leonardo DiCaprio of their genre. Nothing wrong with them, perfectly appealing, boring old superstars whose albums are actually hit or miss because being palatable (for a given value of palatable) was more important to them.

I want the real meat of the genre, the lifestyle bands who managed to eke out their own lasting successes. Ministry, KMFDM, Die Krupps, Gravity Kills, Stabbing Westward, Sister Machine Gun, Skinny Puppy, early Thrill Kill Kult, Front Line Assembly, and tonight's selection Machines of Loving Grace. They are, in my opinion, the Dead Hot Workshop of industrial rock (and by complete coincidence also from Arizona).

Gilt is their second album, and my favorite. The standout song is obviously Golgotha Tenement Blues (a single written specifically for The Crow soundtrack), but the whole album is worth your attention. On the scale of Rock to Noise, Machines of Loving Grace is about as far to the rock band side as you can get (not surprising at all if you know the actual poem), but boy howdy are they cathartically depressing.

The more discerning amongst you will surely notice a very familiar drum sound throughout this album (especially in the toms on some of the deeper cuts), and I'll save you some mental agony and just tell you it's Sylvia Massey (one of the very very very few female producers in rock), who also produced Tool's Opiate and Undertow, Green Jellö, and anybody who passed through Sound City's Studio B in the mid to late 90s, like Paula Abdul or Sheryl Crowe. She didn't just walk into a top tier studio like a lot of producers, if she produced your album she used her personal equipment, samples, and tricks. Her sound is f-ing amazing and I think she's as good as Albini, and leaps and bounds better than any of the Lord-Alge brothers.

Anywho, if you haven't indulged me up to now, please consider doing so with this album. It really is one of my favorites from top to bottom, and a pretty good starting point for getting into the strange marriage of hard rock and dark EDM that is second generation Industrial.

134) Finger eleven - The Greyest of Blue Skies

Every band that has ever existed has one good song. I genuinely believe that statement, and tonight's band is one of my personal least liked bands of all time. I hate them. Every radio single was worse than the one before it, and I wish they did not exist, especially the one that is permanently lodged in my brain, ready to devour my sanity in moments of critical stress (it's Paralyzer, by the way).

Just like last night's album, I loved the soundtrack song so much I went and bought the real album. The song is "Suffocate," the soundtrack is Scream 3, the band is Finger Eleven. Unlike Machines of Loving Grace, I detest Finger Eleven and it's surprising that I still even possess their second album, The Greyest of Blue Skies. I literally haven't heard this album in 20 years, but I remember being really unhappy for listening to it. I'm going to listen to it with an open mind though because I only remember track 7, everything else is practically my first hearing. Keep in mind though, "Suffocate" is a borderline industrial track that I do very much adore, so that's what I'm expecting to hear more of...

Musically it starts out great, but then the vocals ruin it. "First Time" could legitimately be a Tonic song. It's strange for me, but not too bad. Except for the breathy voice 3 minutes in. Don't do that, it sucks.

Tracks 2 and 3 suck. I don't have any words to add, "riding my carousel" is the stupidest chorus I've ever heard. BS&T wrote the only tolerable carousel song, and that's because they didn't say the word "carousel."

I know what is agitating me. They're trying to be Mr. Bungle, but writing pop songs. You can't copy Mike Patton's middle finger project. Fail.

It's like every part belongs to a different arrangement, and they just layered them without any sense of continuity or consistency. Who produced this trashcan collage? Arnold Lanni? Never heard of him. Oooooh, he produced the first 4 Our Lady Peace albums. They suck and I don't feel bad for saying it. At least he consistently produces garbage.

Finally, the song I like. I'm not kidding, this is the first song that sounds complete. The 6 previous songs all sound like they are missing parts, or pieced together from the better parts of worse songs.

Uuughhh. Bones+Joints sounds like audio diarrhea. If I had synesthesia this whole album would be puce (which is "the color of bloodstains on linen or bedsheets, even after being laundered, from a flea's droppings, or after a flea has been crushed"). Falsetto? The end vocals remind me too much of Puddle of Mud, a band I also hate.

God that bass sound is seriously terrible. It's not so bad in the full sonic wall, but by itself it's just gross. I really don't want the whole review to be poop jokes, but it's the only analogy that encapsulates the actual experience: this album takes a dump in my brain.

Ugh, again. "Try walking in my shoes"? That's classic narcissistic douchbaggery. *I'm better than you 'cause I've really suffered.* Eat rat poison.

I didn't think it was possible, but I actually hate this album more now than I did the first time I hated it.

My friend Stephen Hughes ejected and threw his copy of Radiohead's Kid A out the window of the car we were driving before it even finished because he hated it so much, then felt guilty and bought it again the next day to give it a second chance. I could never do that, but it'll be at least 20 more years before I give this god-awful raccoon food a third listen. I might even put a sticky note on it that says "Caution: this album is legitimately so bad that it will actually make you appreciate the talent of Ten Tears After," just in case anyone who isn't me decides to peruse my collection. I still like "Suffocate," but the other 10 songs are just awful.

By all means go give this a listen for yourself, but don't say I didn't warn you.

135) Billy Vaughn - 1962's Greatest Hits

I don't know about you, but today feels like a good day for some elevator music. I probably use that term more broadly than most people, and I rightly or wrongly include orchestral/big band arrangements of popular music regardless of intent. Today I'm listening to Billy Vaughn's arrangements of hit songs from 1962.

I could probably do a reasonable survey of musicians whose master recordings were cremated in the 2008 Universal fire, and Billy Vaughn is one of them. His story is pretty interesting. He enlisted in the National Guard for a year, but then that pesky WWII thing happened. Luckily, he was considered too important as a musician and composer to play dodge ball with bullets and heavy artillery, and pretty easily made a career out of playing any instrument lying around after it was over. He went to college, fell back on being a barber when he couldn't find a gig, and pretty much just made anybody who crossed his path happy and/or wealthy. By the numbers, he was the single most successful band leader of the "rock era," and people paid good money to have his arrangements of hit singles playing in the background. I can't argue, this is quite good. If I only had an adverb and an adjective to describe his style, "tastefully adventurous" might do the trick. He wasn't afraid to let the electric guitarist plink out a full chorus, then play a smooth but hip alto sax line while the choir does a subtle theremin impression. He's no Marty Paich, but this is after all mass market music with a distinct Country & Western foundation. You can tell he's being restrained, but he gets some real boozy jabs in there too.

Don't get me wrong, lots of people hate his work. I disagree with most of the negative things people say because I disagree with their approach to criticism in general. Most critics work from the notion that whatever type of music they are talking about has a canon, and anybody putting out a record gets scrutinized for inclusion. Vaughn sometimes gets told to stick his Country Schmaltz where the sun doesn't shine, but I don't think that's fair. Country Schmaltz is his thing. That's like criticizing Van Gogh for his visible brush strokes; you've completely missed the point, and I'll be the jackass who yells "air ball" as I walk by. Bandleaders who do this kind of thing aren't trying to appeal to you, they are actually telling their own audiences it's okay to like the new crazy stuff the kids are making, it's real music too and recontextualizing it is actually a good thing. Artists make statements about their subject matter, not the other way around. And, let me tell you, "Moon River" is pretty awesome as a harmonica solo.

136) Portishead - Roseland New York

Sometimes I feel guilty for not liking an artist or an album. For example, Tom Waits, or Nick Cave and the Bad Seeds' Murder Ballads, or the third Portishead album, aptly titled Third. I flicked over to NPR on the drive home just in time to hear a flashback of Brian Eno telling Bob Boilen about how excited he was by a Portishead track, and they'll be my focus tonight.

Like I said, I feel bad for not liking Third. After the agonizing 11-year wait, I wanted real trip hop again. I still don't like it, especially now that the other iconic band famous for exponentially extending the space between albums dropped what I consider to be an acceptable Tool album. Double especially considering when Failure finally decided to make another album after a decade plus hiatus, they said to themselves "it has to be a real continuation of Fantastic Planet, or we should just abandon the whole thing now."

Luckily, I'm in charge and I can decide to watch the Roseland concert like it was the last thing they ever did. It's basically both amazing albums played astoundingly well in front of a live audience.

Trip Hop is straight out of Bristol, and Portishead, Massive Attack, and Tricky are its imagineers. The official definition is down tempo, sample heavy, jazz/soul infused hip-hop, with an emphasis on atmospheric/environmental textures. Hip-hop on downers without rap is what it is.

For the uninitiated, Beth Gibbons has a very unique voice that can do things you've never heard before. This performance isn't as harsh as the studio albums, though.

As you'll see, it takes a hell of a lot of gear and people to do this stuff live, but it's glorious. Really, the only things unenjoyable are Adrian Utley's gum chewing, and goofy audience members. If you've never seen it, then you're missing out.

137) The Royal Guardsmen - Snoopy for President

You know what? You can all shove it. Snoopy for President.

I like The Royal Guardsmen a lot. They aren't weird or obnoxious, but their songs are good. They're all over the map style-wise, but it doesn't sound contrived. It's more like they can play whatever style you want them to play, as long you don't mind a completely different style for the next song (they are campaigning across all the constituencies, after all).

Thankfully, they deliver on their promises. An enjoyable listen whenever you're in the mood for lighter (but well written) 60s pop-rock.

138) Female Vocalist Roulette

Let's play female vocalist album roulette. I've pulled 6 out of various crates. I'll shuffle them around and pick a number for tonight's review. Will I like it, will I hate it, who knows? The suspense might malfunction and kill us all!

It won't, guns and women are both perfectly safe so long as you don't pretend they are toys. If nothing else, I am a man of my word. Chamber 3, Barbra Streisand's What About Today, is locked and loaded. Fire at will.

Google tells me 58% of people who told google whether or not they liked it in fact didn't. Wikipedia tells me it's 33.33% of Babs' unranked albums (meaning anybody who did buy it told 12 friends not to buy it), and the phrase "first attempt at recording contemporary pop songs," confirms that nobody likes this thing. So, I should find loads of things to compliment....

I know exactly why people didn't like this album. It has nothing to do with Barbra, the song selections, or the message. It's the same problem The 4 Seasons had. It's 1969, and nobody has any idea how to process this material coming from big showbiz insiders. Is she making fun of the Beatles, Paul Simon, and Bacharach/David? Is she just grasping at a market trend? Am I supposed to suddenly like Vaudeville/Cabaret because it's topically relevant to my life? How dare she express an opinion about war being bad, and question the value of purely material wealth! How dare she implore us to stand up for what we believe in and argue for peace, tolerance, and social equality!

Bah humbug, I say. This is as good as any other Barbra Streisand album (I do have more, you know). Like I was saying about Billy Vaughn, this isn't about Barbra trying to win over new fans, it's about telling the people who already love and listen to her that these ideas and the songs that convey them are legitimate. She's just taking the prevailing musical attitude and incorporating it into her own highly refined persona. Millions of people hate her, but she's still famous, successful, and surrounded by personal and professional praise. I don't like a couple of her interpretations, but I'm pretty sure the 10 highly successful albums before this one (and the 40 something more yet to come) will do her just fine.

Whether you love it or hate it, it's fascinating to hear her try to interpret them (they are real interpretations, not just mindlessly singing pop songs). I don't hear it as mockery, I hear it as acting. She's putting on a little musical with songs from the radio in everybody's living room. The story they build is completely familiar: why is it so strange to be kind, to love one another, and to stop blowing each others' brains out while calling *us* the bad guys for refusing to participate?

Seems like a reasonable question to me, even coming from an out of touch diva.

139) Jack Jones - I've Got a Lot of Living to Do

Tonight's album isn't what you think. I mean, obviously it's a Jack Jones album, but that's not what I'm really listening to tonight. I'm really listening to my all-time favorite arranger blow his contemporaries out of the water.

Jack Jones is primarily known as a pop singer, but 1962's I've Got a Lot of Livin' to Do is one of his forays into big band jazz. He's great, and I really do like his voice. His output is consistently high quality (though the vocal reverb on this album is borderline obnoxious), and that means we can turn our attention to his supporting ensembles.

Three band leaders support him on this album. Billy May only does one track (and his orchestration is boooooooring), so it's really a grudge match between Pete King and Marty Paich. Paich is the winner, hands down.

My love of Marty Paich is well documented (possibly to the point of nausea), but I think you can hear the difference on this album. May's scoring makes his ensemble sound unimportant. The trumpets are always muted, the solos are haphazard, and the recording quality is noticeably muddier. The one exception is "Me and My Big Ideas."

Paich, however, is a genius at putting various subsections of the band on equal footing with the singer. At no point does any instrument just vamp for 8 bars. He never uses the band as mere accompaniment, and every single part serves a vital role in how the song unfolds.

Oh, nevermind. Go give this album a listen just because it's fun. He's a great crooner, and this whole album is highly enjoyable. I'm not ashamed to admit I like him more than Sinatra. I like Dean Martin best, but Jack Jones is a close second.

140) Melanie - Stoneground Words

If you remember way back to our first encounter with Melanie, you'll be pleased to know that I still have no idea what she is. I don't mean that as an insult, I just can't wrap my head around her sheer complexity.

Everything I said about Gather Me applies to Stoneground Words, and more! She's a folk singer, but way more complex than her peers (Joan Baez and Joni Mitchell). This album has all sorts of background musicians, guitars and organ and harmonium and sax and electric bass and congas, and more, and somebody presses the gospel choir button occassionally. Her tonality and song structures are complex, even when the lyrics are borderline silly. She warbles and melismates like she's on the edge of a nervous breakdown. The best story about her is that she completely ignored the fact that the Powder Ridge Rock Festival was totally cancelled, 30,000 people showed up to buy drugs anyway, and she played for that wacked out audience through a PA powered by ice cream trucks like it was a normal Melanie concert.

Stoneground Words doesn't have a pocket. It has two little flaps that hold the record and 5 serrated and folded (but with a hole at the top for hanging on your wall like a calender)12x12 glossy photos of her playing guitar in the desert. It is truly strange, and since I have no familiarity with her doing regular person things, I can only imagine her as a crazy New York hippie who wandered off from the bus tour of southern California and just stayed there.

But back to the music. Her singing still gives me the strangest sense of deja vu. I really don't know these songs, but I completely recognize the sound of her singing them from somewhere else. I guess we'll just have to accept it for the completely confusing conundrum it is until I hear what I'm actually remembering again by chance. I don't really know what it is, but I very much enjoy it.

141) The Supremes

I might be the grumpiest old man in the universe today. 2 days of traipsing through 3-foot snow drifts to feed animals and drive kids around in a blizzard is enough to make anyone steaming mad at the universe. So, let's sip this rum and orange juice together, while I break out The Supremes and soothe whatever's left of this savage beast.

Where Did Our Love Go is their second album. It's the first hit "Motown" album, the highest ranking for a female group ever, 3 number one singles, 89 weeks on the charts, and the first number 1 on the new R&B charts. Diana Ross currently has a net worth of 200-something million dollars, and this is the album that made that happen for everyone involved.

I've already talked about my respect for Motown in general, and Holland/Dozier certainly didn't hand these lovely ladies stinkers. I'm gonna listen to their 10th album too (The Supremes Sing Holland-Dozier-Holland).

Sure, we could delve into the questionable misogyny inherent in this music, the tacit emphasis on "pleasing" a man, even if he's not faithful or particularly worth it. However, I would argue that it's more important to recognize that these songs actually portray a real sense of conflict that stems from that mentality. They are actually expressing the hurt and emotional pain a fickle and unfaithful man causes, thus they try even harder to keep him close and the cycle never stops. Those are the real emotions involved in an inherently sexist world.

Enough of that, it's the Supremes! They were the Primettes, the "sister" act of Eddie Kendricks' Primes. Supremes + Temptations, a no brainer for kicking the music world in the balls and Berry Gordy laced up his metaphorical steel-toed boots (his affair with Diana Ross notwithstanding). It sounds cheesy to say they "paved the way" for the future mainstream success of black artists, but that was the goal: Motown and its two pioneer groups eliminated race from the equation. Don't forget that The Supremes were basically as popular as The Beatles for the entire 1960s decade. This is just fantastic, completely relatable, pop music (even the deep cuts), and you should be embarrassed if you don't love it.

I feel better. You?

142) Stan Getz - Sweet Rain

If you've never heard Stan Getz, the general consensus is that his 1967 album Sweet Rain is the cream of the crop. They call him "the sound" because, well, he's about the smoothest sax player ever. Not lightweight or boring, but double-digit aged whisky smooth.

He's heavily influenced by South American music, and a pioneer of Samba and Bossa Nova based improvisation. Notable highlights from the nastier side of his life include going to prison for robbing a pharmacy for morphine, being abusive to his actual wife and children, and stealing João Gilberto's, the "inventor" of bossa nova, wife. He didn't kidnap her or anything, she just ran away with him when he went back to the states. They didn't actually marry because his real wife didn't want to be bankrupted by divorce (yes, that did frequently happen in a world where businesses didn't hire women to do anything more than answer the phone or type letters).

It's generally hinted that he was borderline mentally unstable, and you might be tempted to read that into his penchant for wild shifts in tempo and style. I've already mentioned that I don't put much stock in that kind of pseudo psycho-musicology, but it's definitely true that he frequently indulges in structural freedom.

The first track is the craziest, but the quartet achieves those radical transitions in a consistent way: the shifts in tempo/meter always follow from an out of kilter riff by Stan himself, or Chick Corea. Like the liner notes describe, it's more a chasing butterflies approach to music that anything inherently schizophrenic.

I find this record quite soothing as the polar opposite of Pharoah Sanders. Getz is squirrely, but in a "oh that's pretty, let's go that direction" kind of way.

143) Dave Grusin's Candy

Dave Grusin is technically a jazz pianist, but he's also a pretty notable film composer (even some movies you've actually seen). But did he make psychedelic noise rock?

Absolutely. I doubt he's proud of it, but I have his soundtrack to a movie Roger Ebert called "a lot better than you might expect [but the book was much better]." High praise, indeed. I don't need to see the 1968 sex-farce Candy. Little known fact: I stopped caring about movies after The Matrix Reloaded (2003), and I abandoned attentively watching them altogether after Occulus (2013).

Anywho, let's attack this for what it really is: a jazz pianist writing symphonic psych-rock that builds toward a Steppenwolf song. That's a reasonable concept, and I don't need to know the actual source of the structure; like the tone poems of Smetana or Strauss. Yeah, a psychedelic tone poem based on two songs by John Kay for a movie based on a book that's a satire of pornography. How's that really any different than Coheed and Cambria? It's not. Good, I'm glad we got that settled.

It's a bit clumsy though. Obviously, the pieces themselves have to fit with the movie timing, and that makes them awkward as tracks on a record. But musically speaking it's great stuff, and I wish it really was an actual album. If I had a time machine, I'd tell him to avoid the movie and just make this a real band.

I think real rock based symphonic music should exist. Not the god-awful things Yngwie and Clapton did with orchestras backing them (or the obvious disaster of U2 and Spiderman the musical), but using the orchestra as a legitimate part of a rock band. Dear composers, learn how to write wacky stuff like this and we all might have a future in the performing arts.

This is exciting stuff, like Spirit and even Beacon Street Union. I'm convinced there's more super obscure stuff like this out there, and I desperately want to find it.

144) Nirvana

Here's an insane story. I was listening to Burl Ives Sings Pearly Shells and Other Favorites, and I had three thoughts. 1) I kind of like Burl Ives, but I don't want to write about this album. 2) I should write about a band's whole discography. 3) let's binge all 5 Nirvana albums.

Why not the standard studio 3? Because Incesticide is their best album, and Unplugged is special. Actually, all 5 albums are completely different beasts, and altogether they paint a picture of a band who cared about only 1 thing: playing songs. The constant thread through every album is the complete exorcism of every ounce of negative energy infesting these human beings. Obviously it didn't work, but you can hear Kurt Cobain exerting every ounce of physical and mental energy just trying get it out of his system.

"Grunge" isn't a thing. Every Nirvana album is both the exact same and completely different. They are the same because Kurt was a professional songwriter from the start; he'd revise his lyrics 30 times before he considered it "finished." Plus, we're only talking about a 4-year time span. They are different because each one had a completely different production crew and aesthetic context.

"Bleach" is basically a demo album, and it most resembles sludgy punk-metal like The Melvins. Nevermind takes it up a notch in a real studio with a proper budget and Butch Vig (from Garbage). But it connected. Everyone who heard it instantly understood where they were coming from, and recognized the unrelenting honesty of just not caring about anything anymore. It's pop but it's sarcastic, it's angry but it's funny, it's polished and highly produced but that somehow makes it more nasty. It's the Ramones if the Ramones could afford a Dual Rectifier, 700 guitar overdubs, and pay someone to watch them play with squeak toys for an hour.

Then they were touring and starting to fall apart, and every once in a while they'd get to record a few songs and that's Incesticide. It's the stuff they liked playing: covers, different versions of songs, new things. It's fantastic. If you've never heard it you have to. Now. Stop reading my blah blahs...

.... Welcome back. At this point, Nirvana is frightening. If they don't make another album, we might as well all kill ourselves (I don't mean that as crassly as it comes across). So, Kurt hired Steve Albini to record In Utero. Why? Because Albini had no interest in sponging off Nirvana. He said here's the studio time I can give you, pay me whatever you think it's worth (actually, Albini still pretty much runs his studio that way and doesn't give a shit if you're famous or good or not. He just takes pride in his own actual work, and tries to make everybody sound as good as possible). Great album.

Then MTV wanted them to do an Unplugged concert. To which Kurt replied, only if we can have effects and play mostly covers. Basically, not an Unplugged concert. But holy crap. Even the same MTV execs who argued about it admitted that it wasn't another dumb Unplugged, it was an actual unique experience, a happening, a moment in time when "the artist" was 100% right, and knew better than everyone.

Then he killed himself. There's been way too much romanticizing of the circumstances of his suicide. Whatever it was he was actually battling won. It doesn't affect my love of his music one way or the other, and the 50 million dollars his accountant manged for him at that moment didn't do it for him.

I've probably heard every stupid self esteem boost ever, like "I used to like Nirvana until I realized I was a better guitar player than Kurt Cobain." Eat me. I simply cannot stress this enough: the skill with which you play your instrument has no bearing on whether I like it or not. Bob Dylan can't sing, Mike Anthony played 3 note bass lines for the entire history of Van Halen (Running with the Devil is basically a pedal E for crying out loud). To paraphrase John Cage, if your child can do it, please for the love of all things earthly and beautiful encourage them to do it in front of a microphone so that I can listen to it later!!!

There is nothing artificial about the whole discography. I have countless bootlegs and demos that you could use as evidence that "they suck," but you're missing the point. The point is "this is what I hear in my head." Nirvana is exactly what I hear in my head, from "Blew" to "Where Did You Sleep Last Night." Every single moment is perfect, every song sounds right, every person who came in contact with them brought their A game, nothing is pretend or fake or contrived. Every word he screams is the result of trying all the words until it physically felt perfect, and I can feel it (meaningful or not, it's the pure pleasure of speech).

When you really sit down and listen to it all in one go, it's flabbergasting. You've heard me say all sorts of creatively critical things, but I've got nothing. Literally nothing. Every single second of the whole discography is perfect, exactly what it should be, and it's glorious.

145) Godsmack

I've always been meh on Godsmack. Something about their debut album feels off, but I think I'm the one who's wrong. Godsmack wasn't discovered, or manufactured, they didn't get lucky. They paid for their first album themselves, but it got so popular that the little label that published it legitimately couldn't afford the scale of manufacturing and distribution. So, they signed with a major label that could invest that much money, remastered and slightly reorganized the tracks, and they're still recording and touring today.

People sometimes call them Nu Metal, but that's just wrong. They are hard rock with industrial undertones, and it is blatantly obvious that they graduated from the Page Hamilton school of guitar riffage. They are Helmet's little brother, who can't decide if he's a cult kid or a biker. It's got the samples and electronics of industrial and hardcore, the dropped-d riffing of the simplest Helmet or Tool, Zakk Wylde-esque guitar solos, and faint whiffs of stoner groove.

Now that I'm listening to it again after years, it's much more appealing than I remember. But, there are highs and lows. Get Up, Get Out! is sub par. There are moments of sonic vacancy in earlier tracks, but the unexplainable void where rhythm guitar should be is inexcusable. It's also lyrically pointless, and they should have just cut it. Granted, this is merely a repackaged demo, but why leave an obvious weak link in an otherwise intriguing album?

I think the thing most lacking is consistency. The production level, the songwriting, the sonic palette, and the orchestration are totally all over the place and it gets really distracting. It's also just wrong for a self titled debut album; it would have been better just continuing to call it All Wound Up.

There's a funny story about that warning label, too. This record was on Wal and K mart shelves for a long time without it, but some guy complained that the lyrics were offensive. The result of course is that it sold even better, because the warning made kids desperate to offend their parents. That's graduate level marketing, but it's nothing compared to Lords of Acid's Voodoo U, which as a teenager I had to buy from under the counter like smut because a naked lesbian cartoon devil orgy couldn't just sit in a music store bin. Maybe I'll write about that album tomorrow.

The potential is clearly there. They are one of the few examples of a band that was going to be famous and make money for whoever put down the cash to package 100,000 copies at a time. In hindsight, they suffer from my personal dislike for the origins of non blues based hard rock at the turn of the 21st century. A lot of terrible crap got made in the early 2000s while we were trying to figure out how to get angry and care again. I heard Godsmack as the start of that mainstream descent into the bad side of genre fusion. I grew up with their actual influences pounding my eardrums, and they sound clumsily derivative to me. That's not fair, but it is true.

Godsmack is fine, I'm just jaded and can't give them the fair start that everyone else could.

146) Lords of Acid - Voodoo-U

Lords of Acid is the EDM project of Praga Khan and which ever female vocalist was hanging out with him at the time. Their sophomore album is considered an industrial album, and now would be a good time to really delve into what that actually means.

When I talked about Throbbing Gristle, I mentioned the idea that this is music from an "industrialized" mindset. Machinery, violence, noise, force, the removal of nature and humanity for mass production and consumption. It very much originated in England, but found a second home in Chicago. From the very beginning it was the genre of the margins of society: LGBT, LaVayan satanism (which is really just complete individual freedom), anarchists (both classical and destructive), and any other marginalized groups felt drawn to the violent clash of sampled drums, chainsaw guitar riffs, electronic chaos, and just talking about the horrible side of life in general. The common thread is provocative (like punk) electronic music emphasizing heavy artificial sound production and repetition over more traditional compositional methods. The sound of machines making music.

Voodoo-U is really just extreme rave music: sex, drugs, sex and drugs, sex and drugs are good, sex and drugs are bad, I have to buy cheap food because I spent all my money on heroin, look at that coked up bitch, crabs actually make me orgasm. There are moments of jungle, house, reggae, and metal, but the overwhelming aura of this album is mechanical hedonism. That hedonism has its good and bad sides, but we're just here to dance until we fall down dead. Stop being such a prude and love this album as much as I do.

147) The Boomtown Rats

Nowadays we associate "new wave" with the synthy, jerky pop/rock of the late 70s and 80s, but at the start it was indistinguishable from punk (especially in the UK). Real punk wasn't an actual musical genre, it was an attitude. That attitude was "this urban/suburban world our parents created is crap." That attitude evolved along two distinct lines, synth pop and alternative rock. The former simply abandoned the whole issue and reveled in the electronic inhumanity of commercial pop (whether escapist or critical, it's meant to be highly refined popular dance music), while the latter delved even deeper into the reason being outcast and miserable isn't any fun at all.

Boomtown Rats are the start of that alternative rock lineage, but they cross over into the Kinks, Cars, Blondie world on occasion. They are an Irish rock band, and Bob Geldof is their vocalist/songwriter. He's much more famous for his charity work (Band Aid, Live Aid, etc.), but his band was the actual foundation of that work. Their self titled debut is a great self titled debut. The songs are all about who they are, what their friends are like, and why it sucks to be teenagers in a world designed to exclude restless teenagers. It's not an overly confrontational or abrasive album, but it is nice and crunchy, loud and distorted, getting into trouble music. If you like the rock part of punk-rock you should definitely check it out.

148) SPK - Machine Age Voodoo

Let's explore the more overtly political side of Industrial. The first two SPK albums are real industrial noise, but their third album is industrial synthpop.

Industrial music has a few characteristic traditions: the heart of a band is usually a guy with a sequencer, acronyms are intentionally undefined (coming up with hilarious interpretations is actually part of the fun), and there's very little indication if any particular idea or topic is serious or ironic.

SPK is New Zealand musician Graeme Revell's journey from industrial noise, through political/philosophical synth pop dance music, to a further career in film scoring (and you have definitely heard his music if you've seen a movie from the early 21st century. Machine Age Voodoo is his first completely synth-pop oriented album, intentionally commercial but built on a definite industrial foundation.

Lyrically, you might feel very uncomfortable with the overtly socialist/communist mindset, and that's actually the point. A lot of the music I throw at you is actually much more intellectually complicated that you might think. The real message is "we feel this way as a reaction to the way we perceive what you are doing."

The ideology of the actual Sozialistisches Patientenkollektiv (the German organization, not the band) is fascinating, crazy but fascinating. Deriving from Marxist economic theory and French Existentialism (specifically Sartre), the SPK was founded on the notion that Capitalist Industrialization is the cause of modern physical/mental illness, and that illness is thus the defining characteristic of humanity. We define ourselves by our characteristic illness and should therefore weaponize illness to fight against the spread of Capitalist greed. Not surprisingly, western medicine in general and Doctors in particular are seen as the ruling class, poisoning us and attempting to eradicate the evolution of our inherent diseased nature.

Obviously, that's a simplified description of the complex theoretical context and you should go read about this fascinatingly bizarre school of thought yourself.

The point of SPK (the band) was psychological disorientation. Original collaborators quit, killed themselves, died from their own health problems, etc., but Revell's turn to commercialized dance music is no less disorienting. The restrained female voice, extolling deadpan propaganda over jaunty but emotionless electronic grooves can be quite disturbing, and that's the point. It's a crazy extremist half of an even more crazy and extremist argument, and you're still watching that fight play out on TV right now, 40+ years later. You've probably picked a side of that argument, and got mad at your friends and coworkers last week because you disagreed about some part of it. You might, and I say this lovingly, be just as bat-shit insane as everyone else.

You know as well as I do I lean diagonally to the left, and that's much different than running toward the center with a pickax in one hand and a malaria blanket in the other. Musically though, this stuff is really fun and interesting and enjoyable.

149) The Boomtown Rats - the fine art of Surfacing

So, what did Bob Geldof and The Boomtown Rats think about America in 1979? Not a lot of positive things, it turns out.

With 2 UK hit albums under their belt, they spent quite a bit of time over here trying to gain some international notoriety, and then they wrote an album about that experience. It's called The Fine Art of Surfacing, and damned if we just don't even bother. We're lunatics.

It's hot, it's freezing, we kill ourselves, and kill kids at school, gossip, play dress up to pretend we aren't miserable, and the only thing we know about all the drugs we take is what color the pills are before we swallow handfuls of them. None of it ever f-ing stops. Just being here is enough to drive you insane. Back to Ireland and some fresh air for us!

He's not wrong. Granted, I was literally a sperm while they were exploring our bounteous insane asylum, but it hasn't gotten any better, now has it? Make no mistake, this is a concept album. The concept is America is insane, but it's not the grandiose vacation adventure of Supertramp. Boomtown Rats got the local treatment, for sure.

I've heard songs from this album before, but the full context makes a huge difference. It's much more new wave (as opposed to rock) than their first album, but it is also much more confrontational in its own way. They were paying attention, and "When The Night Comes" is the most American sounding thing I've ever heard from any British musician ever. Like if Tom Petty and Bob Seger hijacked a Gin Blossoms concert to play a Springsteen song they found on a napkin in a Waffle House trash can.

I'm listening to the whole thing a second time as I write this, and it's a fantastic album. It could come across as condescending, but it's pretty authentic from my perspective. I mean it, this is top shelf of my collection stuff. You can hear everything in there, from The Cars to the B52s and Devo to the aforementioned heavyweights of rock, all from a cynically British David Bowie meets Thin Lizzy perspective. It's borderline clairvoyant. If you've never heard this album, I think you'll be really surprised. I know I am.

150) Thomas Dolby - The Golden Age of Wireless

I finally own a copy of Thomas Dolby's first album, The Golden Age of Wireless. Believe it or not, there are 5 different versions of this thing, and I have the US version of the original. The cover is different from the UK original, they swapped an instrumental track for both sides of his post album single, and used an alternate version of "Radio Silence." These pre "She Blinded Me with Science" versions were never released on CD, I have the mini LP anyway, and I'll never find the UK original, so I'm fine with it.

I talked a lot about him in my previous post, so we can just skip to the album itself. Not surprisingly, it's an album about technology. More specifically, it's about the merging of technology with our lives. Dolby consciously pairs electronic and acoustic instruments, and sings about how we actively use technology in our modern lives, what that does to our mental state, and how we might love or loathe it at a subconscious level.

The common critical reading of this album emphasizes the peculiar nostagizing of the post WWII generation, who grew up hearing the stories rather than directly experiencing that era. Being once over removed from that experience, I both recognize that nostalgia and don't quite understand what creates it. What comes across to me is an almost Noir atmosphere. As though this beta test of true modernity is untrustworthy, something intangibly sinister is happening around the corner but you never quite catch up to witness it.

Quite a few of the tracks are very Bowie-esque, but I'm not afraid to tell you I like Dolby better. This is also the quirky, jerky, paranoid side of New Wave (not punk at all) I've mentioned before, "Urges" being the most overt example.

I'm sure I mentioned that he thought of himself as a mediocre keyboard player and that sparked his interest in electronic music, but he's such an incredible composer that I honestly forget he's making most of this music with various bits of clunky hardware by the equivalent of hunt-and-peck typing. These aren't rock songs with a synth melody on top, they are fully orchestrated compositions built around pop style verse-chorus lyric structures. They aren't full of silly or pointless catchphrases either, the lyrics are highly literate and nuanced.

I think Dolby's music requires repeated listens to fully appreciate. He can come across as weird and obtuse on casual listen, but the more you live with his work in your head, the more you realize how concise and meticulous his music actually is. Everything has a purpose for the song, and the songs play off each other without sounding stale or repetitive. He builds incredible sonic worlds and atmospheres that wiggle and shimmer or lurk and turn sour, but never sound cheesy or dated. I guess what I'm trying to say is it doesn't sound like early 80s synth-pop thrown together by a salaried producer, it sounds like a well-crafted work of art by a serious composer, and that's really enjoyable for me. I really can't recommend this album enough, it's required listening and worth every penny if someone is dumb enough to sell you their copy.

151) Rolling Stones - Their Satanic Majesties Request

I'm on a mission. That mission is to learn to like Their Satanic Majesties Request by The Rolling Stones. I think I can do it.

One, this album is a self-made monstrosity because they were completely drugged up to the point of getting arrested, their manager actually quit and Bill Wyman was close to that point, they had absolutely no one to tell them anything was too much or too dumb, and it was anybody's guess who would show up every day or how many superfluous hangers on they might bring with them. So, the way it sounds is off the table.

Two, it's a complete rip off of Sgt. Pepper and the band unanimously agreed it was a disaster, then abandoned psychedelic experimentation all together afterward. About a month before the intended release they freaked out and just bashed everything together as best as possible. I can totally respect that.

The songs aren't about anything, so there's no need to actually analyze the lyrics. This is just pure studio improvisation.

Actually, that helps a lot. It's really not much different than Pharoah Sanders, or any random Experimental Rock album on bandcamp. If this was the first Rolling Stones album, you could be really interested in hearing them develop and improve. It's their 8th album, so I can understand everyone's agitation at the final result, but it's really not as bad as everyone says it is. Granted, the harder they copy the Beatles the less enjoyable the result, but it's not like they're pretending it's innovative; it's obvious they're copying Sgt. Pepper and that's not necessarily bad.

I think you have to approach this album like you might approach Berio or Rochberg: this is collage music, and its meaning is fully dependent on your own interpretants. Crap, now I have to unpack that comparison. Ok, Peirceian semiotics: the short, short version.

Peirce uses a three-part model for meaning. There is a tangible sign (the representamen) which your mind translates into a more personally meaningful secondary sign (the interpretant), to produce a reaction (the object), and that series can go on indefinitely until you're thinking about what you had for breakfast yesterday but can't remember why.

So, whatever thing the Rolling Stones do, gets associated with other instances of hearing something similar, and it makes you think of The Beatles or whatever, and that association makes you say "aha!" or "barf" or "good god turn it off!" or whatever. If this is all new to you, then it probably just sounds like Jagger and Richards are high as balls but everybody's getting paid a lot of money to be there so no one bothers to stop them.

You know what, forget it's the Stones and it is actually pretty good space cadet music. Not quite as exciting as Dave Grusin, but not too far behind either. It's actually the real song parts that drag the album down, the free improvisation is great.

I know I said the recording/production itself is off the table, but don't ever fully pan your lead vocals. You can do whatever you want with instruments, but hearing full tilt Mick Jagger over my left shoulder is extremely annoying.

I'm not quite there yet, but it's starting to grow on me. The instrumentals are definitely the better part of the album, but the question "why can't we sing this altogether" is a pretty authentic LSD induced sentiment. I'm trying guys, I just think you tried too hard to make it coherent. I'll give it a few more listens eventually.

152) The (Young) Rascals - Freedom Suite and Groovin'

I don't understand this album. Who are The Rascals? Looking at Freedom Suite, I think they're an obscure proto-punk band and this is a massive politically motivated concept album.

Let's go down the basic wikipedia checklist. Rock band? No. Hit songs? I don't know any of them by title. People involved? Nope, don't know any of them either. Lester Bangs called it excessive. No, sounds normal to me. Someone else called it psychedelic. No. It's not "trippy" or "outside the box" or experimental at all. Again, what the hell am I listening to?

This is R&B/Soul. Not "blue eyed soul," straight Soul (doesn't matter that they're white or that there are moments of Baroque Pop). The songs are vague, but they are real songs.

But, this is a double album, and the whole second record is instrumental. The instrumental half is quite fun with a happy birthday jam, a huge jazz inspired drum solo (a good one at that). A 1-minute jazz-funk monstrosity called "Cute" that easily rivals the other full side jams we've listened to from rock heavyweights Iron Butterfly, Vanilla Fudge, etc. All this means they were objectively hot somewhere. Time to dig deeper…

… singles band turned concept album band, big stars covered their songs, had to change their name to The Young Rascals for a while, silly stage costumes and an album called Groovin'. Wait wait wait. I've seen that album in one of these crates. Ha! Found it. Let's call this To Be Continued….

… When we last saw Bottle, he was deep in thought pondering what to make of The Rascals. And now, our story continues.

WHAT IN THE NAME OF WAYNE GRETZKE ARE ANY OF YOU PEOPLE TALKING ABOUT?!? (That's a joke about how popular they were in Canada). The songs on Groovin' are way more psychedelically motivated than anything on Freedom Suite. It's *that* "Groovin'." You know, "...on a Sunday afternoon." They're a "rock band" the same way The Royal Guardsmen are a rock band, meaning a couple of their songs are rock because they play everything: pop, jazz, soul, push the producer out of his chair and turn all the knobs to see what they do.

I understand them completely now. They suffered the same fate as Iron Butterfly. Everyone said "you win." You did the thing that we all like, now please take our money and retire. And, just like Iron Butterfly they replied "no, we take this serious. We want to make more music that we find artistically fulfilling."

All the nonsensical critical blather makes sense now. The people who were happy with their singles had to search for anything negative they could say about their turn toward art over mere entertainment, and the others had to hyperbolize a middle of the road east-coast 1969 album because they did as good a job as they could do. Freedom Suite isn't the greatest record ever, but not liking it is definitely your own fault. I'm the only person in the universe preaching that gospel, so no wonder it made no sense to me at all.

The biggest problem with newspaper style music criticism is that it isn't about the music. Everybody confuses what they like for being good. Everybody forgets that musicians only get to do what they really want to do 1) *after* they make a shit-ton of money for the executive who took a chance on them, and forced them to write/play stuff that would sell, or 2) with the understanding that they won't make much money. Either way, you have to know the difference and approach the music accordingly. That's not what newspaper criticism is about. It's about canonizing or dismissing the upper stratum of consumable media. A payroll critic raves about an album they want to compare other albums to in the future, and pans one they want to dismiss into obscurity; it makes no difference who made it or why so long as it plays into the larger story they want to tell about that artist. I want to find a reason to appreciate it by understanding why it exists at all. Who am I to judge your art without at least trying to understand why you made it in the first place?

Kudos to you, Rascals. You're not exactly a flavor I want in my morning coffee, but you certainly don't suck and I'll still drink it if there's nothing else available at the moment.

153) George Harrison - Wonderwall Music

The first George Harrison solo album, the first solo album by a member of the Beatles, the first album published by Apple Records, the thing that Oasis song is actually about, the soundtrack for a film called Wonderwall.

The film is about a man spying on his neighbor through a peephole. Two different worlds separated by a physical barrier. The album is a literal autobiographical metaphor for George Harrison's infatuation for Indian music, culture, and religion. The tracks are a mix of Indian and Western instrumentation, and it's a very deliberate attempt at creating "world music."

This is what Harrison was doing while John and Paul were making Sgt. Pepper and Magical Mystery Tour.

This is a wonderful album of creative pieces by a serious composer, but it's not a cerebrally cathartic album for me. I find it quite mentally taxing. Partly that's because I don't really like George Harrison's compositional style, and partly because it inhabits the same timbral space as the Jim Carey screech from that scene in Dumb and Dumber. I don't mean the Indian instruments, I mean the whole thing. There's a certain mid/high frequency range to which I am super sensitive, and this album just hammers it. If you can handle it, more power to you.

As an album though, it's not bad. The point is a mash up of two different worlds in close proximity to each other, and Harrison more than succeeds in creating interesting pieces for both Western and Indian ensembles. Everybody who participated in it says they had fun, and if the overall frequency spectrum didn't cause me physical discomfort, I'd probably enjoy it a lot more than I do.

154) Emerson Lake & Palmer - Love Beach

I've been listening to albums that, regardless of how they turned out, the bands very much wanted to make. Let's go the opposite direction and listen to an album that was made under 100% duress by everyone involved.

Emerson, Lake, & Palmer couldn't quit or do anything else until they made one more album. They had basically defected from England because England's tax burden on musicians was ludicrous. I make no judgement on that, but it's a pretty common sentiment and it's the basic explanation for why a lot of them retired to the US or non-British controlled island nations.

They had always had internal bickering and went through periods of hating each other, but this really was the end. Emerson gave Lake Side A to write whatever songs he wanted to write, and used Side B for a large 4-part work of his own. Their lyricist didn't really have time to collaborate with them (and they weren't talking to each other anyway), Emerson wasn't actually in charge of anything but everyone else just refused to participate beyond recording their parts and leaving, so he kept taking lots of drugs and just assembled it all as best he could even though he didn't like any of it (especially the lyrics Sinfield wrote for his Memoirs of an Officer and a Gentleman).

I don't hear any of that though. Sure, Side A is random songs, but it sounds like EL&P. The songs aren't bad, they're just a step back from the massive fantasy concepts everybody expected from them. A WWII love story isn't exactly normal fare for them, but the piece itself certainly doesn't sound like hack work.

The most fascinating story about the album is Emerson's market research. He "set up a booth at O'Hare International Airport." I'm trying to imagine walking through the airport on your way to catch your next flight and being asked to listen to an EL&P album and fill out an actual questionnaire. Robert Stack walks in, punches a Hare Krishna, puts on a pair of headphones and responds "the title doesn't make any sense, change it" before continuing along to deal with Ted Striker's PTSD.

Love Beach is exactly like Airplane or Police Academy or Bad News Bears. You take all the crap you have on hand and you just go through the motions and it turns out perfectly fine. They made their last album, they kept more of their own money, Lake got a chance to write commercial songs like he always wanted to, contractual obligations fulfilled. You can't ask for more than that, and you certainly can't be disappointed with an album that none of them wanted to make in the first place. I find the whole situation hilarious, because the magic of this band isn't *what* they made, it's *that* they made it. It doesn't seem to matter how any one of them felt about it, these three musical madmen playing together just worked.

155) The Best of The Shirelles

Here's a fascinatingly complex story. Imagine you and a few friends sing a song or two in the school talent show. Another classmate, says "you're fantastic and I bet we could all get rich if you make records for my mom's record label." None of you really want to be professional singers, but you're teenagers and Mary's mom, it turns out, isn't joking around.

You record a couple songs, you perform at actual gigs, all the money you're supposedly making is going into a trust fund that you'll inherit when you turn 21, it's all going great.

You're confused when Mary's mom sells her label to a bigger label for $4,000 dollars of 1950s money, and you aren't popular anymore. But, the new label hands you back to Mary's mom who says "that's because they didn't know how to distribute you properly, and we just took them for suckers, wink."

Then you find out it was all a lie, there's no trust fund, you don't get any of that money, but hey you were the first girl group, the first chart topping black artists, you can use that to start managing your career yourself if you want, or you can quit and we'll let Dionne Warwick take your place. Sorry you're sad and stuff. They were mad. They quit and sued. The label countersued. They all let the lawyers work it out, and went on their way.

Meet the Shirelles. Berry Gordy was a lot of things, but his business model was simply a positive refinement of stories like this. Part of the reason I like him so much is that he didn't cheat his artists like that. When he brought on a new artist he said "business is a real nasty thing, but I promise you that you'll get every penny I can negotiate for you." Why do you think so many of his artists stand up when people start talking smack about something he did?

I can totally picture him saying things like "I'm gonna hand you 5 songs, you might not like 'em, but one of them is going to be a hit; I just don't know which one. Yes, I'm going to make a lot of money, but you aren't my only act and I'm not going to rip you off just to line my own pocket. I'm not in it to take your money and run, your success is my success because it lets me do it again for the next band."

Sadly, the Shirelles themselves were unable to compete with Gordy's groups and the British groups of the 60s, but that's not the point. The point: some high school girls having fun had a major impact on the music industry and society at large, but they've all but faded into obscurity now because they got cheated by their deal makers. Critics like to point out that naiveté is a prominent component of what makes their music interesting, and I want to point out that their naiveté is what authenticity actually sounds like. Puppy dog R&B love songs are what the Shirelles were meant to sing, and they are great at it. It's a shame they don't get the props they deserve, but at least they didn't end up crazy, drug-addicted casualty divas like a lot of young girls after them. Give them a try next time you need a little 60s girl pop in your musical diet.

156) Ozzy Osbourne - Diary of a Madman

My friend John gave me the records that have been sitting in his garage for decades and Ozzy's Diary of a Madman is there. How could I resist?

It's his last album with Randy Rhodes, his first album with Sharon being "manager" and like the 47th lawsuit he's settled out of court. She fired and replaced the bassist and drummer because those dirty rat-bastards had the audacity to ask for money to buy food while they recorded their parts for free. The new guys didn't try to pass it off either, from day one they told anyone in earshot that the actual recordings weren't them and the Osbournes finally had to give them something when it was all said and done.

If I didn't know better (wink, wink), I'd say musicians getting ripped off by business executives was pretty standard practice...

Tangent: the written English language desperately needs a sarcastic tense, or declension or something....

Where was I? The best part about Ozzy is he's actually not dark or serious at all. The joke is that he's actually singing about reality. The madman of this album isn't a murderer or a psychopath or a vampire, he's just a normal person dealing with normal boring everyday unpleasant things. We turn to drugs, and rock music, and religion because it's too hard to fight the people who've made it their mission to turn us into beasts of burden for their personal gain. Surprise, surprise, it's the same people in charge of those things as well, profiting from our misery. It's enough to drive you mad....

157) Billy Joel - Glass Houses

Glass Houses is Billy Joel's New Wave Album. No, it's not. It's his Rock album. No. It's Billy Joel's version of punk....

No, no, no. You're missing all the points.

1 - That's his actual house, that he lived in.

2 - New, old, doesn't matter, it's all rock and roll.

3 - Billy Joel stopped writing music because he felt like his turn was over.

This was right smack dab in the middle of his turn, and writing complex stories about actual life was definitely his home field advantage. He's about to throw a rock through his own front window, the album starts with the glass breaking, and he proceeds to live out his rock and roll life in the songs. You feel how you feel, you do what you do, life is what you make it. It's all the same story, go live it.

It really is the same story. The album really is Billy Joel's version of all of it, every possible version of the rock and roll love story. I don't want to grow up, oh crap I already grew up. I don't want to get old and die, oh crap I'm old and... Did I waste my life being reckless? Who's behind the curtain? You. This is your life.

I love all of Billy Joel's work, but I have a special fondness for this album because it and I were conceived and born at basically the same time. Now I have a copy (yay!). It's hard to call it his most diverse sounding album, but there is a wide variety and real sense that the various stages of his life are playing out in the glass-shard vignettes scattered around the floor at his feet.

I think the real takeaway is that it doesn't matter which side you're telling the story from, it's the same story. The only thing that changes is your perspective, and it's going to happen whether you want it to or not. Might as well enjoy the ride.

158) Willy Nelson - The Red Headed Stranger

I've been avoiding a lot of the country albums in my collection. The reasons are many, and complicated, and much too hard to formulate for even my longest winded of single-shot diatribes. But, I love Willy Nelson, and I definitely can't neglect the recent gift of his best selling 18th album, The Red Headed Stranger.

What makes this album special? For starters, it's an honest to goodness concept album (my favorite). It's the story of a fugitive who "killed his wife and her lover." The Juice is loose, indeed.

Jokes aside, his well negotiated deal with Columbia gave Willy full creative control. Now that's a deal. They seriously thought Willy was playing a demo recording of the intended album when he turned it in. What it must have felt like to have Willy Nelson tell you to your face, "tough shit you have to publish it," I can only guess. Then, when it sold millions and somebody made the album into an actual movie starring Willy, it had to sting.

Why is it so good? Because he knew from the start that he had to avoid sounding silly, it had to be stripped down. It had to be raw. It's not a party time, hillbilly, yee haw, rodeo album, it's an I killed 'em in a jealous rage and now I'm an outlaw album. It's an album that's meant to be listened to like I'm doing right now, intently.

Go find some negative criticism of this album, and it will be the standard "I'm supposed to say popular things are bad" crap like "this music has too much music in it," or "all albums have to be as big and polished and generic as possible," or "ugh, I hate it when songs tell a story, if I wanted to hear a book I'd just learn how to read." What really gets me is the notion that vocals, guitar, piano, bass, drums, and the occasional harmonica or mandolin is a "minimalist" ensemble. Who in their right mind would set this story to full strings, banjo, steel guitar, marching band? Just Willy, Trigger, and a harmonica player would be minimal. "Apropos" is the adjective you're thinking of, like 5 guys around a campfire; fitting.

The problem of course is that by 1975 everyone just expected the full Nashville workup, hillbilly jamboree like the TV tells me so. But, anybody with a shred of real appreciation for the actual art of music can immediately recognize the troubodor, singer-songwriter aspect of this album. And, in case you haven't noticed, I'm not spinning much party-time, chicks and hot-rods, getting drunk on a Saturday night rock music either (and when I do, I'm not exactly gushing with praise). I'm not saying that stuff is bad, I'm saying it doesn't interest me.

I happen to really like Willy Nelson, but even if I didn't I couldn't call this anything other than a great album. Like I've said so many times before, technical astonishment isn't one of my criteria for enjoyment. Creating a big, well constructed piece of art from a simple idea *is*. The Red Headed Stranger is a fantastic work of art, and another one of those magical moments when the artist knew better than everyone.

159) Judas Priest - Killing Machine (Hell Bent for Leather)

THREE NIGHTS ONLY! LIVE IN YOUR LIVING ROOM, JUDAS PRIEST SELLS OUT!!

That's stupid. Everybody calls Killing Machine a terrible turn to Arena Rock. What were they supposed to do? Heavy Metal wasn't a mainstream genre in the 70s, but Judas Priest was getting too big to not play enormous international concerts. They had to fill those stadiums, and the only way to do that was to appeal to a much broader audience. The evil gothic priest image wasn't gonna do it, so leather and motorcycles and sing-along choruses seemed like the only possible choice.

Remember, Priest was a pre-New Wave heavy metal band; they were competing with punk and glam and Black Sabbath, and nobody was really sure that this would work in America. That school shooting Bob Geldof felt perfectly fine satirizing? Let's change the title to Hell Bent for Leather and not sabotage our profits off the bat, guys. Why not try an acoustic ballad, yeah of course, make it sound evil, obviously.

Yes, there are a couple terrible songs on this album (Evening Star and Take on the World), but mostly it's dark, bluesy, dangerous music. Too well produced for the die-hard fans? See my review of Metallica's Black album.

Is it their best album? Hell no, but there are some great songs on it. Metal is so diverse and ridiculous because it's founded on the idea of extreme. Faster, louder, meaner, darker, sadder, whatever; take the thing you do and do it more. What it did was prepare us for the bands that would build on it in the 80s (Iron Maiden, Venom, King Diamond). And let's not forget that Judas Priest dropped a pretty great album in 2018, 40 years after this one.

Some people prefer their earlier stuff, some people prefer their later stuff. The important thing is that that's twice the people listening to them!!!!

160) R.E.M. - Document

Oh, life is bigger. It's bigger than you and you are not me. I don't own Out of Time, but I do have other R.E.M. albums, including their fifth, Document.

The first thing you should know is that this doesn't sound like 1987 at all. This album is an entire decade ahead of it's time.

The second thing you should know is that "It's the End of the World as We Know It" is two years older than Billy Joel's "We Didn't Start the Fire."

The third thing you should know is that this album is explicitly about the concepts of fire and labor.

The fourth thing you should know is R.E.M. comes from the same wildly eclectic music scene as the B52s: Athens, GA.

It's not a concept album in the way I've been describing them (see what I did there?). Some critics point to Peter Buck's encyclopedically comprehensive rock guitar stylings, some point to Michael Stipe's ability to write obscure but relatable lyrics that manage to be heavily politically motivated but never seem to cross the line into anger or condescension, some say Bill Berry's incomprehensible approach to rhythm frees Mike Mills to play bass like the melodic instrument it really is, and they're all correct. It really is 4 separate individuals working so well together that it's almost impossible to hear one part without the other three in counterpoint. It might take work to understand what's happening or being said, but the result is still completely comprehensive.

Fire and labor. Fire is a metaphor, and Stipe approaches all the meanings and subtleties of that metaphor like he does with other albums and metaphors. Labor, though, is the real core of the album for me. If you don't know the story, the final track of the album, Oddfellows Local 151, is a joke about the winos near Michael Stipe's house being a labor union (or maybe a fraternal organization). But is that a positive or negative statement? Is the union bad or is the wino sleeping in his car bad? Is there wisdom to be gained from listening to a drunken street sermon, or are these people pitiful victims of their own depravity?

Neither. Or, both. This is simply a document of 1987, and more broadly the Reagan Era. Is it meaningful and valuable, or should you throw it in the fire? Can you really write a love song if the act of writing songs at all is somehow worthless? How can you actually accomplish anything if the people you disagree with make a show of refusing to listen to your side? Someone had to clean up before the party, and doesn't that mean that the work itself is just as valuable as the reward?

Stipe is often considered obtuse and difficult, but that's because he's a gifted semiotician. He takes symbols and signifiers, smashes them together, and forces you to go through the process of building up meaning. Sadly, most people are all too happy to say "oh I understand this part and the rest is nonsense." That's a problem, because the real joy is letting the friction of two contrasting or unrelated ideas vibrate against each other to form a completely new meaning.

I mentioned Peirce a few albums back, but I'm actually a Barthes guy. Roland Barthes was a French semiotician whose ideas were largely dismissed in favor of Peirce in the circles I ran around, but I instinctively think the way Barthes describes meaning and I have to really work to put things in a Peircian perspective. If that sounds like gibberish, I can point you to a few good books on the subject, but fair warning you have to really put some mental effort into it.

Regardless, Document is an amazing album, probably my favorite from R.E.M.

161) Violent Femmes - We Can Do Anything

Oh no! Here it is the end of the night, and we didn't get a chance to jam! And with that Violent Femmes reference, let's listen to their 2016 album We Can Do Anything (which I have on vinyl!)

Allmusic grudgingly says it has a right to exist. Screw whichever useless freelancer uttered those words. If ever there was a band that deserved the label "alternative" it's Gordon Gano, Brian Ritchie, and their current snare drum player. Violent Femmes is literally the least commercial band in existence, and probably the most famous folk-punk band (Meat Puppets are the only other band to reach the same level of renown, but they stray from the genre frequently).

They can be silly, or shocking, or sentimental, or downright dark. John Zorn played in their backing horn section for a while.

This is one of the more stripped back albums in their discography, completely acoustic with a few accents (a lot like The Red Headed Stranger). It's by no means minimal, but definitely intimate. It's not a concept album, but quite literal. They really can do anything, love songs, untrue love songs, songs about midgets fighting dragons, and they aren't done (they made another album in 2019, but I actually haven't heard it yet).

I don't have any criticism for anything they've done. Certain songs might not do it for you (I like all of them), you might hate Gano's nasally voice (I love it), or you might get confused by their most sarcastic or juvenile moments (I completely get it), but you can't argue that they're doing it wrong. They play exactly what they want to play, when they want to play it, and I don't think they ever even read any of the corporate memos their labels sent them.

I'm just happy they're still going. I love love love love Violent Femmes and I'm not sure we can be friends anymore if you hate them. My phone says 11:58, but it's fast so I definitely made it. Enjoy.

162) Emmylou Harris - Quarter Moon in a Ten Cent Town

So, one of my real criticisms of country albums is that they are disproportionately pop albums. All the songs are there to be hits, obviously not all of them will be, but that's the only reason they are there. There's little continuity, no proper narrative structure (I don't mean a story, I mean an unfolding series of events/action). Usually, pop albums amount to a day in the life with ADD. Country, more than any other genre is a hardcore business based purely on record sales. That's not a bias, that's an objective fact; Country stars are either professional songwriters (as an actual job in an office with a paycheck) turned performer, or a groomed celebrity from the start. Country, in any of its various flavors, is not an experimental or adventurous genre, it's a lifestyle genre with a real and discerning demographic, and if it's not going to make money it isn't worth publishing.

That's why Emmylou Harris's Quarter Moon in a Ten Cent Town intrigues me. She's a great singer, with a huge arsenal of vocal inflections. She can be soft and breathy, she can creak like the wisest of grandmothers, and she can hone that rasp to a razor's edge when the occasion warrants it. None of that is particularly strange. What is strange is what happens in the background. The acoustic guitars are clean and quite gorgeous, and that makes everything else sound insane. The electric instruments are so drenched in effects (phaser, chorus, reverb, tremolo) that they take on a real synthesizer quality that I haven't heard before.

I already said Emmylou Harris is great (and the songs themselves are pretty thematically progressive and surprisingly feminist, in my opinion), but this album is a masterclass in unorthodox orchestration. The guitars are soaking wet, there are accordions and sax and strings, and the licks are insane, but not show-boaty. Let's just say that pedal steel and tenor saxophone make a surprisingly enjoyable combination.

The official designation for this album is Country-Rock, but not in the way you'd expect. It's not southern rock like Skynyrd or Molly Hatchett, it's more like they just plugged into whatever gear the new wave band before them was using, pedals and all. Maybe there was a whole scene in the late 70s that I just don't know about, but shoegaze country is not something I've ever heard before. I quite like it, though.

163) Van Halen

I went through the worst of the moldy records tonight, trashed the jackets and washed a few. First up is the quintessential self titled debut, Van Halen. It's still a little scratchy, but no major skips after a quick dish soap sponge bath.

This album is a classic, and most every song on the album is a rock radio staple. It's essentially a live album with some guitar overdubs, and it wasn't until people became interested in what the band was doing afterward that sales finally took off.

Gene Simmons paid for their earlier three track demo. They used that demo to get some big sold-out gigs, and when Warner Brothers bit they took their live set into the studio ('cause that's all they had). The price tag of this album sounds insane at $40k for what it was in 1978 (a glorified set list), but holy hand grenades it's still mind blowing today. You can't deny that Eddie was a genius, and I honestly can't name a more current guitarist who can carry an entire album by him/herself like this one.

Do yourself a favor and actually go listen to the whole album with fresh ears. There are a few tracks I haven't heard before (because I never owned a copy of this album until now), and they are really bizarre in a good way, like they were teetering on the edge of going full on heavy metal a la Judas Priest or Dio.

It's everything a "hello, Cleveland. We are Van Halen" album should be, and man does it rock.

164) Queen - Sheer Heart Attack

We're all just going to pretend that I didn't have a near nervous breakdown today, and listen to Queen's third album, Sheer Heart Attack. I don't plan these coincidences, I just leave plenty of space for them to happen. Most everyone sees this album as the turning point for the band, from a perfectly lovely prog-rock group to the intentionally flamboyant, good naturedly pretentious, and overly dramatic titans of Hard and Glam Rock that we all know and love.

But this wasn't really a calculated move by the band, in fact this album was pieced together out of nowhere exactly like the title might imply. They were on tour in the US with Mott the Hoople (aka the band whose only real fan was David Bowie) when Brian May found out he had contracted hepatitis from pre-Australian vaccinations and they flew back to England. They wrote many of the songs while he was recovering, then he also had a stomach ulcer and they just "left some space" for him to record his guitars and vocals later. Everyone who spent some time around Queen has a story about how serious and workmanlike their studio experimentation was. They "built" their songs rather than simply playing in front of a microphone, and the technicians had an equally long and tiresome workday every day.

It's certainly an ADD record according to Bottle's Taxonomy, but surely the previous paragraph explains that pretty well. Every track is like a whole universe, an experimental composition on the extremities of recording music, the only chance you'll get to explore the depths of the effects rack and construct moving sound images in the stereo field; the rock band itself as an inexhaustible creative force. 75 vocal overdubs to form a choir and hope that the tape doesn't fall apart in the process, splitting May's echo into its own multi-channel, multi-amp ensemble, songs about prostitutes, gangsters, anything else. They couldn't remember who actually wrote what lyrics to Stone Cold Crazy, so everybody got songwriting credits.

People tend to only think of them as the Mercury Theater, but all four guys were every bit equal; take one part away and the absurdity would collapse on itself. Queen is quite intentionally absurd, but by no means a joke. In a way it's the opposite of a pop album, or maybe an attempt to turn pop itself into theater. It doesn't really matter, it's just so enjoyable to listen to that you can't help but smile.

165) Three Dog Night - Hard Labor

When I agreed to be the bus driver for this field trip, I told you there was only 1 rule: listen to the whole album. I didn't tell you the secret second rule, which is always be completely honest (perfectly fine to be wrong, change my mind, skim over details, whatever). I haven't broken either of those rules, and tonight is no exception.

What the crap is *this*? It damned sure isn't 1969 Three Dog Night. For starters, it's not rock. It's the mediocre-est of Blue Eyed Soul. I'm clearly lacking the proper context of the double-digit evolution of their albums, but I certainly don't want to hear it happen in real time.

The prelude is an awful "Entrance of the Gladiators," and the first track (their last charting single) has a toilet flush in it! How apropos. There's a terrible David Clayton Thomas impression called "Put Out the Light" (about as good as Beacon Street Union's Elvis, or Danny Kaye's Louis Armstrong). Yep, that's exactly the organ sound I was trying to emulate for Detective Dog Lawyer, MD. Oh I'd be so happy if we weren't only halfway through. Crap. Crap. Crap. Oh no, Gladiators turned into an actual song about how terrible it is to be famous? Ending with a trumpet impersonating a creaky door closing?

I expected some amount of macho 70's douchebaggery from the giving birth metaphor on the cover (which not coincidentally puts me in mind of Weird Al's "Like a Surgeon" video), but all I'm getting is "making records is hard. Good thing we aren't the ones putting much effort into it, hur hur." Finger Eleven ate all my rat poison, but I still have some drain cleaner left if you guys are thirsty after all that hard labor....

Am I being unfair? Would any of these songs work in a different context? NO!

I'm not wrong, it's crap. They tried disco after this, then thankfully stopped. It doesn't taint my love of early Three Dog Night, it just makes me not want to hear anything after Live at the Forum. My beloved Spirit made a bad album (Clear), but it's definitely better than this. I get horrible acid reflux when I think about Ten Years After, but somehow this is worse. All three heads of Cerberus vomited on my record player, and I don't have enough paper towels to clean it up.

You are of course more than welcome to like it, but I disrespectfully disagree. This is a great band doing a piss-poor job of being a great band, and I doubt that even a lobotomy with a rusty butter knife could change that opinion.

166) Rush - Exit...Stage Left

I now have Rush's second live album, Exit...Stage Left. After my merciless tirade against last night's album, I need something positive to talk about. It's a lot of their best (and best known) songs, the cover art has allusions to every previous album, and it's Rush. They are quite simply masters of prog-rock as an artform. They weren't simply a band, and they didn't simply write songs, they were true composers for their ensemble (the progressive part of the genre).

They aren't simply "jams," the pieces have real complex structures, different sections, moods, functions, Peart's lyrics are more narrative than rhyming couplets (and rarely just verse/chorus modules with an interlude or two).

I tend to avoid live albums for the simple fact that hearing most bands "perform" their music live serves no purpose. Not so here (and not just because I don't have any of their studio albums). Hearing them perform this incredible music is special, in most part because they are amazing players. I don't mean virtuosic, I mean so dedicated to their playing that you can hear how hard they work together. What comes across is the sound of "this is exactly what we think great music is, and we wouldn't dare play anything less in front of you good people."

So, it's a great band working as hard as they can to be a great band, and that really does come across. Not everyone is wired to adore all their stuff (and some of their songs don't speak to me either), but it's all completely authentic; they never half-ass anything. There's no "filler," every track they ever wrote is a sculpture in sound, and I think that really comes across in a live context where the physical battle with sound and gear and audience enthusiasm takes place.

I'll say the same thing I said about Thomas Dolby: any Rush you come across is worth obtaining and listening to twenty or thirty times. Plus, the title is an intentional Snagglepus reference (and we all know how much I like those).

167) Toto - Hydra

I know you only know one Toto song (you actually know quite a few, but that's not the point). It's ok. They aren't everbody's cup of random ingredients, and they are random. Toto is not a concept album band, or a niche band, or a hit after hit after hit band. Like Steely Dan or Spinal Tap, they exist purely on their own terms, and you're either along for the guided tour or you're just saving a little energy for a stop or two on the running board.

Critics pretty much flip-flopped for every album they made, because critics are just making it up as they go. The band thought it was funny, because they were too. Toto isn't subjectable to standard critical analysis. You have to take them at face value as a group of guys who made whatever music their brains produced without any larger plan or ulterior motive.

I resurrected their second album Hydra from the moldy catacombs of doom, but this essay is more about an underlying web of connections that's been lurking in my reviews for a long time, finally breaking the surface and demanding confrontation.

Everyone has this bizarre notion that the music industry is a big complicated network of complicated things that are too hard to explain. It's not. Music business is just business. The things you think are deplorable about the music industry are exactly the same as every other industry. Albums, toasters, interest rate swaps, pork futures, cars, content marketing, life coaching, medical research. If you think that musicians get ripped off by the system, then surely you can't be dumb enough to believe that cashiers, or garbage men, or truck drivers, or construction workers, or programmers, or any other "job" performers are somehow in a better situation. "Business" isn't complicated. Creating the lies and hiding the nasty parts is complicated. Getting people to step back, really look at the world, and change their selfish behavior is practically impossible, so you just find the best compromise between making money for someone else and personal integrity and keep on spinning.

But enough of my midlife crisis fighting the giant water monster, we're here to talk about Toto. Everyone in the band is important, but it's really David Paich's band. How did they get to make albums in the first place? Well, the core members were the studio band for Steely Dan/Boz Skaggs/Michael Jackson/etc., David Paich co-wrote "Lido Shuffle." He's also the son of Marty Paich, whom you might have noticed I like quite a bit.

Good or bad, these guys were born inside the matrix. They didn't have to be their own band, they didn't have to scramble for work, they were already set. Critics liked to pretend they didn't have a unique sound of their own, but that's because you already know Toto. You start to think "this sounds like such-and-such" because it's literally them.

Instead of just being corporate douchebags (which they could have easily been), they used that status to do what they wanted to do regardless of what anybody thought. They wrote obscure stuff about dragons and sci-fi movies and foriegn places and being in love and whatever other fantasy world stuff crossed their minds. Best of all, even critics who were determined to hate them had to admit that they are really talented, and none of this stuff is a joke. Because it's not. It's not cheesy or embarrasing or trendy or cliché. If you don't like Toto, it's your own fault.

    I think there's a very real reason why everything Marty Paich touched is magic, including his son's band. I think it's because he thought creating actual music was the only legitimate part of the whole charade, and it rubbed off on everyone around him. It didn't matter if it was a hit or popular or critically acclaimed or won awards, it didn't matter whose name was on the album, all that mattered was taking it serious and doing a good job.

    A "business" is nothing more than a paycheck. An "industry" is nothing more than a millionaire devising creative ways to never actually give up control of that money; even if you tear it down, you won't actually get that money back. Luckily, the work is your own, and they can't have it unless they pay for it.

168) Bad Company - Desolation Angels

    What am I supposed to do with Bad Company's fifth album? Mike DeGagne tells me it sounds better than their fourth (even though the addition of keyboards and other stuff doesn't make it exciting at all), it's definitely better than their next (and Paul Rogers's last), and it's an unfulfilling listen in spite of its great moments. It sold well, but the next one didn't, so everybody gave up on them, I guess? Is it bad? Is it only underwhelming if you love Bad Company's earlier albums? I don't know, let's find out.

    What the hell are Desolation Angels? I know it's half of a Kerouac novel, but Paul Rogers had wanted to use that title for an album with his previous band, so this album clearly can't be about the actual book. Angels of desolation? Angels of the desolate? Angels who are themselves desolate? Are the band members angels? Are the songs angels? Are they just songs about the clash between fantasy and reality? Is the cover just the four years earlier inspiration for Billy Joel's "Uptown Girl"?

"Rock and Roll Fantasy" (the last hit from the original lineup) certainly sets up an album about how it's all fake and empty and unfulfilling, so where does it go from there? Back to acoustic rock, and that dumb life is a carousel and we want off metaphor (tragically he uses the actual world "carousel," a big no-no in my book as you already know). Another girl left me, time to drink with my buddies.

Parenthetical aside: "Gone, Gone, Gone" is a garbage song. The music is fine, the lyrics are structurally fine, but that goddamned misogynistic idea that a woman is only there to please you and you're going to hire an actual maid to wine and dine makes me want to puke.

Back to the struggle, the universe is out to get us and I just want to go home. "I love you because I want to"? Is that a threat? I can't hear "Early in the Morning" as anything other than what he's saying when he stumbles in at 4am and passes out with his boots still on.

Well, that was Side A. On to part 2, I guess. "Lonely for your love," is self explanatory. He's a touring musician, headed back to Atlanta, GA (just like the women, this is that same empty schtick about the thing in front of you being the "greatest" thing ever). Side B is what I think of as Country Rock, and insincerity is the key idea lurking under the surface. "I'm a piece of crap, but someday I'll figure out how to make you love me." "I'm a rhythm machine (nudge nudge, hur hur)." "Sometimes my conscience tells me I'm useless and all I really need is for you to love me, nameless generic female."

I read an interview with Dave Mustaine yesterday where he said about early Metallica "we just assumed all managers were drug dealers." That's the level of naiveté I hear in this album. I get what they are aiming for, we're all looking for something meaningful in this destinationless trek through life, but this album isn't it. It's not self aware, it's not clever, it's just another dumb group of vacuous Valentine's Day sentiments. But there again, I'm giving it too much credit. It's not intentional, it's onomatopoeic. It's not *about* why we lose the fire and give up, it's what giving up sounds like; we'll just write some crap songs and play some shows, 'cause we can't or won't actually quit yet. Maybe in a few years the next album will be more fun (oh no it won't).

That's the lyrics side, what about the rest of it? The music is fine. The music is great. It sounds like Bad Company. Why the wishy-washy reception? Well, I have the benefit of knowing that it's simultaneously a throwback to early 70s jock rock and about 6 years ahead of it's time. People actually living in 1979 couldn't have that perspective, people in the mid-80s and 90s weren't looking back fondly on the 70s at all, people like me have such a gut reaction to the nonsensical man-child dominated ethos that it's automatically trash. It's a document of a mindset we don't want to revisit, but it still very much exists all around us right now.

That feminist flavor of Emmylou Harris I remarked upon? Yeah, it's the other side of this argument (made a year earlier), and no wonder I find it much more appealing. This isn't Steppenwolf's For Ladies Only, by a longshot. This isn't sappy "you complete me" puppy-dog love, or "I'm a loser, and you *should* leave me" self awareness, this is "it's your job to make me happy or I'll find someone else" drivel.

None of which is intentional. This is one of the least authentic albums I've ever heard, but that's clearly not what they were trying to make. It's simply a reflection of how little they actually cared at that point in their career. DeGagne was right, this is the sound of Bad Company calling it quits, so they probably just should have.

169) The Cars

If, like me, you need an antidote to Bad Company's bad album, Desolation Angels, I've got you covered. It's from my personal stash of trip-killers, and it's The Cars (the self titled debut).

They are self aware, the women are fully autonomous humans (some are dumb, some manipulative, but all independent individuals), and love (however confusing) is exciting.

The Cars had been playing these songs for years in the bars of Boston and the surrounding east coast, so that's at least part of the reason Bad Company's throwback sound was pretty unappealing.

Man, you really wouldn't know that I adore early Bad Company, would you? Don't worry, The Cars made a couple terrible albums themselves. It's like a new theme, bands that start out strong then turn pretty garbage by the end. Oh wait, that's every band. Why do you still put up with my nonsense? Go listen to whatever you like....

170) Bush - Razorblade Suitcase

I'm gonna go on record and say Razorblade Suitcase is better than Sixteen Stone. They are both pretty good albums, but critics have the impossible job of having a strong opinion about the album on top of the stack. So, they cheat. They find something in common with another band, and pretend that's obvious.

Critics hated Bush's sophomore album. They said it sounded like Nirvana (it doesn't), the songs weren't hook heavy radio fuel (sure they are, maybe not your radio, but someone's). They confuse Albini for the source of the sound rather than the giftwrap. They mistake Gavin Rossdale's tangential metaphors for Kurt Cobain's pleasure of speech. They think an album has to punch you in the face to be good. In short, they don't actually care.

Sixteen Stone is a classic alternative rock album. Every song is approachable, recognizable, evocative. It has really crass moments and borderline melodrama (a big seller at the time). It's a great album and I won't argue against that.

Razorblade Suitcase, however, is an art album. It's the album that came from the life of Sixteen Stone. Written while touring, watching your old life fall apart, actually dealing with all the emotional baggage (see, tangential metaphor). He is not the same person for having written the first album, and that can be easy to miss if you have the impression that this type of art is objective.

However similar the instrumentation, a similar taste for primitive power chord riffs, the occasional tourettes inspired interjections, Bush is nothing like Nirvana. They approach the same essence from different directions. Nirvana comes from the garage band mode of making pop songs your own, whereas Bush is a direct lineage rock band searching for something more primitive and aggressive. That's not blather on my part, those perspectives are a well-established part of each band, Nirvana the bored teenage outcasts, Bush emulating their rock heros. I'm not saying they aren't similar, I'm saying the direct comparison comes from a weak surface way of listening.

Razorblade Suitcase is very much like In Utero in one respect, though: it's intentionally antagonistic to its supposed audience. It's supposed to challenge that naive surface listening, that false sense of inclusion you felt, you are an outsider and this isn't *for* you, it's *at* you because you wanted to see deeper.

It's easy to forget that this is a bash it out quick album. Albini may have put a lot of effort into sculpting the finished sound, but the band wasn't sculpting a universe the way

Nirvana did on their studio albums. Gavin writes pretty much as you hear it, but Kurt would start from the most remedial of demo idea fragments and build them into a sort of final version, then play them different live. I don't think I'm imagining the difference I hear in their approaches, I think it's real and audible.

So, why is it better than their first? For precisely the reason critics hated it. It isn't meant to be a collection of hit songs, it's meant to be an album. Nothing, and I mean nothing, ruins an album like a runaway hit single that you just can't put back into context. I can't tell you how many times I skip the big single when listening to an album, and that hurts me deep in my soul. I don't have that problem here (though I do have to ignore the god-awful remix of "Mouth" that my brain wants to remind me of after hearing the original).

The album as a whole is a singular moment in Rossdale's headspace, and that coherence is audible even though the songs themselves may appear scattered or disjointed. What Albini brings to the table is a delicious vibrancy to delicate moments, and that makes the inevitable plunge into noise-rock territory feel both logical and more intense. It's one of the very few albums where a minuscule dynamic range serves a real purpose, and nothing gets lost or pushed into the background. It's borderline lowercase in a big alternative rock context, and that matches the emotional rawness quite well.

One final little bit of trivia to end this rambling incoherent review: those bizarre string arrangements are by Gavin and Nigel rather than some outside arranger. Not bad for a couple of guitar players....

171) John Mayall - Empty Rooms and USA Union

Let's go back to my dad's records tonight for a double header. It's John Mayall's Empty Rooms and USA Union.

I've unintentionally been listening to albums about fictional women. I thought it might be a nice change to listen to songs about a very specific woman, Nancy Throckmorton. Not every song is about her, it's more a chronicle of their relationship, and his experience in general, during his Laural Canyon tenure. The point is when he says "her" or "she" he's talking about a real person.

What makes these albums interesting is that he hired friends and acquaintances he'd been making to be "the band," not because he particularly wanted to, but because Polydor kept demanding albums.

What I've noticed about John Mayall is that people talk about him like he was some sort of mastermind bandleader. They call musicians who played with him "alumni" the same way they might describe someone's tenure in King Crimson. I can't imagine Mayall being anything like Fripp. I imagine it must have been more like "here's the song I'm playing, just do whatever it is you do on top of it. It'll work fine, just play stuff." Flute, sax, violin, piano, guitar, whatever, it all just seems to work.

But back to the relationship theme I've been talking/ranting about. These albums are completely believable. The sentiments and tropes are somewhat stereotypical for blues in general, but the authenticity is quite believable. Bad Company, Bush, even Toto don't sound convincing. They're all just reformulating the standard love you, miss you, want you cliches of rock in general. Maybe that's just my prejudice for Blues. Maybe it's my exponentially growing appreciation for Mayall. I don't know, but it's true.

No, I'm wrong, it just hit me. He's writing *all* of the songs about how he feels about how he feels about her (that's a sentence and a half). He's not trying to paint her into a corner, he's not pretending she's an object to win or lose. He's writing about his actual situation: he's essentially vacationing as a bum in California (doesn't matter that he's a famous musician), the label keeps calling to say music dude, record more music, and he'll go back to England at some point. It's a relationship happening at a complex time in his life, and he had no idea how it would turn out; all he could do was take it moment by moment and live it. That's where the authenticity comes from. He's writing from that unstable, almost apprehensive view of himself as a passing stranger.

Also, there aren't any drums on USA Union; guitar, harmonica/keyboard, violin, and bass. That's it. It's incredible. I should point out the sound of Don Harris's violin is grotesquely atrocious and that's why it's ABSOLUTELY FABULOUS. Not joking, he's running that thing through a wah pedal, the brokenest flanger they could find, a harp amp, a busted mic, who knows what, but it sounds amazing in the context of these songs.

If you've never heard the real experimental side of English Blues, go give USA Union a try. If you're not familiar with Mayall at all, just pick anything. He really is great, and he will definitely grow on you the more you hear of him.

172) Cheap Trick - Dream Police

174 is an odious number. That means it has an odd number of ones in its binary expansion (even numbered binary expansions are "evil"). Phi X 174 was the first DNA based genome to be mapped, the first virus model to be synthesized in a lab, and is still used as a control for testing sequencing equipment and personal protective equipment. 174 is the atomic number of Unseptquadium, a theoretical element formed in the gravitational collapse after a supernova.

None of which matters. Saying random interesting things about the number of essays I've written (which differs from the numbering in bold because Abbey Road and Age Of Aquarius were originally stand alone essays, but I decided I liked them better all together at some point writing this essay) was just a cheap trick for introducing the random interesting

things I'm going to say about tonight's album Dream Police...
...by...
...Cheap Trick.

They got their name from a comment about Slade ("they used every cheap trick in the book"). Each band member has his own consistent character/persona/image/wardrobe, and they ham it up great. I never paid much attention to them growing up, other than noting Rick Nielsen's thing for crazy guitars and sweaters, but I know all their hits and they are a lot of fun to watch.

Their mainstream breakthrough was really interesting. They made 3 albums that didn't really do much, then were blown away by the reception they got in Japan (Beatlemania level excitement). Their live Budakon recordings were meant to be a Japan only release, but got so popular they actually had to postpone the release of Dream Police to publish it in the US.

Musically speaking, they are a straightforward hard rock band. That might sound underwhelming, but they more than make up for the lack of sonic adventure by being quirky and writing interestingly weird songs. They're like your friend's strange older brother, not scary or intimidating, but not exactly living in your own reality either.

Highlights of the tracks include supposed satanic back masking, Steve Lukather (of Toto and any other 80s album you come across, not joking) playing guitar for money but no credit, and occasional Queen-style thousand-overdub vocals.

I wish the album had more of a unified concept, but I'm really just being picky; they have more than enough personality and style to be a great popular rock band playing unrelated songs from their unique perspective. I suppose if I'm really desperate, mild paranoia underpins a lot of their songs (and not just on this album).

Regardless, they really are fun and energetic, and I definitely appreciate their experimenting with orchestral backing in a hard rock (as opposed to prog- or psych-) context.

There's not a bad song on Dream Police, and they certainly don't stay in any one style long enough to get tiresome. Definitely worth a listen if you haven't heard any of their deeper cuts.

173) Noonish Moon - Chapman Street

I am of course biased. I love my friends and I love their music. Right at the top of the list is Steven Stark and Noonish Moon. He is an Oklahoma composer, multi-instrumental performer, teacher, and all-around great guy. Today is the release of his crowd funded EP, Chapman Street, and I'm going to gush about it.

Noonish Moon is his pseudonymous indie-pop project. It's hard to pin it to a specific genre because he's a serious composer writing synthy pop-rock, but it's peppy, indie, dreamy, literate, nuanced, modern feelings music, the kind where a Prince cover seems completely appropriate (and he did one not too long ago!).

I put my money where my mouth is and helped fund Chapman Street, and you're looking at my drawings as the artwork (for which I made a little money). How cool is that!? I also had the benefit of watching the whole project unfold from the beginning and occasionally sharing my thoughts behind the scenes.

The new EP is heavily influenced by African guitar pop (Marshall Munhumumwe/Four Brothers Band style), and a switch from Telecaster to Jazzmaster. Guitar is obviously much more prominent on this album than on many earlier tracks, and metrical confusion is an important part of the fun. I think he nailed it, and it's a fantastic addition to the already established ethos of the "band" itself.

The four tracks are quite different from each other, but unfold in a completely intuitive way. It comes across as a short little love story: a nostalgic memory, an infatuation, a not wanting it to end, and an instrumental that watches them drive off into the sunset. I'm truly impressed at how complete and satisfying the story he's crafted comes across in only 4 movements; it definitely is a single work, a coherent album in my mind.

I know it sounds ridiculous when I say that if I had a few thousand dollars to spend I'd use it to press this EP on one side, and one of mine on the other and hand them out to anyone, but that's a real thing I'd do if I won the lottery.

I implore you to go check out the Chapman Street EP and support great art made from the sheer love of making it. I think Steven and I are kindred spirits in that regard, and I'm beyond thrilled to share it with you.

174) The Doors - Other Voices

Here's a really strange album. Not strange in itself, but strange because it's impossible to contextualize.

Admit it, The Doors without Jim Morrison doesn't exist. You don't have to feel bad for thinking that, because it's true. The problem is that most of the tracks were just waiting for Morrison to come back from Paris and participate. It's a Doors album, but it's not. Some bands can keep going, some bands have to rebrand themselves. They didn't try to replace him, but Ray and Robby aren't Jim and on more than a couple tracks they're clearly trying to be. So, while you can pretend to ignore it, the ghost of Jim Morrison haunts this record because they wrote it for him to sing.

They also made it sound too nice. In my earlier review I mentioned that their "evolution" was as much a product of recording equipment as anything, and this one goes too far. There aren't any "bathroom" vocals, there's practically no reverb to speak of, and there are no edges or corners on anything; if the sound of an album could be childproofed, this is it.

If you can get over the feeling that half the tracks would have been scrapped if Morrison had survived to veto them, it's okay. It's not great. There are cheesy moments. Most critics try too hard to pretend their individual personalities shine brighter, but all I hear is solo album material filling the space where a drunk and deranged Oedipal complex should be. I'm not getting paid, why should I try to make it out to be something it's not. It's not a Doors album, it's 3/4 of the Doors playing new songs. They aren't terrible, but neither is turkey bacon; I can taste the difference, so don't try to spin me around.

I argued when people said Razorblade Suitcase sounded like tracks for the Nirvana album that would never be, and here's my counterargument. If this was the first thing you heard by the Doors you could be into it, but not me. Sorry.

175) Neutral Milk Hotel - On the Aeroplane Over the Sea

It's always sad when I don't bring home an instrument to bang around from a trip to the big city, but I did splurge and buy almost a week's worth of albums to talk about (4 records and 2 CDs). I don't know where to start...

... so Neutral Milk Hotel, I guess. I have no idea what sparked the renewed interest in their second album 10 years ago, and I won't pretend that I knew about it before a couple years ago, but both their studio albums were just sitting at Barnes & Noble. Now they are in my basement.

Every youtube music persona has some grandiose narrative to tell about this cult underground classic, I won't be able to add much of anything other than to tell you that the instant you hear Jeff Magnum sing "two headed boy" it will be permanently lodged in your frontal cortex. Anywho, spin spin spin the black circle (that's a Pearl Jam reference, if you're keeping score).

In the Aeroplane Over the Sea is 32 years and 12 days old as I write this, but it's surprisingly timeless. Nobody actually understands it, and that seems perfectly fine. Let's have a rum and coke and just try to describe it.

It's lo-fi experimental surrealist hipster folk. It's roundabout 20 years ahead of it's time. That's long enough for people like me to hear Mumford & Sons and Of Monsters and Men come onto the scene and say "I've heard this before, by better crazy people." That's not fair, I like Of Monsters and Men. Go check out, Olfar's 2011 album Harbour, but even that's 13 years later than Neutral Milk Hotel. Enough contextualizing; the music Bottle, the music.

This is late 90s crazy guy at the coffee house music, no wonder Magnum had a nervous breakdown after it made him a comparative superstar. He's not Nick Drake, but he's not unlike Nick Drake persona wise. It's not Cake, but it has a very similar flavor, with a Smashing Pumpkins aftertaste. I've listened to this album in various formats and this vinyl is the worst in a good way. The lows are psychotically growly and fuzzed, the clipping is like a bowl-cut (completely intentional 'cause he's definitely yelling but the vocals are crystal clear).

The songs themselves are so incredibly catchy. Whether the themes are dream logic, or interpretations of Anne Frank, or fictional metaphysical mythos, or who cares, this album is fantastic. It deserves every bit of praise and more. It might have driven him over the edge to have to try to explain this insanity on stage every night, but it's gorgeous PTSD-like chaos. Go give it a listen when you have a chance. It's completely unhinged and about as raw as it gets. I'll be listening to their first album in the near future, and we can compare notes then....

176) The Flaming Lips - Yoshimi Battles the Pink Robots

I'm from Oklahoma City. I know the Flaming Lips from before She Don't Use Jelly actually propelled them into the mainstream on MTV (tonight's album simply bouyed them well above one hit wonder status). I've seen them so many times in concert, opening for Smashing Pumpkins, headlining with Liz Phair and Starlight Mints, etc. Next time we're back in my hometown I'll drive you past Wayne Coyne's houses (where his infamous front yard bathtub google maps photo happened). My CD of Yoshimi Battles the Pink Robots has been missing for a long time (it's probably stuck in the busted CD changer in my car along with Queens of the Stone Age's Villians, and some other gems).

Luckily, I found it on vinyl, and I couldn't be happier. Unluckily, the estate of Cat Stevens cried copyright infringement and the Lips still give them a big chunk of royalties from Fight Test (no comment, the most pointed comment of all 'cause Wayne knew they'd bitch and just settled as quickly as possible, but like Cat Stevens needs The Flaming Lips's money).

Wayne says it's not a concept album, the Yoshimi part is literally Japanese multi-instrumentalist Yoshimi P-We (who he thought sounded like she was battling robots, and that's her doing the background talking), but it's actually two concept albums in one. He loses his girl to a robot programmed for empathy, wishes someone could protect him from those evil robots, but then realizes he was the robot who didn't know the difference between love and hate and has to learn to love himself when he escapes the end of the world in a hot air balloon to Mars, 'cause Japan. No, he didn't write it that way, but that's the cool thing about narrative action: it builds itself whether you intended it or not (you haven't been reading your Barthes homework, have you?). Come to think of it, Eddie Vedder famously accepted the fan interpretation of Alive, stating that what he intended when he wrote it clearly isn't how people understand it so he's wrong (what's the Pearl Jam reference count so far?). Maybe I should go back and give you my actual reading of Aeroplane; some other time.

This is an astonishing blend of computer manipulated acoustic guitars and synths and strange trippy rock music. It's weird, but it's incredible, and one of my all-time favorite albums. They experimented with a surround sound mix as a bonus DVD (which I still have), but were completely underwhelmed by the result. It's plenty good enough on its own. Go out and realize how beautiful you actually are, and try to make the best of now.

177) Cage The Elephant - Thank You, Happy Birthday

Fans of the show will undoubtedly know that I have a deep love of serendipitously coincidental happenstance. It just so happens that today is my birthday, and tonight's album is Cage the Elephant's sophomore effort, Thank You, Happy Birthday. I just picked it up because the cover art is pretty awesome, I'd never really heard much of their earlier stuff, and didn't give it any actual thought (didn't even notice the title).

I've written about a bunch of bands that left England to live here, but these guys went the other direction, leaving Bowling Green, KY for the outskirts of London. Strange.

The story I guess is that they did like a Beatles or Prince style thousand song recording session, decided they didn't like any of them, dug deep into their personal side project material and struggled to mash 12 of them together like an imaginary compilation album. I don't *not* believe them, but they hint at feeling a bit embarrassed by their own eagerness to be inauthentic pop punks. The good news is that regretting not putting your real self into your early albums is the most authentic fake persona a pop star can have. Sounding like the Black Keys for your 3rd album and beyond isn't exactly an "authentic" search for your own unique voice (especially when Dan Auerbach *is* the producer) either, if you ask me. I don't know, the early 2010s were pretty abysmal in general so the noisy spastic 3G punk revival sound splattered across this album is actually compellingly refreshing, to me at least. I assume that accounts for a lot of the overly positive critical praise of the time as well.

Is it game changing, culturally significant teenage philosophy? No, but it is highly energetic, and remarkably free of the more contrived emo cliches of their peers. Oh, everything's still miserable, but that's no reason to not be loud and mildly obnoxious about it. They aren't real guttersnipes, but they aren't exactly posers either. I definitely remember hearing Aberdeen, and their earlier breakthrough Ain't No Rest for the Wicked back when they were new, but I have no idea where or in what context.

If I sound wishy washy it's probably just because they didn't actually build on the potential of this album. They got much less caustically annoying; sad because that's the best part of this album. Instead of refining their jackassery, they just ended up being a generic millenial rock band. I really like Thank You, Happy Birthday, but I can't shake that feeling that this is all they've got for me. It's definitely a "talking out of your ass" album, and that's actually what makes it enjoyable. I don't want them to focus or be consistant, I want them to be spastic and unpredictable. Maybe that's just my personal taste, saying "fuck it" and letting things fall out whichever way they do is my thing after all.

Happy birthday, Bottle. I accidentally bought you a surprisingly complicated album from some ex-pat teenagers, 'cause I saw it and thought "this is so up your alley."

Thanks, me! And thank you, everyone who wished me a happy birthday today. And thank you for reading this. Thank You, Happy Birthday.

178) Tom Petty - Wildflowers

You're all gonna cry "blasphemy!," but Wildflowers is my favorite Tom Petty album. I love earlier Tom Petty, but you have to know that I was a die-hard MTV kid. The video for You Don't Know How It Feels was a big deal. I don't know if it was the actual first continuous-shot music video, but it was pretty highly talked about. Plus, the various attempts at censoring the chorus were hilarious; how turning "joint" backward or changing "roll" to "hit" (I assume they were misguidedly thinking like "going to another bar"?) made it any better is beyond me.

Regardless, all three big hits are stellar (It's Good to Be King is very much one of his best songs altogether, lyrically/musically/emotionally), but the deep cuts are really interesting too. Some say the softest tracks are borderline sloppy but they had to wait twelve more years before Highway Companion came out to validate that opinion (that's *my* least favorite Tom Petty album). You could argue that there's a fair amount of thematic recycling (both musically and lyrically) on this album and from this album on later ones, but I think the differences actually justify it (you'll just have to go hear them for yourself).

Wildflowers is the perfect title, because it lets the whole project breathe. It's a metaphor for emotional freedom. It's still mostly the Heartbreakers, but it's not confined to the band's oeuvre. It's not Tom Petty the rockstar, it's Tom Petty the songwriter at large (songs that didn't make the album found good homes with other artists). It's a good mix of hard rock, folk, and country blues. It covers all the moods, and at just shy of 63 minutes, it's practically a double album.

My dad used to say Tom Petty was the best of the Bob Dylan-alikes (better than the original being the implication), and I don't really have an argument. They are quite similar in many ways, but with completely different egos and Tom Petty is certainly more likable. You know my refusal to qualify technical proficiency very well by now, but Petty is inarguably the more melodically inviting vocalist.

This album isn't trying to be anything more than it is, it's a sunny solitary day in a meadow, the songs blossom wherever the wind blew them, nothing is forced or hurried. It's a happy album in spite, or maybe because, of its melencholic episodes. It's a thoroughly pleasing listen, and well worth carving out an entire hour to enjoy.

179) Ramones - Road to Ruin

The Ramones sold out. How dare they pick up acoustic guitars, and sing love songs, and change drummers, and play guitar solos!

Says a moron. It's the Ramones. Road to Ruin. The one with I Wanna Be Sedated (my theme song). It's 60s pop played as loud and distorted as possible at the time. It's where hardcore pioneers Bad Brains got their name, for crying out loud.

And, if your head isn't bobbing hard enough to bite your tongue in half while you talk trash, then you're not listening to it right in the first place. Get outta here with that nonsense.

180) Volbeat - Rewind, Replay, Rebound

I was going to write about something else, but you know who reminds me of the Ramones? Volbeat. They also remind me of Social Distortion and Misfits. I think Volbeat is the closest thing we have to an actual modern day punk band (they're labeled metal about as convincingly as Kenny G is labeled Jazz). They're Danish, and just like Golden Earring (the nearby Dutch), you wouldn't know that from listening to them.

"Die to Live" has totally infested (in a good way) my mental jukebox over the last week or so, so we might as well go listen to all of last year's Rewind, Replay, Rebound on youtube together.

They definitely have a split personality, and the first track highlights their somewhat strange 80s hard rock meets 90s alternative vibe. It's Volbeat light, less filling, tastes underwhelming. Not bad, just not the part that actually interests me personally.

Pelvis on Fire is more like it, and showcases their real Rockabilly roots, with impressive compound/simple meter shifts and the appropriate amount of cool cat ego.

Then Rewind the Exit. Meh. The back and forth reminds me so much of Rise Against: the real tracks are amazing, the emotional pseudo-ballads are bleh.

Then the whole reason we're here. Die to Live with guest vocalist Neil Fallon (I do love me some Clutch). Just a bangin' track, and you can't tell me it doesn't remind you of the spirit of the Ramones.

I don't mind When We Were Kids as much, 'cause the full unique quality of Michael Poulsen's vocals are on display (unlike tracks 1 and 3). Interesting how it builds from an acoustic track to full contemporary metal with a hard rock chorus. It's certainly the most collage like track so far.

Then the surfabilly weirdness of Sorry Sack of Bones. That's brilliant. The song is ridiculous, but in an almost Oingo Boingo way.

Cloud 9 is a big meh again. It has that interesting metal plot twist, though.

We're halfway through, and it's an even-track album for me. We'll see.

Yep, Cheapside Sloggers is more Ramones style catchy as hell old school punk vibes, right down to the constant ride banging. And there's the shift to metal they love so much. Much cooler in this track for sure.

Nope, another odd track downer that just doesn't hit the spot. If the odd tracks were their own album it would be fine.

Parasite is great, like all the best sub 1 minute punk songs.

WAIT. WHAT? An odd numbered track that works (and rocks)? It's track 11 for crying out loud. But, yeah Leviathan is great. Sure, it's a little dumb, but the melody is so good you want to sing along at the top of your lungs (that's the part that reeled me in, after all).

Oh my god. Please tell me you hear it too. The drum open of The Awakening of Bonnie Parker immediately reminds me of the Crystals's Then He Kissed Me. There's the Danish accent! I found Waldo!

The Everlasting is the first real metal track. The youtube video is live, but you can hear they are the real deal, early thrash with their completely unique melodic vocals.

7:24 blew it. If they had switched the last two tracks it would have been a complete sweep.

Verdict? Volbeat is two great bands, but I wish they didn't share the stage the whole time. I stand by my opinion that tracks 1,3,5,7,9,14 are one album, and 2,4,6,8,10,11,12,13 are what I actually came here to hear. The bonus tracks on the deluxe edition don't count.

181) Neutral Milk Hotel - On Avery Island

On Avery Island. It's a salt dome in Louisiana, where Tabasco is made. It's also the first full album by Neutral Milk Hotel.

You're supposed to relate it to Beck, Flaming Lips, and Guided By Voices, all siblings of the musical marriage of John Lennon pop with Syd Barrett psychosis. Sure, you can hear all of that in there, but there's something different happening too. This is the sound of depression itself. The grotesque distorted lows, a middle layer of intentionally poorly recorded cheap sounding instruments, on top of which floats an abstract but clearly personal string of folk songs about how horrible it is to live life as a mere function.

Nobody has much to say about the confusing juxtaposition of dirty and clean recording. Yes, it's a 4-track recording (DIY home recording was the whole label roster's main interest), but Robert Schneider clearly knew what he was doing. The vocals, trombone, and percussion are crystal clear.

It's the fuzz bass and guitars that get the full recycled tape from the garbage can, recorded in said garbage can treatment. You're supposed to be singing those amazing melodies over top of the deep nausea and suicidal malaise. It really is a sad carnival in your ears.

It's not lyrically morose or offensive, but it sure isn't happy or hopeful. Just like the toll bridge to the actual island, you're free to leave but you gotta pay to get back in, especially if you live there.

I love it (just in case my descriptions were confusing you). Lots of people say it's actually better than Aeroplane, but that depends on what you mean by "better." It's definitely sadder, harsher, and less stable sounding; as in this is before the mental snap, In the Aeroplane... after. Obviously, you're not going to crank this up at the gym or at your next patio party, but as a reminder of how much some people hated being alive in the late 90s without a) resorting to faking having a good time, or b) not being alive anymore, it's pretty enjoyable.

182) Prism

Here's an obscure album from 1977, Prism's self titled debut. Well, not obscure in Canada where it went platinum, and the lead track Spaceship Superstar has an interesting story you can go look up if you want.

Here's the deal: it's extremely 70s arena rock, cheesy as all get out, and though I might be imagining it, exceedingly Canadian. But even with all that in mind, it's pretty good. It's uniquely derivative. That sounds like an oxymoron, but it's true. You can hear them stealing every big 70s trick in the book like a burglar with tourettes, but they use them to write pretty original material. It's more like they just assumed that's what everybody wanted to hear. Canada sure did, English and American audiences said "heard it before, ready for something different."

That's kind of sad in a way. Forget that you know Frampton and Supertramp and The Doobie Brothers and Uriah Heep, and forget that in a few years Axl Rose would really dominate the rusty razorblade tenor landscape in the coming decades to much better effect. This is quite good. In fact, the worst thing I've found anyone saying about it is that it's so completely rock radio oriented that it's impossible to love them "in spite" of anything. There's actually nothing to dislike, nothing to defend, every musical moment is the best of what everyone was doing, and actually being awesome is a pretty good way to flush your career down the toilet.

That's not true, they made lots of albums, and as mentioned Canada was perfectly happy to have them all to themselves. It's easy joke that they set their sights on the 3 and 4 spots of the 5 o'clock rock block, and knocked it out of the park, but is there really anything wrong with that?

Picture yourself in the Pinto, cruising past the baseball field, crankin' up the Prism, and creepily combing your moustache (but not actually being a creep). It feels uncomfortable at first, but we're all having a good time so just roll with it.

183) Brother Eye Vs. Hitler

Tonight's going to be a double header. I'm still working on a much longer post about something totally insane, but it's Anthony Artur's birthday and that's the perfect reason to talk about Brother Eye. I've been listening to Brother Eye Vs. Hitler quite often since I randomly came across it in a facebook ad a year-ish ago

Now I have to tell you, it can feel really strange peering into the facebook world of strangers you've met because you like their music, and I often wonder what people like Anthony think about me, the nobodiest of basement dwellers. Luckily, my policy of being totally straightforward whether anyone cares or not let's me feel slightly less awkward when sharing the things I'm listening to right now.

If you miss the good old days of straightforward alternative rock on terrestrial radio like I do, then I've got great news. Brother Eye is fantastic. Now, I'm about as influential as your aunt's neighbor's barber, but go listen to it, and their other albums, and buy them and download them and listen to them on your lunch break like I do. No excuses, you've been told.

All I can say is if I lived anywhere near Pennsylvania I'd go see them play, then post about how enjoyable it was. And, happy birthday, dude.

184) Caroliner...

Experimental music can be difficult to classify. I don't mean the music itself, I mean the adjective "experimental." See, already off to a bad start.

It boils down to rejecting some fundamental aspects of what makes music music. You might reject any or all of the notions of melody/harmony/rhythm/meter, you might reject the act of composing or predetermined logic, you might eliminate the concept of beginning or ending, or goal completion, or instruments themselves, or you get the idea.

On my lunch break today, I learned about California art collective Caroliner.... The ellipses are necessary because every finished project uses a different appendix for unspecified reasons (though it's pretty safe to assume that they correspond to the personnel in some way). General consensus is that their output is Industrial Experimental Psychedelic Bluegrass, and that clearly deserves some unpacking.

You're going to listen to some of it and call it nonsensical gibbering garbage, and you are of course correct, but that does nothing to distinguish it from any other music you might consider nonsensical gibbering garbage (The Incredible String Band, Glass Ox, Conlon Nancarrow,

Throbbing Gristle, Merzbow, Tiger Lillies, Neutral Milk Hotel, or dare I say it Talking Heads). Remember, we aren't talking about good/bad, like/hate, or serious/parody. We're just trying to come to terms with the fact of its existence.

Experimental Bluegrass is simply the obvious context of Banjo forward music, and you aren't gonna confuse this for Bela Fleck or Steve Martin. Psychedelic really just means that whatever you think reality is, this doesn't inhabit it. Industrial, the same way I've been describing it all along, is that ultra modern concept that humanity is now defined by the machinery that enslaves us, the noise, the unfeeling mechanical violence, the anonymity.

The gut reaction is to laugh, like you laugh at horror movies, or extreme metal, or Blood Sweat & Tears. Yet, that shouldn't be the end of engagement. 3 decades of putting records out at their own expense says it isn't a novelty (Fred Firth and Yoko Ono come to mind). Whether or not it's a joke, it's very much an intentional labor; creating it and extravagantly performing it internationally was and continues to be a serious endeavor for those involved, regardless of listener perception (see the story of Richard Benson).

Now, their full albumography will be too much for you to handle, so if you just want to hear their most accessible song (stretching the word accessible beyond all healthy physical limits), take a listen to Burdensome Blood. Sweet nightmares, kiddos.

185) The way we found new bands in the late 90s, part 1 - Epitaph

I took last night off from my unsolicited album talky talk, and I'm sure you all felt a tiny pang in the place where your liver should be. Mostly I was tired and went to bed early, but I also didn't have an album in mind and I wasn't feeling like forcing it. Great news! I've got a hankering to share my woefully small, but authentically collected compilation albums from small semi-independent punk labels.

Shocking as it may seem, there was a time when "the internet" didn't exist, and us music aficionados combed through bins of albums and picked out what to buy without knowing what it sounded like (unless you heard it from an actual friend or from radio singles or whatever).

Luckily, indie labels and labels with non-mainstream bands put out massive compilations for cheap and they were a real time and money saver. I don't mean like K-Tel or Kids Bop other hit re-publishers, I mean small labels with real dive bar bands collecting the best songs and saying "if we could afford radio payola, this is what you'd be hearing after rush hour programming is over."

It was and still is the medium of choice for punk rock, but I've got a couple ambient/acid-house comps as well. Let's take a stroll down the vomit lined alleys of the underground, should be fun.

Let's kick it off with inarguably the biggest of these labels, Epitaph. I bought my aunt Suz Bad Religion's Stranger Than Fiction as a Christmas present, she said she already had it so I got to keep it, I then became a die-hard Bad Religion fan, and it turned out this *is* Brett Gurewitz's label. Thus, I acquired Punk-O-Rama vols. 2 (1996) and 3 (1998), and they were my real introduction to punk in the late 90s. Bad Religion, NOFX, Rancid, Me First and the Gimme Gimmes, Pennywise, Descendents, and on and on and on and on.

These are great albums, in part because this is the cream of the crop. I don't mean that as a slight to any of the lesser known or shorter lived bands, I simply mean that Brett and Epitaph were shelling out the dough to push this stuff into record stores as far as the nowhere that Oklahoma City really is. Unlike a lot of the other albums I'll talk about in the coming days, you could walk back into the same store you picked this comp up in and actually find albums from these bands in stock (no internet, remember). You didn't have to ask a minimum wage cashier to check the database and pay shipping or wait two weeks. That was a big deal.

These are designed to sell more records, the albums the songs came from are listed right on the track list. You'd get little catalogues to order more obscure stuff inside. Like this? Well, it's what we do, we have so much more, and we will send it in the mail to you! That's the kind of business I can respect. It says we care about this stuff and we want to make more of it happen into your ears.

Regardless, if you can't find something you like on these albums then you're just not trying. In reality, this is the world from which Offspring and Green Day catapulted into mainstream consciousness, so go learn some late-century history and find some new old punk rock revival to love.

All these albums are on youtube, so go listen to what it sounded like at a stop light next to my van....

186) Part 2 - New Red Archives

If I had an imaginary cousin named Dixie, she would say:

Bottle, my dear. You must admit that as enjoyable as the Punk-o-Rama albums may be, they very much skew to the pop side of 90s punk. Epitaph may have kept the flames of ironically recontextualized 60s pop blazing well beyond acceptable suburban levels of comfort, but in doing so they gloss over the anger and political antagonism of actual punk rock from the 80s and 90s. Admit it, these are the party boys, but girls are every bit a part of punk.

Geez, she sounds more cognizant and erudite than I do. And, she's right. Punk is pretty much synonymous with the radical lefty anarchistic mohawks and dog collars crowd, but at the center of that defiant display of civil disobedience are the notions of complete equality, personal autonomy, and the radical concept that ideas are not worth killing each other.

New Red Archives (founded by Nicky Garratt of the U.K. Subs) was their champion, and At War With Society was their not so secret 1998 phone book.

Things you'll notice immediately include lower production value, much more anger, a whole lot of "leave me alone," and the vocal breakdown/build up of Anti Flag's "Die for Your Government." It's pretty great.

Things that might confuse you include the conjoining of peace and anarchy (because you don't understand the term "anarchy" in this context), being high all the time isn't cool, or productive, or enjoyable, and ideologies are nasty little mind warping creatures that should be exterminated (by simply refusing to participate).

The left-right spectrum only measures 1 thing, and that is the belief in enforcing social heirarchy. The motto of the extreme right is "conform or die," and the motto of the extreme left is "leave me and everybody else alone" (guess which pole I gravitate toward). The problem, of course, is that it isn't a line. It's a circle, and the Communists end up throwing fire bombs at the Nazis who are shooting at them, and everyday Americans can't tell the supposed difference anymore so they just flip a coin to decide which Halloween costume to wear. PETA is a militant organization, the wealthiest Americans shouldn't have to wait in line behind a bunch of sick people or workman's comp cases to get their erectile dysfunction pills, and so on.

But I digress. This is more ragged, but there're still melodies and structure and background doo-wop vocals like your grandma's Saturday afternoon rock and roll. Sure, it's antagonistic, but for a purpose rather than just to be lazy jerks. Best part? The ladies aren't here to act dumb and look pretty and be your girlfriend; they'll kick you in the balls if you come on like a creep.

One final thing worth metioning is that this is a sort of ten-year retrospective (and we'll listen to a much bigger one in the near future, albeit from a slightly different genre). New Red Archives started out in Brooklyn, New York then relocated to Hollywood, California and finally subsidized into a slightly bigger label about the same time I moved to Iowa. This is a best of the best from their own catalogue, and their early not-exactly-in-it-for-the-money attitude shines through.

Anti Flag is still going as strong as ever, and rightfully so. They are about as famous as you can get while remaining steadfastly underground and independent (wowzers did people get mad at the few major label releases they negotiated).

I'm intentionally not giving you a rundown of tracks, because part of the fun I've had over the last 20+ years is knowing how my own opinions have changed over time. I like some songs I didn't like before, hate songs I loved back then, learned to like bands I wasn't that into, forgot how awesome some of them are, etc. I don't want to spoil that opportunity for anyone insane enough to listen to as much music as I do (I only do it for stuff you might already know, or definitely won't care about how I feel). Tomorrow's album is a real rabbit-hole doozie, but after that we'll go all over the place.

Oh yeah. That's not a sticker. This was a 33-track 99-cent album from the get go.

187) Saturday morning interlude

I haven't made it to Fat Wreck Chords (my favorite of the indie punk labels) yet, but it's still a little too chilly to go work outside so I'm listening to Tilt's 4th album (which I actually haven't heard before).

I love Tilt, and Viewers Like You is great. Straight up 90s sing along punk rock. Intelligent, creative, super catchy. Seriously, go check it out.

188) Junk Records - Goin' After Pussy

Tonight's compilation has probably the most interesting back story. As you might have noticed, these labels were formed by musicians from actual bands and published stuff from their fellow bands (and that will keep being true for most of the rest). Junk Records is the bedroom label of Katon de Pena. Of course you've never heard of him, but it's actually kind of insane that you haven't.

He's the lead singer of thrash metal band Hirax (their most recent album was in 2014, that's 30 years after they formed, for anybody interested in that sort of thing). They were a legit part of the early thrash scene with Metallica, Slayer, Exodus, and Megadeth. He also formed the band Phantasm with Ron McGovney and Gene Hoglan. He's got a real Bruce Dickenson-like dramatic singing style (but with a healthy dose of play it up sillyness) above a seriously thrashing ensemble. He doesn't do the high screachy falsetto stuff, and that's just fine. Oh yeah, he's also black, but that's only intriguing if you're dumb enough to confuse skin color with taste in music. Not that you doubted the thoroughness of my stalker like research, but he posted a photo of pre-beard Billy Gibbons on facebook yesterday.

Anyway, when he started Junk Records he had one goal in mind: find the absolute fringe of 90s underground rock, and publish it. This is raunchy, intentionally nasty, no hope of radio play, mainstream poison, mosh pit bar fight stuff. The whole album is interspersed with actual messages from his answering machine, and it sounds like he was pretty happy being a popular LA nightclub jackass.

If you don't like bad words and sex and generally harmless degeneracy, then prepare to be offended. But, if Guns & Roses were a little too clean, corporate, and well rehearsed for your liking, then this is awesome stuff. It's a blend of shock punk and trashy rock and roll for sure. You're not gonna wake up humming melodies from any of this stuff ('cause there aren't many), but it's not monotone screaming like some people don't seem to like at all (I accept that I'm weird for finding that enjoyable). Good stuff for when you just want to rattle your brains inside your skull until they ooze out of your ears. Throw your empty beer bottle at the wall and crank it up to annoy your neighbors.

189) Kansas - Leftoverture

I felt a little guilty for straying so far from the vinyl that started this whole endeavor, so I washed off a couple more albums from the moldy stack.

First, I'm not going to justify it with a review, but I don't like Clapton's Slowhand. Cocaine and Lay Down Sally are great classic songs, but the rest of the album is crap (Wonderful Tonight doesn't count either way, for reasons I also won't explain).

Second, holy shit, have you heard Kansas's Leftoverture? What a fantastic kaleidoscope of weirdness. Critics who hated it called it a dumb imitation of British prog that lacks the self-deprecating humor promised by the title and cover art.

Bugger that, this is great. It's perfect. Sure, the actual singy parts are datedly 70s faux-folk, but musically it's super adventurous. I feel like people didn't want Kansas to be prog-rock; like the whole time they were just waiting for a half-hour loop of Dust in the Wind, and were getting pretty damned impatient at this point.

Steve Walsh had writer's block, so Kerry Livgren was like "sure, I'll just pick up where my last song left off and go nuts. Chip in whenever something excites you, Stevo." The title/cover isn't a joke, it's literal.

If Emerson, Lake, & Palmer is a little too demented for your liking, this album is a step back from the edge, but still plenty wacky. Magnum Opus certainly is. Don't be surprised if I start blurting "release the beavers!" at randomly inappropriate times.

190) Matador's 10th Anniversary

Bad, evil, naughty Zoot! She's been lighting the beacon again, which I've just remembered looks a lot like the flag of Matador Records. First the spankings, then the indie everything.

What's an independent record label? There are all sorts of technicalities, but it boils down to: not a subsidiary of Sony, Warner, or UMG (the three major corporations that own their entire content, manufacturing, and distribution chains). Matador certainly isn't the biggest, or best known, but they are the most diverse and one of the most influential. They also had a brief flirt with Atlantic's (i.e. Warner) marketing department, but bought that half of the company back after a couple years and currently belong to the Beggars Group for marketing/distribution. For their 10th anniversary in 1999 they published a massive 3-CD retrospective with relatively recent cuts from their 400+ catalogue of releases. You've heard of a lot of these bands 'cause a lot of them are still making great stuff today. Funny story, when the RIAA started waging war against file sharing, Matador had to repeatedly remind them that they were definitely not members of said organization.

Everything Is Nice really is the holy grail of 1990s indie creativity and diversity. There wasn't a full playlist on youtube, so I've done the best I can (a few tracks are missing, but I don't feel like going through the hassle of putting them up there and slogging through copyright junk. 95% is good enough).

It's a mix of everything, some big, some obscure, rock pop hip-hop punk dancy crazy. If gen x-ers were going to make it in their garages anyway, Matador pointed a microphone in their direction. Fun times, the 90s.

191) Waveform Records - Two A.D.

And now (to keep the Monty Python references going) for something completely different...

... as much as I love electronic (synths and sequencers) music in general, I have surprisingly little of it in my collection. It's just not one of my go to genres like rock and metal, 'cause (big shock) I'm not made of money. I do however have the second compilation from English ex-pat ambient dub label Waveform Records, Two A.D. "Ambient dub" doesn't mean anything over here, so they adopted the phrase "exotic electronica" for the steadfastly downtempo, liquid sunshine, aliens and wildlife type soundscape music they broadcast out into the radiosphere. I used to listen to Forest himself DJ Musical Starstreams late at night as a teenager on I don't even remember what station.

This is hour-long attention span, eyes-closed, pretty colors on the back of your eyelids type music. Its sole purpose is to make you feel fantastic, calm, relaxed; assuming of course that you can get past that 3-minute rapidly approaching brick wall urge to skip to the next track. If you've ever wondered how I can sit here listening to album after album from start to finish, well this kind of stuff makes a 7 track 30 minute record feel like tv channel surfing. You can do it, I believe in you. A little nap never hurt anybody anyway, as far as I know. And, the dreams will be pretty cool if you do nod off.

Every track is great, but if you're just not ready for the full scuba dive at least give Coldcut's version of "Autumn Leaves," A Positive Life's "Pleidean Communication," and Biosphere's "Baby Interphase" a try (yes, the album is on youtube). That sample in Pleidean Communication is from Space 1999, starring Martin Landau, by the way. As always, enjoy.

192) Solex - Ahoy! The Sound Map of the Netherlands

If you went and checked out my Matador playlist, you might have heard a couple tracks by Solex. Elisabeth Esselink is a Dutch artist (and record store owner) whose primary medium is sampling (both from records and by making informal field recordings).

Her early work, though unique, is pretty standard hip-hop adjacent, singing over sampled beats, but I hadn't really been keeping up with her work past her first couple albums. So, I checked out her 2013 album Ahoy! The Sound Map of the Netherlands, and wow it's fantastic.

The concept of the album is obvious and mostly explicit, but the full story is worth repeating. She had a boat and a desire to be on said boat for an extended period of time. What better way to accomplish that than to actually make a record on a boat? So, she sailed around her country inviting musicians from every province to come aboard and improvise over a bunch of loops she had prepared. These were all solo improvisations, nobody heard what others had played. Then she took all the recordings including speech and environmental sounds, trashed the original loops, and assembled the tracks into finished pieces.

If you aren't familiar with the peculiar adoration people from the Netherlands have for Rock and Blues (maybe you were sick the week your high school history teacher talked about the Dutch East India company's hostile takeover of Southern Africa, I don't know) then this album might really surprise you. I am familiar with it and it still surprised me. This album boogies and jives, but stays completely loose and unpredictable. That's the cool thing about non-communicative improvisation, it produces intriguing counterpoint you could never strictly "compose." If nothing else, it's a fascinating ethnomusicological survey of contemporary Netherlands. Definitely worth a listen or twenty.

193) Give 'Em The Boot

Let's dig a little deeper into the non-pop/rock side of the 90s punk scene, I'm talking ska, hardcore, and oi!.

What the hell does any of that mean, Bottle? Oh, sorry, I forgot that I never gave you a proper history lesson. I talked about the early punk/new wave interchangeability thing, but there was actually a 3rd ingredient, Reggae.

One of the big questions the twenty-agers had in the 70s was "why are all you people so goddamned racist?" Remember, punk is a leftist enterprise. We're all equal and whatever music you like blends with whatever music I like and that's what we play. Bring your trumpets and trombones, and I'll crank up the distortion. Bagpipes? Yeah sure, bagpipes are pretty punk. This is the stuff Tim Armstrong wanted to sign to his joint venture with Brett Gurewitz, Hellcat Records. Tim Armstrong. You know, Operation Ivy, Rancid. Yeah, that Tim Armstrong.

Look, I'm not a huge ska guy, but there are a lot of great tracks from that world on the inaugural Give 'Em The Boot. I'm much more of a hardcore/street punk guy, so Swingin' Utters and Dropkick Murphy's and Choking Victim are the standout bands for me.

Interesting tangent, Choking Victim broke up and STZA eventually formed Leftöver Crack, then he got real mad at Tim and Hellcat in general and defected to the Fat Wreck Chords camp for CD releases, and Jello Biafra's label publishing vinyl. Not a Scott Sturgeon essay.

This is mainly a ska compilation, but it's still quite listenable. Swingin' Utters "Fifteenth and T" though, that track blew my 17-year-old mind and I still love them today.

194) No Sleep - Every Drop Counts

Sadly, we come to the end of my compilation albums with Every Drop Counts, the sampler No Sleep Records gave me when I bought The Wonder Years's own Sleeping on Trash comp. It's awesome. Go buy a record from one of their bands if you want to hear it...

... I'm kidding. Once again, out of the kindness of my heart, I've assembled a youtube playlist. Not as cool as my actual home-made CD, but still pretty generous if I'm being immodest.

So, what are you going to get? Well, as you can see this is all really recent stuff, so it's a smorgasbord of post-. Post-punk, post-rock, post-emo, post-hardcore, post emotional exhaustion. We don't care about anything anymore. We can't. We're useless, and having fun is no fun at all. I love it, but I've also taken my fair share of anti-depressants (which you might have surmised from some of my "bad day" blurbs). You might find it a little whiny for your taste, but I find it comforting.

This comp is really great because I've been a fan of bands on this label for a while (Wonder Years and La Dispute), but never heard any of these before they literally just gave it to me. Obviously, some of them are going to go on to awesome things and some are going to fizzle out like dollar-store birthday candles, but either way I get to feel something about them. That's exciting.

I'm kind of bummed that my little week-long project is over. I'm approaching the 200-essay mark, and I'm running out of steam. In a way that's a good thing, because I'm finally coming to terms with the death of my dad. If you're relatively new to my nightly album reviews, that's what it's been all about and I once again commend you on randomly opening to this exact page. In real life I'm a super duper not at all talkative person, but writing is actually pretty easy. I don't know what tomorrow will bring, but thanks for reading my personal journal for the last 7 months.

P.S. definitely go check out No Sleep's youtube channel. They put up their artists' full albums themselves.

195) Point Blank - AMERICAN EXCE$$

Geez, I can't even commit to being non-commital. It's snowing here today, so I've fed animals, and played snow princess with the josinator, and washed dishes, and now I'm ready for some all but completely forgotten late 70s/early 80s hard southern arena rock. Point Blank, if you've spent some time listening to classic rock radio, you've heard their hit "Nicole." I like it when a band name serves a grammatical function.

I don't like it when the one hit doesn't actually represent the band. They are actually better than "Nicole." Not to say that's a bad song, but they definitely suffered from the "already heard it" mentality. They sound like all the bigger bands of the era, and it's way too easy to just say "Derivative!" and move on. Let that idea go. Is it silly or boring? No. Is it cheesy or offensive? No. Is it good old mid-tempo Texas-boogie type rock and roll that makes you want to drum on the steering wheel and sing along? Yes, totally.

Sure, the first verse murder suicide of "Walk Across the Fire" is a little jarring. Sure, most of the rest of the album is generic love/break up song type stuff, but at least it's not party party chicks and booze, I'm a rebel, born to lose nonsense. Sure, every single track reminds you of a different song from a more famous band. Why is that a bad thing? I mean they aren't faking it. This isn't hack work. They're good, they aren't jerks. Their core hard-rock sound leaves plenty of space for synths or boogie-woogie piano or harmonica and meandering solos happening under the verses themselves.

I think they just weren't at the top of MCA's list of priorities, 'cause almost any song from AMERICAN EXCE$$ could have been a hit, and wouldn't sound out of place in the rock block at all.

196) The Wonder Years - Sleeping On Trash

Speaking of The Wonder Years (that's a worm hole, not a non sequitur), here's Sleeping On Trash. It's a compilation of non-LP recordings from 2005-2010. It's got tracks from out of print EPs, splits, covers, and demos. It was a way to make a lot of their rarest recordings available in one affordable record.

It's also a good chance to talk about the old school methodology of current punk labels. You've got singles, a "hit" and another song. That's where the term "b-side" for certain tracks came from. This is what labels used to send out in press kits to radio stations, distributors, potential reviewers, etc. Next, let's say you've got 3 or 4 tracks burning a hole in your brain, but not enough time, energy, or money to flesh out a full album. That's an EP.

A split can be any size, but that's where two bands put out a record together. Basically, you're only paying for half a record, while doubling your potential audience.

The point of all of this is to work with what you've got and get it out there for the least amount of money possible. The majors do it to maximize profit, but the indie/punk labels do it to give fans something affordable to buy. See, when you buy a record, maybe a dollar or less of that money made it to the actual band. That's the inherent inflation of retail, it's just reality. When it's all said and done, the cost per unit was 2 or 3 dollars, and everyone who touched it along the way deserves their fair share for touching it, so you end up in the $10 to $25 range for a full-blown product. Not evil. Unnecessary, but that's real life. Indies and bands would rather give the fans what they want (more music) without paying somebody to pay somebody to get it to you, somewhere in the $5 to $15 dollar range. A functional economy doesn't need billionaires to selectively invest in failing sectors, because it's already working properly.

Blah blah Bottle. Get on with it. I like The Wonder Years because their music is good. Catchy pop-punk with hints of hardcore and metal. Lyrically, they are really unique. Their songs aren't poetry, or obtuse, or cryptic, or hyperbolic, or "statements." It's more like listening to someone reading from their personal journal: where we were, what we were doing, how it felt. If anything, this kind of writing errs on the side of hyper-specificity, but I don't mind that at all. I wasn't there, so it's totally fine if I don't know what you're talking about. This band in particular has the vibe that the lyrics could completely change every time they play it. They aren't so much songs, more like monologues. That's probably not a sentiment or reaction anyone else could have, but it's definitely a part of what makes them so enjoyable for me.

197) Meat Puppets II

You seem tense. Are you scared, confused, angry? Are you sitting there wondering why Republican politicians are repeating the talking points of previous candidates for the Democratic nomination? Are you worried that your employer won't sell off their worst speculative investments to pay you for the work you've been doing? Are you not sure how this "grow plants and raise animals you can eat" thing works every spring?

You just need some perspective. I'll feed you, baby bird. Meat Puppets. No, no, not you. The band. Their second album, Meat Puppets II. You're not crazy. These guys are crazy. It's the Kirkwood brothers and a drummer, playing what could only be described as Cowpunk. I suppose you could warp the Venn diagram so that some of it falls within the label Psychedelic Rock, but why? If you like the Oak Ridge Boys, you'll detest this (and vice-versa as my case may be).

Let's start with the cover. What the hell is that a painting of? The desert as a portal to hell. That's pretty obvious. They're from Arizona. It's got a twinge of Van Gogh, but it's predominantly the mash up of paint and drugs.

Is it good? Oh yes, it's phenomenal. I mean if you were a real OG, you'd be mad that it isn't unintelligible hardcore noise like their first album, but those people don't actually exist (sadly, they do). If you think singing should be mostly in tune, and guitar playing shouldn't be sloppy you'll find it hard to digest. Luckily, I have no interest in those things. What I love is pure, unadulterated creativity, and the nutritional value of this album is off the chart. I couldn't write anything like this if I tried for a thousand years, and you couldn't either. This is a 5-star album, 4 if you're in the "has to be 'produced'" camp. This is walk in off the street, do a couple takes and go home stuff.

If you don't know anything about them: Cris and Kurt were children of a legit millionaire, and formed a band. This is just what came out of their brains and fingers in 1984. Go ahead, try to play any of this stuff in a way that doesn't sound polished. You can't (just like their later albums, where they couldn't unlearn the better they got with practice; still great, but lacking the magic spark of being legitimately awkward and sloppy). My point is, this isn't an act, it's not a facade or a character, this is how they played/sang at the time. It's raw genius, without any concept of "popular" or "marketable" or "do we suck?" getting in the way.

You probably know that Kurt Cobain brought them out on stage to play three of the tracks from this album on Unplugged, and he did it because he genuinely loved them. How could you not love this album? No, really, tell me. The record industry is pretty horrible, but this exists. They still play shows. You can go buy a new copy and listen to it until the grooves wear out. Or, you can go listen to it on youtube or whatever. It will definitely change your perspective. Don't be a meat puppet, just listen to them for a change.

198) Modest Mouse - We Were Dead Before the Ship Even Sank

I brought out the Meat Puppets for show and tell yesterday, so it seems appropriate to continue with the post-punk music ('cause tee hee last week I did 90s punk, see how this all just unfolds like I have any idea what I'm doing? I repeatedly tell you I don't, and I mean it, I don't. It's a subconscious thing).

Modest Mouse's fifth album, We Were Dead Before the Ship Even Sank, originated as a concept: Isaac Brock had the idea to write every song about sailors that die in every song, like Kenny from South Park. He couldn't actually keep it up for an entire album, but the core idea is definitely there.

Aside: I'm really not as fascinated with death as my humor and record collection make it seem. You're going to laugh, but I am actually an extreme life loving optimist on the inside.

But, Modest Mouse. They are idie rock, or alternative, or even art rock, but most of all they are anti-facade, exactly like the Meat Puppets, or Violent Femmes. It's ridiculous, or pretentious, or insane, or sarcastic, but it's not an act. They are who they are, and no one has the power to change that. You can't argue one way or the other about them to any avail, and that is as post-punk as it gets. No, I tell a lie. It would be even better if another seriously big post punk musician joined them for this album. Waaiiit, that guy looks a lot like Johnny Marr. From the Smiths. I stand corrected on my correction of myself. This is as post-punk as it gets.

So, on to the music. This album, in Isaac's own words is "a nautical balalaika carnival romp." That's a loaded description though, you have to have a clear picture of carnivals as deranged, frightening, intrinsically ironic social events, like I and most of my generation do.

I might be crazy, but I think their music is much more counterpoint oriented than rock of any type. Listening to

Modest Mouse, you get the sense that you can either bash the guitar with your fist or plink out meanderingly off-kilter melodies, and never the twain shall meet. Vocals are melodic, but the pitches involved have a weighted value of 0.003 (very nearly Sprechstimme to my ears). Loud or soft. Whisper or yell. 50 different flavors of no shades of gray, period. I like that quite a lot, to be honest. Solos start off completely tonal, then a sour note crops up and they veer off into crazy dissonant intelligibility. It's an I'm not ok, pick a path and walk down it because neither is better mentality, and that's a system everyone can work with. Either you love it or you don't, and we don't have to agree at all.

Would it even surprise you at all that his house is filled to the brim with bizarre taxidermied animals that he bought because it was an insane thing to collect?

We should talk about format. By the 2000s, albums had become monstrously behemoth hour plus affairs (80 minutes on a CD, after all). So, if you're retro and publish vinyl too, they end up being double albums. Thankfully, these lunatics take that into consideration, and We Were Dead... is actually the second half. The first half is subtitled We Were Lucky... and that's perfect. 4 songs, 3 songs, 4 songs, 3 songs. I find Modest Mouse vinyl muchly much much more satisfying than the seemingly endless tracklist of CD or digital formats. And the packaging and vinyl itself is thick and sturdy, and real; it matters. It's for people who love it to love it, not impulse junk just to make a dollar. You might be tempted to say "but Bottle, Epic is a Sony label." Yes, but 5th album, and they had just found the mainstream with the previous two. It sold 128,585 in the first week after it had already been leaked online, reached platinum (a million copies) a few months later, and that wasn't a shock. A major *had* to release it; who else could afford to pay for it up front? What lunatic would only publish a single run and make fans wait to get a copy? This wasn't a case of "manufacturing" an act, they were exactly the right band at exactly the right time and the whole industry just stood out of the way and said "thank you" afterward.

I wish I had more than two of their albums, but we'll listen to their debut later this week. Maybe I'll use a tiny portion of my $1,000 RepubliCratic severance check to buy a couple more (ha!).

Let it all drop, indeed. I love Modest Mouse in case you couldn't tell.

199) Nine Inch Nails - The Downward Spiral

If you thought I was being heavy-handed before, then to quote Randy Bachman, "b-b-b-b-baby you just ain't seen n-n-n-nothin' yet."

It's NIN time. The Downward Spiral. I've been known to make semi-disparaging remarks about NIN, but that's only because they are the Five Flavor Fruit Punch, or Gin and Tonic Blossoms, or [insert ultra famous band from a much larger scene here] of industrial rock. You should know full well by now that I love Trent Reznor and his tech crew, but they are the Made-in-China American Flag on the iceberg that sank the Titanic. You say "industrial," I start yip-yapping about my beloved genre, and you have that deer on the highway panic attack that screams "Nine Inch Nails, I only know about Nine Inch Nails, and honestly only one or two songs from The Downward Spiral 'cause I heard Johnny Cash cover "Hurt" but I didn't really get what all the fuss was about, and actually I haven't really listened to the whole thing, I'm sorry I brought it up, can we talk about sports or cars or anything else instead!?

Calm down, dude. I'm the one who got overly excited and rambly. We can work this out. We'll just listen to it and try to describe some of the flavors.

First, NIN is Trent Reznor. He invites various people to physically help him create his music. This album is Trent, flood, and Adrian Belew (plus a few others on random tracks).

Flood is a British recording engineer/producer. You might know Adrian Belew from his long running stint as the front man of King Crimson, or as the guy who makes animal sounds with guitars. There's no trickery here, this is an album fully devoted to portraying what it's like to lose your goddamned mind and sink lower that you thought possible, then kill yourself.

      It's not actually a narrative concept, more random but comprehensive scenes from inside the feelings of uncontrollable self destruction. Humans as pigs is a central theme, but you have to know a lot about pigs to fully appreciate that metaphor; take everything you know about how people use pigs as a metaphor, add the general observation that they show no obvious signs of comprehending death, and really imagine thinking those things about yourself. Uncomfortable yet? That's high school level listening.

      Let's jump right into graduate school seminar territory. You own some good headphones, right? Well, you need some. There aren't just two or three layers to the production. There are full parts stacked on other parts at different volume levels, and they constantly shift around the stereo field. It seems counter intuitive, but you have to turn the volume down a little and listen deeper than you've ever listened before. You'll start to notice that the loud thing happens on the left, while 4 even creepier things happen quieter on the right. There's whispering of lyrics from other songs, spoken sections, abrupt cuts, samples you could easily miss at louder volumes. In short, it is completely disorienting, and the thing you thought you heard distracts you from the other things that are happening. Thought there couldn't possibly be acoustic guitars, clean piano, and high-low vocal overdubs? Oh, they are there, along with a thousand other interesting things you haven't heard yet, like the vocal counterpoint on the track "The Downward Spiral" where he just plays with the sound of "wow-ow-wow." Note the coda (or more accurately interlude) melody recalling the melody from "Closer." Yes, this album has multiple Leitmotifs.

This is 65 minutes of the most mentally exhausting sonic and thematic turmoil. The relatable thoughts are inflated to grotesque absurdity, and the actual suicide is understated as "hurt." You should feel like you need a sandwich afterward, because all the nutrients have been sucked out of your body through your ear holes, but you're way too nauseous to actually eat it. It's fantastic!

And I get to go back to work tomorrow, and listen to people say confusingly hyperbolic nonsense. Yay.

Now doesn't that make you feel better?

200) Steven Stark - I Wonder What the Radio Plays

It's a thing I do now, so let's all take a moment to say Happy Birthday, Steven Stark.

You can find his first album on most any online platform, just give it a search.

It's an album of great songs with interestingly complex harmonic twists, catchy melodies, and enough abstraction to find relevance for whatever state of mind you find yourself in. I don't just mean your current frame of reference, but how you felt back whenever your particular "then" might be, and in the future when other things have happened. It's an album to have, and experience, and come back to, and most of all enjoy.

He usually describes himself as "compositional pop" but he has a very distinct indie rock personality too. Not the crazy kind like I've been showcasing, but the calmer rational side of thinking outside the box. Or maybe it's an adjacent box. I don't know, I'm just spitballing here.

I do love the fact that however many years later I have finally achieved that magical $20,000 baller lifestyle of our youthful fantasies, and we'll just sweep all thoughts of inflation under the corner of the rug for now (we'll come back and bag it up later).

And so, my lunch break comes to an end and I go back to business as usual for 4 more hours. It has definitely been an enjoyable break on a rainy boring day, thanks to my long-distance friend. So, in the words of Cage the Elephant, Thank You, Happy Birthday.

201) Black Oak - I'd Rather Be Sailing

You know what I haven't done in a while? Record roulette. That's where we grab a record I know absolutely nothing about, and hope it doesn't 'splode in my face.

Wheel of morality, turn turn turn, give us some music that we've never heard... Black Oak's I'd Rather Be Sailing. They look like Southern Rock to me, and they're fully committed to The Lonely Island's I'm On A Boat schtick. It's 1978, so there's not going to be a T-Pain guest spot, but there're "syndrums" and glockenspiel, and everyone plays guitar (some with e-bows). I won't know if they are actually from Arkansas until two or three paragraphs from now, but Capricorn Studios is the "birthplace of southern rock" so I feel somewhat vindicated in my judging of the cover photo. Time to walk the plank, I guess.

Sweet baby buddah, I choked on my drink trying not to laugh. It was just shock, and I'm still getting used to his voice, but Jim Dandy Mangrum is unique. I just wasn't expecting the opening at all. The electronic toms are ridiculous, but yeah this is perfectly great southern rock, four tracks in.

You probably suspected it wouldn't be about boats at all (I wouldn't mention a SNL sketch if I took it serious), didn't you? It reminds me of other stuff, but not explicitly enough to give it a name. Oooh, that's a nice sax intro on "You Can Count On Me (I'll Be There)."

So, first half impressions: it is in fact southern rock, but there is also the unmistakable influence of disco and soul. Eureka! I know what I'm hearing. It sounds like a disco remix of drunken Blood, Sweat & Tears leftovers. That sounded insulting. I didn't mean it that way, these are just my tasting notes, to borrow that metaphor. I probably wouldn't want to drink it on a regular basis, but I'm not dreading Side B. See you on the flipside...

... aw maaaan. They went soft rock. That blows. I expected the e-bows to be lap steel imposters, but I didn't want easy listening. Don't get me wrong, it's not bad at all. Underwhelming, but not unlistenable. Side A had so much potential, and then they just James Seals-ed the second half. The first half is almost so close to the edge of prog territory, but then you get rick-rolled into a Gerry Rafferty concert. It's like a Georgia Satellites concert where they don't play Keep Your Hands To Yourself, or Greg Allman refusing to play I'm No Angel. Why did I even put pants on for this?

This one gets a green participation ribbon, and a "thanks for actually being from the town you named your band after." See, I told you I'd look it up eventually. I'm the one who's disappointed, you guys did fine.

202) Steppenwolf - "At Your Birthday Party"

There can be only one album for tonight. I wasn't saving it for any particular reason, but for all the obvious and secret reasons it's Steppenwolf's third album, "At Your Birthday Party" (the quotes are actually part of the title). You remember "Rock Me" as the finale of the Candy soundtrack, right? It also has a fantastic little instrumental called "Mango Juice."

I don't feel like concocting some clever essay, it's everything I want it to be. Steppenwolf could have played "wheels on the bus" or "baby shark" and I'd still love 'em. I love the sound (as feeble as the mix/master might sound compared to other albums). More than any other band, you can hear them playing. Who cares what the actual word for word lyrics are?

As it stands though, there are quite a few pertinent statements. Perhaps most relevant is a sentiment my father taught me (if maybe not quite so succinctly): it's never too late to start all over again. That's some good advice right there, though it might take you a while to tease out all of its possible implications.

Miss you like hell, dad. Happy Birthday.

203) George Szell and the Cleveland Orchestra's Debussy - La Mer

Only half a record tonight, because Debussy's La Mer only takes up one side. This is George Szell and the Cleveland Orchestra playing Debussy and Ravel (I'm not interested in hearing Ravel right now).

La Mer is a tricky piece. It's not a symphony, it's not a symphonic poem, it's not "impressionistic," it's not what Debussy was known for writing up to this point, and nobody had much nice to say about it until he conducted it himself. The general reception ran along the lines of "how the hell is this 'the sea?' It's just half an hour of scribbly nonsense."

I'm sure it won't shock you that I find classical music criticism even more odious than rock criticism. Let's ignore them and take a more Bottle-ian approach.

It took a year of looking at Japanese paintings and daydreaming of childhood memories for Debussy to write it, and for him that was a rush job. He didn't want it to be an actual symphony, but he didn't want it to be overly pretentious fluff either. What have you got to work with? Waves? Light? An unpredictably violent briny death? Mermaids? I can hear all that in there, same as any Disney apprentice tracer. More importantly, the sea has its own moods and men can never control or predict them. On that score, it's brilliant. The movements don't follow a formula, they just unfold; things happen, other things happen afterward, there's continuity for sure, but no immediately observable logic. The calm is not actually calm, it's a tense vibration waiting to explode. We are fascinated by the sea because we cannot truly inhabit it. We can endure it, harvest from it, explore it, traverse it, but it will always be a force that we cannot control. Everything in the piece happens in waves and ripples.

I hate the way it ends, but I don't have a better suggestion. It has to stop at some point, and big crescendo with a plop is a pretty standard "it's over."

204) Whitney Houston

Oh, you're in for a real treat tonight. Or, a brain hemorrhage. Either way we all have a lot of fun. That's a moderately oblique Men In Tights reference, everyone who didn't get it takes a shot.

True story, my dad had a hard time pronouncing certain words, and I could swear he consistently pronounced her name Whitney Useless. I don't think that's fair, because she didn't actually get a choice in the matter. We aren't talking about Cher, or Dionne Warwick, or Barbra Streisand. The title and the voice are the only part of this debut album that belongs to Whitney Houston. This is a Sony stables production, a producers album, a Berry Gordy style "one of these songs will hit it big" type album. Jermaine Jackson, Kashif, Michael Masser, and Narada Michael Walden in a fight to the death to see who will emerge victorious in the pair this new kid with an established duet partner grudge match of 1985.

Walden won, by the way. Much as I hate to agree with the critics, "How Will I Know" is the definitive cut from the album. That's because Walden (about as hardcore R&B as it gets) said "yes, obviously you can sing anything, why not sing this thing that will make you an untouchable pop idol?"

Admit it, "How Will I Know" is a freakin' great song. It's bubbly, it's fun, she's 22 for crying out loud. Sure "Greatest Love of All" is a monumental ballad, but don't tell me for a second that it's the thing you actually want to hear her sing.

What the critics hated about this album was that the other 3 producers treated her like a generic R&B vocalist. "Here's a good song, just sing it like you do, blah blah, sounds great, ok what's my next project?"

What's the other thing you actually remember from Whitney Houston (music wise, not Bobby Brown and 75 kilos of cocaine and baking soda)? That's right, The Bodyguard. Also Narada Michael Walden. She had one guy making her look good, and a hundred other people looking to cash in on her talent. They cashed in, and she cracked. Get it?

It comes down to this: Could Whitney Houston sing? AND HOW! Do I like 93% of the songs people told her to sing? HELL NO. Am I capable of ignoring that and fully enjoying this album? ABSOLUTELY. Would I choose Donna Summer's The Wanderer over this? EVERY DAY OF THE WEEK. Do I know all the lyrics to every song and would I sing along out loud without a hint of embarrassment? OF COURSE I WOULD!

I'm a walking contradiction and I ain't got no right, to quote a Green Day chorus.

P.S. my dad used to hum along too.

205) Cyndi Lauper - She's So Unusual

Why not keep the fun going? You know who made her major label debut 2 years before Whitney? Cyndi Lauper. But She's So Unusual isn't actually the start of her story.

Cyndi Lauper was the singer of a band called Blue Angel. They were a NYC club band, but only one of their two albums actually got published. Their A&R guy's boss's boss's boss over in Germany got fired, and the new guy just dropped the whole roster. Blue Angel kept on playing clubs but fired their manager after a sideways Studio 54 gig. He sued them for $80k and that bankrupted her, so she just worked at a retro clothing store and kept on singing whatever she felt like at all the clubs she already made a name in, and a new manager finally scooped her up. Being the savvy New Yorker with two functional middle fingers that she is, she made sure that she was an equally credited arranger of every song, got her own songwriting credits, and didn't actually pay for any of it herself.

You can call it new wave, or synthpop, or whatever, as long as we all understand that this is the same universe as Boomtown Rats, Blondie, The Cars, Devo, a direct descendent of the preppy, nerdy, strange side of punk. Cyndi Lauper was a punk. Captain Lou Albano was her best friend, he starred in all her videos and she'd be ringside at his wrestling matches. My cousin Tom actually met them at a pool hall one time. Blue Angel was generally regarded as neo-rockabilly, but that's just a nit-picky portion of the punk/new-wave spice melange (Dune reference, drink 'em up). Actually, I legitimately don't hear a difference between this and early Prince or B52s or any of the weirdest stuff from the late 70s to mid 80s. It's good time 80s dance music, and synths were the thing at the time.

What else? Oh yeah, that's an Annie Leibovitz portrait taken in Coney Island, and Cyndi's own dress.

Now for how I really feel. It's freakin' awesome. You know the hits, but the deep cuts are spectacular. Kiss You, with it's bizarro spastic take on Love Potion #9, Prince's When You Were Mine (an insanely weird song in its own right), and the gender switched title track which is actually a duet between regular Cyndi Lauper and her 1920s gangster moll impression.

I don't want to ruin all the surprises if you've never really, I mean *really* listened to the whole album, but something is genuinely off-kilter about every track, in a way that you can hear isn't like anything else. Critics are quick to point out that nothing after this quite achieves the same level of spectacular in her career, but I think that's missing the point ('cause if you haven't noticed, she just kept on doing whatever she wanted to do). Whitney Houston or Madonna is the wrong comparison. This is a Red Headed Stranger type album. This is an I know what I'm doing and I'll let you make a lot of money too if you shut up and move the faders like a good boy album. Who gives a crap if I sell another record after how big this one is gonna be? Right place, right time, right personality, the industry followed her lead not the other way around.

206) Linda Ronstadt - Mad Love

You know who else made a New Wave album in 1980? Linda Ronstadt.

I feel very conflicted about reviewing this album. First, I know I heard a lot of her growing up, but I only remember Different Drum. Second, I've got a lot of Linda Ronstadt records (not even half her discography, but closer to ten than two), but I don't want to listen to all of them just to throw a few fast balls by you at the moment. Third, this was her umpteenth platinum and/or Grammy winning album, so my opinion is worth even less than the normal nothing. Fourth, I don't do the like it 'cause she's cute kind of listening, so I might hate it even if the tomatoes and beer bottles start flying at my head.

I do know that this was a try something different 'cause the last one didn't do much album, and nothing before or after resembled it at all. I also know that the only tracks anyone cared about were the Elvis Costello covers. But, there's no crying in whiffle ball, so batter and bottoms up.

Great news, I don't hate it. Bad news, this isn't in any way New Wave. It's New Wave aware, but it's really just a variety-rock album. Worse news, I do at some point have to listen to all of them, because it's not really a trendy cry for attention either. My first listen, I'm getting an experimental vibe for sure. The country is still there (I'm well aware of her connection to Dolly Parton and Emmylou Harris), along with the mishmash of new wave/hair metal guitar work. This isn't punk, but every so often she gets the inflection just right and you can totally hear how it could have been punk if she didn't rein it back in right away. There's a little bit of Pat Benatar bite in there too, but not at all in a copycat way. Again, it comes across as an experiment, but it's certainly not awkward or cheesy like you might anticipate.

I reserve judgement. I really will have to do some more research to formulate an actual opinion. I suspect she really is in a league of her own, and I'll have to figure out where they hold spring training before I start filling out my tip sheets.

207) Ministry - Psalm 69

Sadly, another great drummer left us Tuesday after a long battle with cancer. I've talked about Bill Rieflin in multiple contexts (not in this book, at large), and I could play any number of albums from Ministry or KMFDM or NIN or all of the above (I am an industrial rock/metal kind of guy).

Let's skip the jibber jabber and just listen to Ministry's Psalm 69. Rieflin was the first phone number on Alain Jourgenson's call list for everything, and Psalm 69 is my favorite (not Ministry's best, but we've already established that I can like whatever I want to like when I feel like it, and it's not so secretly because he finally started actually caring about guitars again with this album).

It's got everything. Drugs, politics, war, Aleister Crowly, Gibby Haines (from Butthole Surfers) makes a guest vocal appearance singing Jesus Built My Hotrod.

You might be thinking what does any of this have to do with William Rieflin? It doesn't. Bill was always a behind the scenes guy. He was an amazing drummer who just liked making other peoples' music come to life, especially my beloved Chicago Industrial. Actually, now that I think of it, his wife painted the cover of KMFDM's Nihil, their only non BRUTE! cover, to the best of my knowledge.

RIP William Rieflin. You were a big part of some of my favorite music.

208) David Bowie's discography, 1 - David Bowie

I'm going to have to tackle this at some point. Maybe not today, maybe not tomorrow, but soon...

... Well, now that it's raining through yet another clump of my increasingly rare days off, I guess I might as well start. If I'm going to go album by album through his entire discography, you might as well hop on at the start and take the whole trip with me.

As far as I know, David Bowie's self titled debut is pretty much gone from our collective consciousness. That's a shame, because it's quite enjoyable. It's a collection of interesting, sometimes strange, stories and character songs, and I suspect it's exactly the context required for understanding his later career. I mean, so many of his albums are actually David Bowie portraying a character, sometimes fictional sometimes pseudo-(auto)biographical.

It's 60s pop pretty much across the board, but highly literary. That's not to say there's a coherent narrative or theme to any of it, but the songs aren't sing along mottos or messages, it's all very much David Bowie singing. David Bowie the performer, here's what he writes, sings, thinks about, for your listening pleasure. I don't think he's really trying to communicate anything more than the conflict between the individual and the public; the one verses the many, self vs. other. There is, however, a definite post world war mentality. I'm not sure if it's part of Bowie himself, or just intrinsic to his generational Britishness. We'll see quite a lot more of it though.

Part of this gigantic listening project is to change my own opinion: I like some of his stuff, hate a few specific things, but a lot of it I just haven't bothered to care about. I thoroughly enjoy this collection of early songs, I love the arrangements and tunes, I like his theatrical vocal style. We've already established that the psychedelic baroque-pop of the Beatles makes me moderately angry because they didn't seem to actually care about what they were making. I get the complete opposite sense from Bowie, he clearly cared that the actual songs were good. They are. I can't single any one out for being great or terrible, they are all great.

209) 2 - David Bowie aka Space Oddity

Like I said earlier, this is just me listening to David Bowie's whole discography and trying to get something out of it (I don't know what). It's not a history or a critique or anything scholarly, though I'll keep my look up random info research methodology going. His second album has been repackaged a few times, but it's the one with Space Oddity.

If the first album is Bowie as Cabaret singer, this is his folk rock album. The story is Deram dropped him after the first album, and Space Oddity is the song his brain puked out when the people around him finally got him to write something and convince a new label to publish it. That's definitely a recurring theme in his biography. He's a songwriter/singer/what-have-you, but the people around him have to actually force him to get up and actually do something. You also get a very clear picture that, especially with these early albums, it's a "what's the state of mainstream music? Oh, sure I can do that too, here it is" kind of game. Remember how psych rock gave way to folk rock in all the 68-70 albums I talked about, how everybody wrote something about space in 1969, etc.? Whether it's true or not, that's where my perception of Bowie comes from; this is exactly the same as what everyone was doing, but with Bowie's own take on the subject.

Like the first album, the central theme sure seems to be the individual vs. the larger world he lives in, the one against the many. Major Tom, a Jesus figure, a shoplifter, an ex-boyfriend, all characters who suffer in whatever particular role the world at large looks to them to fulfill.

Basically, I think you have to actually join the cult of David Bowie and pretend he's a deity of some sort in order to get past the fact that he's endlessly singing "please don't join my cult, because I don't want to be your god." Maybe that's too specific. Maybe he's really just trying to point out the very real phenomenon of the most famous and successful people being cripplingly self-conscious and fighting a daily battle with their own inferiority complexes. Everyone forces you into a box, and there's nothing you can do to make that enjoyable.

Is that a fair assessment? I don't know, but once again none of it sounds like hack work. It doesn't sound clumsy or heavy-handed, nor does it sound egotistically whiny or pretentious. Every song sounds like he meant it, like he did it on purpose, this is just the subject matter he's interested in and he doesn't care if you like it or not. It's quite good, I don't hate any of it, but it feels very straightforward. There's no hidden message or agenda, no artistic ideal he's struggling to express, no sense of failure to achieve something.

If you haven't noticed, the better an album is the less I have to actually say about it. Every song is great, I can't agree with the critics when they single out Space Oddity and Cygnet Committee then throw the rest in the trash. Those songs don't stand out, none of the others are "less" in any way. None of the songs contradict his artistic perspective. He's 24 for 24 as far as Bottle is concerned.

210) 3 - The Man Who Sold The World

And then David Bowie got married. He and his wife would sit on the couch listening to the rest of the band jam, and every once in a while he'd get up and play some random chords or go to another room and write a whole set of lyrics in 10 minutes, and that's The Man Who Sold The World. It's his hard rock album that nobody cared about until Curt Cobain broke the rules of Unplugged to specifically use distortion for the solo on his cover of the title track, thus confusing an entire generation of children younger than me who thought Nirvana wrote it.

That's the standard rock history 101 description. Bottle will of course add that that's what mainstream music was doing: Led Zeppelin and Black Sabbath were trying to invent heavy metal without a trail map, and Bowie said "yeah, sure, I can do that too I guess, if you guys aren't going to leave me alone." We still haven't left that "David Bowie's version of it" feeling I keep mentioning. You may or may not know that nobody actually cared until Ziggy Stardust (still another album away); sure he had fans, but remember how nobody gave a crap about ZZ Top until Eliminator? Same difference.

The original cover art is a cartoon of a cowboy carrying a rifle in front of an actual insane asylum, but Bowie wasn't sure so he hired a photographer and really played up the lying on a couch context. Not surprisingly, the songs are about insanity and war and Lovecraft and technology, and if you're thinking Thomas Dolby is about 10 years younger than Bowie and this is about 10 years before Golden Age of Wireless then you're right here in the confusion seat with me, and that's why I think it might be a British thing, 'cause this is what Dolby would have been nostalgically channeling.

Regardless, Man Who Sold The World is considered pretty dark and bleak. I don't disagree, but it's not actually different from the first two albums. The studio experimentation has always been there, the individual/social antagonism is nothing new. Really, the only new thing happening is that now the direction the world is going is the problem and he doesn't want to be a part of it. Basically, as soon as you grow up you realize all the rules are gone and everybody is actually a monster, that's why all the things you remember from your childhood are creepy as hell.

There's that Christ figure again, but this time it's a computer that comes to the same conclusion: stop trying to create an idol to blame for your own foolish need to suffer.

The original title was Metrobolist (yes, a play on the famous Metropolis). I don't know, I think Man Who Sold The World is better. It fits with the "reality is pretty terrible and I'd rather live in my own imagination, at least I *know* that's not real" theme of Bowie's work so far.

If you're wondering where the stuff I don't like is, we haven't got there yet. We're in "classical period" Bowie now, and it's all quite enjoyable. Everybody good so far?

211) 4 - Hunky Dory

Hunky Dory. Enter the androgyny, the conflict between objective fame and having no idea what you're actually trying to do, humans are crap and it's time for a better species. This is full on piano-man and the spiders from mars pop-rock. Yeah, great, everything's fine.

It's still very much character driven, but those characters aren't really related to each other except in the context of "kids" vs "adults." That's what it's all been about so far.

I still don't think there's much subtext here, because the overriding sentiment is "the fact that your generation had to have the fight with the Nazis at all is pretty good evidence that we're garbage animals in general" and it's explicit. Forget your mind and we'll be free.

This is my wife's least favorite Bowie album, but I think it's fine. The silliness is maybe a little more obvious than before, but I think that's to be expected. Bowie's on record as saying this is the first album he actually got public feedback on; people actually told him this is good stuff. No wonder he kept this lineup and worked the reluctant messiah theme up to a fully coherent concept for the next one. It certainly does seem (even if it is in hindsight) that he'd been doing the same thing the whole time, he just couldn't figure out how to package it up to crack the public consciousness. Who would have thought that actually being a cohesive, straightforward rock band would connect with people? That's real crazy talk.

Ah crap, Bottle the Curmudgeon woke up. Isn't it possible, seeing as this is your first major label record, that maybe more than 120 people have heard it now. Maybe they saw your albums in actual shops and said "oh I guess he's famous now, I should at least give it a listen"? It doesn't matter how many critics say this is pretty good stuff if no one can actually see it sitting on the shelf. I don't like being sarcastic and grumpy about it, but yeah it costs millions of dollars to make music available to the masses. Somebody has to have those millions to spend, and they inevitably want it back with interest.

The irony, of course, is that's exactly what Bowie's previous 3 albums have railed against, and he's right on the cusp of becoming the rock idol he's been criticizing and saying he doesn't want to be. We're still miles away from the sellout music he publicly regretted making in the mid to late 80s, but we've finally reached the point where I can't tell if he's doing it on purpose or purposefully not noticing that he's doing it. Still all good songs though. I like all this stuff, even if I can't point to anything in particular. Changing his style and appearance is an integral and intentional part of every one of his albums, probably because the underlying concept is the same: I don't want to find the thing that makes me super famous, but I'm going to keep searching until I do, so here's album number 4.

212) 5 - The Rise and Fall of Ziggy Stardust

...And here it is. The thing that finally made David Bowie a superstar. Does anybody really care if Ziggy Stardust is Jimmy Hendrix? My question is why did it take 5 albums to figure out that actually *being* the character who the album is about would be what people needed to finally get it?

We're in David Bowie's version of Lord Sutch and Alice Cooper theatrics. His running joke during Hunky Dory was that he was "the actor" and all I can say is "duh?." Like any good Barthesian narrative, we get to say "hello saxophone, we look forward to where you'll take us next."

Aside: you've been reading your Barthes, right? This is mandatory narrative logic. His example is a book with a parrot I can't remember the name of at the moment (the book, not the parrot). His point was that there is no room for illogical occurrences in proper narrative. Introducing the existence of a parrot is mandatory if the parrot matters to the plot. If you didn't introduce the parrot, we'd call you a crappy writer.

Anywho, I said I couldn't tell if any of this is intentional or coincidental, and I can't anymore. Elaborate stage costumes and rock theatrics are the norm. Bowie's take on the subject just happens to be spectacular. Now he's a rock genius, and everybody's looking up his back catalogue and saying "holy micky mouse, he's been doing it the whole time." Graven image of a cow? Life On Mars? Bueller? Bueller?

Alien rock star with a message of love in the face of a doomed planet. The complete lack of subtext is driving me absolutely bonkers at this point. Every single thing is so on the nose it's like he just snorted us all up it.

Spoiler alert, he's going to go a little crazy, move to a foreign country for a while, sell out, rebel against that selling out, make weird crap that I personally don't like very much, finally make an album I do like very much, start planning his next project and die. It's like they gave him the script in 1967 and said the part is yours, have at it. Everyone else tried, but didn't have the determination to actually finish the movie.

He had to be making it up as he went, right? It's not logically possible to do all this stuff on purpose, is it? Am I the only one who finds it this hard to reconcile? You can't possibly map out your entire 50 year career in advance, you have to just go step by step asking yourself "what's the next logical step?," then doing it.

I'm getting ahead of myself. This album is awesome, but you already knew that. Bowie's first 5 albums is enough work for one day (and yes, I've been doing it all day long with breaks for lunch and dinner and talking to my family, and running to town for grapes). We'll see how many I get through tomorrow....

213) 6 - Aladdin Sane

Welcome to day two of my Bowie binge. Aladdin Sane is, in his own words, "Ziggy goes to America." It was written and recorded in the middle of the Ziggy Stardust tour. Like all the best coincidences, Bowie's brother had been diagnosed with schizophrenia, he felt both intrigued and appalled by America in general, he loved playing for thousands of people but hated the bus rides with complete strangers in between gigs. Not surprisingly, the album is a bizarre mixture of classic rock & roll, avant jazz, and technological noise. Also not surprisingly, the characters continue to be the casualties of society at large.

I haven't mentioned it before, but there's been an increasing sense that these seemingly incidental characters are actually the superheros, the stars, the real idols. I mention it now because it's right there at the surface. Ziggy Stardust is the famous person, but he's surrounded by people who don't know him, asking a truck driver for his autograph in a seeming post riot Detroit, and directly addressing the clash between the being on stage and the agitation of the endless wait between shows. He's very much the actor, and everything is a movie, but the making of the movie is a very different experience from watching the movie.

I like this album a lot. In part because I love the saxophones and boogie rock juxtaposed with the introspectively incoherent jazz piano, but also because it's a fractured take on a fractured subject. He's found the character, he's doing what that character is supposed to do, it's everything he already said it was going to be, and he's getting increasingly impatient to retire it and move on to the next thing. Art imitating life imitating art.

214) 7 - Diamond Dogs

Like all good method actors, Bowie found out that becoming the character drains you of your actual real-life personality. It's time to not be Ziggy anymore, but the nose candy isn't just an extravagant indulgence anymore either. Welp, time to fire the Spiders, set Orwell's 1984 to music and call it Diamond Dogs (I'm skipping Pin Ups because it's a cover album).

Orwell's estate wouldn't let him actually stage it as a musical, so he just reverted to his own post-apocalyptic version of everything. Thank goodness for the paranoia and anorexia of cocaine addiction, gives it that realistic touch you can't get anywhere else.

Everyone points out that this is his last glam rock album, but remember he's just moving with the trends and putting his stamp on it. But, like he's been doing all along, he's imagining a world in the near future that he doesn't want to be a part of and then going a different direction. Right now, he's still in his Rolling Stones phase and he's about to go Soul while everybody else goes punk.

But I'm getting ahead again. This is more great, now super trashy, rock and roll. Some say that's because Bowie isn't as good a lead guitarist as Mick Ronson. I disagree, it's 'cause he's coked to the gills and he's watching himself be the rockstar casualty he started scripting 7 years ago. This is the part of the movie where he hits rock bottom so that he can vanish for a while and "recover."

I'm not making that up, by the way, it's track 7, Rock 'n' Roll With Me. Now more than ever, he's very clearly writing these songs and singing them at himself, then living them out. I love this album, but we've reached the second sticking point in my familiarity with Bowie. The next few albums are uncharted territory for me, and I really don't know what to expect. I do know they lead to the 90s Bowie that I didn't much care for as a teenager. Guess we'll see how that plays out.

215) 8 - Young Americans

I can't improve upon the words of the man himself. Young Americans is "the squashed remains of ethnic music as it survives in the age of Muzak rock, written and sung by a white limey." In other words, Plastic Soul. Hello Luther Vandross and John Lennon.

Music first, lyrics after had always been the way Bowie preferred to work, but he took it to the next level on this record. He'd bring in funk and soul musicians, they'd work up the shape of a piece and once it was put together Bowie would write lyrics that night and they'd just record it live. The band didn't really know what a song was going to be until it was already done and they had moved on to the next one. He even invited the die-hard fans who congregated outside the studio in to hear previews of finished tracks.

Bowie wanted Norman Rockwell to do the cover art, but didn't want to wait 6 months for him to actually paint it, so scrap that; gotta get it done quick so I can run away for a while.

Obviously, running away from the direction rock was heading is the whole point, but it's another one of those good across the board albums. Once you're used to the style and mindset, it's great stuff. Different, but high quality. And right on cue, Fame tells us the super funk mixed with Krautrock is coming next....

216) 9 - Station To Station

I think Station to Station is best summed up by a pretend letter from Bowie to himself scribbled on a napkin that he didn't remember writing.

Ok. You're the Thin White Duke for this album. It's basically Pierrot, but it's really the way you looked in real life while recording Young Americans because your diet is coke and milk and peppers. It's not your fault we're in the middle of the neo-nazi renaissance and everyone's going to forget that you A) are the rebellious child of WWII, B) chose your side like 4 albums ago, and C) only pretend you're secretly a fascist. It's not just the cocaine talking (even though we both know you're doing enough of it to kill 3 elephants), LA is a god forsaken wasteland just like you said it would be, and you have to go back to Europe. You'll pretend you don't know it's going to happen ('cause you'll be doing like 3 other massive projects that won't see the light of day), but you'll end up in West Berlin and we'll get back on track at that point. Just stick with the paranoia and fear of fellow occultist Jimmy Page, and get through the worst of the slander 'cause sarcasm won't exist for like 5 more years, but you're so out of your mind you don't realize it. Gary Neumann will stand up for you, while you fall over and shatter like the snorting mirror you just dropped.

Note to self: I get the breakneck acceleration of these last couple albums, frantically rushing face first toward the brick wall finish line. It's making me antsy too. I need a break. Gimme like 6 hours before we delve into the Berlin Trilogy. Clear as mud?

217) 10 - Low

Ahhh, what a sweet sweet breath of fresh air Low is. For starters, it's a terrible album. He's never made one of those before. I love it.

No, those things aren't contradictory at all. He had the psychological car crash that was The Man Who Fell To Earth. The music he was writing because he thought he was the composer as well as the actor was rejected, exactly the way Fame told him it would be. He's got a drug habit to kick, France and Germany are way cheaper to live in for his self rehab (he doesn't like heroin so West Berlin's rising opioid epidemic is quite helpful in that regard), Iggy Pop and Brian Eno are there to help him explore things he sucks at (namely electronic soundscapes and dance). It was going to be a bad album any way he chose to approach it, and the fragments of brand-new experimentation are what he has to work with.

We're listening to the soundtrack of his life after all, and you can't have the comeback until you live through the fallout (maybe not coincidentally in the actual iconic epicenter of your WWII fueled neurosis, where nobody actually cares about a burned-out British pop star).

To recap, he's done the naive martyr, the reluctant martyr, the Indulgant, and the Crucified. Now we sift through the rubble and rebuild. We're all conscious of the bizarro absurdity of burned-out Bowie shaping Iggy Pop's transition to solo artist when the Stooges and Iggy were the model for the Spiders and Ziggy, right? Now they are sitting in the same German apartment looking at each other saying "I don't know, what do you think? Brian, what would you do if this were a Roxy song?"

So, obviously I say it's a terrible album but think it's great, and that should probably remind you of McCartney. That album had song fragments and instrumentals too. That album was rage fueled spite turned giddy DIY experimental glee. Freedom from the machinery of your own creation.

I swear, it's impossible to slough off that "here's Bowie's version, better than the original" feeling. You can't really predict what thing he's going to act out next, but you know it's going to be an award winningly convincing performance.

218) 11 - Heroes

Bleechggh. I thought we'd ease into it a little more smoothly than that. Who invited Fripp? Don't get me wrong, I adore Robert Fripp, but to quote 21 Pilots, "stay in your lane, boy."

I've made no secret of the fact that there's a whole segment of Bowie I hate. I could never describe it properly, I always felt it was like the music was doing one thing and Bowie was intentionally doing something different just to sound out of touch. No, it's the sheer SMUG. It's Bowie looking you dead in the eye and saying "HA! I WIN. I FIGURED OUT HOW TO MAKE YOU NOT LIKE ME." The gall and bile. The betrayal. "Heros is ironic." No shit, Sherlock.

I am pretty much the only person in the universe who hates it at this level, everybody else say "oh my god, spectacular, what a fruitful collaboration, Bowie's back and better than ever." Baaaarf!

It's not a smooth transition at all, it's an incredible hulk style "I told you so" album. It's bad narrative. It's crank phone calls acted out by puppets passing as entertainment. It's crashing the car on purpose to get your photo in the Sunday paper.

You're welcome to like it, but I seriously don't want to keep going. It's exactly like a Roman Polanski movie, the first half is great and you should seriously just walk out of the theater. I want to just skip ahead to Blackstar and be done with it all. But I can't, I'm a completionist. What horror movie youth hostel nightmare does Lodger have in store for me?

219) 12 - Lodger

No, see this is great. Why did I have to sit through Heroes? For one line in Fantastic Voyage? Just to remind yourself what the war was about and which side you wanted to be on? Completely unnecessary. Seriously could have just skipped from Low to Lodger.

It's his Britpop album. Oasis and Blur directly borrow from it. To say Bowie is ahead of his time is an understatement. He quantum leaped forward back at Diamond Dogs. What he's really doing is finding underground music scenes and being the mainstream frontrunner by about 5 to 7 years, before anybody else is actually willing to invest in "right now" music. I call it "here's what your younger brother is working on in his bedroom" music.

Now that we're moving forward again, please don't make another "Heroes." Let the crappy parts just be random moments I don't like, not monumental sculptures of rusty car parts on the courthouse lawn....

220) 13 - Scary Monsters

One more. That's all I've got in me. Remember, I've listened to 13 David Bowie albums in 2 days. Scary Monsters is a good stopping point though. We're back to proper Bowie writing songs about himself, but it's 1980 so it's got Japan, and we're about to watch the whole world give David Bowie levels of cocaine a try. Fripp is back, but he's being used in a proper context this time. We're still using Eno's compositional tarot cards, or pictionary I Ching, or whatever you want to call it, and Bowie's just yelling out other guitarists for Fripp to try to imitate, but he's had to take a different approach for himself and actually write this stuff down, edit it and, "compose."

What everybody seems to forget is that he's the adult now. They forget that it's all an ego trip that he's writing as he goes. Before he was the kid and didn't want to grow up to be a monster like all the other adults, so he invented new monsters, but now he *is* one so he has to point out all the repetition and "been there, done that" that he was there and doing.

There's a hint of that smugness from Heroes, but at least he's saying that he's still trying to run away. He's still saying he knows he's following the script, but looking for an escape route. He still says don't look up to me, I'm not the trendsetter you think I am. I'm not the hero, just another one of the monsters. It's very explicitly a recap album, and it's pretty thorough. Once again, after you wrap your head around which chapter of the story we're reading (think Robert Palmer, Phil Collins, creepy dad 80s), it's great. The sellout is coming, but I really, really don't know the next few albums so I'll be as surprised as you how I react to them.

Maybe tomorrow, I'm a little tired and we're only halfway through this epic. Or maybe in an hour I keep going. How am I supposed to know?

221) 14 - Let's Dance

Welcome to day 3. I'm back at work, so the deluge is going to slow down to a trickle.

You could just say Let's Dance is Scary Monsters part 2, but it's not really. Bowie changed record labels, so while it is a continuation of Scary Monsters musically (it's actually a refocusing of Young Americans, now with Stevie Ray Vaughn), it's the start of the real 80s Bowie that I don't actually have physical copies of; youtube it is.

Critics say this is the last "old Bowie" album, but it's the first hit songs album. To say Bowie now had 17 million dollars is a misunderstanding of corporate finances.

EMI started a new ledger called "David Bowie" and allotted $17.whatever-million to it as working capital. Bowie's new job was to make a profit from that by being David Bowie. He hired Nile Rogers, said "Darling, make me some hit records" a lot, and most everyone thinks it's crap. I didn't invent my earlier Phil Collins comparison, that's exactly the name Bowie used to describe this period of his career.

They are still working with material from the Berlin period, and first on the list of hits is China Girl, from Iggy Pop's album. Nile assumed it was about doing speedballs (cocaine and heroin at the same time), so that's why Bowie's version sounds like a Studio 54 party. Iggy of course wrote it about an actual person, Kuelan Nguyen.

Why does he need hit records? Well, nobody liked the "solo" albums he made, and the Tin Machine side project was just a tangential creative outlet to make himself happy. Bowie proper is its own subsidiary corporation now. It's not 17M in Bowie's bank account, it's 17M to pay to producers and studios and musicians and marketing and TV time and fly around the world to do all this brand stuff. Every penny gets recouped before Bowie gets his first penny.

Obviously, I'm at work and I can't really listen to it like the others at the moment, but none of this is bad in my opinion. It's undeniably 80s, or what the 80s would become, because Bowie actually lives 5 years ahead of schedule. I don't get the embarrassment about it, it might not sound like he wanted it to sound, but it's still listenable to me. Modern Love is a great song, and the faux disco vibes don't bother me at all.

Except for 1 thing. You know how Bowie's voice just kind of floats along in the verses of the title track, Let's Dance? Like he's not really connected anymore? That's the Bowie I don't like. That's what I hated about Heroes.

Honestly, I hear this as the right way to do "Heroes." I suspect, however, the next couple won't be as enjoyable for me, but I've been wrong a time or two. Who knows?

222) 15 - Tonight

Tonight. Meh. Half of it is fine, half of it is terrible. Loving The Alien and I Keep Forgetting and Neighborhood

Threat and Dancing With The Big Boys are all fine, but he should have never waded into reggae.

Here's what's happening in my head. The music is doing its thing, and it's perfectly fine, but Bowie starts doing this terrible bobble-headed Reno nightclub lounge singer thing, and it feels like cigarette burns in cheap red polyester, dingy shag carpeting, Twin Peaks Red Room in Reverse creepy.

Plus, now he's thinking about "the fans." That's a recipe for suck because the fans you think you're writing for aren't your actual fans. I know it's going to get worse, but maybe there's some hidden good stuff? Maybe?

223) 16 - Never Let Me Down

I was actually feeling pretty good about the first two tracks of Never Let Me Down. Then he did that low register lounge thing and proceeded to do exactly that.

This is the worst of the spandex workout unitard, Paula Abdul, 80s. It sounds like 1987, and that's a problem. 20 years, but for the first time he's not ahead of the crowd. This is the crowd. For Bowie, this is stale. Let's call it like it is. This is purple headband, dancing in the street, workout video music. I've got nothing else to say, he's allowed to be embarrassed by this one.

224) 17 - Black Tie White Noise

Then David Bowie woke up after a 6-year nap, got married again, and kind of wrote the music for the after party: Bowie's take on House.

I seriously didn't know this album existed, and a quick glance at the charts of 1993 is enough to know why. This was the year of In Utero, Counting Crows, Onyx's Slam, Janet Jackson's sexy comeback, Lenny Kravitz, the most famous Meat Loaf song.

Black Tie White Noise seems intentionally underground and obscure by comparison. You know what he did with the break? He learned to play the saxophone himself (he'd almost been proud of not playing any part of the music before).

You know what else? It's good. I'm as shocked as you, this is freakin' good. He's using his full vocal range, but he's not doing the airport lounge singer shtick. It's high-end nightclub, art dance, Ace of Bass type stuff, but yeah I'm totally on board. It's posh but it's not pretentious. It really is David Bowie's take on the dance club dj set, and I could listen to this every day.

I'll go back to hard copies after this, but consider Black Tie White Noise exactly what I was hoping I would find. Great stuff.

225) 18 - 1.outside

I'm mildly trepidatious about 1. Outside. It's supposedly his return to rock, his return to making this crap up on the fly in the studio. Buuuut, Eno's back with his uno cards, and we're in David Lynchian, Lost Highway, insane asylum territory again (3 years ahead of schedule, if anybody's keeping track). The song "I'm Deranged" was my first experience with the great music/floating hologram of David Bowie's 3rd quarter. I didn't like it then, I didn't like where it came from, and the casting couch is full of uncomfortably familiar faces. Maybe I'm wrong, and I'll "get it" this time around?

Oh, ok, it's an actual story, a fake diary to not be a boring real-life diary of a touring musician, the product of actually visiting an asylum. He's back to being interested in the fringe, not the center of it all (that's long-range foreshadowing, wink). There's definitely an industrial undercurrent I didn't know he explored (again, didn't know this album existed). Why didn't I know about it? Probably because it's very Thrill Kill Kult analogous and I was clearly interested in the same underground happenings as Bowie, not actual Bowie.

Yeah, I totally get that detached feeling in this context. It's not Vegas crooner this time. In the real world I started talking about Derrida for no apparent reason, and it turns out now is why. Stupid fake psychic subconscious guiding me along. It's a new take on "alien." It really is a standing beside yourself, institutional kind of horrifying.

I really like this. It's the right balance of sleazy and horrifying, making it extremely horrifying. Yeah, this is straight up industrial rock, and if you don't believe me jump directly to track 6, "Hallo Spaceboy." This is my home turf, no wonder the mainstream didn't care, and us weirdos never bothered to look into it. Why would the goth kids care about Bowie? I wish I had, for this one at least. Definitely check this one out if you've never heard it. It's dark and beautiful and terrifying, and I'll definitely be listening to it again and again.

226) 19 - Earthling

Finally, I get Earthling! Seriously, I just couldn't understand Bowie's drum and bass album. It's that standard tandem album broken up by the inconvenience of touring we've heard at least 3 times now.

The dark industrial of 1.outside obviously morphs into the hardcore d&b, jungle, borderline Prodigy sounding rave music.

Yeah, 3 for 3. These albums connect like they never did before. Everybody says it really was 70s Bowie in the studio again, just going for it, and happy, and making it happen. I can tell, he's filtered all the bad parts out. This is exciting stuff, every bit as exciting as Ziggy or Diamond Dogs were in their own contexts. I'm not ashamed of hating it before, I'm just very happy that it's finally connecting. The thread of avant-jazz sax and piano under all these albums is not unnoticed either.

I know we've been here before, I get excited and then Bowie blows it. Even if that does happen again, it can't be as bad as the first two times. Partly because we're close to the end, but mostly because the whole project was worth it just to connect with these albums in a way I couldn't before. I'm super thrilled.

227) 20 - Hours

Hello day 4, Hours is the drive to work soundtrack. This is very clearly Bowie's alternative rock album. Not the happy side of alternative (like that's a thing, pfffft), the sleepily lethargic technological side. It's the same place Radiohead went, and then Muse, and all those unhappy 20-somethings born in the computer age.

It was the first downloadable mainstream album ever, born from a video game project. It's also the last entry in the EMI ledger, and he'll take another extended break.

I very much like it, but it has that "end of an era" feeling. It's not exciting, but it's not supposed to be. Not stale, just run down. I'm good with that.

228) 21 - Heathen

So, we've officially made it to the 21st century. Bowie lives in New York, he's got some old friends and some new friends (all famous, every Bowie album is pretty much a supergroup), and they are making their typical angsty Bowie in New York kind of album. It's a comeback album, because we left off at the standard Bowie imagines where society at large is headed (spoiler alert, it's war and death and pointless destruction), and he doesn't want to be on that bus (he's already been on that bus, because he lives ahead of us, remember).

The recording is pretty much done, and wouldn't you know it some lunatic crazy people fly airplanes into the World Trade Center, so now he has to mix and master and distribute this premanatory apocalyptic new stuff while the city around him sifts through the rubble.

Right place, right time is almost always coincidence. That's because whatever came out today was written basically a year ago. There's no such thing as "psychic," just people who are very in tune with the way a particular Zeitgeist will logically unfold. Humans, for all their apparent instability and chaos, are inherently logical creatures. If we're going down, we're going down with gusto. Here's Heathen, for our lunch-nap dining displeasure.

You know the airplane scene in Hackers where Orbital's Halcyon + On + On starts playing as he looks out over the clouds. Yeah, it could just as easily have been the song Sunday. Cactus sounds like a leftover Blur song. Oooh, that haunting 40s nostalgia of Slip Away is just gorgeous.

I won't spoil the rest of the joy of hearing them for yourself. Well, other than to say it's a split personality album like all the rest. America vs. Europe, reminiscence vs. foreboding unease, everything is the same and everything is different, I lived it all before but knowing that doesn't change the experience of living it again, and more. It's a very full and complex piece of art, coincidentally published at a time when the whole world was ready to hear it (maybe misunderstand it slightly; it's about Bowie, not the world). An album for an America that didn't exist yet, but inevitably would. Zeitgeist.

229) 22 - Reality

Reality check. Bowie's been living and dying and resurrecting and doing it all over again for ever. It's time to retire. So, right on the heels of Heathen he makes his retrospective retirement spectacular.

Why? Because reality is over. The world finally caught up with Bowie. Existence is just a stream of digital factoids and humans have no ability to reconcile any of it into a coherent meaningful existence. There's no ego to build out of that, it means Bowie really is nothing more than his discography. There's no knowledge anymore. He has to just wait. And wait he does, for 10 years. But that's in the future. Where are we now?

Art rock. The splotchy, colorful, scribbly, weird fonts and out of order typesetting kind of art rock. The Picasso meets Warhol wacky postmodern revival. We reinvented a word for it, that word is quirky.

New songs, very old songs (he'd been nursing "Disco King" since the 70s, but it never found a home until now). Now, I've really thought about it and I don't think I'm making this up: this album is the composed death of David Bowie. It's hospital clean, he's sewed up all the wounds and the smell of freshly applied antiseptic floats on the air. Ben Gibbard has started the night shift behind the wheel of the death cab, my friends of friends the Starlight Mints are shaking hands with surrealism. There's no underground anymore, so there's no mainstream either.

Time to retire, with all these flashing lights and blurry images. We want an encore, but it sure sounded like he wasn't going to do one. By the end you get a very clear sense that the next character David Bowie was going to inhabit was himself, at home, no more pretend, no more show, no more ego.

So, he undoes his bow tie, pours a double scotch, and sings a song to death itself in his best Sinatra impersonation. Man, Bring Me The Disco King really is an amazing finale. We know he'll make 2 more albums, but we didn't know that then. This was the end, and he did it in style.

230) 23 - The Next Day

Then 10 years later, like he was breaking double-secret probation for the occasion of his 66th birthday, Bowie made another album. He cheekily called it The Next Day, and if you've keyed in on my tendency to get ahead of myself, the first single asked Where Are We Now?

Unlike everyone else, I giggle and clap at whiting out the cover of Heroes. It's meant to "subvert" that iconic album as "an obliteration of the past," and obviously I couldn't be happier, I hate that album.

And for 2013, Bowie gives us trash rock. The world is garbage (you all know that's exactly how I felt 'cause we moved to Iowa in 2012 while he was writing it). There's a little bit of subtext, in that Bowie is implying it's garbage because he wasn't making albums, but that's clearly the joke.

I remember when the video for The Stars came out and it was awesome. We had celebrities again, but they were trash. This whole album has that "Bowie's version is better vibe." We are all real people, don't worship the worst of the fakers for a cheap thrill. The humor has a darker side, though. It's the real sadness of mortality. The past is dead, and I will be too. I don't know when, but I'll keep going until there's no more day and night for me.

The thing we've learned from all of this is that Bowie knows what he's doing, and though he still has so many things to say, he is waiting to die for real this time. We couldn't know that, he'd always been saying it so it just felt like normal split personality Bowie.

There was a group of critics who call it mediocre, and to that I would say yes there is a context in which this album is mediocre. If you listen to it as just an album from 2013, then it's meh; not that spectacular, merely good enough against the background garbage that is his subject matter to garner some obvious hyperbole. If, however, you listen to it like I just did, as the "I can't take it anymore" outburst of a retired superstar, then it's pretty great. If you've got the entire discography in your head, it's pretty obvious that the world at that moment was acting like something David Bowie has an opinion about. If you listen to it at face value, it's pretty freakin' sad and you know that he's going to wait until he knows he's dying to make the next one. You're not psychic though, so feel what you feel. Any kind of rock in the wasteland of 2013 was worth trying to like from my point of view. Like I've said before, once the context finally clicks, you'll realize it's high quality across the board.

231) 24 - Blackstar
Shhhhhh.

232) Epilogue
I don't do April Fool's Day. Mostly that's because I live in a permanent state of post-ironic confusion. Every conversation with me is like:

Me: [states piece of information that will be important for person in the near future]
Person: are you shitting me?
Me: no.

I just spent the last 5 days listening to David Bowie's entire studio discography (minus Pin Ups), and boy are my arms tired. My first time around, I liked early Bowie a lot. Then, as with all things, I went off in my own direction, and paid no attention to him for 20+ years. Then he made Blackstar (which I bought as a present for my wife, 'cause she likes Bowie) and died two days after it was released. It's a fantastic album, and I've known I needed to tackle this enormous project for quite a while.

What I found out was that 1) Bowie really was awesome, 2) there are only 3 albums I don't like, and 3) I'm actually a lot like Bowie (in my own perception of myself).

Bowie made movies. Some of them were actual movies, but some of them only manifested themselves as a recording project, a tour, and a moving on to the next project. He imagined what kind of character he could play, learned to live in that character for a couple years with an ensemble cast of current and future superstars, then started over again. Some of those characters were really nasty. All of those characters were commentary on the world he lived in and where it might lead us in the next few years.

In one way or another, everything he did boils down to a deep look at conflict. More specifically, the kind of social and political conflicts that created the Second World War: the conflict between order and chaos, the conflict between what you want and what you have to do to obtain it.

Books and books and books could be written about this stuff. You could go deep into the analytical and philosophical rabbit hole. You can approach his work in any way you want and get something out of it (good or bad), but I think the core theme is "history repeats itself." Or, to quote the man himself, "Same old thing in brand new drag."

This was an exhausting project. I both do and do not recommend trying it yourself. Maybe don't try to cram all 24 into 4 days. Pace yourself.

233) Offspring - Smash

Let's see if we can squeeze in an album while my cheesecake bakes.

Ignition is my favorite Offspring album, but it may or may not have died an unsavory rodent induced death in the cd player in my garage. I still have Smash, though. My friends Chris and Sam and I used to listen to this and Green Day and other analogous things while we were playing pool, or cruising around Bethany late at night like little hooligans (we're big retired hooligans now, but that's beside the point). Bad Habit is still the official road-rage anthem, as far as I know.

I'm not going to pretend that I care about Offspring past Ixnay On The Hombre (my t-shirt from that concert has mostly peeled away into oblivion at this point) but their early stuff is incredible. They deserved to be 1/5 of the 90s punk revival. They don't appear to like LA very much, and I can't say I blame 'em. It sounds like a terrible place. I think I was in one of their airports once or twice but I didn't get brutalized, so I can't really comment.

Sweet Euterpe, what a glorious collection of harmonic vibrations plucked from the universal quantum wave field. I could start an Offspring tribute band tomorrow, that's how engrained in my brain this album is (I dare you to explain the spelling change for the past tense of the verb ingrain; I turns to e because screw it I quit).

Damnit, timer went off. I don't want crunchy cheesecake for breakfast tomorrow. Hold on, be right back...

... ok, I'm back. All 5 bands are important in their own way, but Smash was the first Gold record for Epitaph, now quintuple platinum or some ridiculous figure (I probably accounted for three of them because I've dropped a lot of CDs in my time on this planet), so it's undeniably praiseworthy. Not bad for a bleach-headed microbiologist in training (he finished his PhD in 2017). You may or may not know that quite a few of us punks are highly educated, with advanced degrees in something or other (too bad I didn't have platinum selling album royalties to pay for finishing mine, har har).

Smash didn't make an impression for its family friendly lullaby ballads. It's loud and fast and the songs are so incredibly scream along pleasing to hear, even for the ten-thousandth time. They recommend a glass of wine, but I've secretly replaced Bottle's coca-cola for apple-cherry juice (folgers crystals style), and whaddya know, Mikey likes it.

234) Weezer

Somebody sent me a super secret awesome thing today, and I'm so stoked.

I don't think I've ever said that phrase out loud before, but as soon as I formed the words Weezer's first album started playing in my head. Then, because my brain doesn't simply accept a thought, I started thinking we did The White Album, The Brown Album, The Black Album, so yeah, The Blue Album. But then, there's STP's Purple. Crud, that just leads to albums whose titles aren't on the actual album, so we have to include Pearl Jam's Vs. and we're right back to six degrees of conflict with David Bacon, I mean Bowie (go ahead count 'em). But again, as last night's album taught us, you gotta keep 'em separated.

The Blue Album. I'm not ashamed to say I don't care about anything after it. From Pinkerton to last years' cover of Africa with Weird Al, I know exactly the song Hash Pipe. Give Rivers Cuomo (pictured here slightly left of center) his 20-million dollars and say "thank you" for me.

When I was quarantined with mono (of the Nucleosis Monos) [that's a dumb rhetorical joke that only I find humorous, but try as I might I couldn't find any way to reference Epstein-Barr, and believe me I tried] for what felt like 17 years (but was probably only 3 or 4 weeks) in 9th grade, I basically did only 3 things: eat rotini, drink Earl Grey tea, and listen to Weezer. Whew, that was more parenthetical that topical (like this whole essay).

This is another sing along because every song is head bobbingly amazing. This is like top ten in the history of recorded music. If you can't enjoy every single second of this album, you're an uncultured swine. I'm kidding (I'm not kidding).

As you can tell, either the ADD is working overtime, or there's not enough rum in this drink to shut the p(nmi)t up. I'm tired of being snarky old Bottle, so moderately spastic p(nmi)t will have to suffice.

Did you know Rivers wanted to be a professional soccer player like his hero, Maurice Larcange. Sadly, Rivers was a crummy accordion player, so he settled for playing power chords in a band like the rest of us plebes. That's a joke, I say, that's a joke, son, as my hero Foghorn Leghorn used to say.

I guess what I'm trying to tell you is I got an electric guitar, I play my stupid songs, I write these stupid words, and I love everyone. I've also got cheesecake, but you already knew that. Have a nice weekend playing with your imaginary friends. Mine are going to help me record a new piece of music. Oh no, I've said too much (I haven't said enough), but you have the listening schedule for the rest of the weekend. Feel free to get a head start.

235) Stone Temple Pilots - Purple

Stone Temple Pilots managed to hold my attention for 3 albums, but I never really cared about any of Scott Weiland's other bands after they booted him. He basically lived his life like the Thin White Duke, an irritatingly narcotic personality. All 3 or their first run albums are great in their own way, but Puple is my favorite.

I've said before that I don't consider grunge an actual genre, and I really don't. I will however accept it as a qualifying adjective. Like Nirvana is a grungy version of the Ramones, Pearl Jam is grungy arena rock, STP are a grungy Rolling Stones. Alternative rock is my preferred description, because they present alternative viewpoints, explore generally taboo subjects, and exude a "this is what we are, take it or leave it" attitude.

Why are we in mid 90s heavyweights of flannel territory? Well Bowie was all cocaine and so was Scott. Maybe I'll run out of direct Bowie influences on the music I choose, but that project was so massively all-consuming that the ripples will carry on for quite a while. I'm highly susceptible to these kinds of haphazard chains of thought (like I'm sure you never noticed, huh?).

I should do a cocaine vs. heroin amongst musicians comparison sometime. That's like a graduate level seminar in its own right.

STP is probably the most compositionally complex of this weekend's bands. The DeLeo brothers played highly harmonically and rhythmically adventurous music that somehow maintained an incredible sense of cohesion. STP has an almost jazz trio feel in comparison to their peers. It's rock, but somehow much more than rock; it feels improvised, but so coherent that it obviously can't be, this is thoroughly composed and highly structured but so far beyond generic that it seems almost magical. Not one single note sounds haphazard or out of place. Not surprisingly, Brenden O'Brien is the producer behind all of the biggest stuff from this period and STP, Pearl Jam, Black Crows, and Red Hot Chili Peppers made him one of the go to guys for about a decade. He's like the evil corporate mirror doppelganger of Steve Albini who somehow manages to make records sound amazing in spite of how goddamned loud they're going to get mastered.

One of the magical things about these (dare I say) Post-Nirvana bands is that they all inject a self-deprecatingly humorous commentary on how ridiculous it is that they are making huge corporate mainstream albums. This requires a new paragraph with some historical context.

Welcome to the new paragraph (that's a joke on Jello Biafra's disclaimer for Offspring's Ixnay). Brett Gurewitz didn't originally want to sign Offspring. Buuuuut, he's a record label, he heard Offspring's first album published by soon to be defunct Nemesis, heard Butch Vig's dumb luck in engineering THE NEW THING, put two and two together and said "I don't want to be poor anymore." Weezer didn't even have to go through the hassle of being undiscovered, and tomorrow's Pearl Jam only needed Eddie Vedder to move from LA to Seattle before the remnants of Mother Love Bone got their advance.

They all knew they were riding the profit train to hate-my-corporate-overlords-ville and they put in ridiculous intros and spoken sections about parties you don't want to go to and jokes about this record being "like Johnny Mathis." It's a joke, so we might as well have fun while we're being the butt of it. I eat it up like birthday cake on a random Tuesday.

Even as obtuse as "Kitchenware and Candybars" is, I know full well the actual song is a tongue in cheek homage to Something In The Way from Nevermind. Cellos and being a homeless loser on the last track? Subtle reminders that you yourself are bipolar, but not suicidal. You're telling me you seriously didn't notice? I told you, Weiland was a prick.

Regardless, the unnamed Purple (what's the title? Neverind) is a fantastic album of great songs. You have to accept that there's some real nastiness lurking underneath the lyrical obscurity, but once you do it's fascinating to hear it play out.

236) Pearl Jam - Vs.

I like Pearl Jam's first three albums, but I just couldn't get into No Code, or any of their stuff with Neil Young, or anything after. Their second album is my favorite. I have a weird thing about loving second albums, and Vs. might be a good indication why.

The story goes like this: Ten was a huge deal. They are famous. They start out jamming with their new drummer for the second album, but Brenden O'Brien moves them to high end LA. Eddie Vedder, being the method actor he really is, can't stand it because A) it's too nice, B) that makes it impossible to get into the insanely negative head space he writes from, and C) how is any of that rock and roll?

Long story short, he starts living in his truck and his band mates try to make it as miserable an experience as possible for him, and everybody is super excited because once he actually gets some lyrics penned down, they're a good enough improvisational jam band to just go wherever he takes them. The end result, in their own words, is HEAVY. Ten wasn't a paddle-boat ride across a placid pond, but it was mentally and expressively very restrictive, because it was very much an already finished work of Vedder's unsavory subject matter. These songs are still negative, but the narratives lend themselves to much wider musical possibilities; punk, ballads, some funky stuff like they used to play, you get the idea.

Let's be honest, Ten is a little too much to talk about even for the moderate level of intellectual freedom I've given this project, and you definitely don't want to read what I might have to say about it. But child abuse, learning disabilities, rats being better than people, sheltered small town living, that's pretty safe subject matter.

If Purple sounded cerebral and well thought out, this sounds like four guys smashing their faces into the wall while their singer has a seizure. Yeah, they are just letting it all spew out into the room. It's fantastic. Even the slower stuff sounds made up on the spot, just a couple chords and everybody following Vedder's lead when it's time for the chorus or shift. You can't compose that feeling, it's full on winging it captured by microphones; albeit well placed ones.

This is not an album with musical coherence. You can tell that they made it one song at a time, not in any order. What holds the whole thing together is a common anger and dispair; this stuff is bad and there's nothing we can do to fix it except just rage until we're too exhausted to think anymore. It's the kind of heavy that doesn't really exist outside of sludge metal like Crowbar or the deep cuts of Pantera. Believable anguish is a whole lot harder to really explore than zombies and devils and sensational gore.

Amazingly, everything here is likable, catchy, singalong-able. It feels like a collective experience, these guys just happen to be the voice for it. That feeling starts to fade with Vitology, but it's very much true for Vs.

Quite literally, the band didn't want to be famous, they wanted to get through being a blip on the mainstream radar and get back to just being a self-contained rock band. No more videos, no release parties, stop jacking up the price of tickets, and please forget about us as celebrities. They just released a new album. I haven't heard it yet, but they seem much happier after exiting the brightest of media spotlights. Grungiest arena rockers I know.

237) CST 470 - Nielsen/Brubeck

I feel like I've already used up most of my allotted wordy-words today, so let's just enjoy this George Nielsen/Dave Brubeck split. Bop and Cool Jazz. CST 470 if you're a catalogue kind of guy. Very nice.

Now that I look, it's not on youtube anywhere. Give me an hour or so...

Geez, that only took a minor eternity. It's like there's a teenager hogging our upload stream with video game commentary, or something.

Anywho, please enjoy some cool jazz on me. I filtered out the usb squeal, but left the clicks and pops for that authenticity you've come to expect.

238) Seether - *Disclaimer

South Africa has given us some amazing things. Die Antwoord, Charlize Theron, an alternate reality where Nelson Mandela died in prison and people's names are spelled differently, Leonardo DiCaprio's abysmal accent work, but they also gave us the musical venereal disease that is Seether. Seether, the International Nickelback.

*Disclaimer: You think I'm going to be biased. Obviously, I hated it the first time around and I haven't listened to this album in decades, but I am always willing to be wrong. However, before we start I'll tell you that I have absolutely no problem with their first hit single "Fine Again." Perfectly lovely song. Sure, I may have enjoyed making fun of the final vocal cadence. Who didn't? Let's all listen to it with fresh ears.

We're going to ignore the fact that I put it in my computer, and my computer vomited it back out immediately. I have to reach around and put them in backward, and it actually happens a lot. Pure coincidence.

Not a coincidence, this thing was produced with 10 different potential faces on the cover, I got shaved head asian guy. They tell me there's an edited version, but I like swear words. Press play.

Whaaaaaat? Gasoline starts us off with what I assume is a gender reversed description of Lisa "Left Eye" Lopez's (she was "the rapper" in TLC) arson trial. I mean, you're intentionally demeaning her so it seems appropriate that she hates you. I'm trying to conceptualize it, but you treat her like crap because she pretends to be a starlet, but she's actually horrible so it's totally normal? Everything about this song is gross.

How is the first lyric of a song called "69 Tea" (which by the way is stupid all by itself) about being in an insane asylum?!? Did you yahtzee all of the song titles or something? Well, at least you don't care that you're lost. That's something.

Ok, we need to take a moment to talk about something I find absolutely unacceptable in pop music (which is what this is, it's not rock or metal, it's pop), and that is the word "pills." The word pills makes me think of that episode of Saved by the Bell, where Jesse was taking diet pills so she could study for the SATs. I am a discerning drugs in music listener and you better be specific. Speed, hypnotics, advil? And what does any of that have to do with oral sex, or caffeinated beverages?

Yeah, "Fine Again" is great. I could listen to this awesome song 25 times in a row and still function like a human being. It's right next to Finger 11's "Suffocate" on my broody 90s mental anguish mix-tape. Good job guys, thumbs up.

Speaking of Finger 11, that's a diarrhea bass line on Needles. And "needles" is some kind of metaphor, but since I can't figure out who or what the subject of the song is to begin with, it's just jibber-jabber. Is the needle singing the song, who is he hurting, how is he already dead?

Do you know that I'm lying when I say that I'm wondering if you know I'm lying about wondering if you've already killed someone? Oh, you're going to kill me now? Thanks "Driven Under," that helped.

I don't even have a joke about "Pride," it's just nonsense.

Is "Sympathetic" a song about the suicide note he's going to write? No really, is it? I seriously can't figure this nonsense out.

That's a goddamned Green Day joke! No, screw you guys. Next song.

Baaaarf! Guitars shouldn't sound like that. I can't do it. I literally pulled my headphones off and went for a smoke break.

Don't try to pass it off as a "lost in translation kind of thing." Half of Die Antwoord is in Afrikaans and I understand what they are trying to say. This is buzz-word WASPy parents listening though the bedroom door fake emo garbage.

7 albums? Are you kidding me? Are there no other South African alternative rock/metal bands? None? This is it? I

hate Puddle of Mud, but I'd rather listen to them any day. At least they clearly don't take themselves seriously.

No stars. Hate it. And super thanks to my friend Sarah for suggesting this brief moment of delightful suffering!

239) The Black Dahlia Murder - Unhallowed

Tonight's album is going to hurt a little (assuming you actually go listen to it). That's because you don't like death metal. You don't think screaming and growling is an acceptable use of a vocalist's instrument. You think there are certain things no one should write songs about.

So, tonight we'll turn the tables. The Black Dahlia Murder's 2003 debut, Unhallowed. Cannibalism and death and demons and anything you can think of that might make Tipper Gore's skin crawl. But, as I've tried to teach my children, sticks and stones may break my bones, so please don't throw them at me.

It's just music. Yeah, if you forget that it's just music then you might turn into a psychopath, but the same can be said about two people fist-fighting over the last bag of potato chips.

More to the point, I find sexism and racism and hypocrisy appalling, but that's all the last two firing brain cells of every 1 out of 3 people I see in a day (in real life, or on TV, or on the albums I've talked about) can seem to produce. I listen to it and think up clever ways to tell you it's garbage.

Don't think of it as screaming, think of it as a highly refined and methodically practiced vocal technique meant to convey anger and produce fear (you can't wing it if you want to talk to your friends tomorrow, or do 27 interviews to promote your concert that night). Some people are good at it, some people sound ridiculous. I consider this one pretty good, because Trevor Strnad is one of the very few people interested in bridging the Atlantic Ocean's distance between American Death Metal growls and Scandanavian Black Metal shrieking.

You're supposed to feel uncomfortable, or at least recognize that it's supposed to make you feel uncomfortable. It's art. Evaluate it. They work just as hard to do a good job as Twang Smackman and the Banjoettes, and I have no doubt you noticed that not once did I insult anyone from Seether's musicianship or personal life last night. I insulted their content.

240) Go Gos v Bangels

I know what question you've been dying to ask this beardly visage. You want to know which greatest hits album from 1990 is, well, the greatest; Go Gos or Bangels?

Geez, that's a tough one to call. I mean, they represent different worlds, right? The Go Gos are hanging out at the mall with their friends shopping for funky hats, while the Bangels are secretly stealing their boyfriend and going to the drive-in. Contradicting my rule that it's always Chad's fault, it's not Chad's fault. Chad likes rock and roll more than new wave inspired pop. We all knew Chad was a jerk, and it only makes sense that he gets a little bad karma heartbreak of his own to chew on when it's all said and done.

I'm not an image guy, but it's no secret that the Go Gos are "cute" while the Bangels are "sultry." The Go Gos are Claire's Boutique, the Bangels are the makeup counter at Nordstrom. If you're asking me to choose between Belinda and Susannah, I can't. I'm not cool enough for either of them.

What I can do is make up some ridiculous comparisons and end up saying they're both awesome. Let's see how that plays out.

They both have 14 songs, they both sing about a mildly embarrasing dance craze, and they both have ballads. No clear winner in the prelims. Susannah Hoffs has an incredibly interesting breathy voice, but I like Belinda Carlisle's almost nasal punk rasp just as much. A few songs on each are a little silly, but nothing I would call bad or nonsense. It's all catchy, it just depends what kind of mood you're in that day. They're both great, unless you just want to forget the entire 1980s decade altogether. There, I can't help you.

241) Alice In Chains - Dirt

Tonight, it's Alice In Chains' second album, Dirt. It's about the Egyptian goddess Sekhmet, the lion headed daughter of Ra whose fiery breath shears the land to desert. I'm joking, it's about Layne Staley's herion addiction, and how that basically defined him as a person. It's about other things too, but it's an explicitly autobiographical album from the perspective of a serious junkie.

It's also a real-world coincidence kind of album. Remember how Bowie's Heathen was interrupted by September 11? Well, AIC were tuning their guitars when the verdict of the Rodney King trial was being read, and LA decided it was time to have a riot. Back up. I hate that phrase, police officers were the defendents on trial and they were excused from punishment for unnecessarily beating the shit out of him, which they were filmed doing. Eventually, two of them saw the reverse angle of prison. Needless to say, Jerry Cantrell's afternoon run to the gas station for beer was a little more frightening than he expected, so they picked up their friend Tom from Slayer and hid out in the desert for a week before starting to record.

This isn't grunge either. It's alternative metal... fine, grungy alternative metal if you're just unable to stop chasing that dragon. His relationships are crap, his dad's nickname really was "Rooster" during the Vietnam not officially a War, and the second half is Layne's own journey from naive acupuncturist to a guy who wished he wasn't addicted to heroin anymore. If we're being honest, his equally alcoholic bandmates probably weren't the most stable of support systems. Not bad kids, just stupid ones, as Axl so succinctly put it.

If there's a moral to the story of Dirt, it's that we're all pretty good at trying to kill ourselves, and that's pointless considering we're going to die anyway. They never meant this album to be a glorification of how miserable they really were, and they didn't like it when fans bragged about how high *they* were while asking for autographs. More tragically, that's not an ironic situation. It's the reality of idiotic reverse pathology: telling people how horrible something is just makes them want to do it more.

242) 3rd Bass - Derelicts of Dialect

Suddenly, over the loudspeaker I heard an album that I think is spectacular. If you remember 3rd Bass at all, it's going to be their hit "Pop Goes the Weasle," a dis track making it very clear that 3rd Bass doesn't want you to put them anywhere in the same paragraph as Vanilla Ice, unless like I'm doing, you're making it clear they thought he was an embarrassment to humanity at large. Don't worry, they equally hated MC Hammer.

You need a proper historical context for this album. Hip-hop came from the Bronx. It's the melting pot of Jamaican turntablists, clever word play, graffiti, looking fly, and jumping up and down like teenagers do with their black/white/latino/jewish/whatever friends who are equally stuck in the inner-city. Two turntables, some old funk and soul and jazz records, a microphone, and your hype-man showing off some cool new dance moves. Everyody had something to like, because everybody was involved.

Naturally, some coked up white guys in the 80s with ugly ties to match their ugly personalities said "we can make a lot of money if we push this already popular scene into the mainstream, and they put their lawyers to work figuring out how to water it down, bottle it up, and scrape 90% off the top.

Meanwhile, a couple kids who loved it to begin with decided to start their own label in their dorm room and called it Def Jam. Those kids were Russell Simmons and Rick Rubin. I don't want to do a whole Def Jam history, so I'll just kind of gloss through the relevant chain of events.

Russell and Rick invested their time, and energy, and money putting out recordings of actual people they knew making good music because they loved it. A hardcore punk band who dabbled in hip-hop to great success made their first album and it blew up. Like, big time. That band then proceded to ditch their actual friends at Def Jam for all the friends named Ben at Capitol records, and three other guys from the Bronx inhereted the war of real hip hop vs. mainstream douchebaggery. There's a real love/hate relationship between the Beastie Boys and hip-hop in general, but everybody pretty much agrees that 3rd Bass was the real deal. They were hip-hop kids to begin with, and they had no interest in selling out just for notoriety. They made 2 great albums with no intention of gaining mainstream popularity, broke up, and proceeded to live their own lives like friends do. I've long since lost my cassette of The Cactus Album, but Derelicts of Dialect is one of my most valued posessions. Yes, the official genre designation of this album is "golden age of hip-hop." It's a masterpiece of plundephonics, collaboration, social critique, and the art of assembling an album. It is specifically modeled after the albums of A Tribe Called Quest and De La Soul, as in "this is what real hip-hop is supposed to be."

I don't want to do a breakdown of all the tracks, because that really would take away some of the joy of listening to this album for yourself.

If you are one of those people who think rap should be outlawed along with skateboarding and driving really slow, then all I can do is quote LL Cool J saying "I don't think so," give you the gas face, and remind you that everybody's invited to the party, even your dad. The only rule is: don't be phony. Peace.

243) Alkaline Trio - Good Mourning

If you thought I had a dark and morbid sense of humor, I've got news for you. I'm a Positive Penelope compared to Alkaline Trio. Here's their fourth album Good Mourning. Spoiler alert, Kenny dies in every episode.

You might be tempted to think this is just tasteless misery for the sake of gloom, but the sheer scope of describing everyday normal occurrences in elaborately morbid ways is pretty impressive. And the puns, oh the glorious puns. Lydia Deetz ain't got nothing on Matt Skiba and Daniel Andriano.

Musically speaking, these are some of their best songs. The melodies are fantastic, the words are fun to sing, they've got one leg in the punk world and one in the alternative rock world. If I could only take one album with me to the waiting room for eternity it would be Spirit's Twelve Dreams of Dr. Sardonicus, 'cause this one's surely already in their jukebox and I want to impress Juno, my caseworker.

244) Marianne Faithfull - Weill

Let's listen to some Kurt Weill. No, my spelling is correct. I'm not talking about the ex The War On Drugs guitarist turned indie-folk hero, I'm talking about the German composer responsible for the music part of Bertolt Brecht's Epic Theater.

I need a gimmicky thing though. I've dragged the socialist/communist stick through too many puddles of mud already. I know! You're already familiar with Jim Morrison's take on Alabama song, so why not hear a completely different bizarre version of it.

Luckily, I have Marianne Faithfull's album of Weill's music. The whole Seven Deadly Sins and some other stuff (the aforementioned Alabama Song, a couple things from The Threepenny Opera, and one from Happy End.

Before you even bother to ask, she's the "da - da di - da" from Metallica's The Memory Remains. She was also the leading female of the "British Invasion" but that gets mansplained away as "Mick Jagger's girlfriend" a little too often in my not particularly humble opinion.

If you've been keeping score, she's on the anorexia/heroin side of the dodge ball court. She is raspy. It's awesome. She very much reminds me of Angela Lansbury's Mrs. Lovett from the original production of Sweeney Todd (I have that too, 'cause it's my favorite musical, duh).

I suppose we can't avoid the fact that Brecht was pretty critical of capitalism, I mean he goes as far as to write a whole opera that essentially calls it the hedonistic side of a schizophrenic personality. I say it would do you some good to get a view of what other parts of the world think about us without trying to defend whatever stupid ideas you thought were important, but what do I know?

The Seven Deadly Sins exists because a bored rich English guy offered to completely finance Balenchine/Kochno's Les Ballets 1933 if 1) his wife had a part in something, and 2) Kurt Weill was involved in some way. Weill said "get me Brecht!," and they wrote the whole thing in a ridiculously short time. If you're a ballet afficianado, this is in between Diaghilev's death (thus the Ballet Russes's bankruptcy) and Balanchine's founding of American ballet schools so that they could stage his own productions.

The joke of this essay, of course, is that Marianne Faithfull was a bit of all over the place. But I really enjoy listening to her earthy, crackly voice. My apologies to every opera singer everywhere, bel canto isn't my thing. This is fantastic. She's the best Pirate Jenny ever.

245) Primus - Sailing The Seas Of Cheese

My brain feels like dog food. I don't want to write about an album tonight. Thankfully, Les Claypool saved me some effort and made his own gravy.

246) Terrible! Disko and Blue Mink

I've been a little down lately. Not for any specific reason, just the normal hills and valleys of third-winter and universal cacophony. I want to hear something terrible.

I've got just the thing. Disko. Not with a "c," with a "k." This isn't your typical boring old compilation album of 70s cheese, it's a cover-band album from Pickwick Records' in-house, third string, not at all suspiciously anonymous Disko Band. 50 cents is practically grand larceny if you were expecting the actual original recordings, but if you want to belly laugh at rhythmic bungles, out of tune horns, and the worst falsetto ever committed to tape, then this is easily worth the 7 dollar cover charge and 3 drink minimum.

You get 2, count 'em 2, kung fu songs (I assume that's Carl Douglas's entire oeuvre), a mediocre Rock The Boat, and all the sweaty polyester you can imagine. I promise it gets worse and worse as the album progresses.

Why am I so happy about it? Because it was clearly recorded in an afternoon by a bunch of shysters, who almost certainly tried to deduct cocaine under "office supplies" on their expense reports. Lou Reed was a staff songwriter and session musician for Pickwick early in his career, and that's how he met John Cale in the first place. See, something interesting fell out of it after all.

It's not supposed to be good, it's supposed to fluff up the discount bin, and for making your friends look like they smelled a dog fart it's spectacular. You'll be limping back to your table from the disco round in no time.

It took forever to get the copyright claim fixed because "Do It" is the actual B.T. Express version, and I let youtube cut out a chunk from it to make the video viewable. I don't blame 'em, I wouldn't want my name on this thing either.

... Which begs the question, what was England exporting from their own charts in the post-Beatles early 1970s? Blue Mink, apparently.

It's a little funky, but it's interesting. You can find tracks from their US release Real Mink on youtube, but they were a compilation band in and of themselves. Their albums were really just random songs as far as I can tell. They don't suck. This really was pop in 70s England.

That was a let down. Sorry. I'll be more creative tomorrow.

247) Green Day Discography 1 - 10,000 Smoothed Out Slappy Hours

It's time for another full discography. However, this one will be controversial. This is *my* Green Day. Everything after American Idiot is a different band. I don't feel like I have to defend that statement. I don't dislike current Green Day, I just don't care about their last 3 albums. Maybe in 20 more years I will?

My CD of Dookie is currently hiding; probably somewhere unpleasant.

Johnny Rotten thought Green Day were weasly little posers, but I think Public Image Ltd. was a terrible band, and the one Sex Pistols album isn't fun, even for me, the guy who can learn to like anything. Nobody's going to win that coin toss, 'cause listening to Lydon's opinions on anything is like desperately trying to forget that you said the opposite thing a year ago. Rotten says whatever thing will make the person he's talking to confused and upset. That's his character, he wants to be centrist compared to whichever bias you throw at him, and he's counting on you not actually listening to him. He's just a walking attitude trying to get you to actually do what you yourself believe. Respectable, but annoying as hell. So, Johnny Rotten can suck eggs. Here comes the ham. That's a Dr. Seuss joke.

Their first album is actually their first 3 EPs compiled into one album. It sounds like it was written by teenagers because it was written by teenagers. Keeping that in mind, it's quite enjoyable. The songs get better with each album, but they thankfully stay completely emotionally juvenile throughout. The Ramones didn't want to grow up, and Green Day said "us neither, poop jokes and sad break ups and sarcasm 'til we're 40 and start wearing eyeliner like we're teenagers going through a Robert Smith phase." How can you not like these irascibly mopey little snot-rags as much as Letterman did?

248) 2 - Kerplunk!

Hello, Tre Cool. Welcome to Green Day. We've just jumped 10,000 light years away from our first album, and we're gonna do it again after this one, so good thing you hopped on the bus now. Kerplunk! Here's our second album. Lookout, we're gonna sell 10,000 copies on the first day, drive all across the country and stress your limited production budget by quintupling that figure in a couple months, and move to a major label where we belong.

I told a similar story with Godsmack and Offspring. This band was going to be gigantic. I could save this story for later, but it's relevant now. Green Day was in it to win it from day one. You can get all pissy about them moving to Reprise (aka Warner), but Lookout couldn't support them after Kerplunk! "Sellout" is factually wrong.

Imagine you are a company. Let's pick an arbitrary number, say 2 million. That's your credit limit, period, no negotiation. This next album is going to sell an astronomical number of copies. It's going to cost 7 million to produce enough copies to get through the first week, and that's like half the people who already planned to buy it. You can't publish it. End of story.

Not the end of the story, because that band is going to keep selling records so fast that you can't even retain the rights to their first two albums. If you shut your entire business down, let go of every other band in your catalogue and did nothing but produce the first 2 Green Day albums, you still couldn't meet the demand. The royalty checks to Billie Joe alone are more than your entire payroll. Anyone you might borrow money from would take one look at the projections and say "why the hell would I loan you money when I could just publish it myself for a jillion times the profit?" That's the ugly reality of business.

Is Kerplunk! Really that good? Yeah, it is. Green Day isn't a joke, no matter how much you wish you could hate them. They are that good, and we're still climbing the mountain. They won't plateau until Warning, and my friends and I stood out in the rain in Tulsa for more than an hour just to get into that show so we could get a little closer than 90 miles from the stage.

Obviously, I'm biased because I like them, but so did 100-million other people. They weren't an underground band. They weren't a gimmick band either. They earned their popularity by being good.

Back to this final indie hurrah. They don't sound so much like teenagers anymore, because Billie Joe is one long nap away from turning 20. The cool part of Green Day is that their albums happen in real time (for me, I got to grow up listening to them grow up). They break out early, make some great stuff in their 20s, weather the doldrums of actually turning into adults, and emerge out the other side a fine band I don't care about anymore. They don't need me to care anymore. We haven't reached my favorite yet, but Kerplunk! has pummeled my eardrums a few thousand times. If you've never heard it, you definitely should.

249) 3 - Dookie

So now here's Dookie. A&R guys are taking the trio out to dinner, Disneyland, begging for the money this thing will bring anyone who touches it. It's all done and in their heads and fingers, Green Day isn't pitching ideas to anyone, they've been playing whatever songs they wrote yesterday to fans screaming "when can I give you all of my money?!" It's just a question of who's tolerable enough to talk to on a daily basis. They didn't just sign to whomever, they went with Frank Sinatra's Reprise because they liked Rob Cavallo's actual work with the Muffs. They wanted to sound like the Sex Pistols or Black Flag, and they had it remixed until they liked it.

They were the darlings of Gilman, and the punk scene in general. They may be dumb, but they weren't stupid enough to think they could ever go back after they signed page 12, and initialed here, and here. We started out as punk, sure we miss our old friends, but we want to be a mainstream popular rock band. Hate all you want, that's our goal. I believe it was Freddy Mercury who said "get on your bikes and ride!"

As far as I'm concerned, they were always alternative rock, it just took two albums to get good at it. All the songs are personal stories, but they tap into something everyone can relate to; boredom, confusion, anger, stepdads you hate for no actual reason, girls who were cool then dumped you, etc.

The real shift in this album is the realization that you just don't know how to feel about it anymore. That's the difference. If the first two albums sound naive and juvenile (they certainly do to me), it's because they are too tied up, they are closed little stories; here's what it is, here's how I feel about it because that's the way I'm supposed to feel about it, nothing to question, life is a book and I have no say in any of it. Dookie, though, says here's how I feel, do you feel that way too? Am I making it up? Yeah, we do. No, you're not.

By the way, this is punk. These are 60s pop songs about not at all 60s subject matter played loud and fast and distorted and yelled out at the universe asking why or how could anyone enjoy all this confusingly stupid stuff we do to each other and ourselves. There's no answer for that one, it's not any better today, is it?

The real reason the "real punks" didn't like it is because it wasn't political anymore. There's no fight, we're not growing up, we're just burning out. Nobody else cares, why should I?

Is it selling out to describe how you feel when the people who also feel that way aren't achieving that same level of success? Or, is it that making a lot of money doesn't change any of that stuff, it just let's you peter pan your way around it? Or, does being likable make it appear like you're exploiting your own scene? They haven't actually said anything nasty about anyone. Were they just mad that Green Day wasn't looking for an excuse to not be awesome?

I feel like a loser. You're not a real loser, screw you, you can't hang out in our clubhouse anymore.

I'm so confused. I give up, this is awesome.

250) 4 - Insomniac

Green Day think Insomniac is their most honest album. I think it's their best. It's also my favorite. It's about their own immense internal conflict.

The only thing they want to do is make more music. Caffienate themsleves to the bursting point, bash out a 2-minute masterpiece, take a nap until their fingers stop bleeding, and do it again. Why? Because they are proving to themselves that they deserve their success. We worked for it. We are in charge. Why do we believe that stupid story that we're flash in the pan posers?

Every song is a story by a narrator who hates himself for actually acting like a loser. Billie Joe is auditioning amps for every song because he wants it to sound exactly right, but his inner teenager is sneering at how pretentious that is.

So, what are we talking about? I don't want to be a trust fund loser. I don't want to be a meth-head. I don't want to drink rage-a-hol. I don't want to have panic attacks. I don't want to be an image. I don't want to be a bitter old man who feels like he wasted his life. Yeah, that might have ruffled a few Berkely gutter-punk tick infested feathers that couldn't recognize their own hypochriphal narratives.

Critics didn't understand this album. You can tell because they say "it's good, but not as good as we want it to be. They should have done all the things these other bands did so we can play the who's better than who game." They missed the important part: it's not about them. It's about what feeling like a walking contradiction actually feels like. It's a story, but everyone forgets that it takes place in an imaginary world inside Billie Joe Armstrong's head.

It's Dookie part 2 in every respect. Part 1 was "I feel like a loser," Part 2 is "I'm going to stop acting like one."

I believe it was me who said if we're all going to act like 12-year-olds, then I'm going to be the best 12 year old ever.

251) 5 - Nimrod

Yay, Dookie/Insomniac is over. Let's go tour Europe. Oh, wait, we don't actually like being the big arena rock band we tried to convince ourselves we wanted to be. Ok, let's make another album instead. We should just have a bunch of unrelated songs this time. It'll give us a chance to do weird crap like the critics wanted us to do for the last album. I've always wanted to hire a violinist to play 1 intro to a song about my newfound alcoholism. Ok, fine, bring the rest of the quartet and I'll write an acoustic ballad. Oooh, I could write a real nasty hardcore thing, and snarl. And that surf rock sound check instrumental we've been playing. We'll call the whole thing Nimrod.

Aside: Billie Joe constantly writes about break ups, and it tickles me to no end that "She, "Good Riddance," and "Whatshername" are about a girl who literally left him to join the Peace Corps.

The album itself is influenced by The Clash and Bikini Kill (London Calling and Reject All American, respectively). I don't have any of their albums, but Kathleen Hanna is quite interesting on her own terms.

Did you know Nimrod was the great-grandson of Noah, and it was incorporated into English as "hunter." They were probably using it in the Bugs Bunny insult sense, though.

Self deprecation and not wanting to be a grumpy old man? Yep, still consistent. Random things for a random album. Seems fitting.

252) 6 - Warning:

Warning: we've reached the end of the second chapter of the book of Green Day. It has been a 10-year roller coaster of ups and downs, popularity and rejection, redundance and experimentation. It's time for something new. I sure hope Al Gore doesn't lose the election to an ultra conservative frat-boy who invites the corporate vampires into our fragile politico-economic landscape. Last time that happened we went to war for the opposite of a good reason (which 20 years later, we're still not officially engaged in fighting), not to mention the 4 times before that.

The result is an incredibly spastic mush of acoustic guitars, retro pop quotations, cabaret stories, and fables about growing up. To borrow the Conan O'Brien gag, in the year two thou....sa...nd, Green Day made a sort of folk punk album. It's just another Green Day album, but it's hard not to compare it to other things like Meat Puppets or Violent Femmes; it's pop-punk with a whole lot of acoustic instruments.

Critics bring up Brecht-Weill, people start saying dumb things like file-sharing is killing record sales, and say all sorts of generic maturity vs. professionalism vs. whatever statements that clearly indicate they don't know how sarcasm actually works. Yes, the word "sarcasm" vaguely means "saying the opposite of what you mean," but that's only the technical device, not the actual meaning. The actual meaning of using sarcasm is something along the lines of "you have created a context for this conversation that forces me to respond in a way that isn't true, I am forced to respond but I'm not in control so all I can do is try to get across that the whole context is absurd because any response is an untruth."

Punk isn't mainstream anymore. They can go back to Gilman. A little part of the world has scabbed over and our arms won't fall off.

And I hear you say "Bottle, where is all this coming from? I can't follow your story."

And I say "sorry?" I'm reading Billie Joe Armstrong's diary. I tend to take lyrics from before, and after, and around the thing I'm listening to and recontextualize them into some more meaningful statement. Billie Joe the narrator is dealing with all the false dichotomies in his own mind. Some of them are forced on us by society at large, some of them are our own special sado-masochistic creations, and we sure do tend to drive them staples deep (see, I reached all the way back to Tre Cool's song from Kerplunk for that one).

If we've learned anything from all this, it's surely that I don't think the way you think I think, and that's confusing. But, isn't that exactly what quoting Tony Hatch's "Downtown" as sung by Petula Clark on a pop-punk album published by Frank Sinatra's record label is meant to convey? You're welcome.

253) 7 - American Idiot

Dirty little secret: Green Day had this little subconscious gremlin in their minds that they should model their career on the Beatles.

Hello, Rob Cavallo, you unofficial 4th member of the band, you. They asked Rob what they should do after the stuff they demoed for the next album was stolen, and Rob said "was it any good?" Green day said "no."

Let's make a concept album! That's exactly what the Beatles would do at this point in their career. I have to tell you,

I like this album a lot. Buuut, Billy Joe decided to go to New York City and hang out with Ryan Adams for a few months. I don't mean to brag, but I was like 8 or 9 years ahead of you guys in figuring out what a little weasel he is.

Rock opera about a teenage anti-hero, blah blah blah. The real point is that Green Day was never a political band, but Warning couldn't help but be about hoping the W didn't become president. 4 years later it's album time and by the way please don't re-elect Wal-Mart for president. I have a lot of those explicit anti-Bush albums, mostly because that's what prompted some of my favorite bands to make another album at all. Sadly, I don't like most of them because they are too overt. American Idiot on the other hand is coincidental, and I like that very much.

So, let's tie up some loose threads. I don't like what the Beatles did after their big concept albums, and I don't care about Green Day after this one. Here I am just trying to listen to my favorite music because that's what I do, but it all just keeps circling back to four years ago when I said please don't vote our country into the Trump-dumpster, because even though I can't predict the specific stupid things he's going to do, I know exactly how the structure of the story unfolds, and it's going to make me a grumpy old man. I don't like being a grumpy old man. I'm not good at explaining why it happens like that, and you wouldn't listen to me anyway, so we'll just see what happens together, I guess. Either way I'll keep plugging along like I always do because I've been trying to do the best I can to be a good example while everyone else runs around being a jerk. I don't have to change my life because the President is a moron, I only have to remind the people around me that I don't play that game.

What a lovely Saturday. A tad windy, though.

254) The Cars - Panorama

You know who else felt really conflicted? Ric Ocasek. The Cars was a magic awesome breakout, but after Candy O went platinum, the critics were like "you're just a vapid trendy pop band making awful, emotionless, new wave garbage," and Ric was like "screw you guys!"

They went from being a bar band nobody cared about to being the center of the universe to being told that they weren't living up to everyone's expectations.

What expectations? We're just a band. You liked one thing we did and somehow it's our fault for tricking you into thinking we're awesome? Sounds to me like you guys are the ones who don't know what you want. We aren't beholden to any rock cliché, or pop standard, we're "alternative" in every sense: cutting edge technology, shaking things up, living the confusing life. Wanna see how weird and creepy and sarcastic we can be? Hello, 1980. Here's a Panorama of how bizarre this all is for us.

255) Paul McCartney - Memory Almost Full

We should shake things up a little. Here's Paul McCartney's 2007 album Memory Almost Full. Go listen to it.

You tell me: is it good, or is it a vacuous piece of twaddle that only superficially connects to anything in reality housed inside the CD jewell case equivalent of hostile architecture?

Objection. Leading the witness.

Sustained.

Did you, or did you not start MPL as the umbrella company for your own post-Beatles publications, then just buy as many smaller rights holders as possible to make yourself the largest private copyright holder in the world?

Yes.

Did you, or did you not start recording Memory Almost Full, get bored or frustrated or whatever word you want to use, record, publish, and promote an entirely different album, then think "oh, I guess I should finish this thing I abandoned a while ago," and licence it's distribution exclusively to Starbucks so that you incurred little or no financial liability?

Objection!

Noted, but I will allow it on the grounds that the inherent snark of the question does not factually contradict the witness's previous public testimony, nor does it force the witness to agree or disagree with the sentiment. The jury may disregard the prosecutor's tone of voice in this instance. Please, answer the question, Sir.

Yes.

Is the artwork meant to depict various ways in which you are "falling out of your easy chair?"

Yes.

Are we wrong to interpret the partial inclusion of lyrics and redirection to your own website as indication that the exclusive licensing deal with Starbucks did not provide adequate monetary compensation for your indisputable copyright to the reprinting and distribution of your typeset lyrics?

No.

The prosecution rests, your Honor.

256) Steven Stark - Country Wrong Turn

I have a nasty little secret. I don't own one of the albums by my friend Steven Stark. Tonight was the perfect chance to remedy that situation, 'cause yesterday I criticized Paul McCartney for running off to make a different album in the middle of making an album.

Come to find out, CD Baby closed their web store last month. In the apocryphal words I put in Ric Ocasek's mouth, "screw you guys!"

I'm so bummed that I forgot all the hilarious things I was going to say. So, to my friend Steven I say, you know where I am over on the darkside of bandcamp, and there's more than a couple beers waiting for you when you get here.

257) Korn - Life Is Peachy

Tonight's album is a doozie. Before I say anything else, I need to make it clear that this album isn't critqueable. It's simply a fact in the space-time continuum of the universe. It's Jack Harkness. It makes us time lords queasy, but we can't do anything about it.

Life Is Peachy. You can feel the sarcasm burn your retinas when you read those 3 words. There is no pretense to Korn. There's no artifice, no gimmick, no image. Listening to a Korn album is essentially watching Jonathan Davis's regression therapy. The world fucked him up, and his friends and a lot of meth, cocaine, and alcohol made the world well aware of that fact.

The outrageous metaphors have to be outrageous. Whining, screaming, and tazmanian devil-ing are about the only way you can vocally express it. Every member of the band is playing a different genre. You're supposed to watch it happen and become very aware that that is a world in which you do not live. You can't possibly understand it. A hundred other bands tried to get close, but Linkin Park's Hybrid Theory is as good as it gets. Nu Metal is what we call all the bands that tried to copy these two. Maybe I'll write about that album sometime.

I don't want to ruin your entire evening, so we'll just leave it at he was molested, he tried to tell his parents, and they said he was a liar. That's Korn. If you think the entire biography of Korn is a work of fiction, then you probably think you work for money, or that firemen are trying to save *your* house by putting out your grease fire, or that the grocery store makes your food, or that restaurants in China are somehow different from restaurants in America, or that "placebo" is a synonym for "guinea pig." Yay, topicality!

You can like it or hate it or desperately try to ignore it, but Life Is Peachy is an entire multi-discipline Doctorate in its own right. All that being said, I hate hate hate hate hate that goddamned clicking!

258) Ferrante & Teicher

I don't know about you, but after a hard day's night of moving objects from one location to another I like to pour myself an adult beverage and watch a pair of
piano pugilists fight to the pain (my family watched The Princess Bride last night, so I watched the whole thing in my head during the gap between the fire geysers and ROUSes, because I've got 1.21 gigabytes of memory, and it's nowhere near full), for my own amusement. That's a lot of references for one little sentence.

Nobody has to die, I just have to find a bunch of random ways to blender up all my standard character tropes with things that happened in my real life and let you have a go at trying to figure it all out.

Ferrante and Teicher have the hilariously underwhelming distinction of receiving honorary memberships in the University of Central Oklahoma's chapter of Tau Kappa Epsilon. Take that, you wannabe practical physicists and uneducated novelists!

I am joking. These guys were legitimate Julliard prodigies, and they had massive success as arrangers, performers, and local music store employee annoyers. I have like 300 of their records, which is good because there's that really annoying Universal Fire again. If I didn't know any better, I'd say gathering a whole bunch of unique and important things into a tiny little space and forgetting about them is not such a great idea (it's the forgetting about them that's the problem).

Ok, I'll stop. I'm gonna go with Ferrante & Teicher By Popular Demand because I want to hear their version of "Goldfinger." You would seriously have to be paying attention to know that Barthes uses Goldfinger as the example of the "narrational level" (the novel has three unconnected narrative episodes that form its underlying structure). I'll forgive you if you thought it was because it starts with "The Greatest Story Ever Told," but you should really know by now that I'm not *that* immodest.

Ok, I'll stop for real this time. I just find Pops style symphony concerts really enjoyable, and I like piano almost as much as I like guitar. This is easy listening in the best possible way. Perfect for when you're just flat out tired of watching whatever ridiculous things other people are doing out in parts of the world you didn't want to visit in the first place (not you guys, you're amusing yourselves like you should be, you know what I mean), or listening to coworkers from the other side of the building complain about things they thought were super awesome a year ago.

259) Color Me Barbra

It's Friday, and you know what that means (it doesn't mean anything); it's Tickle Me Elmo, I mean Color Me Barbra!

That's a really complicated joke, because you have to know that the title itself was a reference to the fact that this was Barbra Streisand's first TV special *in color*, at a time when color television was still considered a novelty. You also have to know that I'm using both definitions of the word "novelty," and that you can play around with assigning each to both. It's 4 jokes for the price of one, and I'm practically givin'em away (which is itself a TV advertisement style commercialism trope).

This album is hands down fantastic. The real question is how could you possibly not like it even just the tiniest bit?

But it's showtunes! Yeah, the best songs from plays with songs in them.

But it's silly! Yeah, who in their right mind would want to sit in a crowded theater on a Friday night and not have a good time?

But it's Barbra Streisand! Yeah, she's l33t.

Look, Babs is a Broadway superstar because she's incredible. You can hate Broadway musicals as much as you want, but it's an art form. You have to work within that context.

If I were gonna pick some songs to sing from some musicals on this brand-new thing called color television that only rich people can afford to buy to amuse themselves, I'd probably pick ones that are exciting, ones I'm really good at singing, ones that the people who pay me money tell me are spectacular.

Pretend I'm the opposite of me, an uneducated, drywall punching, sexist, racist, homophobe who thinks about nothing but how I can exploit someone else's talent and personal drive for profit. Oh wait, this is the early 60s and those are the rich people handing Barbra Streisand their pocket change 'cause she's awesome and people will give us lots of money for just letting her sing some songs from musicals in front of a couple cameras.

My point is, you can't logic your way out of Barbra Streisand being awesome at being Barbra Streisand. You'd just have to use all your time and energy trying to ignore her existence, but then everyone would say "you seriously don't know Barbra Streisand? She's amazing," and we're right back where we started.

I mean, you could not be in the mood to listen to her, or have an inner ear problem that makes certain notes give you a headache, or you could feel like she can't quite hang on to the French accent for certain words, but those are all your own personal problems, nothing to do with her. She's up there differentiating vowel sounds depending on the lyrical context, using different timbres to convey shifts in character emotion, deciding whether or not to be dead on pitch or glide into a note for emphasis. If you're hung up on how dumb a song about animal crackers is, then you aren't really taking any of this serious, now are you?

Bernadette Peters is the Queen of Broadway.

I disagree. She's very good, but Barbra Streisand is the Queen of Broadway.

Barbra Streisand sucks.

YOU SUCK!!

For the record, I really do like Barbra Streisand. She's objectively awesome. And then you're like "aha! I see what you did there. Barbra Streisand and Adam Sandler are both Jewish celebrities."

No, no, no. The structure of the review itself led me to that specific lunchroom dialogue because we're acting like 12-year-olds, remember. All the things that match up because of that are coincidences. Acting like an adult means trying really hard not to screw up other people's lives, keeping everything going as smoothly as possible, being cautious, and polite, and patient. San Dimas High School Football rules!

For that one, I took "12 year old" and "O'Doyle rules," changed "year old" to "-th grade," and filtered them through my time traveller trope to get Bill and Ted's Excellent Adventure. Coincidentally, also about school. And that's how Dennis Miller's tangential comedy style worked. I didn't count or anything, but that Dennis Miller reference was from like 200 essays ago.

My whole point to begin with was that my brain runs laps around the playground because it's a spastic hyperactive child, but I try really hard to not act like that in real life (I save it for these things that I hope you find amusing).

And now that you're completely lost in my ADD thought stream, I'll tell you the real secret that ties this whole thing together. I've literally spent all day concocting this essay in the attempt to emulate her humorous version of the Minute Waltz. You try to perform that thing in front of a live studio audience for national television broadcast, and then tell me Barbra Streisand sucks.

Have a great weekend, everybody (I say as I wave like Forrest Gump).

260) Joe Walsh - You Bought It - You Name It

You know who didn't care about his solo albums? Joe Walsh. You Bought It - You Name It is generally considered his worst. I love it.

Joe Walsh is insane. He wanted to record this album with an actual mobile truck. The producer he hired said no, so Joe fired him and did a non-dolby recording at an old ballroom on Santa Catalina Island. It's got a WWII ship on the cover, Joe sings about random crap like not wanting to go to war in the middle east, big tits, and video arcades.

Who listens to Joe Walsh for the lyrical content? Dear Robert Christgau, all of Joe Walsh's albums are his comedy albums. He famously said something like "if I knew people were going to like Rocky Mountain Way, I would have done a better job." You listen to Joe Walsh for the guitar playing. Jimmy Page, Eric Clapton, and Pete Townshend all said "yeah, he's phenomenal."

For listening to a guitar player play random stuff he just thought up, this is a pretty decent record. And, Theme From Island Weirdos is just a great little piano piece with weird guitar parts and seagulls in the background that ends with an infinite loop of said sounds from the Pacific. It's a pretty coherent project about being a dumb American. What's not to love?

261) Joe Walsh - There Goes The Neighborhood

Why didn't critics like You Bought It - You Name It? If you read reviews, it's because they liked There Goes The Neighborhood, and it's follow up was somehow not as good, or silly, or...

What? This is actually sillier. It's medium rock (as opposed to hard or soft), those weird talk box lines, "things," actual life vs. being rich and being self quarantined from the world for fun and profit. He's guarding his pile of trash.

The real difference is that this is normal quirky (ordinary average) Joe Walsh, but the follow up makes it sound like you weren't actually paying attention. That's right, I think critics felt embarrased to admit that they didn't actually notice until Joe cranked the amps up and said "who cares? Nobody." They liked his soft rock stuff and ignored the fact that he was always telling you it's just stuff, it's not important.

Joe Walsh is actually a pretty convincing (albeit obtuse) punk stuck in a middle-aged office manager's Tuesday afternoon. He's his own career long midlife crisis.

In summary, I think you have to take There Goes The Neighborhood and You Bought It You Name It as a 2 part story: all this grown-up stuff is just stuff and it's dumb, so I'm going to lock myself up in my bedroom and play guitar really loud. I may play a professional human on TV, but I know a fellow inner 12-year-old when I meet one. Joe might be insane, but at least he's not daring you to drink from the bottles he found under the kitchen sink.

262) Pink Floyd - Dark Side Of The Moon

I did my regular humor album thing about Joe Walsh this morning, but I just want to hear Pink Floyd's Dark Side Of The Moon. It's about a lot of things, but it's mostly about being Pink Floyd without Syd Barrett, and why. It's a contender for greatest album ever, and deservedly so.

It's always impossible to describe why something is excellent, because it usually feels like magic. It's that feeling like every single moment is a complete surprise, but exactly what it should be. No one needs to explain this album, the same way Clare Torry doesn't actually have to use words on The Great Gig In The Sky.

The album is itself a complete life. Each side is a continuous multi-movement work. You couldn't possibly skip a single moment of the journey. This is just pure musical pleasure in my book.

You don't need a reason or an explanation, you only have to keep going and remember where you've been. After all, we are only ordinary men....

263) Carpenters (the Tan Album)

It's Monday, and you know that doesn't mean much of anything, so let's play an album with the word Monday in it. I bet you thought I used up all my color albums with Weezer, but I've got one more hiding in here. It's The Tan Album, Carpenters (though mine's starting to look a little pink in anything less than bright light). It's the last one. The red and green albums don't count because Weezer isn't allowed to make it their personal gimmick, and The R.E.D. Album doesn't count because 1) that's it's actual name, and 2) this is my game, not The Game's game. If you've got a legit color album I don't own, I'd be interested....

Sadly, Karen's exceptional cover of Klaatu's Calling Occupants of Interplanetary Craft isn't on it, but her first take sight reading of Richard's edited version of the lyrics to Superstar from a napkin is. I've got a Delaney & Bonnie album hiding in here somewhere, but that's a different story for a not very Monday afternoon.

When last we met the Carpenter siblings, I said they had mental health issues and that they were just too innocent for the exploitative world they lived in. It's a pretty common trope to blame the downfall of otherwise lovely human beings on the sleazy underbelly of corporate business, but it's equally true to say most everyone confuses permissivity for influence. Record execs are pretty terrible, but they are generally working with active junkies. "Stop injecting lighter fluid into your eyeball for two minutes and play f-sharp in the chorus... I'm gonna need at least 4 points and a children's album if you want me to put up with these guys for the next 3 weeks.... I don't care whose girlfriend you are, touch that $12,000 compressor and I'll chop your fingers off... Richard, I hope you brought enough skittles to share with the rest of the class. Karen's great, she doesn't eat anything and three takes at the most. I love these goofballs."

Seriously, if Saturday doesn't make you laugh uncontrollably, then you aren't human. You think I'm making fun of Richard again, and yeah I am, but I don't mean it as an insult. He had to know that juxtaposition is so incredibly jarring, right? It's exactly the same reaction I had to The Incredible String Band. Karen, dear sister, your talent knows no limits and I have made these arrangements to highlight the real strength of character in your impressive contralto range, now please excuse me while I tap dance across the stage in my purple tutu.

You might not be able to tell how much I love the Carpenters. I truly do, they are fantastic. I just can't reconcile the sheer difference between Richard's composing for her vs. himself. His songs are fantastic, but they are so bizarre when interspersed between hers. Take Druscilla Penny. That is an absolutely amazing song, but Karen just sang Superstar reading from an actual napkin, and we segue right into One Love which is like Bacharach/David level awesome, and then *do* go into a Bacharach/David medley that's better than either the originals or any other subsequent cover ever.

Sonny Bono should have hired Richard Carpenter to write his albums, they would have been AMAZING.

If you ever thought I was joking when I say "buy it and I'll pay you back with interest," I'm not. You find me some more Carpenters on vinyl and I will make it worth your while.

264) Syd Barrett's Pink Floyd

I'm having a bad brain day. I am of course my own proverbial Bottle of Beef, but day in day out of hearing dumb crap from people who get paid to be important wears on a guy like me, you know? So, before I let any more of it spill out into the world, here's more of it.

From Richard Carpenter to Syd Barrett. Richard was a Quaalude brand methaqualone enthusiast, but Syd preferred his Mandrax style, cut with a little Benadryl (diphenhydramine). Neither of them were what you really think of when you say "drug addicts." Syd was always going to burn out, the acid just accelerated him toward the realization that it would be a lot better for him if he did it quickly. Both of them were essentially self medicating the obvious symptoms of severe underlying anxiety. Richard finally realized it was a serious problem and got help, Syd just shut down and retired to a life of painting and gardening in solitude. That sounds dreamy....

Fans of Pink Floyd will know that as Syd began his downward belly flop into the sea below the sea, the boys brought in their mutual friend David Gilmour to eventually replace him as lead singer/guitarist/cruise ship navigator, get the airplane back up in the air so to speak. They just didn't pick Syd up on the way to the studio one day, and that was that.

That must have been weird? Apparently not, Syd's toboggan ride continued at its own pace and he liked Gilmour so much he asked him to produce his two solo albums. They needed other musicians, so the other members of Pink Floyd came and played too. It's like at some point he just forgot that Pink Floyd was *his* band, and asked his friends to help him make some music. He famously just showed up at the studio while they were making Shine On You Crazy Diamond and silently watched them work before retiring forever.

So, what do you get from Piper At The Gates Of Dawn and A Saucer Full Of Secrets? You get an LSD day-trip through the mythological English countryside. Gnomes, and space, and doctors, and the first take of Scarecrow recorded the day after they watched the Beatles record Lovely Rita. You get massive, almost frighteningly nebulous soundscapes followed by quaint English folk. Viscious and bitey electric guitars, then recorders. It doesn't sound funny or silly like when the Carpenters do it. It's disturbingly matter-of-fact, like these completely unrelated things just happen one after the other because there is no reason why they shouldn't.

Early Pink Floyd was a jam band. They would get up on stage and just improvise for hours, Syd would act weird and the crowd would eat it up. Roger, Nick, and Richard were boring old non-psychedelic terra-naut architecture students and the whole art-school freak-out mind-melt thing just kept getting more and more fightening/frustrating.

Everyone has a story about how they felt like Syd didn't respond well to suggestions or criticism, but that's clearly because there wasn't anything he could change about it. He wasn't "crafting" anything, he was just letting whatever was in his head come out into the real world. I doubt it made any more sense rattling around on the inside. Sure is fun to listen to, though. And, as strange as it must have been to follow Syd's unpredictable lead, they spent a whole lot of time and thought and energy trying figure out how to do it without him. I don't think Roger Waters ever did, actually. His Pink Floyd was completely centered around the loss of Syd, and eventually he too had to reluctantly hand the whole thing over to Gilmour. The band did indeed have a life of its own, no one person made it what it was, no one could stop its evolution, and I think that's what I like most about them.

On a tangential, real life note, I'm not really interested in drugs per se. Caffeine and nicotine in moderate doses are plenty for me. I even take way less ibuprofen than anyone in my life actually recommends. But, I am fascinated by the phenomenon that so many musicians ascribe such power and importance to their drugs of choice. I think thinking is capable of producing most of those effects all by itself, but the aluminum foil wearing Governor of Iowa (Reynolds, get it?) and the President of our country sure do seem to make the people I meet in the real life, whom I'd much rather stay home from, antagonistic to my cause.

265) Heads or tails?

I'm a very psychosomatic person. Mental stress makes me physically tired, aches and pains stoke the flames of my, let's say it, excessively morbid sense of humor. Tonight's album review could go in two different directions, but if I'm gonna sell my soul at the crossroads of metaphor and hyperbole street, I'm also going to bore the devil with an extended analysis of how both paths are essentially the same and my perseverance along either hinges only on the mindset from which I choose to approach them.

I go through periods of loving and hating both Marilyn Manson and Social Distortion. They can be exactly what I want to hear, or they can come across as total poser hacks that I have to ignore for a while. They both wear makeup.

Marilyn Manson is essentially a protege of Trent Reznor but fails to be either metal or industrial at almost every turn, and Mike Ness can't decide if he's a greaser, or a hick, or a gangster, but he's really just a grungy version of all of them. What I'm saying is they are both potentially enjoyable and have their moments of amazing, but as franchises they might as well be the third Matrix movie: if you paid me to care, I'd still say "pass."

I saw Marilyn Manson in concert for Antichrist Superstar with my friend Vinh, which means I stood in the parking lot of the state fairgrounds for an hour waiting to get overly frisked by security, yelled at by activists, squeezed like a sardine in a sea of sweaty goth kids, have my poster stolen by a 12-year-old who could run surprisingly fast, and get called a heathen the next day in algebra. Fun times. I haven't seen Social Distortion except for old video footage.

Manson is a commercialized exaggeration of my thing, he's the shock-rock imitation pancake syrup of industrial, but my palate demands actual boiled sap from a maple tree harvested in a galvanized bucket from a real forest in Canada.

Mike Ness strikes me as the Billy Idol of Rockabilly. Or like if Johnny Cash were Emo. Give me the Stray Cats or Reverend Horton Heat any day of the week. I'm not gonna stand here and say that's a fair assessment, but don't throw the tomatoes so hard that I can't slice them up for a sandwich later.

Musically and lyrically, both these albums are great. If this was it from either of them, I'd be perfectly happy. But, they aren't. The things they did before them are better. The things they did after are corporate franchise work disguised as artistic license. These are two of the very, very few albums I bought as a demographic, and I traded most of that stuff for cash to pay off my first round of credit card debt. I'm not saying that's the source of my bipolar opinion of either band, but I am saying it's real when I listen to them and some times I just can't ignore it.

There I go, walking across the median after punching Satan in the nuts. Bonus points if you can tell me the year they were published without looking it up.

266) Helmet - Betty

You tell me a story. Tell me about Wilma's Rainbow of peaceful colors. White, brown, black, blue, and the elusively invisible purple. Tell me about those weasley Weezers who tried to sneak red and green into Betty's kitchen, and ended up ruining her biscuits. Tell me about the feeble Silver Hawaiian and his run in with Sam Hell. It doesn't have to be good, or nice, it doesn't have to make sense, it doesn't have to even be a story at all. I just want to hear you tell it.

267) Death Cab for Cutie - Plans

Death Cab For Cutie is one of those bands that graduated from indie to major because they needed it (I've talked about several). It was Ben Gibbard's secondary solo project, it got bigger and he put a full band together, then their 4th album got really big and they were in the position to actually shop around. Plans is a great album because it was the album they were going to make regardless of who actually paid for it. They were also smart enough to completely distrust "corporate economics," and told their real fans to buy it from them online instead of waiting for it to hit Wal-Mart shelves.

In other words, Death Cab for Cutie did it right. They didn't "sell out" in the way most of us understand that term. They used Atlantic for a label's real purpose, which is to finance the "mainstream" distribution of their own work, the work that built them a real fanbase, a fanbase they cared about and didn't want to abandon. I'm not actually in that fanbase. I liked their radio singles, but I've already mentioned that the mid to late 2000s were well below my tolerance for gas station quality coffee, and I only bought Plans what, 4 years ago?

But, I can recognize authenticity even when I don't personally care about the product. It's the 5th Death Cab for Cutie album, and the bells and whistles are just that. Better equipment, smoother mastering, glossier paper for the booklet, still the same band and quality of writing.

I like the morbidity, the melancholy, the downright sadness, but there's no snark to buoy it anymore. There's no fight, no "but it could be better," no hope anymore. You don't get to fly off the tracks like Neutral Milk Hotel. You don't even get the chance to go insane anymore, it all just sucks and then we die.

Don't misunderstand me, this is beautiful, musically amazing stuff, but do you hear any hope? All I hear is hope that we might someday have hope again, and my-lanta that's depressing. Maybe generations younger than me find some catharsis in it, but I sure don't. If you've ever wondered what underlying psychosis chooses the album I listen to next, my best explanation is that the kind of day I had just injects an album straight into my subconscious. Nothing actually bad happened to me today, I just woke up with an unrelenting malaise toward the American version of humanity. I know what happy looks like in my imagination, but I'll be damned if I can figure out a way to get anyone else to participate.

I like doom and gloom when it has a funny or sarcastic twist to it, but this is just emotional misery. Plans: what's the point of even making them anymore?

268) Gin Blossoms

I'm going to argue that Gin Blossoms have two albums. Obviously, they made more than that, but 2006 to present is the ironic happily ever after of their story. The story itself goes something like this:

Band from Arizona tours all over the country, gets record deal and continues to tour, breaks up for 10 years, reforms and still plays shows. They're just a band who had a few years in the mainstream spotlight while alternative rock was the most popular genre for suburban teenagers. They are the softer pop side of said genre (some might say power pop), as evidenced by Robin Wilson's ever-present tambourine, but that's a needlessly fussy distinction.

Like most bands, they came from a scene and their scene was centered in Phoenix/Tuscon, AZ with more than a couple exceedingly long road trips through El Paso to the Gulf of Mexico. You could argue that their mainstream success was due in large part to the Seattle breakthrough, but only in the sense that the major labels were really keyed in on the commercial potential of Alternative Rock in general. It proved to be highly lucrative, didn't it? I would argue, however, that these guys happened to be out looking for a deal at the right time, and they got their taste of corporate finance, pointed their handlers to their real friends back home, and everybody got a little shot of Southwest flavor on their musical scrambled eggs.

Their first album is from 1989, so we are talking exactly the same time frame as Nirvana, Pavement, Pixies, all bands who one way or another were just following REM's lead. That first album doesn't count because they reworked half those songs for their real first album New Miserable Experience. Believe it or not, it took an entire year for anyone to really latch on, but the singles magically skyrocketed into the Top 40 in 1993 and they were off to the races.

The title alone is worth the cover charge. It's the kind of sarcastic self awareness that's just too big to fit in the trunk of the death cab, so Ben just sighs and resigns himself to buying new deodorant when he gets there. Go ahead, try to say "new miserable experience" in a non-sarcastic way. You can't. It's either gallows humor, or insulting the mopers, and either way my brain giggles.

Hey, Jealousy. Long time, no see. What you been up to? That sign says "next exit Allison Road, your sister is named Allison, I'm gonna have an epiphany in a few weeks and make that a hit song." And, they cap the whole thing off with the schlocky country joke "you can't call it cheatin'; she reminds me of you."

Then comes Congratulations...I'm Sorry, which would be a great title if it weren't literal: it's Congratulations (on the success of New Miserable Experience).... I'm sorry (that you had to choose between your friend Doug and making another record). Doug's alcoholism was so bad that he couldn't stand up to finish recording the first album, and they had to fire the founder of the band or get dropped from their deal. He started rehab, but killed himself as their second album hit shelves without him. That's a downer of a story, but I tell it to give some more context to the downfall of my musical generation that I've been hinting at all this time. The 90s and 00s were one of the most dismal times in the rock music psyche. I don't think it's much of a secret that the real mainstream music machine exploits the most generally troubled and vulnerable artists for profit. A&M didn't give a shit about Doug Hopkins, the lead guitarist and songwriter of Gin Blossoms, and they definitely weren't interested in watching their latest investment fall apart without capturing it on 2-inch tape. Sure, yeah, a mediocre album generates less revenue than a great one, but compared to no revenue at all it's a no brainer business 101 decision. To quote the entire chorus from Less Than Jake's "How's My Driving" off Losing Streak:

> Fuck Doug
> I'm not going out like this
> he said man I'm all I got
> and I won't be missed
> and this makes
> this makes no sense to me
> ain't the way
> the way it's supposed to be

That's why there are only two Gin Blossoms albums. You'd need a decade-long break after living that new miserable experience, same as anyone else. But, like I've said before, time heals most wounds and scars are the mementoes that prove you've been doing stuff.

I'll try to find a happier album tomorrow. I promise. If you're inclined to read too much into my mental state like I've warned you not to do, just remember that there's usually a snarky joke hiding in there. It might not be a funny ha-ha joke, but I haven't pulled the discounted price stickers off.

269) They Might Be Giants - Flood

It's Sunday. I promised you a happy album. So, surrealist absurdity it is. A brand-new record for 1990, They Might Be Giants' brand new album Flood. Greatest album ever recorded, g'night folks.

I'm kidding, I actually have too much to say to possibly construct a coherent essay; good thing it's nonsense already.

Two Johns from Brooklyn with synths, guitars, and a taste for absurdity. They are both serious composers who take being unserious very seriously. This nice A&R lady from Elektra was a big fan, so she negotiated a deal for them where they didn't get screwed. They got a budget, a couple producers who were more than willing to both go wherever the songs took them and prevent them from getting carried away and ruining their own songs. That's a surrealist daydream in itself. I mean, they blew 66% of their budget on 4 of the 19 tracks, forgot verses to songs, and had a few technological mishaps along the way, but the end result is spectacular.

It's another case of using a label for its intended purpose, professional level assistance in making your art, a rolodex full of professional contacts who can use your art in new and exciting ways, and a contract that gives you the freedom to do what you already know you want to do. Bottle's school of music business teaches only two rules: 1) if you aren't already making money by playing music, a record label can't help you, and 2) a deal that takes your money is a bad deal; their job is to expand your audience. All a record label does is play your music for people actively looking for new music; it helps a lot if you're agreeable to other synchronization projects like cartoons, or jingles, etc.

Anywho, part of the magic is that it's just 2 guys with synthesizers and imaginations. They programmed all their music in midi so they could perform it, and that means you can just patch it to other things in the studio and go to town. I have exactly the same model of drum machine that they used to make this album. There are lots of real musicians too, but the core of the whole album is synths and samples that cost nothing to create.

There are two great things about TMBG music. First, the music comes first and they jostle and shove words into it. That's a big part of how the nonsense gets made. Second, they aren't trying to be funny. If you try to be funny, it will get old quick and no one will come back once it loses its punch. If, however, you sing "minumum wage" in an overly grandiose manner followed by mashing 2 samples together to sound like a bullwhip, it will be hilarious for all eternity. A song written from the perspective of a nightlight? Fantastic. A song that compares your own trip to Berlin to a Bing Crosby/Bob Hope movie? Genius. A cover of Istanbul/Constantinople? Awesome. Unreliable narrators and unexpected narrative settings and creative misinterpretation of metaphors and being reincarnated as a bag of groceries? Comedy gold.

Not all my essays are good, and Skip the Editor might say "scrap that one, or at least rework it" but the best ones are the same kind of freedom of thought you get on Flood. Ideas create new ideas, you just let them build themselves and pick out the ones you enjoy. The secret to their success is that anyone can find humor in it. Absurdity is a nutritious snack for everyone. Here, I'll share some of mine.

270) Sublime

How's that Kurt Braunohler joke go? Something like, He says "I can play the guitar like a mother f-ing riot," then proceeds to plink out the most awkward amateurish solo imaginable. It's a good joke, but he's wrong. That's a great little solo exactly how it needs to be played, on par with Paul Gilbert's inconspicuously astonishing 8 bars in the Mr. Big classic "To Be With You."

The story of Sublime is pretty dismal (shock and awe, you gasp), but I watched it play out in real time. This little ska punk band from Long Beach, CA made two pretty popular independent albums, then stepped up to the big leagues for their 3rd (coincidentally the album that most critics say is single-handedly responsible for the 3rd wave of Ska). Damnit, I'm building up to the 3 strikes you're out baseball joke and I don't want to do it.

Anyway, major league self-titled album, but Bradley is such an enormous heroin addict that they kick him out of the studio before it's even finished, and he overdoses and dies before the masters even made it to the manufacturing plant. He's dead, the band doesn't exist anymore, the singles skyrocket up the radio playlist to every hour on the 10s, and us highschoolers are like "this is freakin' awesome...oh that sucks."

Neil Young said "dear everyone, please stop shooting up and dying," and everyone replied "heroin good. Got it. Thanks, Neil."

Look at it from my perspective. I'm 16/17, my musical heroes have been killing themselves since I was old enough to understand the concept of suicide. My actual friends are being treated for ADD and Tourette's and they kill themselves. Now, you might imagine a few different ways that might mess me up psychologically, but you don't have the other perplexing part of my personal experience of being alive.

My whole existence has been subdivided into segments of doing what I thought I was supposed to be doing, then being told "you're too smart to be here, and you need to leave." I don't think that was anyone's actual intention, but rejection is rejection no matter how absurd the context. I'm perfectly happy to talk about it, but I don't want to ramble on about my bizarre inverse inferiority complex. The point is my adolescent brain said "oh, clearly it's the being important and famous part that makes the universe a miserable place for people to exist."

All of which is beside the point, because we're here to talk about a Sublime album. I think his point is that we're all miserable, we can't do anything about it, and we end up destroying ourselves looking for a quick bit of fun or relief. Why do I say that? Let's delve into it a little. Apologies for not having the booklet anymore, I've recklessly listened to this album a time or two.

1 - The image might look cool, but my life is crap.

2 - It doesn't do any good to dwell on the negative, you just keep going as best you can.

3 - here's a story about Annie, who's dad actually encouraged her to be a prostitute. What could I possibly do to fix that messed up reality? I'm Gregg Allman (I'm no angel, get it?), I could kill him, I guess. It's your life, it's not like I'm any better, so I can't really tell you to run away.

4 - let's face it, somewhere deep down I like destroying myself.

5 - Remember Offspring and Alice In Chains's fun during the 1992 LA Riot? Here's Bradley Nowell's sarcastic song about using it as an excuse to rob liquor stores and steal the guitar he's currently playing. Zappa lived through this riot too, but he already stated his opinion about a previous one, and I think he would have been at least a little pleased by the sheer snark of this song.

Again, I could keep going, but I've already talked your ear off and you can go hear the rest of this fantastic album any time you want to do so. My friend Rocky, who I haven't seen in an unacceptably long time, listed this among his 10 influential albums, and I couldn't resist.

You might be thinking "holy crap how can one little album elicit all this logorrhea?" Yes, that's a real word, and my answer, as always, is I am a Bottle of Beef.

271) The longest windup I've never intentionally created

I write about other stuff I'm thinking about on facebook, and here's a two-day long train of thought:

1) I think there is a fundamental flaw in our conception of the scaling up from "sole proprietor" to "company" to "corporation." That flaw is what I would call the ownership of labor. As we incorporate into larger networks of relationships, we tend to confuse division of labor with acquisition of labor to such a degree that we begin to personify the incorporation itself.

That's an incredibly dense paragraph, and requires very strict unpacking. First, this is a theoretical model. It cannot be elaborated by specific examples until its constraints are fully defined. Second, real life examples are difficult to show because we all, to some extent, participate in the flawed reasoning I am describing.

A sole proprietor is what you might call a dictionary capitalist. An individual who owns the means of production for whatever product they produce or service they provide. The success or failure of that real person is not dependent on the labor of others within the limited context of the business; we assume that he or she already possesses the resources necessary to complete some objective. We also remove any speculative endeavor. For example, we assume that a carpenter isn't simply making a table in the mere hope of selling it, i.e. the carpenter is making a table for an established trade (be it money, or simply to have a stable surface for some purpose). The purpose for labor already exists.

Now imagine that the need for tables exceeds the individual's ability to produce them, to the point that a second fully independent carpenter is needed to make a second table at the same time. This brings us to a point of contention that we must understand. These two carpenters are not competing to win the reward, their labors must be essentially identical. This relationship can be accomplished in different ways. The first carpenter might view the second carpenter as an employee, or as a partner. Either way we call the resulting combination of labor a "company." However, if the first carpenter views the second as an employee, then there has been a tacit assumption that the conjunction of labor itself is fully owned by the first carpenter. He mistakenly thinks of himself *as* the company, when in fact he is merely half of the labor in this abstract combination. In other words, there has been a division of labor, but no recognition of that division.

Now imagine that the need for tables has grown larger than the ability of the abstract company itself to acquire materials. It becomes necessary to form a larger combination of companies. One company acquires the necessary materials (chops down trees or whatever) and a second company manufactures tables. This abstract union of companies is called a corporation.

If the very first carpenter still believes that he owns all of these divisions of labor, then he will mistakenly think of himself as the corporation. He will in essence be the primary beneficiary of all subordinate labor while assuming complete responsibility for the continued operation of the corporation at large.

In essence, he has elevated the value of managing the abstract network by refusing to acknowledge the divisions of labor, thus devaluing the labor itself.

Note that we are still operating in a fully abstract context, without any application of real-world forces (money, scarcity, environment, deception or fraud, law, etc.). My choice of making tables was merely an example I think everyone can wrap their head around. I have limited it to only 1 division of labor at each stage to make the inverse relationship between labor and management as visible as possible.

It's easy to jump ahead and say Bottle thinks corporations are evil, or that I'm some nefarious 'merica hater, but don't. I want to understand my understanding of this phenomenon and the only way I know how to do it is put it down in writing and let you see it. If some part of my thinking doesn't make sense, feel free to ask me about it. Am I missing something? Did I skip a logical step? Am I making a false assumption somewhere? Those are the things I would like to talk about. That fundamental understanding is what I see lacking in most public discourse, and why I refuse to participate in most of it.

2) In theory, a corporation is simply an abstract body of rules and procedures used to coordinate separate but interdependent companies. That's why we say cities and states and businesses with multiple departments are all "incorporated." They are generally managed by a governing body that is wholly separate and generally unconcerned with the specific business of any particular subsidiary company. Instead, the only concern of a corporation is the continued interaction or transaction between these companies.

There are no "employees" from the corporation's perspective, only functions. To use yesterday's table making example, there is a function that produces raw materials and a function that produces tables from those raw materials. The corporation cares only about the success of the process: obtain-transfer-produce.

Should one of these stages fail in some way, the corporation has only 1 decision to make, replace the failing component or dissolve the corporation itself. I say replace for lack of a better word; I simply mean correct whatever failure is taking place in some way without eliminating the component function itself. Remember, there are no people involved in this model, it consists only of two functions and a link between them. The corporation exists only to monitor that link and decide how to correct or remove the failure.

For example, a failure to obtain resources might entail relocation, substitution, or elimination of that subsidiary function. That does not necessarily mean that the function ceases to operate, in only means that it is no longer considered part of the corporation's resources. A failure of transaction might involve bringing the two functions into closer proximity, or adding a third function that manages the transaction itself as a subsidiary company. A failure of production is essentially the same as a failure to obtain resources.

If your brain is buzzing with examples of how people have misused or misunderstood this model, I don't blame you, but please push those thoughts away for now. I am only concerned with the fundamental structure, not its real-world manifestations.

At this point, I have outlined 3 unequal functions. They are unequal because 2 of those functions exist in isolation, while the third monitors the interaction between them. They are also unequal in that 2 of the functions are regulated, but the third is not. There is no overseer who determines if the corporation itself has properly assessed the interaction. Nor can there ever be a "regulator" of the corporation, as inventing one will simply be redundant to infinity; a check on the check of the check....

The real lesson in all of this is that the structure of this corporate business model is inherently uneven, and biased toward successful transaction over either component production. The corporation itself inherits an invention of pure human imagination; the overriding rule of self preservation. For the corporation, it is more important to sustain successful interaction and it will subsume all external forces into that unequal relationship.

As I asked before, have I made a mistake? Am I missing a step? I am after all building a theory from the ground up, and I can only draw from my own self-taught knowledge of systems in general.

Or, enjoy any of the delightful albums from the band that helped make the electric guitar an acceptable instrument for public consumption, the Ventures. I say, Let's Go! No thinky words, I promise.

P.S. No, this wasn't an elaborate ruse to bring my separate trains of facebook thought into a productive but pointless pun on "business venture," but you can be assured that as soon as I realized I *could* do it, I knew I had to, and I enjoyed a hearty giggle on the inside.

272) Republica

My friend Sam and I shared a tiny little inside joke today, and the telescope my wife ordered so she and Jupiter-jos could look at the stars arrived, so I thought I might try to share the galaxy of thoughts those completely unrelated things created in my brain today. And wouldn't you know it, there's a specific album hiding in there. Is it good? Ghastly green gravy, no, it's probably a faint unremarkable blob in your collective memories. But does Bottle love it? Indubitably.

The secret is just a boring old number, but its source is a leather couch in a coffee shop in Bethany, Oklahoma and a guess the number game I programmed on my TI-86 graphing calculator. I also made a little picture book with the final punch line being a drawing of my middle finger, and somehow the phrase "el pavo de Diablo" and white-chocolate mochas for me and shots of espresso for him figure into it. And terrible cult classic movies, and playing doom, quake, and freddy pharkas frontier pharmacist which took up too much ram in the end stages and he would have to rewrite the bios to not run services so we could keep playing. And that's like an impossibly miniscule fraction of the memories I have with my best friend.

You have to understand something about me. I have never heard anyone describe memory the way I experience it. It's not photographic, or idetic, or any of those other trendy words. The best analogy I can come up with is cinematographic. I can literally watch my memories with the part of my brain that processes vision in the same way people have described a musician's brain acting like they are physically hearing music. My joke has always been that I have no concept of time, because all of my experiences are just there in chronological order. I only have to pick a starting point. It could be seconds ago, or years. Obviously, if a scene was boring, I probably stopped paying attention and don't remember it, but there's only like 3 or 4 times in my life I've ever been officially "bored." One of them I left Sam's house and drove east on 23rd street just to see what was out there and ended up in Harrah, OK before turning around. So, not boring at all. I most definitely get overwhelmed, but never bored. Consequentially, I forget that long spans of time have passed since I saw or spoke to the people I love, and it makes me sad that I can't really fix that problem.

But enough about that, when I think about all that stuff, I also think about Republica. Did they disappear from the universe because they sucked, or because we just didn't care about alternative electronic pop/rock? Let's find out.

Why yes, Saffron, I am weird. I'm also confused as to why we are on the rooftops, and what exactly the "it" is that we are supposedly having. Oh, you're ready to go now. Ok, where?

Hold your horses right there. What did I do? We were having a confusing romp on the rooftops and now you're ready to fight. You're the one who was ready to go. I'm driving in city traffic and you're mad that I'm concentrating instead of jabberjawing? And why are you mad that I have a job?

You called yourself that, I certainly didn't say it. Are you just mad 'cause I'm not rich?

Ok fine take a train to a random city and eat chinese food, then come back and complain that you didn't have a good time.

You want me to objectify you? Is that sarcasm? I am very confused.

Thanks for saying I'm pretty and that you forgive me. Oh, you meant your ex-boyfriend? No, me? No, him? I'm not even sure we ever dated, or that you broke up with me. What the hell are you talking about?

Yes, of course we are all trapped in our own lives. I know what you mean, but I think you could express it better without the backup singer.

Look, I still don't know what the hell is going on here so I feel very uncomfortable with your explicit sexual advances.

It's like I'm not even here. Hello, hello, am I in an M. Night Shyamalan movie?

Who the bloody hell is Holly!? Never mind I guess you're ready to go again.

Listen, it has certainly been an interesting evening and I'm not opposed to maybe trying it again sometime. Maybe I'm just not the kind of flashy or extroverted go-getter guy you're looking for right now. That's ok. I've got your number, you've got mine, one of us will call the other in a couple years to catch up.

What an awesome trip down memory lane that was. Thanks, Sam. Wish I were closer and could hang out with yuhs (that's my Garth Algar impression). G'night everybody.

273) Grimes - Geidi Primes

What the hell is Grimes? I don't mean who, I mean what. The best answer I have is Grimes: because...Japan.

You might know her because you heard me randomly mention her when I was talking about something else a long time ago. Or, you might know her and her "partner" as recipients of the annual Name Your Child Something Even More Ridiculous Than The Prince Symbol Contest (I hear he's famous for something or other, but I live under a rock, or at least surrounded by rocks). Or, sadly, you probably just read that she's Elon Musk's girlfriend and cared no further. I don't care about that, I'm the internet's least interested music nerd. I know her from her 2012 album, Visions, which I randomly stumbled across and said "whaaaaa?"

I'm currently listening to her first album, Geidi Primes. I guess it's a concept album about Dune, that isn't actually about Dune at all. She didn't expect anyone to ever hear it, and feels moderately embarrased about having to constantly answer questions like "what the hell does any of this actually have to do with Dune?"

Most of her music is just electronic dance music, albeit weird and unique. This album, though, is highly experimental, amateurish, and thoroughly enjoyable. What I don't understand is her symbolic imagery. I get the japanese "super-flat" quality, to borrow an actual phrase from the contemporary art world, but I don't get the juxtaposition of Sailor Moon cosplay and albino boa constrictors. Or body builders and motocross. Or cowboy hats and angel wings.

And a falsetto voice that I can only compare to the singing mice from Babe. And she's got that same out of nowhere singing lisp as Richard Carpenter. It's barely noticable when they talk in real life, what the hell is it supposed to mean when they amp it way up while singing?

I generally don't beg you to suffer like I do, but damnit I need some outside assistance. Go listen to all her albums, so we can at least be completely befuddled together.

274) The Don Ho TV Show

I don't have to defend liking Don Ho, I don't have to defend moving from Grimes to Don Ho, the complete opposite ends of any musical spectrum you care to develop, but I do have to defend him from being seen as a "commercial sellout," from the perspective of his fellow Hawaiians.

He was an aviator for the joint Navy-Air Force transport command until he left the Air Force to help his ailing mother run her bar back home in 1959, coincidentally the same year Hawaii became a state. He always enjoyed playing and singing, and he started doing shows for tourists. He naturally got more and more popular as tourism became a major industry in the state, and made recognizing WWII Veterans an integral part of the show. It's easy to see why commercial pop was his focus, he wasn't trying to be a musical artist, he was just catering to drunk people who wanted to be entertained; a little bit of Vegas on a tropical island. Does he go a little too far and step across the line into embarrasing cultural exploitation? Probably. Did it hurt his career? No. Did he care much that his fellow Hawaiians were less than enthused? Well, I'm currently hearing his version of Aquarius/Let The Sunshine In, and no he clearly didn't give a fat flying fig newton. I don't take him as a cultural representation of his Hawaiian heritage, I see him as Hawaii's Dean Martin or Frank Sinatra, and a boon to the state's economy. If I were 30 years older, I would have paid to see his show too, 'cause I not so secretly like crooner schlock quite a bit.

If you haven't figured out by now, I do everything my way.

275) Symbolic Americana

I knew I still had some records up in the attic, so today I went up and retrieved them. I don't have a turntable or needle for 78s so I left that stack up there, but I brought down a big fistful of 33s. Some were given to me, some were picked up on random trips to random places, some were obtained in let's call it a dubious manner. I honestly don't know where this one came from, but I have it so let's give it a spin.

You're looking at all the information there is, the jacket has 4 wonderful paintings, and the label gives you some unhelpful information about where it was recorded. It's called Symbolic Americana and it's by Phillip White Hawk playing a hybrid Lute/Guitar and singing. Time to fire up the google machine.

Discogs tells me it's Sunhawk SR-4211, Phillip White Hawk is a Cherokee singer/songwriter, the first half is a reissue of his Returning Of The Medicine Horse LP, and it's from 1976. Percival, IA is a bit south of Omaha/Council Bluffs (thank you google maps). That's all I've got.

Or is it? I mean, I'm a guy who makes music for the sheer love of making music, clearly he is too. I'm a champion of ordinary people, and all my album reviews address that in some way. The ones I hate the most are the ones that obscure the actual humanity of their creators.

This thing, though, is amazing. I justified Don Ho because his intentions were obvious: help the people he loved by catering to tourists with money. I don't have to justify this in any way, it's an expression of pure love for life and I can't believe how amazingly lucky I am to be able to share it with you.

Please enjoy this 1976 recording of Phillip White Hawk that has taken 6+ hours to get online for you. I've split it up into 4 separate sides for a more authentic feel, and to ease the burden on your short, modern attention spans. Please be aware that it has an enormous dynamic range and the Lutar is mixed significantly lower than the vocals (i.e. don't crank up the volume just because it sounds quiet until you know how loud it actually is).

276) Herbie Mann - Memphis Underground

Tonight's album is an interesting fusion of jazz and R&B from 1969. It's actually 4 jazz soloists and a backing band. The backing band was the house band at American where it was recorded and Herbie Mann brought along two guitarists and a vibraphone player, and called it (not surprisingly) Memphis Underground. He played other instruments too, but he's generally regarded as one of the first specialized jazz flautists.

If you don't consider yourself a jazz aficionado, don't worry. This album sounds like a funk/soul record with soloists rather than singers. You definitely know the Isaac Hayes classic Hold On, I'm Comin', and Herbie, Roy, Larry, and Sonny do a pretty ripping take on it.

If the strangeness of the ensemble doesn't reel you in, perhaps a real proper distorted noise solo will. If you thought Free Form Guitar from Chicago Transit Authority was too tame, or that Pharoah Sanders was too restrained, you're in for a real treat. The second half of said Hold On is absolute armageddon. No, I'm not exaggerating, it sounds like Hendrix or The Who or anyone just destroying their gear for the hell of it. Magnificent. There's more of it on side 2, and a hot plate! (I mean octave pedal, you remember that obscure George Plimpton gag from The Simpson's, of course you do) if that only made you hungry for more.

It's on youtube, give it a try and I think you'll be pleasantly surprised just how nutritious and delicious it really is.

277) More flute, this time with funny trousers!

We've edged past 11:00pm and you though I was gonna forget about an album. Nonesuch! You know me better than that.

Let's stick with flute, and hear some C.P.E. Bach. These are old-school sonatas for this new-fangled side flute thingamabob and harpsichord. 3 movements: slow, fast, faster. Frederick the Second approved, gallant, major keys, one theme at a time, and well under 4 minutes a movement, please and thank you.

Bye bye Poland, see you again in a hundred something years after Napoleon defeats Prussia. It's like musicians don't understand why everybody loves war, or something. Nevermind, just put on your evening pantaloons and enjoy Rampal's take on some lovely duets from Bach 3.0. Two thumbs up from me.

278) MC5 - Kick Out The Jams

I suppose I have to do it. I've been postponing it for ages, but I have the holy grail of Detroit garage rock self indulgence. The soundtrack of the White Panther Party, the reason Lester Bangs existed famously enough to get mentioned in an REM song: the first MC5 album, Kick Out The Jams.

Lester's actual review of the album isn't anywhere near as scathing as people pretend it is. It is a decadent album, it was way overhyped, but it is easy to learn to love it and change your mind. In fact, the only thing you can't do is get over the sheer shock of Wayne Kramer's falsetto on Ramblin' Rose. I still laugh every time. I can't help it, it's so shocking it's funny.

What are we really dealing with here? Well, it's proto-punk, it lives in that weird space between Ziggy Stardust glam and the Sex Pistols grotesque downward spiral. These guys were the real deal. They actually made more money playing shows than they did at their day jobs, so they quit going to work. They upstaged Big Brother and the Holding Company and Cream when they opened for either. At no point did they ever need to make an actual record. But, when they finally did it was a big deal. Remember that DNC riot from the liner notes of Chicago Transit Authority? Yeah, MC5 played for 8 goddamned hours there 'cause nobody else dared step out on stage. That reminds me of that hilarious Melanie concert powered by ice cream trucks. Man, the late 60s make our modern day hissy fit over public health and safety look like a kindergarden scuffle over who gets to sleep on the pink yoga mat.

    This is a Bottle review, so I'm allowed to call you a moron if you think Corporate America is doing a good job at any of the things they are doing on publicly broadcasted radio. I don't need a pundit to tell me how stupid the words these 4 and 5-digit morons vomit on a daily basis, I heard them say it (for the record, I'm a 3 digit moron and those numbers refer to the average daily balance of your checking account). If you're even the tiniest bit comforted by anything a broadcast personality says at the moment, then please unfriend me in real life.

    Now, before you get all defensive about your 0.3% dividend for investing in the hedge fund that invested in Sandra Marmaduke's Mailboxes By Mail, or Bankrupt a Trucking Company and Sons, please remember that that money was withheld from someone else's paycheck. In real life, owning a company is the way you document losses from your actual income to lower your tax liability. Finding just the right amount of failure is the key.

    Sorry, I got sidetracked. What Lester actually learned later was that these people were good people, and that the ridiculous spectacle was the whole point. They were a band of crazy working-class people who truly believed that this was as good a dream life as anyone could ask for. Look, you and your

4 friends aren't practicing every night in Kyle's garage to not wear sparkly capes and be sheer mayhem. No, you're in it to hear 500 people scream and dance around like maniacs while you act as ridiculous as possible.

To be sure, there's a heavy left political spin. However, that spin is much more clear and direct on this album than most anywhere else. It's not militant, it's not offensive, it's simply the notion that being rich doesn't make you better than anyone else. Especially when your money came from the labor of people you pretend are somehow "less" than you. MC5 spent all that money making their show bigger and even more ridiculous because that's the whole point of it all.

Plus, I must have like the best pressing ever because this is probably the third best live recording I've heard. Go read forums. Everybody says it sounds tinny and overproduced, and I'm like whaaa? The Stones' vinyl mastering is crap, this sounds great. It's supposed to sound like the speakers in their amps are about to shred, that's not fake tube sag, the vocals are actually audible, and the crowd noise isn't making it unlistenable at all.

Anywho, if you've never actually listened to the first MC5 album Kick Out The Jams, you really should. It took me 2 or 3 times to warm up to it, but yeah, it's a great little piece of anarchy sure to exacerbate your tinnitus in a good way.

279) Rod McKuen - The Single Man

The humor of this trope hasn't worn out its welcome yet, so what the hell is a Rod McKuen?

I've got a second appropriately socially distanced glass of Malbec perched conspicuously atop my composer's notebook with the associated bandcamp album in the background, the googlemaphone is primed and ready to deliver the ancient wisdom of the skin fleshed tome that is wikipedia (that's a pretty weak Evil Dead/Army Of Darkness reference), and away we go.

The first thing is technically a song, but the second thing is definitely a poem, and unless I'm mistaken that's a terrible Clint Eastwood impression. And wouldn't you know it, wikipedia leads off with the fact that he sold more albums than books of poetry. In all honesty, I can see it. Once you get used to it, his singing is actually quite charming. He's no Sinatra or Torme or Martin or Ho, but he does have a certain charm. He's no Emerson, or Blake either, but that's just the wine talking.

Yeah, he's Kermit the Frog's Clint Eastwood impression, I can't unhear it.

"I'm down to the last of the wine." Now that is the most serendipitous coincidence that I didn't plan in any way. I swear, I didn't know that was going to happen. Not a joke, that really is pure random coincidence.

I'm not doing it justice, this album is actually really cool. No, I'm not a fan of his poetry in particular, but the musical accompaniment is legitimately fascinating. I can see and hear why he was really popular in the late 60s.

I checked, and you can find most of it on youtube. If you're 30 years or more older than me you might not think he's obscure, but for me this is insanely obscure. 3 or 4 more listens and/or glasses of wine and I'd be all in. No, I take that back, the orchestration on this thing is incredible. "Arranged and Conducted By Eddie Karam." If this bizarre album is any indication, he's a pretty close second to Marty Paich in my book. There's choir and strings and horns and harpsichord. Yeah, harpsichord.

You taste like almonds? Did I mention I'm not a fan of Rod McKuen's poetry? I'm not, he's worse than James Seals. Any of you guys know some more albums Eddie Karam worked on? The music is gorgeous!

280) Mothermania

I did a quick calculation, and my LP/CD collection is larger than 818. It's probably a little over 1,000 physical discs actually, and I've barely written about 300 of them (280 essays with many multiple album days). Wouldn't it be awesome if 20 or 30 people gave me a dollar every day for writing them? It would. Is it ever going to happen? No. For starters, I don't care. For second breakfast, it's not like you can run over to your local record store and buy any of them. For elevensies (my wife started watching The Lord of the Rings yesterday and these things creep into my essays like I have a cinematographic memory, or something), the fact that I've listened to about 500 different albums all the way through since last September is just beyond comprehension even for me, and I'm the one who listened to all of them. You guys would owe me thousands of dollars at this point. You're welcome, here's tonight's best of the best.

I should have done this last Sunday, but whatever. I have one more Mothers Of Invention album and it's the perfect opportunity to delve into some behind the scenes stuff about Zappa's recordings. Tonight's album is the "best of" called Mothermania. The back cover is completely in German. Geil!

It was considered redundant by critics, and Zappa publicly distanced himself from it for a long time, but the story is more interesting than that.

They made 4 albums for MGM/Verve and that was the end of the contract. So, Zappa created a semi-independent label called Bizarre. Essentially, they worked out a deal where Bizarre was the publisher and Verve did the marketing and MGM was the distributer. Verve felt like they had lost money publishing the first 4 albums, so part of the deal was that Zappa would make a compilation that Verve could use to recoup their money. He did. He remixed and remastered material to form a brand-new continuous mix. Each side really is a 20ish minute work, pieced together from earlier pieces. It's the only one Frank himself ever made.

What made him mad was that they pushed it through as quickly as possible and got it into stores before Uncle Meat. That meant that anyone walking into a store would see both the new Zappa owned album next to a cheaper, not owned by Zappa "best of" album. Which one are more people who don't actually know the difference going to buy?

However, it's hard to stay mad when the actual project is a realization of something you've been saying all along: all this stuff is a giant modular monstrosity that can and should be played around with, rearranged, and heard in various combinations. That's what appeals to me.

Believe it or not, Zappa and Prince had a lot in common. They both fought really hard to get back their masters, they stored them all in the hopes of doing more with them, but died before they really had the chance to actually get somewhere. They also had no real plan for how anyone should actually execute decisions about their estates. I don't know the exact difficulties with Prince's vaults, but I do know that Zappa's estate was basically bankrupt, to the point that Ahmet and Moon had to actually sue Dweezil for playing their dad's music just to pay some leftover bills. I'm sure I've mentioned my feelings about our convolutedly moronic copyright laws a time or two. I know the idea of royalties for the heirs of great artists in perpetuity sounded good in Sonny Bono's brain, but that brain also produced Inner Views, and both those things are so shortsightedly preposterous that I can't even.

The reason you don't see Mothers reissues too often is that they just don't have the money to manufacture physical copies. Great for collectors looking to sell for profit, tough luck for anyone looking to buy physical records or CDs. The worst Zappa LP with giant visible gouges will fetch $20 *if* you happen to stumble across it.

And really, what's the point any more? You can't sell new physical music anywhere because it would cost trillions of dollars to cater to everyone's tastes, and the moment an independent label does find a niche market, the majors come smashing down the door to keep themselves afloat. Fat Mike wrote a lovely song called "Dinosaurs Will Die," but UMG, Sony, and Warner are putting up one hell of a kamikaze death fight.

I feel like a broken record harping on this major corporations thing, but we have to make it stop at some point. There are enough cars sitting on dealership lots to satisfy us for the next 15 years, we're killing thousands of pigs a day because we can't find truck drivers or slaughterhouse workers willing to work for pennies, UPS drivers are trying to make triple the amount of stops in a day than a month ago, "illegal immigrants" build our McMansions, America is destroying itself just like Dave Mustaine said we would, and everybody's too busy demanding that someone else cook them a steak to be bothered.

That's my sermon, and I'm stickin' to it. Contact your local vegetables, and call them by name.

281) DLP-185

Remember that garbage off-brand disko album from Pickwick I shared a while ago? Well, here's a fairly legit compilation from their subsidiary Design Records (the one Lou Reed worked for). Some lesser-known songs from the Kings of '62 and The J Brothers (not the Phillipino pop band or the construction company). You're seriously telling me the google mapped part of the information sewer highway doesn't have anything to say about a completely non-famous New York singing group from a discount republisher with Lou Reed sitting in on guitar and providing something akin to lyrics?

Oh, sure, it's janky as all get out, but you gotta do some real 3rd page search engine scuba diving research before you chuck things in the trash can. This is a little treasure of long forgotten b-sides and throw away songs in my book. I wish I had the ability to share it with you, but these things are definitely catalogued in youtube's copyright cross-check library. We wouldn't want to gyp Neil Sedaka of that sweet sweet 1/7,500 of a cent revenue from his agent's nephew's girlfriend's little brother's razor blade manufacturing company's youtube ad campaign, now would we?

That's ok, I can guide you through imagining it. Take your grandma's old AM transistor radio and put it in the microwave on high for 20 minutes. While that's exploding, take a nail file and ram it in and out of your left ear. Once you're properly bleeding, imagine Johnny Rivers singing about a hole in a bucket, and that's what listening to a dirty ¼-inch thick plate of recycled tire rubber from the 1960s sounds like. Acetone would make a dramatic improvement. There's no bass to speak of, it's pure eye watering mids and crackles. If stucco made a sound, Pickwick would have tried to sell it at Woolworth's.

Yes, of course I'm exaggerating, it's what I do. But no, this is not an audiophile grade, from the original master recording type beast. It's a genuine imitation department store Christmas present for your least favorite nephew type album. Love it!

282) The Sandpipers

I couldn't leave my friends with an album they couldn't go hear, so how about some 60s folk from the Sandpipers' second album, The Sandpipers.

They were a trio who suspiciously always had uncredited female back up singers. Always. Live, recordings, sometimes two of them, and this one time they snuck a photo of 5 whole people on the back of an album. Sometimes they even let the ladies sing actual words instead of imitating a flute in the ensemble. Not the lady on this particular cover. No clue who she is, but she's pretty. That'll sell. Suspicious, indeed.

They were famous for singing all sorts of random crap in foreign languages. It's actually pretty enjoyable, and I gotta tell you I had no idea how prominent the harpsichord was in 60s pop.

Have you ever heard a Spanish translation of Yesterday? Well, what are you waiting for!? Imagine talking to your friends and slipping in a mention of The Sandpipers singing "Michelle, me amore" with full on Mariachi accompaniment. I'll feed you, baby bird. I know you don't care for those youtube ads, but I'm not gonna mail you my vinyl. Such is life I'm afraid.

283) Baja Marimba Band - Those Were The Days

I was right in the middle of writing about two other albums, but while I was searching for the second one I coincidentally came across this album. It's funny because the other day I was looking at my friend Tim Verville's website and somehow came across some class notes where he mentioned Baja Marimba Band. They'd drive a modern-day PR lady to spike her wine with Tylenol3 (that's the one with codeine). Cultural appropriation aside, this is just great fun from some serious studio jazz musicians having a laugh.

I've got a bad habit of starting a review then chasing butterflies, and I'm like 3 deep right now. Hopefully I can circle around and finish some of them. Until then, please enjoy the Tijuana Brass's younger brother, Chuck Barris's go-to game show theme song performers, the Baja Marimba Band. Those were the days, indeed.

284) Burl & Bylan - Pearly Shells and Nashville Skyline

Thank you for your patience. We here at Bottle of Beef pride ourselves on our selection of hold music. Please continue enjoying Baja Marimba Band, have a glass of strawberry wine, and Bottle will be with you shor....

Hello! Sorry for making you wait. I've got two more albums for you tonight, but this time the connection is completely musical. I'll get to that in a second.

On paper, I should like these two records the other way around. The one I hate is the one I'm supposed to like. The reason is actually quite simple. I learned how to play every song on the second album from a transcription without ever hearing the originals. I know it sounds trite and condescending, but the version in my head is so much better than the actual thing that it's really uncomfortable to listen to it.

On paper, there's no reason why I should like Burl Ives. So, I'm gonna pull out my "I don't need a reason" card. Burl Ives is great, end of story. I'd go as far as to say there's something wrong with you if you don't like Pearly Shells, or any of the other favorites on DL 4578, played at 33 1/3. Like the mythical phoenix rising from the ashes, F(x) is its own derivative, I mean the album itself contains all the standard vinyl speeds. That's one of those complicated inside jokes from a high school math textbook that even I barely remember. Side A ends with a hanging for murder, but the real murderer's telltale heart finally broke him, so they hanged him too. And some high school english to boot!

What was I talking about? Oh yeah, the pedal steel solo on Pearly Shells ends with the same melody Dylan uses for the lyric "no light will shine on me" from One More Night off Nashville Skyline. It's a common melodic ending, but I can't stop myself from making the connection. The only thing worse than normal Dylan is Dylan actually singing. They say it was

Dylan letting Nashville have a stab at making a Bob Dylan album, but blech!

Not to confuse you, every song on Nashville Skyline is great, but anybody else singing would be better. Maybe I can trick my brain into hearing Burl Ives sing it. That'd be cool. Short of that, I'll just go back to my internal memory of learning the songs from sheet music.

I'm not intentionally looking for a nostalgic tour of my younger days, but to quote a very familiar song from my earlier mention of Baja Marimba Band that you probably didn't know was originally by Burt Bacharach and Hal David (admit it, you thought some 80s pop band wrote it), there's always something there to remind me.

In practice, you might prefer listening to them the other way around, as I very much wish I had done.

285) It's the end of the world as we know it (for bluegrass, at least)

I'm going to tell you the weirdest story. It came out of last night's random encounter between Burl Ives and Bob Dylan. Now, I've told you I avoid country albums for lots of reasons, but it's really just the simple fact that country gets to be so formulaic that's it's just not interesting anymore. Like if every track on a blues record was 12-bar, or if every pop track was I-V-vi-IV. That wouldn't be bad if they told a story with a real plot, or shed some interesting take on the human condition, but "I drink beer and I drive a truck, my girlfriend left me, and...," I don't give a flaming flamingo.

But that's not to say I don't like or appreciate the music, I just don't want to carry it around in my head all day. But again, even the most remedial music history that mentions Bluegrass has a couple paragraphs about Flatt & Scruggs.

So, here's what's been bothering me. Blonde On Blonde is a deservedly historic album (1965), and Nashville Skyline (1969) is probably Bylan's most polarizing album. For a start, it's full-on country at a time when the entire universe was looking to him to bear the flame of liberal rock and roll. Rock fans were obviously aghast.

But here's Kris Kristofferson saying it was a breath of fresh air, a let your hair down and stop being so uptight sucker punch to Nashville in general. The Grand Ole Opry got a little bit hipper. 1969, Country will never be the same and Flatt said "Skrugg this" and flat out refused to be a part of it anymore. I have their penultimate album from 1968 and it's been nagging a hole in my brain.

You've seen the cover, Nashville Airplane. It's a corporate gimmick, the notes on the back ham it up calling the producers flight control and the musicians the crew and their agent the stewardess, etc. It's silly, but it's fine. But it's got 4 Bylan songs on it, including the lead track from Blonde On Blonde. Hearing Flatt & Skruggs sing "everybody must get stoned" is worth the ticket price alone, but then Bylan goes all in with Nashville Skyline. They were Columbia label-mates, how could it possibly be any form of coincidence? It would make more sense the other way around, but just like dead men release dates tell no tales. Bylan was the man who shot Lester Flatts' metaphorical Liberty Valance, or maybe Bylan was Valance and Lester was Jimmy Stuart, but Earl Skruggs would be John Wayne, but that doesn't quite work right…

… and that's why late at night when a wisp of cloud floats across the quarter moon you can hear the faintest of conspiracy-tinged whispers on the southwest wind; as if to say "my name is Bottle, and Bob Dylan is the Yoko Ono of Bluegrass."

286) Mantovani v Mancini for the championship title

… and the orchestra he rode in on, I mean
… and his orchestra!

It's time for another grudge match. This time our contenders hail from the world of film and television soundtracks. In the blue corner, weighing in at 1962, the Menace of Venice, Annunzio Paolo Mantovani. And in the red corner, needing no introduction, at a close 1963 (those few months aren't going to make or break him), Henry Mancini. They touch gloves and head to their corners. We're in for a real treat tonight, folks. These heavyweights of film score are true titans. Gonna be a great fight. There's the bell, and they come out swinging.

And it's Mantovani on the attack, with a vicious left hook. Some referees might frown on leading off with your opponent's own piece, but Bottle is no stranger to back-alley brawls and he knows this London release has a different track order from the first run Decca version, so he lets it pass. Plus, it didn't really connect, I mean there's a reason Moon River and Drunk Trumpet are two different Kid Koala pieces.

Mantovani is certainly testing the waters, but he sounds a bit shrill. He'll loosen up pretty soon, though. Ooh, the accordion connected. That's gonna leave a mark. The Mancini crew will definitely be checking that Welk over his right eye at the break. He's moving high and low, checking for any signs of weakness, but a strong showing overall from the challenger from Italy. We'll see how Mancini responds in the second round.

Let's take this interlude to say both these men have impressive pedigrees. One or the other might seem more famous to you, but both men have cast their influence far and wide. A little bit of trivia for you, we've got a secret highlight reel showing Mantovani's little joke about David McCallums Sr. And Jr., "We can afford the father, but not the son!" But that's an album for another night because we're back to the action.

Mantovani came out strong in the first round, let's see if Mancini can turn the tables (covers mic: I don't care if anyone got it, that's a damned fine joke if I do say so myself). Green Onions? That's certainly an interesting approach. But my word does it work in his favor. Mancini's saxophonist wiped the floor with Mantovani's trumpeter, and I can see the judges scribbling furiously. If he can keep this up, he'll be taking home the belt for sure. He's really turning up the heat with the horns and bass flutes, hoping to counter Mantovani's accordion. And the tenor sax sends the Italian reeling. He's got him up against the ropes and we're barely halfway. Just when you thought he'd reach maximum sultry he switches gears with his own take on Ellington's C Jam. He's not letting up folks, we may have to call it early out of mercy. Oh no, he might have got a little too cocky with that much too mushy Rhapsody in Blue. He's ahead on the scorecards, but running out of steam is the wrong way to keep it out of the judges' hands. Cheers seems to be working, though. That tiny setback might not be a problem after all. Oh my goodness! Can you believe it? That Lonesome came out of nowhere, and the challenger is stunned. Now Mancini's just toying with him, turning down the treble for a deep dark grammaphone style coup de gras.

And it's all over! The Mantovani camp has thrown in the towel. They trained hard, and it shows, but Mancini was just too much. Any lesser opponent and the outcome would have been different for the challenger, but Mancini pulled out all the stops and retains the title of heavyweight champion of the 60s film score conducters league.

What an incredible evening that was. From all of us here at Bottle of Beef, thanks for watching and we'll catch you on the flip side.

287) Joe Cocker - A Luxury You Can Afford

Now, some of you die hard collectors might find it painful when I do this. Tough. You can keep your mint in-box cabbage patch dolls, or your complete set of micro machines. One of the greatest joys in the life of any Bottle like myself is opening a never been touched cut record from the glory days of the 99-cent Target bin. Luckily, that is a luxury I can afford.

And what an appropriate coincidence, it's Joe Cocker's 7th album from 1978, his only release from Asylum. Well, now that the cardboard cut under my thumbnail is bleeding appropriately, and I've just lowered it's apparent value from $30 to $6, let's give it a spin.

Oh man, that's good. It's British Big Band Blues (duh), the kind you might associate with your parents' 20-year high school reunion (unless you're younger than me, then that won't make any sense at all).

If you only know the couple super famous Joe Cocker tracks, you're really missing out. I've always thought of him as a good version of Eric Clapton singing. This album has his take on Procol Harum's hit Whiter Shade of Pale, among other great tracks.

British Blues, like every other genre they were enamored with, lived a life of its own. Seriously, Black Sabbath essentially created heavy metal from it, Mayall and Clapton gave it a seriously broody personality, but Joe Cocker somehow gave it this sophisticated night show vibe. He's not pessimistic or condescending, he's not cheesy or mopey, he's not really drowning his sorrows, he's got this lovable loser crooner thing that really appeals to me. He's raspy when he should be, but not to the point that he sounds beaten. It's actually much slower than you might expect, but I can hear that almost like patiently waiting for the upturn, like there's an underlying optimism that things will get better. Maybe that's just me? It's not an early looking for fame kind of album, it's for the already all-in fans of Joe Cocker.

Now for the downside, this thing is too long. Not musically, physically. Never been played, but that last track and a half are absolute garbage. The first four tracks are absolutely gorgeous, so it's hard to say the pressing itself is bad. I've heard good records that deep toward the center, so

I'd say the lacquers were crap right from the start. A half-assed rush job with no volume compensation wouldn't surprise me at all. No one cared about this record, Cocker was already as big a superstar as he was ever going to be (we're a decade past A Little Help From My Friends and 4 years past You Are So Beautiful after all), and in the middle of label hopping through a string of live albums. Every bit of that is pure shame, in my opinion.

Joe Cocker is just the bee's knees, and you should really give this one a listen. It's on youtube, so truth in advertising, it's A Luxury You Can Afford. Cheers, my friends. May your reopening of 'merica be less unpleasant than the one I've been driving to work in this whole time.

288) Shinola, I mean K-tel's 20 Hits and stuff

I'll wager every crate combing curmudgeon has at least one tragic story where they forgot to actually double check the record itself, only to feel the bowel clenching despair of finding a K-tel compilation inside of a truly collection worthy cover. Mine's Blondie, but at least the record had one Blondie song on it. So be it.

It's much less horrible if you go at it intentionally, and tonight's record at least has a novelty jacket. It's Jukebox Jive from '75.

You know K-Tel, the Canadian infomercial company. Compilation albums, the Veg-o-Matic, Miracle Brush. Sure, they're Winnepegan hosers, but at least they put out the actual original hits, unlike Pickwick or Kidz Bop.

$6.99 on 8 track!? Quick, Marty, get us back to 1975! What do you mean the flux capacitor is broken? Fine, fetch me that 45-year-old dinner plate, I wanna hear some Clyde McPhatter. You don't know Clyde McPhatter?! The Drifters? The godfather of Doowop? What kind of music history are they teaching you kids these days?

But how does it sound? Oh, absolutely terrible. What did you expect from a TV commercial? It's quieter than most records of the time but somehow there's nasty sibilance, they made absolutely no effort to even plug in a VU meter to try and normalize the tracks. Oh god, how did they make Runaway sound like that? The track itself is panned like 75% left, and the right channel is just pure slapback highs. It's definitely a stereo mix, so it's not like it's unintentional. I feel like someone just drove an ice pick into my right temple. Rock Around The Clock is better, but Devil With The Blue Dress On/Good Golly Miss Molly sounds like you need some new brake pads and probably rotors. Yeah, this whole album sounds like a short-range FM broadcast at dusk when the signal interference is at maximum crossover talk radio annoying. The record itself is clean as a whistle so it's definitely poor-quality source tapes.

Wow, Side B is even worse. There's actual phasing and the left channel disappears completely. I jumped to other tracks just to make sure it wasn't my turntable or computer. Nope. It's not even up to the Stones' level of terrible mastering.

But man, I love Lou Christie's Two Faces Have I. He's a pretty close second to Frankie Valley in the awesome falsetto department. I suppose David Lindley's Carol Channing impression from The Load-Out/Stay is untouchable, so maybe he's tied for third with Rick Davies' David Hodgeson impression on Goodbye Stranger. I'm being ridiculously picky, I know.

So, should you pay even a dollar for this thing? No, absolutely not. Five 1975 dollars equates to 23.85 today, and full price for a shitty comp is highway robbery with a side of involuntary manslaughter. They should pay you for even considering flipping it over to look at the back for the actual track list. But, the majority of the songs are great and it's fun to hear what cheap commercial make a quick buck garbage sounded like half a century ago.

If you've ever found one of these lumps if coal in your stocking, then I can empathize. Nothing spells disappointment like K-Tel, but if you're expecting the terrible it's pretty impressive how creatively bad these things can be. Good night and have a pleasant tomorrow (1975 was the year Saturday Night Live debuted, and I bet you totally glossed right over my earlier SCTV reference to Bob and Doug McKenzie. You wouldn't believe how much research I have to do to sound like I'm talking out of my ass...).

289) Promises, Promises

Here's an interesting idea. Let's see if we can piece together the plot of a musical from just the songs. The only thing I know about Promises, Promises is that it's Burt Bacharach's first musical. I know a couple of the songs, but I have no idea what the story is. Should be interesting.

Overture time, themes and stuff, excellent. Party on, Wayne. Sounds like Bacharach, which is to say, Austin Powers levels of campy (Mike Meyers movies are tonight's cinematic sub-theme, apparently. I assume that's just the residual effect of last night's adventures in Canadaland). Onward!

He's not so thrilled with his lack of achievements. But he's gonna be somebody.

3rd floor apartment. What weird timeshare agreement have they got going? Quick inflation math: 637.50 a month for a downtown apartment, and your neighbors "borrow" it for an evening. Yeah, pretty dismal digs, my dude.

Girl who doesn't notice him sitting in the friend zone bleachers. Pretty clever song actually, using the buildup but lack of resolution to mimic his nervousness.

No clue what the secret is, pretty creepy.

She likes basketball?! I like basketball! Match made in heaven.

She's gonna break up with her crummy boyfriend? Or, maybe she's just looking to get out of town?

Who's this random guy wanting things?

Oh, it's Christmas. Ok. Have the two main characters even met yet? Who's that pretty lady walking down the sidewalk? Oh, you mean the girl that likes basketball? She likes basketball!? I like basketball!

It's Christmas, in case you forgot. What fact? Are they drunk in a bar on Christmas?

No clue who she's singing about.

Oh, that's why they all share the same apartment one night a week.

Did you know it's Christmas? I had no idea. That clears up so many questions.

Pickin' up chicks and takin' 'em back to my 3rd floor apartment.

Cheating cheaters cheating on their cheating spouses who cheated. Love stinks, love bites, love is a battlefield, I'm so glad I stopped lying and don't have to lie about lying down with liars and I can save $600 a month by switching to Geico, I mean not renting an apartment so I can have affairs once a week. Merry Christmas, everyone!

How'd I do? I don't actually care enough to look up the plot, but I am curious.

OK, I finally did look it up and HOLY CRAP HOW DID I NAIL THE INSURANCE COMPANY SETTING!!!???!!!

290) Earl Grant - Ebb Tide, etc.

Today's one of those days that makes me run back and quadruple check my karma score-card. I thought I should have been on the upturn, but clearly not. That's my problem, not yours. So, tonight we'll just eschew all the words and listen to multi keyboardist Earl Grant be awesome. We're in for stormy weather tonight, and it just so happens that's the first track on his most famous recording, the Ebb Tide LP.

He was born in Idabel, OK in 1931, and ignoring the risk of uncomfortable innuendo, my dude can manhandle an organ like there's no tomorrow. That's not a joke, the jacket blurb says, and I quote, "[he] coaxes even the most subtle tones and innuendos out of his instruments...." The album itself is like the greatest blues/jazz organ recital with full orchestral accompaniment.

Sadly, my copy has lots of skips. Even more sadly, he died in a car crash on a trip to Mexico at 39. Worst of all, that damned Universal fire again. On the bright side, some other really nice person uploaded their copy to youtube, rice crispies and all like I would have done.

Go give it a listen. It's a gorgeous album that's practically its own lofi production studio. Seriously, this is an incredible album that everyone should get to enjoy. I wish my copy wasn't so beat up, but I don't really mind bumping the needle every once in a while. Cheers.

291) Jan DeGaetanni - Charles Ives Songs

What self respecting music school burnout wouldn't snatch up Jan DeGaetanni's 1976 recording of songs by Charles Ives? Not this one, certainly.

It's hard not to pretend that Ives is a major influence on my own music. The vacillation between bombast and melancholy, modality and dissonance creating strange textures.

What's harder to believe is the sheer coincidence of blindly picking a musical set at an insurance company, unknowingly making a Geico joke, my car breaking down, picking an organist from Oklahoma who died in a car crash, then randomly picking Ives (the most famous insurance salesman of a composer I know) out of my own top shelf collection. They are all very much coincidences, but you have to admit it would probably give a less aware person the heebie jeebies. Or, maybe that subconscious part of my brain is even more powerful than I am willing to accept. Either way, I don't wanna go back to work tomorrow.

Dear millibillionaires, please find a more useful and productive way to divide your wealth among us plebes than buying sports teams and supercars and pedophile islands.

Did you know Ives paid for the publication of his 114 songs himself and gave them away to anyone interested? That certainly seems more worthwhile to me than opening a chain of sub edible fast-food restaurants, or bulldozing a neighborhood to reroute a 9-lane highway, or funding a remake of the Wizard of Oz, or whatever. Did you know John Malkovich lost his entire life savings to Bernie Madoff? I hope Elon Musk's rocket doesn't kill those NASA astronauts.

I wonder what Ives or Copland would think of the plight of the common man today. Probably "who in their right mind elected Scrooge McTrump's kid for president?!" More than likely they would be as confused as ever at how the machinery and wealth of our ingenuity has done nothing to elevate our spirit or good will. We delight in the suffering of others, and we argue at the highest philosophical level about how to keep it going for eternity. The wealthy are too dumb to do anything but under pay their laborers for the promise of more labor, and we elected a perpetually bankrupt grifter to spearhead our ultimate downfall.

We've come a long way from the tigers in their circus cages of Ives' day, only to thrill at watching it happen all over again, and hope that lady murdered her husband. I'm rambling, I apologize. For whatever reason, I can't help feeling like we would be better off without the endless cacophony of modern industry, the epilepsy inducing strobe lights of fictional reality, and the constant reminder that the common man is a burden our economic overlords are unwilling to bear. Let the laborer pay the manager what his services are worth, and find out how much or how little value it deserves.

292) Julian Lloyd Weber - Herbert, Elgar, Sullivan

I waded back into the classical music pool yesterday, and I'm just not in the mood for modern day songs about our ongoing WWII reenactment. So, here's an obscure recording from 1986 of pieces written well before things like bombing other countries were even possible.

What's Andrew Lloyd Weber's little brother have to say? Quite a lot actually, because these were some impressively obscure pieces at the time. Victor Herbert actually played his own premier of his second cello concerto, then wrote some super famous operettas that completely overshadowed his other stuff, Elgar wrote a Romance for a bassoonist friend (and also made a cello version that no one ever heard until Webber's performance of it in 1985), and you know how common bassoon solos are.... Then there's the obscurest of all, Arthur Sullivan's mostly incinerated cello concerto. Julian and friends had to reconstruct it from 2 surviving copies of the cello part, and Charles Mackerras's memory of conducting it back in 1953.

This record is actually worth double digits according to discogs and ebay, and my copy is I'd say very good. Not that I want to sell it. I want to listen to it. He's really good, and these three pieces are quite lovely, even if their respective composers abandoned them for much more entertaining and lucrative things (their opinions, not mine). No, I'd go further. These are great pieces of music written around the turn of the 20th century by composers in the midst of trying really hard to learn how to write great music. That means they weren't just slapping down habitual tropes and phrases that they already knew would work. They're trying out big ideas, and working hard to make them sound awesome. Herbert's concerto inspired Dvorak to run backstage, give him a hug, then scamper off to write his own cello concerto. Elgar's writing a solo for his actual friend, and Sullivan is trying to be Mendelssohn 'cause he hasn't met Gilbert yet.

The album itself isn't on youtube, but I'm pretty sure videos of Julian Lloyd Webber performing the pieces are, and they are definitely worth checking out.

293) Alexander Brailowsky- Chopin 24 Preludes

Here's another interesting album. The 24 Chopin Preludes played by hardcore Chopin enthusiast Alexander Brailowsky. He's famous for filling the space between WWI & WWII with six-night concerts of Chopin's complete works for piano. The first time he did it he actually used Chopin's own piano for quite a few pieces. I'm sure that's where Coheed & Cambria got the idea for their Neverender concerts. Almost certainly. Without a doubt.

But seriously, can you imagine touring all over the world with the entire Chopin catalog in your head every night? That's hardcore. I'm too tired to run up to the attic to fetch my scores, so we'll just lean back and watch the pretty colors flicker on the backs of my eyelids. Quite a relaxing hobby, I highly recommend it.

294) I finally snapped, 'cause I'm a pisces

I didn't want to have to do it, but you forced me with your stupid Boston Tea Party memes and inability to understand that doing half a job is worse than not even bothering to start. You brought this upon yourselves, you whiny snowflake canned bean diet secretly brony posers.

I wish I had Edward Bland's Concerto for electric violin, but I don't. I've got his stunning orchestrations of incredibly famous songs on the most nauseatingly commercial album ever created by a charlatan astrologer, a hair stylist, and a fashion designer. Pisces is the sign of the poet or interpreter. I'll accept the latter title, but not because Carroll Righter says so. I'll side with Killer Mike on this one and say, oh ok Ronald Reagan was his fault.

Put on your Oscar De La Renta unitard, rub some Paul Mitchell conditioner through your hair, and say it with me: astrologer to the stars, my ass. Ooooh, he wrote a book just for me? What human love can compare to the compassion of a fish, indeed? Good news everybody, I have the psychic quality of spiritual understanding. Blah blah blah, paradox, contradiction, you got me. I'm a total February/March.

All I can say is, poor sweet Edward Bland. I hope they paid you more that they paid for that green bikini, or to have a stylist glue her hair to her face. It's not listed on your official web page's discography, so I'm guessing they pretty much robbed you. It sounds so good, it's a shame they marketed it as sushi, but almost surely paid you for skunk bait.

See what you made me do? Are you happy with yourself? If you want to burn down main street, burn it down.

But, they were being jerks! So are you. Stop fighting.

You're all morons. I'm a moron too, but at least I have the decency to admit it. You can't "prevent tragedy," you can't "police the population" you can't tell me that vindictive violence is more righteous than the original violence. You can't solve anything. You suck. You're useless. America is crap. It's a garbage country. If you are even the slightest bit offended by that opinion, then you clearly can't tell the difference between an opinion and the real world. I the person am not my opinions. Stop demanding that I have them. They suck.

My opinions are garbage. Your opinions are garbage. This album is garbage, but the pieces of music on it are phenomenal. A person sat down with a pen and scribbled musical notes on a piece of paper that 90% of you can't read, because some old charlatan practical psychologist paid him money to do it, which last time I checked is the only thing grocery stores take in exchange for food, and if I never post another goddamned thing on facebook ever again it's because I can't stand how garbage everyone's ideas are and how desperately everyone needs to feel like they belong when you can't even name more than 3 people who live on your street because you're afraid their pit bull might snatch your newborn baby out of your swimming pool, and muslims, and lizard people, and toxic waste in my cat food, and we never went to the moon, and there's always some nefarious plot to steal plutonium from Lybians in the parking lot of a shopping mall, and…

    Have you had enough yet? I have. It's all garbage. There's a symphonic transcription of My Favorite Things on this album. That's ridiculous and awesome at the same time.

    It's all just words. The words you use affect the way you think. Did a police officer who should have already been removed from active duty kill a man? Yes. Did Amy Klobuchar recuse herself from prosecuting him a long time ago? Yes. Is Donald Trump the child of a Ku Klux Klan member who was repeatedly investigated for profiteering and defrauding the general public by selling his government contracts to himself? Yes. You elected him president of the United States of America. I did not. I didn't particularly want Hillary Clinton to be President, but I voted for her in the hopes that we could avoid the last 4 years on non stop garbage coming out of everyone's mouth and brain.

    If you want my opinion, burn it to the ground. Destroy everything so that future generations might not follow in our idiotic footsteps. Or, maybe, shut up and actually attempt to solve a problem. How? Work a little, save a little, have some fun. Last time I checked, you don't get a prize for dying last. Racism is alive and terrible and I see it every day, but I suspect that killing people is like eating pringles because I don't want to do either of those things.

    If you don't want my opinion, why are you reading my facebook posts? I've many times over proved that these things don't lead where you expect them to, and it's your own fault at this point. Did someone burn your house down today? No? Then stop complaining and help the guy whose house burned down today. I'm sick of being the whole world's dad. GET OFF MY LAWN!!

295) EJ 1011

I have another sealed record. Hows about we unprotect ourselves from it?

Woody Guthrie had a lot of interesting things to say about Fred Trump, but I don't have any Woodie Guthrie albums. Instead, I'll share a record I do have but wasn't already on youtube.

I wasn't saving this record for any special occasion, but now's as good a time as any to open a factory sealed 1981 pressing of some 70+ year old live Jazz recordings, a few made during the final years of WWII.

I don't have any morals or fables or jokes, I'm just sharing an amazing collection of live music from real musicians facing exactly the same tired old useless racism, sexism, and bigotry that we're still watching a large portion of our country defend because they don't know any better, or maybe they do know better but just don't care. I care. Here's Billie Holiday and Charlie Parker and Art Tatum and friends making a hard day's struggle feel a little less painful. This round is on me.

The only bad track is the last one, Art's Blues. Everything else is pretty good quality for live recordings from the 40s, in my opinion. Enjoy.

296) The Believers - A Salute To Motown

It's time to play good or garbage. Tonight's album is A Salute To Motown, by The Believers. I'd love to give you some historical or biographical information, but I can't find any. The best I can tell you is it's a Dick Glasser/Al Capps production. They aren't completely unaccomplished musicians and/or producers, but Bottle tells me it begs the question: two white guys making A Salute To Motown that hasn't even made it to a wikipedia page, and has nothing but sub 3/5 ratings, what could go wrong?

No, see, this seems totally legit. Unlike that abomination The Astromusical House of Pisces, or Disko Hits!, or the others, this is good. 1970, we're still the better part of 2 decades away from Berry Gordy cashing in his $132 million by selling Motown to EMI. Capps and Glasser only take production credits. All the tracks are Jobete Music tracks, the musicians are anonymous but really, really good.

So, what is this? It's a funky, upbeat, borderline disco instrumental album of famous Motown songs. The songwriters get their royalties (via Mr. Gordy himself), Motown gets some fresh capital and a broader potential market, this seems like a legit deal from top to bottom. I want there to be some scandalous thing wrong with it, but I can't find it yet. So, until I get some further information, this is awesome. Go check it out if you can find it somewhere. It's great, all the stars, extra credit for the vibraphone solo and raunchy funk guitar work. Seriously enjoyable, and an impressively high-quality recording.

297) KMFDM - Angst
albums in response to the death of George Floyd

Sundays have new meanings that they never had for me before. It is a day of contemplation (every day is that for me, I am for lack of a better word a philosopher, but they are different now). I do not have a record for it. I have a CD that comes close.

For me at least, KMFDM is a drug against war. And, KMFDM sucks.

298) Feliciano!
albums in response to the death of George Floyd

Quick! I've insulted our president's dad with publicly available information, insulted our president by insinuating that he has been manipulated and lied to his entire life, and Mark Zuckerberg is going to turn all of my already public facebook posts over to the Trumpstappo. What album am I going to listen to tonight?!

I have another Prism album. No, it might be bleh. Crystal Gayle, Nancy Sinatra, Linda Ronstadt? No. Um, um, Anita Kerr's The Sea with Rod McKuen using wordy things? No. Aw, man I don't know. I feel like I have to use this platform for good, for new experiences, for delving into some personal part if my past....

I know. It's time. It's time to admit it, and share it with you. I never heard a single nanosecond of anything by Jose Feliciano until after my dad died last September. There were Feliciano tabs in his guitar case and I just ignored it. I knew he was blind, I knew everyone was blown away, and I just didn't even bother. Then one day a couple months ago I put it on and HOLY HAND GRENADES! Three is the number thou shalt count, and the number of Feliciano albums in my record collection thou shalt count is 3! With sharp pointy little teeth, even. If I had any flexibility left, I'd kick myself off the bridge.

Let's listen to his self titled exclamation point. Puerto Rico is a US Territory. The population of Puerto Rico are US citizens with no representation at the federal level, just like Guam and the Virgin Islands, or the residents of DC, the actual location of the federal government. Your so-called awesome country discriminates against its citizens at the level of basic geography. I watched a youtube video of some absolute moron yell at a lady who rented a pavilion in a park for a birthday party for informing him thusly. I give everyone the same high level of respect, and a lot of you throw it in the garbage, piss on it, then complain that I handed you piss drenched food. And you have the audacity to get mad at me for saying "don't piss on your own food"?

All these yous and yours are obviously rhetorical. No wonder Julie Tippets said he was the tits, or the bees pajamas, or whatever word you whippersnappers use for awesome. Feliciano is amazing. He just detuned and retuned his low e string in the middle of And I Love Her! He's better than Mark Knopfler. Not that it's a competition, but damn!

I could have been listening to him for the better part of 30 years, and I hate me even more now. I suck. Feliciano is amazing.

Join me before it's too late. Jose Feliciano, copy and paste his name if you have to, just don't let president manchild demand the national guard hunt you down like dogs before you hear his version of Bacharach's Always Something There to Remind Me. I know you thought Naked Eyes wrote it, I already made a joke about it, just go find any good thing you can get your hands on before that moron forces SETI to call the Omicronian War Gods of the Ketsick galaxy to acid rain on us, or summons the ghost of George Lincoln Rockwell to the Rose Garden for tea, or who knows what nonsense.

299) The worst album ever?
albums in response to the death of George Floyd

I once told you that England considered Lord Sutch and Heavy Friends the worst album ever recorded (I disagree). We have a contender for that title too. It's a sort of strange mash up of compilation, tribute, and soundtrack, and only two bands came out of it without giant bleeding gashes across their cheeks. Put it this way, Aerosmith didn't cover Come Together just because they felt like it. Interesting tangent, Run DMC didn't really want to cover Walk This Way, and they thought it was corny and weird. Turned out ok in my opinion.

So, let's see if the movie soundtrack to Sgt. Pepper's Lonely Hearts Club Band deserved to be a "return platinum" album complete with an Atari-like trip to the landfill to dump all that wasted PVC. Another interesting tangent, I sure as hell couldn't figure out how to play that infernal ET game when I was a kid.

I'm not particularly keen on the Beegees or Frampton but "Euthanizing the population" for buying it at all might be a little overboard. Dare I compare it to the frighteningly real risk of Trump trying to federalize the National Guard?

Then again, I haven't listened to it yet (that's sarcasm, giving Trump a WWII style lobotomy couldn't make him any less dangerous). Critic Dave Marsh is responsible for the euthanasia hyperbole, send your hate mail to him. Tangent 3, we should do the Megadeth discography (that ends with not at all funny pun Youthanasia as far as I'm concerned).
I'm stalling, I don't want to listen to this thing. But I will. For science!

It leads off with Aerosmith's Come Together, exactly what you would expect 'cause it's not from Sgt. Pepper at all. Huh, George Burns, alright. Ugh, yeah that's Peter Frampton not rocking at all. I believe he expressed reservations about many aspects of this endeavor, but actually it's fine. I mean, it all sounds more like Lionel Richie than either Frampton or the Beatles, but that doesn't make it bad.

Oooooh. That's bad. Barry. No. Yeah, all anyone is going to remember is Barry Gibb ruining A Day In The Life. I never want to hear that again, ever. I'd count how ridiculously long that last note was, but I said never.

Much better. Billy Preston is exactly the kind of frontman the Beatles thought they were poorly imitating. This is better than Paul's original version of Get Back.

Disco for the title track? Pass. Ugh. 3 more sides? Once more without the gorgonzola (funky cheese, get it?) We might need an ellipsis...

... So, there are some lessons we can learn. First, disco was not an "authentic" genre. There is great disco, but great disco didn't start out as something else (with the possible exception of Meco's Star Wars thing). Doing a "disco" version is almost always bad. Second, the Beatles were imitating R&B, Soul, Blues, etc. You hand their music to a real band like Aerosmith, Earth Wind and Fire, Billy Preston, anybody, it's going to be amazing. And it is. You hand it to a performer with their own bizarre approach that no one would ever expect, it's incredibly interesting like Alice Cooper's Because. But if you hand a random nonsense Beatles song to the Beegees or Frampton and they try to play it straight it's going to suck. And suck it does.

Who gave them a ring modulator?! Was it Carl? Who put Carl in charge? (That's an old bottle of beef joke). The Daleks sing the Beatles!

Everybody criticizes Steve Martin's Boris Karloff impression, but I counter argue with I Am A Dentist from Little Shop Of Horrors. Unique. Weird. It works because he's the right kind of silly.

In summary, half this album is crap and it's the half with any of the Gibb brothers, Peter Frampton, Dianne Steinberg, and Sandy Fajina. That's a typo, Farina, I apologize. Sgt. Pepper was nonsense to begin with, the whole concept was that the Beatles didn't want to be the Beatles because they were just making up nonsense to sell records. What better concept than an imaginary band playing nonsense songs. We all know that backfired like a rusty '78 Pinto, and you can hear it happening on this album. You can't take it serious, but they sure tried.

Still not the worst album ever, but definitely make your own heebie-Beegee free playlist of the actual good parts. Don't tell 'em Bottle sent you, they'll make you pay full price even with a student id.

300) System Of A Down - Toxicity
albums in response to the death of George Floyd

But seriously, the sentiment that some people need to go home followed by the sentiment that those other people need to get back to work followed by criticizing people for not working when you then describe them as unworthy of having a job followed by asking me what I think is a recipe for getting a big fat earful of what I think. I think you're a moron.

I also think it's the perfect time to listen to System Of A Down's Toxicity. It's a great album. Even my wife likes this album. It's great.

It asks the most relevant questions I can think of: You. What, do you own the world? How do you own disorder? I suggest you just listen to it.

The Armenian Genocide was the systematic mass murder and expulsion of 1.5 million ethnic Armenians carried out in Turkey and adjoining regions by the Ottoman government between 1914 and 1923.

Lots of people denied it and still deny that it happened, just like people deny the Holocaust.

The best story about the early days of SOAD is that any time they played, 200 people would show up 5 minutes before their set, mosh and cheer and be thrilled, then just leave before the headliner even took the stage.

Listen to them speak. The follow up to Toxicity is called Steal This Album! and it's not a joke. Unfinished demos of tracks that didn't make Toxicity leaked onto the internet, so Daron and Rick Ruben finished producing them out of guilt that their real fans were hearing unfinished tracks.

America the nation has a lot of unpaid parking tickets. But I don't like alternative metal, wah. I don't like mayonnaise, but I have to actually refrain myself from quoting Bruce Willis in The Whole Nine Yards every single time I order a sandwich, and I still eat as much of the sandwich as I can because mayonnaise isn't going to kill me, I just prefer not to taste it.

Some of us have to constantly remind the people we randomly encounter that we disagree with their politics and philosophies while treating them with the same respect and consideration that every person young or old deserves. You can think whatever you want to think, but the moment it distracts me from my work I will politely ask you to stop, often I don't even have to ask I just lift my head up and crack my neck like I'm tense and trying to loosen up. Don't whistle while I work.

Call me crazy, but I don't think the boys like LA all that much. What is it with cities where dollar bills are more useful as cocaine straws or stripper tips than currency? How is that fun? I'd rather use my energy at home than to haul air conditioners back and forth in an un-air-conditioned warehouse, but I'm a beast of burden like the rest of the actual working class so silence me for my radical ideas of tolerance and compassion. Eat a bag of dicks, Corporate America. I realize Louis C K isn't the most PC comedian to reference, but I've been avoiding the 3 Bill Cosby albums in my record collection. Sometimes it's the things you don't say that are important.

Perspective. Learn a new one every day.

301) Megadeth - Countdown To Extinction

Show of hands, how many of you remember when CDs were housed inside a plastic theft protection case that you had to cut off with scissors when the cashier couldn't find the little doodad tool to remove them? Ok. Keep your hands up if you remember when they were housed inside a full color printed cardboard box with the cover art printed all around it?

I do. I don't remember if tonight's album did or didn't, but I do remember Master of Puppets and Ride the Lightening were in full regalia when I got them, so quite possibly. Which came first, the oversized card board box, or the plastic thingamajig?

I could write a hundred different essays about Countdown to Extinction. Some would be funny, some historical, some about the actual songs, some very painful to read or write. Some of those I'll save for when I do the discography. Tonight, I would simply like to talk about my personal connection to this album because I am the only person who could have this relationship with it. The only connection I want it to have with current world events is that I think humanity (whatever that is) has a completely dysfunctional, unhealthy, and possibly unresolvable relationship with the concept of death.

    My oldest friends will remember my period of medicated clinical depression, but the process that led to that breakdown started much, much earlier. I met my beautiful wife of now 17 years at the end of that process as I was building a new human being out of the ashes. I was not, nor have I ever been suicidal, but my doctor and I decided on using Celexa because I was afraid that I might become suicidal. The insomnia and irrational sadness had grown too frightening and debilitating, so I sought professional medical help. Still here today so I'd consider it either successful or unnecessary. Counseling and therapy were available to me, but I personally chose not to pursue them. I am not a psychiatrist or psychologist, so that is as much as I will say about that (perfectly happy to talk about it in a different context, though).

    I'm getting to the album, be patient. I already told you that this was the first CD I ever had, because Symphony of Destruction just clicked with me. And, my fascination with the complicatedly intertwined history of Metallica and Megadeth is something that really did spark my love of learning. That sounds silly, but I assure you it's true.

    So, this essay is about Uriah Golden. We were school acquaintances as children. He lived a difficult and somewhat violent childhood as a human being trying to live with Tourette's. We were not really friends, but not really enemies either. Then one day in I think it was 9th grade Oklahoma History class, he said "hello me, meet the real me" and I, not even bothering to turn around continued "and my misfit's way of life," and he was completely elated and that was our connection as human beings. We didn't hang out or anything, but years later when he killed himself, I understood quite clearly that he had reached the end of his ability to fight against the forces of nature he had battled his entire life. I do not wish to offend anyone by saying this, but I find no shame in losing that battle. He was no less of a person for losing that battle. I have a memory of my connection with him that I find beautiful, if bittersweet. If I were to say that my moderate depressive condition taught me anything, it is that the will to carry on can only come from inside, but that no man can fight alone forever. I truly believe that the sadness I feel for his situation is the sadness that the world could not accommodate him, or rather dissuade him from believing that he was a burden to the people he deeply loved. I do not believe that he was somehow less of a human. I do not believe that was his fault. It is a fact. I do not believe his suicide was selfish, or vile. Rather, my dealing with these ideas is a part of my own humanity and my own will to keep going. If there is good in me, then surely Uriah Golden played an important role in that development, and for that I would sincerely thank him if I could. I cannot, but I do it in my head whenever I think of him.

I hope that was not too unpleasant of a read for anyone, and I further hope that it gives some new perspective on the reason I end this essay with my inevitable macabre sense of humor by saying that it doesn't hurt that it's a kick ass album to begin with.

302) Aesop Rock - The Impossible Kid
albums in response to the death of George Floyd

Look look look look! It's finally here. I still say their paper mache recreation of The Shining is the best way to listen to Aesop Rock's The Impossible Kid if the record itself isn't on your top shelf.

I love this album. The songs connect with me. He's amazing. The Weathermen, The Uncluded with Kimya Dawson, Malibu Ken. I'm not one of those people pretending like I've known about him for ever, I'm not one of those underground or die guys, I'm not here because NPR sent me or because his vocabulary is in a different zip code from most hip hop, I'm here because I'm a scholar of music and the easiest way to broaden your horizons is to actually go listen to things other people say are awesome or amazing. I heard Dorks and it was the same feeling of "yes please, more of this" just like Symphony of Destruction when I was a kid.

If you were to say Bottle, point me to some hip hop you think should be mandatory listening I would say in no particular order start with Aesop Rock, 3rd Bass, Run The Jewels, Cut Chemist (a turntablist), The Avalanches, and Deltron 3030, and go from there. Follow the youtube rabbit holes, or read liner notes, or check out associated acts on their wikipedia pages. You can't find stuff you like until you search for it, and you don't know what will reach out and grab you. And, you literally have nothing to lose. These people want to share their hard work with you, and they won't be mad if you happen not to like it. They don't want to hear you yell "you suck!," but no one else does either. They aren't trying to ruin your afternoon, don't be such a dork.

And as for the idea that you can "hate" a genre, I give you all of my positive reviews of country albums. You don't have to like a specific example of something, but using that as synechdochal evidence that an entire art form should be eradicated from existence does in fact put you in the same ballpark as Hitler, Stalin, Amin, Mary I, but I digress. If you can find rhyming Sprechstimme agreeable in the broadest sense, then it's quite easy to distinguish between what you may or may not personally enjoy vs. saying perhaps I am not qualified to voice my opinion on this particular issue. In any case, if you asked me what I thought, I'd just say "why? You clearly don't care. Let's talk about something else." Luckily, I can't hear you, so I'm free to just ramble to my heart's content.

I love this album. There's a Star Wars reference, a cat, death, stories about his brothers, his past vocations and hobbies, his brother liked Ministry!? I like Ministry!
That joke is funny because the original thing I used this joke for was She Likes Basketball from Promises, Promises, but Blood Sandwich starts off with a story about his other brother Darrell playing baseball, and those two sports placed against each other in the context of the Bob Newhart Show forces you to think about racist stereotypes that are engrained in your own thinking. I'm lying when I say I don't put much thought into these essays, but I assume you knew that. The fact that I throw them together in 30 minutes to an hour every night belies the fact that I've been thinking about how I might frame a particular album for months. That's the musician in me. I've been practicing in my head 24 hours a day, and the actual writing is a strange type of performance art that no one gets to see. In all honesty, it's like a jazz jam session, or one of my weird loop pieces. Some nights I'm just off, and I say sorry for bombing tonight, please check me out tomorrow when I try something different. Rehearsed spontaneity.

Sorry, the Josinator interrupted me to ask "what's a wire?" and I'm pretty proud of saying "it's like string made out of metal."

Where was I, oh yeah, being completely open to new experiences and different ideas and being patient and friendly and ooh bubbles. Sorry Josie is blowing bubbles.

I give up, this album is awesome, go check it out. It's my turn to blow bubbles, so in the words of Biz Markee, bye bye now.

303) Bad Religion - Suffer
albums in response to the death of George Floyd

I want so badly to just run away and listen to something totally irrelevant, but it's impossible. That is the trouble with giving a narcissist power. Donald Trump lives in an imaginary playground in his own head where he never has to deal with caring about other people. He does whatever he wants to do and says "see, isn't this great? Everybody's happy. This is what you want. You want me to be in charge. I'm doing what the American people wanted me to do."

When a band does that they suck and they make terrible albums. He sucks and he makes the world terrible. He thinks the whole world revolves around him, and the whole damned world now revolves around him. He's the only thing we can pay attention to anymore. He's your company's douchiest executive. He's supposedly Billy Madison, but he's not. He's Eric Gordon. Billy Madison learned that he would be a really crappy executive and gave control of the company to whom? Anyone? Bueller? Matilda? No one?

CARL!!!! He said no dad, CARL. It's like you're not paying attention at all (which is exactly what I told you to do). I spent all day wrestling a weed whacker and all I got was this lousy bottle of beef joke.

Trump is a bad religion, so we all... anyone? Anyone? SUFFER.

When I bought this album (at a Borders of all places), the cashier said "this is a seriously good album." It is. I told you a long time ago that No Substance was my favorite, but Suffer, Recipe For Hate, and Stranger Than Fiction are tied for their best.

I've also told you that I think religion itself is a bad theory, but System of a Down's theory that spirit runs through all things doesn't do it for me either. I'm somewhere in the middle. Don't take that personally by the way, you can and should hold and practice whatever theory of the universe helps you exist in it. All I'm requesting is don't prey on me (that's from Recipe for Hate). I will gladly talk about any aspect I feel I can say something about, but I am an anarchist and organization feels incredibly uncomfortable to me. Anarchist in the classical sense, I believe in mutually agreed construction rather than centralized authority. If I can work around your ideas I will, I'm very adaptable. I can't work around Trump's ideas. They are garbage, and I'd light one of his hotels on fire after letting everyone else out and repeatedly warning them like Milton from Office Space.

Bad Religion doesn't like LA? I'm shocked!

When? has a really great opening lyric: I've seen a lot of things in 5 years....

The real crux of the issue though is the title track: the masses of humanity will always have to suffer. Greg Graffin's Zoology PhD dissertation was an in-depth study of the intellectual contradictions that plague the field of evolutionary biology. Specifically, the religious beliefs of prominent biologists throughout history were often highly contradictory, and sometimes downright damaging, to their research. Again, I'm not condemning anyone's religion. Whenever I can finally get someone to understand that I didn't even know what Christianity was until I was like 8 or 9, we start to talk about all the substitute things I used to fill those (call them) spiritual questions of existence, namely music. That's not a joke, when a friend tried to explain it to me in elementary school I though it was like a soccer team or a parent/teacher conference or something. It made absolutely no sense to me, so being repeatedly called a heathen was funny in my book. A few personal experiences did contribute to that breakdown I mentioned, but those might be the only subjects I won't talk about in any context (nothing sinister or evil or unlawful or gross, but highly psychologically damaging nonetheless).

Anywho, my point is that Punk Rock is meant to be confrontational. We sing about things that make us mad, and being mean about it is an unavoidable side product. We aren't mad at you the person, we're mad at an idea that stops us from functioning like human beings, and we take it out on the institution that espouses that idea. Much different than sending your army out to taser people who are already frightened for their lives on a daily basis.

So, to sum up, I live out in the corn/soy fields of Iowa, only go to town to make money to buy the things I can't make for myself, and treat everyone I meet like they are my equal in every way, black white asian middle eastern hispanic orange short tall fat obnoxious sleazy high schizophrenic young old male female dogs cats chickens plants. The only things I hate are bad ideas. You can be wrong or dumb until the universe implodes (and so can I), but the only thing I won't let you do is mess up the brain I've delicately rebuilt half a dozen times thus far. I'll politely ask you to stop, and if worse comes to worst I'll just go for a walk outside until I calm back down and can be assured you'll leave me alone for a couple hours. Being mad is like asking that vampire of depression if he'd like to come in and throw trash on the floor.

I'm making it sound worse than it really is, but I've been called an enabler a time or two, and not in a nice way. For the record, I'm not an enabler, I just assume that you know what's best for you and sometimes that's not the case at all. Thanks for letting me recline on your couch.

304) Saturday Night Fever
albums in response to the death of George Floyd
Let's talk popularity, not sales. The yardstick, or measuring device of pop music has pretty much always been Billboard, so your awards ceremony features The Beatles, The Supremes, and the Beegees. Today is my day of thoughtful meditation, so I'm a day late and a couple hundred thousand dollars short. I guess you could say I had my own Saturday Night Fever (that's a reference to the suburban child on fire on

the cover of Bad Religion's Suffer). I also can't pass up the 21 Pilots joke by reminding you that I told Barry Gibb to stay in his lane after he mangled my actual favorite mash up of half-finished Lennon-McCartney songs, A Day in the Life. For years I misinterpreted that song on purpose, I thought Lennon was talking about some unexplained psychic phenomenon in Lancashire where people thought they were witnessing holes in the fabric of reality. I knew he was talking about potholes in the road, but I like a good absurdist thought experiment probably more than anyone. So, let's listen to the only disco album physically preserved by the Library of Congress as a significant cultural artifact. Sometimes truth *is* stranger than fiction, thanks Greg!

Some history, the Beegees were a serious British band that came out of the Skiffle scene and rose to international popularity (like all the 50s British kids of that era). Their harmony, and Barry's falsetto, came straight out of R&B, and since they were super popular, they tried to keep up with the times and gradually morphed into disco like everyone else. They were over in France working on their next album when some movie guys interrupted them to get music for their gritty, urban, tribal coming of age story. They loved the stuff the Brothers Gibb had already recorded and only asked that they amp up the disco on a couple more tracks. The official Beegees statement about it is that they kind of felt like they lost an album by making that deal. They didn't even know the basic plot of the movie, and said no at first. Travolta said he was dancing to Stevie Wonder and Boz Skaggs (neither of whom particularly wanted their music appearing in this film).

Do I like the Beegees? Meh, not particularly. Barry doesn't crack the top 5 of my goofy white guy falsetto list.

Are the Beegees' songs on this soundtrack phenomenal? Yes, absolutely. Say to yourself, I'm going to listen to the Beegees. Man, this is good stuff.

What about the rest of the album? Some works, some doesn't. A Fifth of Beethoven is pretty classic, Night on Disco Mountain is borderline. The contrast of wedding reception funk and overly dramatic orchestral writing is actually perfect for the themes of the movie itself, but the innards of the pieces are clumsy and boring. Great idea, mediocre execution.

Kool & the Gang's Open Sesame might rub you the wrong way, but we're already up to our necks in potentially crocodile infested waters with what look like bizarrely buoyant bricks covered in plastic wrap floating everywhere, so maybe we just skip that one tonight. We came here to dance out our frustrations, not have an actual knife fight a la West Side Story.

As Jim Henson so aptly put it, dance your cares away, worries for another day, let the music play, clap clap, down in Fraggle Rock. We're still a decade away from whatever town made that illegal in Footloose (based on Elmore City, Oklahoma if you didn't know that useless trivia).

Context is everything. We live in a postmodern world, and that means we have to define it as part of every conversation. My context is I'm a dork in nowheresville, hiding in my basement, ragging on records. Much as in pains me to say it, this is a good soundtrack. I don't want to listen to it 25 more times, but it gives some much-needed context to that gastrointestinal discomfort of Sgt. Pepper.

305) Less Than Jake - Losing Streak
albums in response to the death of George Floyd

This is the old dude, Howard J Reynolds, and you're listening to Bottle of Beef.

As is my prerogative, I'm invoking the second record rule. No, it's not Bobby Brown, I just wasn't happy with liking Saturday Night Fever and it's still early. So, let's listen to my favorite Less Than Jake album, Losing Streak. They're from New Jersey, and they're glad about it (like the 4 Seasons). It is the Garden State, after all. I'm lying, they're from Florida and that's how you know the barbershop quartet intro is unadulterated sarcasm (the fact that their name comes from being told that they were annoying the pet parrot is a pretty dead giveaway as well). Johnny Quest thinks they're sellouts, but I suspect he just doesn't like ska. I do.

They really did have a super fan in his 60s who came to all their shows and banged around with the teenagers in the mosh pit, so they invited him to tell a story about getting caught naked during an affair with a married woman. It's like the punk version of Skynyrd's Three Steps. They manipulated the index file so you had to physically rewind track 1 to hear it, go too far and you'd wrap around to the last track and have to start all over again. Fun times.

You think it's a non-sequiter, but as soon as you hear the first two lines it'll make complete sense. This album makes me happy; I could listen to it on a loop for days. I still don't want to go back to work tomorrow, but right now is pretty swell. Cheers.

306) Rod McKuen and Anita Kerr - The Sea
albums in response to the death of George Floyd

Tonight's album is a chance to explain one of those completely hidden behind the scenes things that happen all over my nightly album reviews. You probably didn't even notice.

In my review of Feliciano!, I said "Anita Kerr's The Sea with Rod McKuen using wordy things." Why? Well, Rod McKuen wanted to work with her, so they talked for a while and whatever, and when she played some of the drafts she had written he threw his words in the dumpster and started all over because this album was her piece now and he was the contributor. No power play, no chauvinism, no ego, just Rod McKuen saying lady, this is fantastic and I need to start over. He says so right on the jacket. Bottle (that cartoon of a skeptic I am) says that sounds like something my enemy would say. That's just what they want you to think. That's how they getcha.

So? Who cares? Let's pretend it's true. Conspiracy theories are way more work than actual research, and I repeat my initial question: what the hell is a Rod McKuen? What reason would he possibly have for lying? Exaggerating a little, maybe, but you'd have to live in a strange parallel universe to say "I hired some chick to write the music and they made me include her photo." The Sandpipers had to sneak their female members into the photo shoot through the back door, cue them to do the photo bomb, and their producers were still like "I don't think so." You have to read that in the voice of LL Cool J 'cause I straight up talked about it in the 3rd Bass showcase showdown (which reminds me, I eventually have to talk about Beastie Boys' Check Your Head at some point). Why did I do that? Because I mentioned Less Than Jake's Never Going Back to New Jersey last night and the "I don't think so" is his response to the rhetorical question "are you going back to California?" Nobody likes LA. They go out of their way to include it at every opportunity. There's a Tool album for that (remind me to do the Jack Nicholson Joker joke for that album, and there's The Shining connection).

Man, that's a lot of preliminary work for an album I literally have not yet placed upon the lazy susan. What do I do if it sucks? Same thing we do every night, Pinkie: try to say something absurd.

Zoinks! Jinkies! There's a whole lot of light jazz style borrowing going on. Snippets of famous melodies, twisted and squirrely, but totally enjoyable. Rod is much more James Garner than Clint Eastwood on this one. He's deeper, more growly. He's reading love poems, I'm more interested in her trumpet solos. Yeah, sure he's rugged and sensitively masculine. If I were sexually attracted to men, I'd fan myself (it just so happens that I'm not, but he's definitely dreamy). Ooh.

No, I don't think about the rain much at all, but I really wish he sang more, not just occasional tra la las. I called it charming on the other album, but he just said "these are the days of dancing six feet apart" and she's totally riffing on Bacharach's Raindrops Keep Falling On My Head. It's not fair! 1 - it's awesome, 2 - it's ridiculously pertinent because yes, the numbers of Covid-19 cases are high enough here that I wore my mask into the liquor store today, 3 - it's 1967 and Nostradamus he ain't!

Never mind the world indeed! I'm tired of dancing too.

Oh man, she's good. No, the music is just gorgeous. I've joked about karaoke versions of records before, but I'd pay actual money for a version of this without Rod McKuen. He's not bad, but I totally believe the story of going back to the drawing board. Phenomenal. Seriously phenomenal. More Anita Kerr, please. I'll be doing some youtube exploring for sure. Any leads are most appreciated. Definitely check her out when you get a chance.

307) Tool - Aenema
albums in response to the death of George Floyd

This town needs an Aenema! LA. It's a hole. It's the land of competition. It's too big for its britches. It's also the epitome of everything we love or hate, it's that nagging bad idea that we're all raging against. The problem is that there isn't a word for it. We can't name it, it's too big to conceptualize so we pick at the edges and try to dig a hole through 6-foot stone walls with a grapefruit spoon. I can name it. I've said it so many ways. I've held it up, I've dissected it, I've picked at it and laid its nervous system out for everyone to cringe, and gasp, and photograph. Winning. It makes me gag.

Trump is nothing more than another minuscule little blip in the annals of a bad idea. He's not even good at it. In fact, he might be the least successful proponent of manufactured competition ever produced. It might be the fundamental schism of human consciousness, the original absurdity. As grotesque or uncomfortable as you might find the imagery on any of their albums, that's how I feel about the concept of winning, and the merciless lengths we will go to to achieve it. So, I say, I'm not even playing.

Tool is a tool. Maynard told me so. Use it for whatever purpose you need to use it. So, I have. Thanks, Maynard! No winners, no losers, shit happens. The less of it I, or anyone else, has to step in the better. I'd rather wake up and smell the coffee. I want to go home, but it's 2 outs, men on 1st and 3rd, suicide squeeze, guess I'll have to either plow the catcher down or weasel my way around the tag, assuming the ump gets the call right. I thought little league was supposed to be fun, but there're bleachers upon bleachers of screaming people, like a 12-yea- old is supposed to carry the weight of the whole observable universe while running on slippery dirt. Man, I'm just a kid. I can't believe I gotta worry about this kind of shit. Sorry for being such a party pooper.

308) Dixieland Jazz Party

Alright, I'll bite. What's ridiculously bebowlered British clarinetist Sir Mr. Acker Bilk and his newfangled Leon Young String Chorale (legitimately called "experimental" at the time) have to say about New Orleans Jass? Not the card game, that's how everybody spelled jazz before 1917.

This is his first international hit record, Stranger On The Shore. Interesting note, he lived long enough to get tired of it and never want to play it again. If you thought I was wordy and obtuse, check this out:

> Customarily, Mr. B heads a small Ensemble devoted to the Purveyance of that extempore polyphony or "Jass" associated with the Inhabitants of the City of New Orleans. There are nevertheless (as the Sage has aptly

remarked), more ways of destroying a Feline than suffocating the Beast with Cream.

Kudos on the German style capitalization of nouns, raspberries to this not being Dixieland in any Way, Shape, or Form. Clearly there's a second album in our near future (wink). This isn't bad by any means, but his excessive vibrato is, shall we say, a little machine gun. If you love the clarinet, you'll probably enjoy it more than me. Still interesting, but I like accordion better. It's a nice experiment, but I want horns and upright bass.

Now let's saunter over to something a little more authentic. I've been to New Orleans a time or 6 (including my honeymoon). Drum solo? S'il vous plaît. See, now that's a Nawlins clarinet solo (or at least the New Jersey version of one). Here come the trumpet and trombone marching in. Acoustic guitar!? Bucky Pizzarella? Is that a typo, or an intentional spelling change? Don't care, this is great. This is worthy of putting up on youtube, so I did. You'll like it, I promise.

309) Starlight Mints - The Dream That Stuff Was Made Of

We interrupt your regularly scheduled programming to bring you this important bulletin:

CF: do, you, you, uh, you remember that scene in Bartman, I mean Batman Returns when, uh, when you're dead and the cats start eating your face off?
MP: yeees?
CF: that was awesome.

Now replace Michelle Pfeifer with Elmer Fudd, and the cats with Chase from Paw Patrol. Decidedly less awesome. I thought we were finally done with Billy Madison, but nope. I paraphrase:

What everyone just said is one of the most insanely idiotic things I have ever heard. At no point in your rambling, incoherent bickering were you even close to anything that could be considered a rational thought. Everyone in this room is now dumber for having listened to it. I award you no points (the points don't matter anyway), and may God have mercy on your souls.

Watching the world argue about Fox News tasting great, but Twitter being less filling is a terrible show to air at Thursday prime time. I religiously watch only UHF. Again, Michael Richards had his run in with people finding out he was a douchebag, but I wanted to find the marble in the oatmeal and drink from the fire hose. I want to teach poodles how to fly. I don't need no stinking badgers. Red snapper *is* very tasty.

I like Starlight Mints because, like Chris Cornell said, it doesn't remind me of anything. No one's coming for your guns, because in real life people just kill each other. No Pulp Fiction monologue before hand, no blanks and ketchup packets, just dead people. Ask Brandon Lee. Stop romanticizing, or should I say fetishizing it. I'm trying to count to twelve like an adult.

I'm lying, Allen Vest has some of the best words, in the best order, that make me think of everything, and all 4 of their albums are so indescribably soothing that I'll just invite you along for the ride. See you tomorrow, nonsense 'merica the TV miniseries.

310) Roland Shaw is James Bond in his office arranging music from Bond Movies

Max Power. He's the man that you want to touch. But, you mustn't touch.

Wouldn't it be funny if I had an album of orchestral arrangements from James Bond movies. I'd probably hide it in Kentucky, or employ an army of sadistic female jujitsu specialists, or hide it in a cello case, or who knows. I'm joking I'd take it out and play it. Roland Shaw was a British composer/arranger famous for working with Mantovani, making this record, and a new one for every new Bond movie. Sweet gig, wait for a new Bond movie and make a new compilation album. Money in the bank.

It's good, too. I mean, Goldfinger is my favorite Bond theme, but this album is great across the board. I wish I had more of this kind of stuff. I'm sure it's on youtube so go check it out.

311) Head East - Live

Which direction should we go? Up, down, clockwise, widdershins? I know! Let's Head East. I am, after all, the king of wishful thinking.

That's hilarious because that song is by Go West, not Head East. Thankfully, they're from Illinois, so they could have gone either way. They changed their name from something dumb to something cool because their roadie (the awesomely named Baxter Forrest Twilight) had an all-night acid trip that culminated with the Teletubby Sun Baby telling him that they should change their name to Head East. Who could argue? It was probably more like king god from Monty Python, but I assume the Teletubbies are an acid trip to begin with, so I totally get it.

They're great. The only reason I don't have any of their studio albums is that I'd have to buy all of them and I struggle with the fictional concept of money already, so I just don't. Forget Skynyrd or Molly Hatchett, when I want 70s pseudo-southern arena rock I head toward the sunrise. That baby has a lot of interesting things to say.

312) Cleopatra

Speaking of power struggles, nepotism, egomaniacal self proclaimed dictators bent on world domination, imperialism, celebrity scandals, ludicrous investments that eventually turned a profit, my wedding anniversary being the Ides of March, rebellion, the chance to reference The Princess Bride (you've been studying your Agrippa, right?), and the deluge of nonsense that we subject ourselves to by opening this horribly creepy college yearbook turned corporate espionage simulation called book of faces, here's the bland and completely forgettable soundtrack to Cleopatra!

313) Romeo & Juliet, like a version style

Prokofiev, Berlioz, Tchaikovsky, Gounod, Bernstein, and who? Nino Rota? The Godfather guy? 29 years of Fellini films? Ok, I'll give it a whirl. They tell me "What is Youth" is pretty earwormy. Can't be any worse than Cleopatra, 'cause that was yesterday and like yesterday it's gone (I barely remember *that* I listened to it). Here we go....

Conducted? He conducted that intro? Are you sure? Nice trumpets and fighting, though. Yeah, yeah, iambic pentameter. Shameless self promotion, I really do have a choir piece where I take a couple lines from the start and a couple lines from the end and make a coherent question and answer. If you have a choir and an email address, I'll send the score to you. Really, I will.

Actually, his music is quite good. It's a nice modern approach to period writing; a kind of romanticized take on 16th/17th century secular music. I can taste a "minstrel" flavor in spite of my pirate's rum and fruit juice. The voice acting is pretty generic. I once had a friendly argument with a professor about Baz Luhrmann's William Shakespeare's Romeo & Juliet, where I said the silliness of the guns and gaudy colors against the original text was an important addition to give the characters their precise teenage mentalities in the late 20th century, talking like that in an ironic display of juvenility. He didn't totally buy it, but I stand by it.

There's a whole lot less music on this album than anyone might expect. Lotta reverb, though. As you might suspect, I picture them descending the staircase in Young Frankenstein, rather than visiting Friar Tuck, I mean Lawrence. I do like the incidental music for the mutually assured destruction of Mercutio and Tybalt. I like it a lot. Brass vs. Strings. Hit the road jack, and don't you come back no more.

She pronounces pomegranate wrong, in case you were wondering. "Pommygranite," ew.

No really, the reverb on their dialogue is a little overboard in my opinion. The movie sets might make that more agreeable, but on record it's honestly pretty annoying.

The music is quite good, if somewhat sappy and a little too Greensleeves-y for my taste. Plus, there's just not enough of it to warrant an actual soundtrack. It just comes off as a scattershot audio book to me. On the other hand, I'll probably remember what it sounded like two days from now, so that's at least better than yesterday's soundtrack. I don't feel punished, but I wouldn't tell you to rush out and find it, either. A good solid "I listened to it without getting mad."

314) Speaking of...

Speaking of a thing from a thing that's comparable to other things. This one's got everything.

That's not true. It's missing 1 incredibly important statement: Radiohead's Exit Music (for not just any film, but this exact film). Ok computer, I saved my latest draft, start printing.

It's an eclectic collection of all sorts of confusing topics that every human on the planet should have a deep connection to; we've inherited the ridiculous wars of our parents (who by the way equally inherited their wars all the way back to a rock and a choice to throw it or not), with no instruction manual, half the pieces of a bunch of other equally nonsensical games that don't exist anymore, and an almost palpable urge to meekly scream "we hope that you choke" at anyone who disagrees with us.

If that paragraph comes across as extremely heavy handed and in bad taste, then please remember that I'm smashing together all of the rhetoric of current events, past events, and albums I've mentioned, and just letting them sit on the page for you to view. If there's a moral, it's that there's nothing new under the sun, and we need some refreshments (I'm feeling fizzy, fuzzy, big, and buzzy, tee hee). I'll be waiting with a pack of sandwiches, and you're more than welcome to come find me. I'm unarmed, so please don't come at me like I'm some kind of love fool. Everybody is free to feel good, and I'll help you out whenever I can. That's what I believe.

315) Refreshments, like I promised.

You look tired. Working all day out in it. Well, come in and have a seat. I cleared off a chair for you, the fan is whirring away. I promised you libations, commestibles, a revitalizing tonic or two. I promised you Refreshments. Never reneged before, and I don't plan to start now.

Like I've said so many times, there ain't no morals to these stories at all. The good guys and the bad guys really don't work past noon around here. We can have some fun pretending, or you can chase me with a baseball bat and put me out of my misery. It's not a bottle, and there's nothing sour to bite on, but I'll tip this fizzy-fuzzy rum and coke and say cheers. Here's to life.

No? Well, you know what they say: you can lead a horse to water...Kidding. Don't mind me, I really am carefree. What should we listen to tomorrow?

316) Oh, by the way...

Oh, by the way, tonight I begin listening to Pink Floyd's Oh, By The Way. It's their 2007 boxed set, so it doesn't have The Endless River. Maybe I'll listen to that one at the end, maybe I won't. Depends on how the story unfolds.

The real question is do I point you to the three albums I've already listened to and discussed? Do I pretend they never happened? Do I revise them to better suit my current place in the universe? Perhaps I simply remind you that you can flip back to them. Yeah, I like that.

We're currently in the midst of the second wave of a coronavirus pandemic, there's a heavy duty fascist uprising taking place, people are tired of hearing about how horrible they make each other feel by not caring about how they feel, and I'm in the mood to remind you that the day before Trump was elected president I publicly said I was high-tailing it to the Bottle of Beef bunker to make some music and wake up the next day to whatever ridiculous ridiculousness would happen if we elected him to be president. It was like bizarro Christmas where everyone was thrilled that Aunt Karen got drunk and microwaved Timmy's hamster 'cause that meant they were free to just scream at each other like unsupervised children. Trump is a useless moron, and the fact that any human on the planet follows his lead is proof positive that we shouldn't be a country any more (why am I thinking of Neil Young right now?). He was elected president to accomplish exactly what you are watching the world be at this very moment, and he's done such a good job he just might get reelected. I have a conspiracy theory. He was elected to win the civil war the other way around this time. That's just my loudmouthed opinion. I've been promised an actual surprise Father's Day gift tomorrow, and I'd prefer you didn't explode us into space in the middle of the night.

Deja vu all over again. Down the escalator we go. Let's skip the formalities and get down to what we're here for: The

Piper at the Gates of Dawn. It's perfect. It's alternatingly silly and underwear soilingly frightening (that's a mouthful of a sentence right there). Enjoy along with me, my friends. All the sides of the moon get alternating sunlight and darkness, space cadets ahoy!

317) A Saucerful of Secrets

Nick Mason says A Saucerful of Secrets is his favorite; a cross fade from Syd to David and the birth of the collective Pink Floyd we're about to explore. I don't disagree.

Critics say it's not as good as their first album, they call it mediocre. They are wrong.

If you thought Pink Floyd was Syd Barrett, then this won't sound the way you want it to sound. If you wanted a magic folk fairytale, you'll be unhappy. But, if you want a highly refined and balanced album of psychedelic rock, not too silly, not too dark and depressing, made by a group of kids trying to figure out how to work together in the midst of falling apart, it's pretty awesome.

Some of them thought they should stick to the 3-minute make us a little money pop song format, some said slow build rock symphony skip a few decades to post-rock soundscape-ville was the way to go, some said build it like a house, some said let it happen the way it wants to happen, all of them contributed and the whole process is captured in this album. It is obviously Beatles aware, but intentionally different. I'd compare it to Iron Butterfly without the William Morris celebrity slush fund.

Yes, it's a heavily produced album, but it sure doesn't sound that way. It sounds performed. They live inside that kaleidoscopic echo chamber. Wright does most of the lead vocals, but he is in no way the "frontman." This isn't music for the sake of words, or sing some nonsense in between the guitar doodles, it's 4.5 guys interacting to form an experience much larger than themselves. This is the sound of "a band" with its own personality, and any individual part is just a way to tap into that collective consciousness.

Nicky said it best, it's the actual birth of Pink Floyd from the primordial ooze.

Congratulations! It's a Pink!

318) More

I took a pill in Ibiza. Thanks, but no thanks, Mike Posner.

More is a fascinating album. So fascinating, I'm actually not sure if I'll even talk about the music in this essay. It's the soundtrack to More, the film about Ibiza's heroin crisis. The prop drugs in the film are real, cause why buy stuff when the cast and crew can just empty their pockets? The soundtrack is not real, or is real but isn't a standard soundtrack. It's a Pink Floyd album made by watching scenes from the movie and timing them with a stopwatch so they would fit into the scenes of the movie like they were just playing in real life. Pink Floyd didn't have sync studio money, and Barbet Schroeder wanted contemporary European music playing when a character flipped on a radio, or a tv, or put on a record, or sat in an office with loudspeakers, or whatever. So, it's a newly Syd Barrett-less Pink Floyd album inspired by Barbet Schroeder's images of 60s narcotic induced free love on an autonomous island that technically belongs to Spain. Long story short, Stefan couldn't handle Guns 'N Roses levels of heroin and died, and Nazis are still a thing. I'm not known for agreeing with Roger Ebert, because he graduated from the school of "my opinion equals the director's intent," so I find it hard to believe Schroeder was actually saying let's all go to the lobby and find a dirty syringe. I suspect it was a much more boring moral about moderation and temptation that he had in mind.

If you'd rather watch scenes from the movie while listening to one of my favorite Coil tracks, Careful What You

Wish For, because I can give you that option. I'm going to stick to the script and just listen to it as a Pink Floyd concept album, the concept being make some music to fit what real life music should be playing during this scene. According to my own peculiar brand of Structuralism, whatever I come up with should bear some fundamental resemblance to what the Floyd were thinking at the time. Or not, I'm just as happy to be wrong.

Yeah, you need the context of a soundtrack. It doesn't have to be this film, it just has to be about some observable clash of cultures. Nature vs. noir, folk vs. party rock, acoustic vs. electric, it's all an entry way into that world of cinema: the real and the depiction of the supposedly real refusing to blend together like peaches and gravy. You're gonna give me a weird look, but it could just as easily be the soundtrack of Harold and Maude. 2 minutes in and you know it won't have a happy ending, you just don't know how we're going to get there; funny from a certain macabre perspective, but definitely not cathartic.

Look at it from both sides, like Joni Mitchell told you to do. It's not Pink Floyd, it's Pink Floyd's version of the world in the late 60s: rational working class English musicians writing the music for how the rest of the world experiences Pink Floyd. Is it Middle Eastern music, or the American surf guitar version of Middle Eastern music? The real world can't tell if it's silly or sinister, I can't tell if it's silly or sinister, so it must be that both exist simultaneously, or neither are true. Perhaps reality lies somewhere in that murky middleground where you are what you eat, and more isn't necessarily better. Fun to listen to, though.

319) Umm....

Ummagumma isn't a Pink Floyd album either? I'm so confused.

I'm not confused at all. I told you that Richard Wright was not a front man. There's no Richard Wright's Pink Floyd. He's not the team leader, or manager, or anything, he was just the only one with ideas that they could actually accomplish at the time. It turned out that halfway through he regretted making it a no-cooperation endeavor, and the other three didn't enjoy it, but for good or bad it's their 4th album.

Pink Floyd makes concept albums. Real concept albums. The act of making the album is explicitly their conception of what album they should make. Some of them are movies, some of them are statements, this one is a double album about 4 guys living two simultaneous double lives as performers, recording artists, members of a famous band, and people with real lives that may or may not cross over those boundaries. And, the soundtrack for Gigi on the cover is relevant. It is, go look up the plot of that movie and you'll see why Nick Mason's wife and Roger Waters's girlfriend are here.

Totally cool thing about this boxed set: the Ummagumma labels are on the wrong discs. Now before you go all "don't buy this cheap gimmick garbage because that only encourages them," (yes that what the internet trolls really say about this boxed set) think about everything I've ever told you. Every single original album in my collection has the tracks listed out of order (because they had to start printing before the track order was actually finalized to meet the release deadline), this is published by EMI not some skanky 4th floor knock off label, it was manufactured in Holland because that's what the Dutch had for a dowry when they entered the EU ("Made in Holland" is a sign of higher quality and actual money being invested in their working-class sector). Of course the packaging is a gimmick and some random guy in a factory made a mistake, but what the hell would *you* sell if you needed to generate new revenue quickly? It's 2007, and nobody even knows if Pink Floyd is going to do anything else. 7 years later they made an album that I haven't even heard yet, but I certainly wasn't gonna go through the hassle of finding every album at full price. 14 x 16 is a hundred more than I paid for this and it's a handsome box on your favorite bookshelf. My point is you're all mad about the wrong thing. These big labels spending real money to make and distribute albums is the good part. EMI owning the band's music and giving them a sliver of the real profits while every Carl at the office makes more is the nasty part. Musicians don't become producers because they love mentoring young artists, they get paid whether that artist makes a hit or not. That's how it works in the pyramids; 4 for me, 1 for you, got any more songs you'd like Carl to record?

    Where was I? Oh, the live half is over. Time for the solo sides by each member of Pink Floyd without any help from the other three.

    Ummagumma was a made-up word one of their roadies used as a euphemism for sex, and Gigi is about a lady who refuses to be anyone's mistress. Not as cool a story as Head East's Teletubby themed christening, but London is already east of Turville (the actual town where the Vicar of Dibley was filmed). Alice loved the Teletubbies. Do I have to explain everything?

    Richard Wright and his 4-movement keyboard extravaganza, go! Timpani and synth strings, check. Piano tremolos and stereo panned cymbal twiddles, check. Percussive nonsense, check. Slow weird thing that would be right at home on one of my stupid albuHOLY SHIT! I peed a little at that fade out to complete cacophony. I forgot the 4th movement does that. It's quite a jolt. Eternal punishment for self-aggrandizing craftiness and decietfulness, indeed.

    What's Roger Waters and his plus one have in store for us? Ostinato of bird sounds, a lovely little folk song followed by his stethescopian approach to chaotic music concrete, devolving into a kind of poetic rant in a strange and almost highlander dialect. It's just a couple standard Roger Waters tracks. They could have been on any Pink Floyd album 'cause that's just what he does when left to his own devices.

Now, understanding David Gilmour's contribution requires you to do a little pantomime. First, have your name constantly spelled wrong on your band's albums, then bend your elbow so your right forearm is parallel the floor, palm up, half way make a fist, and shake it side to side. He thought this whole concept was dumb. He asked Richard to please write some good lyrics for his music, Richard said no, so he recorded 1) a lovely acoustic guitar track with wanky wailing high pitched noises and background oohs and aaahs, 2) an ominous electric guitar track with Waters-style random noisy bloops and blips, and 3) a song about wishing he could either fly away or be a kid again with like 27 lackadaisical vocal overdubs run through Abbey Road's least enjoyable reverb catacomb speaker/mic combo. I actually kind of like it.

Nick Mason cheated. His wife was an actual flautist, and he's a real percussionist. Gilmour tried, but Ringo he ain't, and Wright and Rogers didn't even bother; two timpani and a ride doesn't count. It's not exactly the kind of party I want to attend, but Grand Viziers aren't exactly the garden party kind of people in the first place.

It's still a worthwhile album, though. If nothing else, you get to really hear which parts of your favorite Floydian slips come from which ego. No, it's not in the top 13 as far as Pink Floyd albums go, but every institution has its Rincewind, and Ummagumma is very clearly the looking glass version of A Saucerful of Secrets. Looking glass, Alice, Terry Pratchett, subconscious connections centered around my familiarity with English arts and entertainment, are you starting to see how these things are born from the primordial ooze inside my brain? If so, then please don't tell me, 'cause I don't wanna know (hello Refreshments reference, long time no see). I'm more surprised than ever at how intricately connected these improvised essays are getting, and I literally just noticed that my original completely unintentional choice to mention that my copy of The Carpenters was fading to pink in between two Pink Floyd albums happened.

So, to recap: I'm insane. Pink Floyd only works when they freely mingle with each other, and tomorrow morning we get a good look at the backside of a cow. Solid work Bottle, I'm impressed.

320) Atom Heart Mother

So, we can get back up and do it all over again.

Where do we even start with this thing. I mean, it's got a standard album structure for the time, the recording process was a nightmare, they hated making Ummagumma so much that they did it again and wouldn't let Gilmour leave until he wrote his song for the b-side, the titles are from the same type of tangential metaphors *I* use even though Pink Floyd isn't my inspiration for doing it. I guess we just pick some of those things apart and don't make any effort to steer the ship at all.

Concerts and soundtrack contributions, snippets of melodies from jamming live, new studio equipment that they weren't allowed to run spliced tape through. Waters and Mason had to record the whole 23-minute suite in one go from memory because they couldn't read music (that'll be important), then head back out to play shows while Ron Geesin tried to make up an orchestra/choir piece above it while leaving space for Gilmour and Wright to solo on it later. The orchestra didn't like Geesin or his music much, so John Alldis (the choir director) had to take over and guide them through it.

Why so much strife over a meandering rock symphony with Western undertones? Well, Pink Floyd *are* the quintessential studio improvisers. Like most rock musicians, they can't read music and they just have to sit in a room and argue until everyone has memorized what they are going to play. That doesn't work when you've got an orchestra and choir with headphones not wanting to play "avant garde" nonsense.

What do we name this monstrosity? Newspaper article about the first lady to have an atomic pacemaker installed. ATOM HEART MOTHER. Subtitles relating to the cow artwork. Side A done, everybody writes a song for Side B. David doesn't actually know how to just write songs? Guess we'll slide sandwiches under the door and he'll either figure it out or die. Record the roadie making and talking about breakfast. Album done, we all hate it, why'd we do it that way?

I love it. I think this is a much better album than Ummagumma. Not concept wise, but music wise. I've more than once stated that writing a thing is not the same as playing the thing. This sounds like Pink Floyd the band again. Saucerful was the last time that happened.

We're right in the middle of Pink Floyd being the machine. They are grinding away: album, tour, soundtrack, tour, album... they don't have a goal, it's just more more more. The standard prog album is this: full side work, other stuff on the other side. Why? Because that's the real-life structure of a band. Work hard and build this monumental work, but hey there's all this other stuff that happens too. We split into multiple personalities, but come back and try to work together. That's the structural foundation of relationships, paths crossing and brief moments of holding all that chaos open for everyone to freely mingle before closing it down and heading off in different directions, having hopefully changed a little in the process.

See why I timed them out to listen to this one on the morning of Father's Day? I didn't, it's coincidence.

I like this album a lot. It's music for the sake of music, and everything else is just packaging.

321) Meddle

Do not meddle in the affairs of wizards, for they are subtle and quick to anger.

But Bottle, where does the connection to Coil fit in? Pink Floyd's album covers were designed by the art collective Hipgnosis. Remember that weird zydeco infused thing by Hapshash and the Colored Coat. Yeah, a design house focused on album art. A group of artists making steady money from labels by doing real design work (something major corporations take away by monopolizing the production process and preventing artists from freely working with other artists). Peter "Sleazy" Christopherson himself didn't make any Pink Floyd covers that I know of, but he was a member of that collective. He was also in Throbbing Gristle, then formed Coil with his superfan turned boyfriend, John Balance. There's a ride at Disney World for that (sing it with me: It's a small world after all…).

Somewhere in the middle of the Atom Heart Mother tour they realized they had absolutely no idea what they should do next. So, they experimented with various ways to waste everyone at Abbey Road Studio's time, and energy, and patience. Execs popped by once in a while with booze and pot, but eventually the boys decided that the antiquated 8-track equipment was the problem, and took their accumulated bleeps and bloops to smaller studios with newer equipment that would let them build pieces in smaller sections and use them like legos.

Third time's a charm? It is basically the same album as Ummagumma and Atom, big thing on one side, other stuff on the other. Prog-rock is starting to feel a little formulaic, at least from an "I dunno what to do next" perspective. How many more albums until Waters starts taking it personal?

But, wow, what an album. Crappy American promotional efforts aside, I think we all in retrospect hear this as the first monumental musical statement from the band. It's epic. It's unbelievably good, as in how did these mortals make such magic when we know full well they were just twisting knobs to see what they did? Fantastic. Yep, just step back and listen to them work, because we haven't even made it to the stuff they're going to make on purpose.

Oh yeah, the cover is supposed to be an ear under water, but Storm Thorgerson thought he did a crappy job of turning his own idea into reality. Yin/yang, win some lose some, I think an actual ear would look pretty dumb, to be honest. And because I can't resist, fearlessly the idiot faced the crowd, indeed.

322) Obscured By Clouds

Obscured By Clouds. Obscured by Pink Floyd is more like it. After More, Barbet Schroeder made sure that they would make the soundtrack for whatever film he made next. They said "yeah, sure" and went on tour and started writing Dark Side of the Moon, then had to find some time to stop off in Paris on the way to and from Japan to actually do it. Same game plan: time out scenes from the film with a stopwatch, make some music, force David Gilmour to write a song 'cause he'll have to do it full time after Roger Waters' over inflated ego explodes after a few more albums (and he needs all the practice he can get), end up making fully formed tracks, getting mad at the film company and changing the name (forcing the film company to add a subtitle to the film because the direct connection to Pink Floyd was important), then finally getting back to missing Syd.

It's an often over looked album. Partly that's the nature of the project itself. It comes across as some throw away tracks for a film in the middle of the beginning of the glory of the kingdom of Pink Floyd. Still, you can hear how far they've come since More. It's better throw away music. They're really starting to care, and it shows.

This is the last Democratic Republic of Pink Floyd album. Not to spoil the plot, but Roger is about to self proclaim himself dictator, miss his friends, build a wall, start to build another wall from the leftover bricks but turn it into a story about how the world betrayed his dad by having the Falkland War at all, fire Richard and demote Nick to the FX department, then quit and years later realize what a total pratt he was.

For now, just enjoy some really nice but not particularly epic Pink Floydian faux country rock songs from a film about an accidental voyage of self discovery while travelling through the unincorporated tribal lands of New Guinea. I've used this joke before, but because Japan.

323) Dark Side of the Moon (this time in context)

Greatest things of all time lists are dumb. But, Dark Side of the Moon certainly belongs on all of them. This is the first Waters album. By that I mean, he came up with the idea that all the songs should be written about a single idea: things that make us mad.

This was an album written to be performed as their next tour, assembled on the road by playing it bits at a time. They bought some new gear (9 tons worth to be exact), moved rehearsals from a Rolling Stones warehouse to the Rainbow Theater, and premiered the whole thing for the press a year before it was released. Believe it or not, recording all those clocks was an Alan Parsons project. I don't care who you are, that's funny right there (Larry the Cable Guy, who'd have guessed that was rattling around in my lunatic of a brain?).

It's about conflict. It's extravagant, but it's concise. There's no beating around the bush, there's no speculation about what kind of furry animal is bustling in the hedgerow (it's a rabbit). These are all the things about modern life that drive us insane. They think of it as generally good, but a tad childishly naive. I take it personal, so let's pick it apart.

We start with the overture. A real overture: snippets of things from the songs you're about to hear, a direct statement about the overall concept that needs no explanation, and away we go.

Roger Waters had a farm, e-I-e-I-o. And on that farm he dug a hole, e-I-e-I-o. With a run run here and a soundtrack there, here a thing there a thing everywhere a pointless thing. Roger Waters had a farm and sat there waiting to die.

He didn't really have a farm, but his first attempt at a midlife crisis was pretty much that simple. We aren't preparing for anything, there's no goal, we're just running around and around killing time and each other while complaining that we aren't accomplishing anything. Eventually, we all give up and try to be children again anyway. Humans are insane, and it's contagious.

Black and blue; who knows which is which, and who is who?

The moral of the story is that all the bright and beautiful and good is right here waiting for us, but some deep flaw in our collective psyche prevents us from realizing it. Perhaps, what really connects us is the fact that we all have those negative emotions and the only thing we have to do is recognize them. But, like rabbits, we just dig a hole and sleep and run around and dig another hole until we finally snap. It's hard to disagree with him, and you certainly can't argue with the album it produced. I've got my plane ticket to crazytown, meet you at the clock tower.

324) Wish You Were Here

It can be really confusing to read about these middle albums, everyone talking from their own perspective of having lived it as though each album is a separate thing, a project they sat down and hashed out. We, however, are watching them live it, and it's a completely different thing. Waters' Pink Floyd is tangible because we can see him take control, get angry at everyone else for making it harder to create, and finally explode. The other three think they're still just a band, but Roger is writing about his real life internal existential crisis. We're talking about an 11-year chunk of time where they have enough money to not care about having to make money. Roger's goal wasn't to become a millionaire and get drunk by the pool every day, but it also wasn't to grind and vacation, grind and stare at hotel walls for 6 months, watch label execs cash in on his hard work and say things like "gravy train" and "fame and fortune." He wanted to be happy again, and he wasn't getting what he wanted.

Anywho, Wish You Were Here is the actual dark side of the moon. If Bowie was saying party over here, I'll be over there (thanks, Aesop Rock), Roger was screaming "why am I at this party? Let me go home!"

Nick Mason's marriage was falling apart, so he was quite the party pooper, Gilmour was Syd's replacement, so you can completely understand his mindset being "your idea is really great, let's just make sure the music does it justice this time," and Richard was just glad he didn't have to work as hard to come up with ideas (he didn't like his own ideas).

Music's awesome, though. They deserve all their success in that regard. Gilmour can whine about Shine On being split up by the other 3 songs all he wants, at the end of the day it's an unquestionable masterpiece.

325) Keep the change, you filthy Animals

I mentioned that Pink Floyd was a twisting knobs in the studio kind of band. Now that their original deal with EMI is over, I can tell you that their deal was a lower percentage of sales in return for unlimited studio time. I can also tell you that that's not a deal: it's the made-up thing that Pink Floyd thought was a good trade off. In reality, from a bookkeeping standpoint, the band pays for everything. A record deal has always been, and will always be, a corporation buying a band's music outright and using it to turn their own profit. When that profit is really good, they let you keep the change. Pink Floyd got to keep millions off the trillions of dollars their music actually generated. We can argue about expenses and legal fees and what have you, but Jason Newstead can tell you that once he passed his probationary period, they let him in on a little secret called money management (not of the venture capital variety) and he never had to work another day in his life before the Black Album even hit the shelves, because James and Lars may have their personal quirks, but they learned really quick how to effectively scream "get off my lawn!" Some people watch their friends nose dive into an empty swimming pool and say "no thanks, I'll keep every penny you drop and save it for later."

Still though, Roger has a point. Money is only useful for spending, and how many people really dream of being super famous and homeless at the same time. I own 4 mansions and 12 airplanes, but I actually live at 37 different Ramada Inns with our lunatic road crew. Yay.

I'm getting off topic again. Roger Waters read Animal Farm one time and said "Storm. Make me a giant inflatable pig so I can hate our fans and use that anger to write a rock opera."

Does anybody like Animals? I've heard it a couple times, but I can't recall any of the songs except Pigs on the Wing. Maybe I can and I forgot they were from Animals. Either way, not a high-profile album in their catalog.

Except for its relationship to punk rock. It's Johnny Rotten's fault. He started it. He didn't mean to, he just didn't realize that he was the inventor of sarcasm by writing "I hate" on his Pink Floyd t-shirt. He liked Pink Floyd. I don't know that he himself ever read Animal Farm, but Waters and Lydon both clearly agreed that Conservative 70s Britain was pretty terrible. Nick Mason thought punk was awesome and gladly produced The Damned's second album at the same church complex they turned into a studio after the EMI deal was over for Animals.

"Dogs" is Gilmour's best work according to critics (and his only contribution since he left to be with his wife and newborn baby like an adult, and Roger and Nick accidentally deleted all the other stuff he had recorded beforehand), so maybe I should give it a proper listen. But before we do that, I'd like to get off track again.

The one good thing about our messed up international copyright laws is that you can't copyright an idea. Otherwise, describing England's social classes as different animals would have been prohibitively expensive. Where's my inflatable pig, Stormy storm?

Issues of "dinosaur rock" aside, the inflatable pig exploded more than twice. It wasn't supposed to explode, but inflammable gasses are flammable. What really set Waters off was the suspicion that they were getting ripped off at the door. He hired a helicopter and did a crowd calculation at Soldier Field. Turns out 20,000+ over "sold out" capacity meant over $600,000 flew right over their heads and landed in someone else's pocket without exploding shrapnel into the crowd. Gilmour said "welp, now we've done everything, guess I should look for something meaningful to do." Oh, we're not done yet Davey boy. Not by a long shot.

Oh yeah, we're listening to an album of theirs or something.

No, I'm sorry. David Gilmour is a lot if things, but a good Brian May style guitarchestra player isn't one of them. This is not his best anything. Whatever song he thought he was soloing over might be good, but this is like bizarro Doobie Brothers meets the Eagles. It's a stepping stone, sure, but there's way better Gilmour before this, and in the future.

Look, look! I was wrong. "Sleazy" is credited with photography. Industrial meets prog at last!

I can't disagree, "Pigs" is just a rehash of Have A Cigar. It is.

Ok. The story makes sense, I guess. Predators, despots, and the general public are sheep who eventually rise up and put a stop to all of it. It's totally relevant (then and right now), but the album isn't good. It's not *bad* bad, but it's throwaway soundtrack type stuff. They aren't getting along with each other personally, and the music suffers. Gilmour wasn't there to make the end result not suck, but instead of realizing that he needed his actual friends, Roger decided to build a wall....

326) The Wall

Everybody knows The Wall. Waters hated playing arenas so much that he said out loud to an actual psychiatrist that he wished he could build a wall between the band and the audience. They hired Bob Ezrin to help flesh out the story, and the rest is history.

There's a lot of important background stuff going on with this album. Roger had two ideas, one became his solo album, the other became The Wall. That's the simple part.

The hard part is that Pink Floyd had a history of handing their money to real sleeze balls. They needed to make a big album to have money because NWG was about to lose all their money, but leave the band with the 80+% tax liability for earning it. It's pretty damned hard to pay a couple million in taxes when your actual bank balance is zero. Finally, Gilmour pulled the plug and became the band's financial manager himself. Every check from here on out has David Gilmour's signature at the bottom. End of discussion. He didn't particularly want to adult that day, but he was the only one who was going to do it.

Gilmour and Ezrin combed the ideas' hair and made it look pretty, and the whole band was super excited. Brick by boring brick (thanks, Paramore!), building the wall. Buy new equipment, Roger fires Richard after demoting him to overnight production, but David keeps him as a salaried musician for the tour. April 6th 1979 was the deadline to become ex-pats to save their money. Hi ho, hi ho, it's off to France we go. Divorces and yelling and Gilmour trying to be everybody's dad, and hey it turns out that Pink is the disembodied psychic humunculous of Syd Barrett that lives inside Roger's brain! Look, Ma! Nazis are still a thing. We're definitely not in Kansas anymore, Toto.

Somehow Gilmour made it all happen. Hello, Michael Kamen and all the various New York orchestras/choirs! You remember Michael for writing and conducting Metallica's S&M in the future, right? There's a ride at Disney World for that!

Columbia literally tried to coin-flip Waters for royalties, but Roger finally won that argument when Brick #2 made them shut up and start counting all their new old Nazi gold coins.

This is all spiralling out of control like a wounded Vickers F.B.5. Kurt Loder loved it, Robert Christgau hated it, no clue what Tabitha Soren thought. Everyone unanimously agrees that it's ridiculously extravagant and pretentious. The proof is in the pudding, but you have to eat your meat first. Let's just listen to it...

... man, that's good. Just incredible. Forget that it's basically happening in real life at the same time. This is what Pink Floyd was progressing toward. All the weird individual components working seemlessly together to paint a ghastly portrait of a fractured psyche. This is some of the best and most delicately painful solo work by Gilmour. It is an undeniable work of art, if uncomfortably close to non-fiction. It's a major achievement of recorded rock music, whether you like it or not. I personally can't see how you could not like it, but go ahead if you don't. It's on par with Jesus Christ Superstar, the sun and moon of rock operas, as far as I'm concerned.

327) The Final Cut

... and then out of nowhere, Margaret Thatcher cared very much about Argentina's invasion of the Falkland Islands. So much so, she waged her own private undeclared war. In the end, I think everybody agreed to just pretend like they own it, but don't actually kill each other anymore.

Pink Floyd was easier to settle, it turned they didn't file their paperwork properly from the get-go, so some dude in a powdered wig said "figure it out yourselves, ya whiny children." Gilmour got Pink Floyd and Waters got The Wall. Roger eventually apologized for being a jerk. Score one for due process diplomacy.

What happened after The Wall boils down to this: Richard was out of the picture completely (don't worry, he'll be back), and Nick didn't care anymore. David and Roger, sittin' on a couch. Roger's plan was to use tracks that didn't actually make it onto The Wall for the soundtrack to the movie version of The Wall. Then along comes Maggie. Scrap that, let's make an album about the Falklands (not technically a) War.

Jorge Louis Borges famously described it as "a fight between two bald men over a comb." Bald Margaret Thatcher, that's a funny mental image. 907 pointlessly dead people, and both countries still to this day pretend they own it? That seems lame.

Gilmour's response was "dude, we all sat here and decided those songs weren't good enough for the last album. Are they suddenly awesome because you don't like Thatcher? That seems lame. Let's make an actual new album with actual new music that *is* awesome."

Roger replied "I don't see you offering up any bright ideas."

David calmly said "yes, we all know I go through periods of objective laziness. Now is one of them. Do it if your mind's made up, just don't waste too much of our money."

Roger that, Roger did, and when it was over, he decided Pink Floyd was a deflated pig balloon, and he got quite a shock when David replied "great news, I not feeling lazy anymore. Shove off. Nick and I have a new album to make. We met this great keyboard player named Richard Wright, don't know if you've ever heard of him. Toodles."

I've honestly never heard Roger Floyd's The Final Cut. Guess it's time to see what all the fuss was about.

Great news! It took exactly 1 minute for me to hate it. I'm with Gilmour, this blows. It's way too on the nose, and it's whiny. It should have stayed a solo album like everyone pretends it is. I haven't even made it to track 3 yet. Aw, another crap "Dogs" solo from Gilmour. You can tell exactly how little he cared because he didn't even dial in a tone. He turned on the crappiest amp and squinted like he was constipated.

It would make a fascinating aesthetic study. It's sombre and serious and reverent music, but Waters' delivery screams smarmy bile. "That's how the high command took my daddy from me!" ? "Jesus, Jesus, what's it all about?" ?? Low octave vocal underdub ???

I'm calling Finger 11 on this one. Narcissistic douchebaggery. Eat rat poison.

Don't misunderstand me, I completely get where he's coming from, and I clearly have a lot of ideas and feelings in common with Roger Waters, but this is too much. This isn't Pink Floyd. It's not clever, or intelligent, it's pretentious. The pretense is that we're supposed to feel sorry for Roger. This isn't what he meant with Dark Side of the Moon, this is "feel sorry for me, I command it." Kevin Hart impression: I'm a grown ass man being childish.

It's a good thing he had no plans to tour it, because I could not even begin to imagine how uncomfortable it would be to see it or perform it live in a bar, or theater.

All of which is a shame, because there's some truly great music in here. It's the specific lyrical content that's the problem. Finger 11 and Seether look a little less horrible by compsrison, and that's an atrocity.

Oh god, another ghastly ragged melodic guitar solo. The melody for "Fletcher memorial..." is amazing but "a final solution can be applied" reminds me of a hardcore Jesus fan named Shireen Salyor. Remember that baby nailed to a tree? Yeah, that's how this makes me feel. How can you walk around the universe legitimately feeling and thinking that way? It's how Emerson felt about An Officer and A Gentleman. It's grotesque.

Sell it to Rolling Stone? Even Kurt Loder couldn't like this one. Footnote: Kurt Loder wasn't just a nobody MTV personality, he was *the* editor of Rolling Stone in the 80s.

Final verdict? Congratulations, Ummagumma! You just cracked the top 13!

Do not go listen to this album. Forget it like everyone else did. Really. I'm serious. It's a complete waste of awesome cover art. As soon as my own tears evaporate, we'll move on to (spoiler alert) my two favorite Pink Floyd albums.

328) A Momentary Lapse of Reason

I don't care if A Momentary Lapse of Reason is basically a Gilmour solo album made by his backup band. I don't care that it's undeniably 80s apartment rock. I don't care that it's just songs. I don't care that it's more like a midi programmed performance by the animatronic Chuck E Cheese band than a Pink Floyd album.

I care that it's Pink Floyd again. Richard is there. He only added some background chord filler, and he's not an official corporate member of Pink Floyd, but $11,000 a week is a ridiculous amount of money, so who cares?

We think of these bands as just some dudes making music, but they aren't. They are executives with a board of directors, sub-managers, staff, phone calls, and business meetings (probably less formal than where you work, but identical in the legal sense). Roger quit the band, and he doesn't want to hang out any more, but he still has his share of the business, and he is "Director of Pink Floyd Music." He can object to what Pink Floyd does, and it matters.

Also, we live in digital recording nirvana. They just got MIDI, but they are still making the album with tape. Want to tweak the phaser settings? You have to re-dub that part, put it back in the mix, and listen to how it sounds. Tape operator was an actual full-time job, because someone had to physically operate tape recorders and itemize the recordings and literally do everything by hand. After the recordings are done, they dump it into a digital machine to play around, but it's still a physical machine with buttons and knobs and the ability to permanently delete a month's work by setting your beer bottle in the wrong place, or tripping over an extension cord. The concept of "undo" doesn't exist yet.

Tack on lawsuits, and label execs saying "this isn't Pink Floydy enough," and Roger spying on them, and there's some serious stress involved. They can't fail, or it really is the end. No grand concept or story, no political pomposity, songs that people right now will like and that most of our fanbase will tolerate. The three remaining members of Pink Floyd wanted to make an album, and this is what they made.

Learning to Fly was almost certainly the first Pink Floyd song I ever heard when I was 7 or 8 because it was Pink Floyd's radio single. I love it. Yes, the album itself is undeniably 80s dad-rock, but it's not Bowie's sellout 80s pop, it's rock.

More importantly, it's a u-turn back into the sunlight 'cause Roger's turn to the darkside left a nasty aftertaste in everyone's mouth. No more turning away. Keep your eyes on the skies, and help each other out. We can't make the war machine stop grinding if we're constantly fighting each other.

Take the best of what the people in your life have to offer, and keep learning to fly. I can't think of a more relavant message, dinosaurs of dad-rock or no.

You know what seals the deal? What's been missing from the last few albums? The Noir. That feeling that something isn't right, but you can't quite name it, and you won't see it until it jumps out and tries to bite you. That sound that whispers "sabotage," and tells you to be wary. Something is rotten in the state of Denmark, and we need to sniff and snuff it out. Whether it comes from the real-life stress of making it, or from the natural melding of minds, or if it's simply a tonal quality that just plain sounds good, it's back on this album, and it's what makes Pink Floyd awesome in my head.

329) The Division Bell

I don't think anyone would really argue when I say The Darkside of the Moon, Wish You Were Here, and The Wall are the 3 best Pink Floyd albums. The Division Bell, however, is my favorite by miles and miles.

The main theme is communication, but it's really about making choices. The Division Bell tolls for the call to vote. Yea, or nay. We've come full circle. Build the wall, or tear it down. Rise to the challenge, or run and hide. Make a product, or record your friends playing hours and hours of music (who cares if they are technically in the band or not?) and see what develops.

It's the last Pink Floyd album. They planned to use leftovers from it for other things, but it wasn't until 6 years after Wright died that they finally made The Endless River. Everybody got songwriter credits (making the various producers and agents mad), because everyone contributed to writing the album in their own way. David says, no more cocaine for me, thanks.

It's Gilmour's best everything. Marooned is improvised. I've heard it a thousand times and it still brings tears to my eyes. And High Hopes is just a heartwrenchingly devastating sonic monolith stretching forever off into the endless river.

330) The Endless River

Which brings us to said Endless River. It's a beautiful piece of music.

After The Division Bell, they did have Andy Jackson edit the leftovers into a large ambient work called The Big Spliff, but they never released it. Finally, in 2012, David and Nick revisited the material and decided to actually do it. It's a lot of things, and you can go read all the various things said about it, but everybody gets it wrong in some way.

David Gilmour always said and believed that Pink Floyd didn't belong to any person. Pink Floyd was the group of people making the album, in the flesh or in spirit, part of the band or a hired hand. He kept reluctantly inheriting more and more of it, until he was finally done. This is David Gilmour's last Pink Floyd album, and fittingly it's an instrumental collage with a final song written by his wife.

Pink Floyd played music. It's his way of saying hello to all the people who want to listen, and goodbye to all the people who helped make it happen. So, to summarize my thoughts, don't confuse the meaning for the machine. The machine will grind you up and spit you out. You can fight it, rage against it, be its victim, or if you're hopelessly optimistic, find some beauty in the journey.

331) Poe - Haunted

You ever read any Poe? No, but I like her 2nd album a lot.

Wanna hear an hour and 15 minutes of existential torture that'll have you running for you safe room but too afraid to walk down the unlit hallway to get there?

Here's Haunted, the companion to her brother Mark's book House of Leaves. What do you mean you haven't read it? Were you raised in a forest talking to tay-tays? It's Jodie Foster movies, hurrah! Useless Jodie Foster, as my dad used to call her. That's not fair, she was a legitimate multi-lingual child prodigy and deserved to go to Yale. Silence the bleating. Put on your hazmat suit, be the brave one, and make contact with your local purveyor of ergodic literature. I'll run up to the attic and fetch my copy while I wait for you...suitably terrified? Let's go.

The samples on this album are mostly from Daddy Danielewski's audio diaries that they found after he died.

We start off with the creepiest answering machine message ever created. Edgar would be impressed, assuming he got past the initial astonishment of telephones and answering machines (he died 27 years before telephones existed).

Now, as far as magazine criticism goes, yes, this album is too long. Every album from 1995 to 2015 is too long, but this is all you're ever gonna get from Poe, so hit pause and walk a lap or two every 20 minutes.

The business/legal side of Poe's career chewed her up and spat her out, preventing her from doing pretty much anything except charity work. It's a fascinating horror story, but I'll let you read about it on your own.

She's all over the place, musically speaking, but if you need to compare her to something it's unquestionably Garbage meets Solex.

Lyrically, the album is a fascinating blend of autobiographical ideas through the lens of the characters in the book. You get an interesting double-sided perspective of the subject matter that Mark actually used for the structure of his next novel, Only Revolutions. For House of Leaves/Haunted, though, the most obvious connection is Tad/Zampano leaving behind a difficult to understand body of quasi-fictional work for everyone else to decipher.

Imagine what she could have accomplished if a couple of rich people just paid for it in good faith instead of using her as a bargaining chip in a pointless profit war. But nope, we get a bunch of already rich people complaining that we don't have enough money to buy their stuff, so they just pass their stuff and money back and forth to each other and tell us we're the lazy ones.

At least we got this masterpiece of grungy alternative hip-pop. 4 thumbs up. It's even bigger on the inside.

332) Dan Vapid and the Cheats - Two

The winner of tonight's random bandcamp search is Dan Vapid and the Cheats. Not gonna lie, I was expecting complete garbage when I searched for "tweezers." I don't have any idea what I actually did, but this was the 4th thing that popped up, and since I have the attention span of a squirrel, let's go for it. Random is random, even when you get it wrong.

Not joking, this is the 6th thing I've wanted to buy on vinyl today that's been completely sold out. On payday. That blows because holy shit this is good. It's punk, old school punk. 50s/60s rock and roll with massive distortion and super catchy music and melodies.

Now, Screeching Weasel is one of those bands that everyone has played in at one time or another. That's a Chicago thing for sure. Dan Vapid is tied for most prominent not a weasel with Dan Panic at 6 albums each, but Mike Dirnt is probably their most famous bass fill in. Not important.

I can't repeat it enough, this is awesome. Go check it out. Seriously.

333) Robert Maxwell - Shangri-la

You know what you need? Light Pop-jazz harp and orchestra. Robert Maxwell is famous for writing Ebb Tide, Shangi-la (Jackie Gleason's theme song), and making the harp not quite so weird of a solo instrument. Ok, maybe it's still weird to hear a 1963 pop harp album, but who else is gonna tell you about it? No one. Just me.

I think Robert Maxwell had the right approach. He was on TV a lot from what I've read. Remember when Zappa went on TV and played an upside-down bicycle? I think he was just tapping into the camp and humor of it all, and this album has it too. It's campy. In a great way. It's not a joke, there's some incredible orchestration and playing, but it's fun, it's lighthearted, it's bubbly, it's entertaining, at least what I think of as being entertaining in the early 60s. There's lots of playlists of his stuff on youtube. Go find some and have a smirk. You won't regret it.

334) Scritti Politti - Provision

I once said that "best of" lists are dumb. "Worst of" lists are much better, and I'll explain my reasons. 1) it eliminates albums you just hated on instinct or genres you intentionally avoid, 2) it forces you to evaluate a body of work you have internalized (that is, you know something about), and 3) it forces you to consider your own opinion without pitting you against the nebulous idea of other peoples' preferences.

I posed the question "what's the worst album you've listened to all the way through?," and I got some great answers, mostly things that were really disappointing. I have a worst album. It's the worst album in the Bottle of Beef collection. I actually bought it *because* it is terrible. It has no redeeming qualities that I can think of, and that is really saying something.

Let's look at some of the official worst albums based on critical reviews (but only the ones I've actually heard, so no

Kevin Federline, or One Direction spin offs, or novelty stuff). For that, we go to wikipedia's "List of music considered the worst/albums."

Shaggs - Philosophy of the World: no, incredibly influential album, and technical proficiency has no bearing on musical merit.

Lord Sutch and Heavy Friends: no, I reviewed it, he's my spirit animal, plus it's good. Embarrassment after the fact because "it might hurt my career" is grade a bullshit, every single one of those people had fun making it.

Attila - Attila: no, Billy Joel didn't go full on "hurt my career" and that saves him in my eyes, but it's a completely acceptable album for the time and place and world in which it was created.

Elvis and Lou Reed don't count. Adding Metallica into the mix doesn't count either. As far as Guns 'n Roses goes, The Spaghetti Incident is way worse than Chinese Democracy because everyone expected Chinese Democracy to suck.

I already did the soundtrack version of Sgt. Pepper, and it was like 40% great.

That's it, the rest are disqualified.

What makes an album terrible? Well, it has to invalidate its own existence. It has to be so egregiously horrible that it drags the universe down with it. It can't be funny, it can't be insane, it can't be derivative, and it can't be ill advised. Every one involved had to be serious, it had to sell well (in context), and it had to be followed by a decade of hiding out in the country to live down the mental anguish of creating it at all.

I've mentioned it before (not in this book). It's Scritti Politti's Provision. I believe I called it "audio gonnorhea." I did call it that. If we were playing the "girl/baby" drinking game we would all have fatal alcohol poisoning before the end of Side A. That's not even the bad part. This album actually transcends irony, rockets past cult level ideology at ludicrous speed, and somehow includes a trumpet solo from Miles Davis, who I assume was too high and too broke to care anymore. A sub 2-million dollar estate when he died unexpectedly after fighting with multiple doctors' recommendations? Miles Davis deserves every accolade a musician could possibly garner, but he lived like buying enough cocaine to never sleep again was a challenge he was ready and willing to accept. Bill Evans famously used the word "corrupted" when talking about labels and fame and pop/rock stardom. Not the point. Let's dive right into it.

What the hell does any of this mean? No seriously, this is an actual honest to sincerity communist love song album. Oooh girl, baby baby, I love you, but in the communist way. Love (in Communism), Green Gartside. He started his own communist club in high school. The band name is a rock-bandification of "scritti politici" ("political writings" in Italian).

The Tupamaros aren't hard core enough? For those of you who don't know, the Tupamaros were an Uraguayan organization that sprang out of the steep decline in value of agricultural exports to Europe in the 60s. The post civil war government of Uruguay had a trade deal with Europe, and it was pretty freakin' awesome from an economic standpoint. Uruguay was a first-world track country through both, count 'em both, world wars. But after Hitler suicided himself, food prices dropped significantly, and the economy of Uruguay went to shit. The Tupamaros started off peaceful and had massive support, but by 1970 they had morphed into a militant guerilla army that directly attacked the government and military, and subsequently got squashed like bugs. Now, before you pick a side in that fight, remember that in 1984, yes you read that year right, Uruguay had it's first democratic election and the people of Uraguay decided that the whole thing would best be left to the past. No more dictators, let the communists out of prison, act like adults. Not that I'm scolding you America, but Uruguay figured it out in

19goddamned84, and we're so back-asswards we're finally having that same childish fight in 2020? Really?

Scritti Politti didn't always suck, you just can't buy any of their non-sucky records. They were originally a new wave band like everyone else. But, Green had some serious anxiety issues and turned to synthpop in the hopes of hiding in the studio and never having to perform again. This album was what finally broke him. It got to the point where they were programming kick drums in raw time code, he couldn't even form coherent sentences as you can clearly hear, and after it was done, he went back to the Welsh countryside for 10 years.

Everyone describes his writing style as essentially wordy and obtuse, but I just hear him as a nonsensical Michael Jackson. He puts the emPHAsis on the wrong syLLAble and constructs awkward half thoughts that sound like they are supposed to convey some underlying clever secondary meaning, but most definitely do not.

Musically speaking, one could argue that this is gobbledigook, and no one would disagree. Bleeps and bloops are the hallmark of good synthpop, but this sounds like everyone thought those bass lines were killer and expected everyone to dance. He wanted to make this, and not in the ironic "taking down capitalism from the inside" way you might imagine. SPK gives it that much needed dead inside/last hope of surviving feeling, but this is (and I apologize for using the term because I do not have a more accurate one) retarded.

You should absolutely go listen to this monstrosity and feel free to tell me I'm wrong. But, and I can't stress this enough, don't pretend that it's intelligent because you and I both know that's a fist squeezing a deflated globe, but it contains the lyric "Hot sugar returns to toy town" in a song subtitled Lovesick.

I'm glad that's over, now get me the hell out of here.

335) Prelude to the first half of the Megadeth discography

Ok. Megadeth time. I only care about their first 7 albums, my Megadeth stops at Hidden Treasures. The reason is complicated.

I've mentioned it before, but 1995 is kind of a tipping point in my mind. It wasn't that grungy alternative rock killed mainstream music, or that the internet was starting to make an impact, or even that major labels started wildly flailing around and preventing bands from getting popular without their support. What really happened is that my generation finally said "screw it." We were tired of even trying to succeed in the world of business. Pick a person who "achieved success" and I'll point to the guy or gal he ripped off to achieve it. Corporate America reached a tipping point where the wealthiest Americans said to themselves "it's more important to profit from pumping disposable garbage into the world and use that money to feel happy, shoot tigers, and live by the lake than it is to care about the working class and their families," and we responded by saying "I'm already miserable, so have fun watching us get worse." I'm not saying we were right for giving up, I'm simply pointing out that we did. I might be the youngest gen-xer on the planet, but age is unimportant. To paraphrase Ron White, I've got a lot of quit in me. You can pretend that this country is functional, but our economy is a lottery economy. 25 years later, we think it's pretty awesome that the kids of today have the spark and gumption to start fighting back again. We're going to keep encouraging them, by the way. Not because we're right, but because "bite me."

Sadly, 1995 is the point in time where Dave Mustaine lost his way. He started looking to cash in on his metal stardom and reach for the mainstream radio alternative rock money, and I said "meh, guess I don't care about Megadeth anymore." Oh well, I'll survive. That's not to say Megadeth hasn't produced some good songs in the last decade, it's just that I don't care. There's no value in it for me anymore.

These albums though, I completely understand. First-half Megadeth exists for only 1 purpose: to be "x-er" than Metallica. See you later tonight with their debut....

336) Killing Is My Business...

You know what bothers me the most? In 1995 Lee Hazlewood actually won. He quoted Melanie (look what they done to my song, ma) and complained that Megadeth's version of These Boots Are Made for Walkin' was vile and horrible. Yes, that was the point. The only character being defamed was Dave himself. Killing Is My Business... is the result of Dave being sent home mid-tour for being the worst drug abusing alcoholic in a band comprising drug abusing alcoholics. His sales pitch was "whatever Metallica does, I'm gonna do it louder, faster, nastier 'cause I wrote most of Kill 'Em All and I want revenge." Capitol Records said "ok, here's $8,000." They immediately spend half that on drugs, fired their producer, asked for another $4000, and produced it themselves. I don't think it sounds terrible at all. It sounds like early thrash metal. Dave is the bad guy. Vic Rattlehead, the victim of anonymous torture, is their new mascot. It's not satanic because this is just the evil side of the coin: you're doin' swell, but I feel like hell.

People make a big deal about him getting fired, but Dave has pretty consistently said that he was mad that they didn't say anything. Not once did they mention that his substance intake and behavior was scaring them, they just sent him home one day. He thanks Slayer, Anthrax, and Metallica in the liner notes. They are the Big 4 because they all invented thrash together, trying to one-up each other for the sheer love of heavy metal. Megadeth will go on to much more coherent social/cultural/political statements, but we have to start somewhere. From Kill 'Em All, we get a little more refinement. If killing is my new job, then I've got plenty of work to keep me busy, and I better get started. Hi everybody, we're Megadeth, rattle your head 'til your brains fall out.

337) Peace Sells...But Who's Buying?

First off, Gar and Chris weren't fired for "substance abuse issues." Yes, Dave and Dave were really frustrated that those non-Daves were too high to show up for recording sessions because Dave and Dave were homeless, but they were fired because they stole the band's gear and fenced it so they could buy more heroin. Chris eventually got clean and played on another Megadeth album that I don't care about, but Gar died. Peace Sells, but Who's Buying?

1986 is the year of the Challenger explosion and the Iran-Contra Affair. It's also the year that Dave Mustaine said "look, this supposed 'american dream' thing is pretty much dead. Anyone with eyes can see that the hardest working people aren't getting anywhere because they are paying Corporate America to let them live in peace. You can't succeed by working hard and earning it, you succeed when someone finds a way to profit from your success." Said another way, make me money and I'll let you keep the change.

But that's not all you get. Call now and we'll throw in a hyperbolic story about cheating on the girl you were dating because she let you stay at her place (homeless, remember) but you were actually in love with someone else. First 10 callers get some generic witches and satan-adjacent occultism, sure to make those wealthy religious conservatives squirm! Disclaimer: not responsible for any future embarrasment caused by the decision to convert to Christianity (we're looking at you Dave #1). Yeah seriously, at some point after I stopped caring, Dave Mustaine decided he wanted to be born again or whatever and felt really uncomfortable playing any of the occult stuff. But again, the whole point of Megadeth was overreacting as a mirror image of "civilized society." It's just a form of escapism. The statement was "this is how *you* see me, and it's not true. Real life is brutal, and I have to go to ridiculous extremes to show you how disconnected from it you really are."

Now, I will agree this is a better album than the first, but does it sound 3 times better? This album's budget was $25,000 (a suspicious man might think the first album generated revenue for someone, huh?). I mean, sure some of that went to the artwork, and a lot of that went to the new producer, but at least to my ears studio gear in the 80s sounds like studio gear in the 80s. Everyone is using pretty much the same equipment, indie or full subsidiary: Marshall amps and Jackson guitars, a match made in some boring but awesome board meeting on a Thursday.

Remember kids, you're paying back every penny from your own future profits, so expect to get out exactly what you put in.

This is considered a classic thrash album, one you're supposed to listen to before you die. I can't argue, it's good. Thrash is miserable time, unhappy music. It's not a party, it's a coping mechanism. Hyperbole warriors ho!

Is it their best? I don't know. Sort of, I guess. I mean, there's much more enjoyable stuff in the future, but as far as messages go, the question is pretty apropos: we, the lower class, are the ones advocating peace and civility, why are we paying you to not take our houses and happiness away? That doesn't seem civilized at all.

338) So Far, So Good, So What

Hey Dave, who should we get to play now that we've fired our heroin junkie drummer and guitarist? Gee, I don't know Dave, I met these two heroin junkies who can play for us. Why didn't you say so, Dave? Geez, we could have already hired and fired them by now.

But seriously, they didn't even make it all the way through the tour for So Far, So Good, So What before they had to go home for more drugs, or less drugs, or who really knows. Dave Mustaine is not good at keeping track of what he ate for breakfast yesterday, how could he possibly keep track of all the blurry faces he fired in the 80s. It's not like he himself was sober for 10 consecutive minutes during the whole decade.

It does sound much better than the previous two, but sadly the songs just aren't as good. Topic wise it's great, nuclear war, depression, drunk driving, censorship, and revisionist history, but it trades some speed for heaviness and that's a loss in my book. Not a bad album at all, just not as concise and face smashing as I happen to like from revenge metal. Hook in Mouth is the best track on the album, in my opinion. Censorship isn't about album covers or naughty words, it's about suppressing ideas that differ from yours without considering their content or merit. It's about taking away your ability to think for yourself.

339) Rust In Peace

Finally, we get to the classic albums with the classic lineup. That's not to disparage the before and after, it's just to say that for most people, this is Megadeth. May all your nuclear weapons rust in peace. This album came from a bumper sticker quote.

Is it better than Peace Sells...? I don't know. Peace Sells is an underground/fringe album, Rust in Peace is a mainstream metal album. Thematically, I think they are the same. Every Megadeth album is the same, the songwriting just gets better (up to a very specific point when it's very definitely over).

Dave Mustaine is an Eddie Van Halen type riff guy. He just wanted to write songs and play lead guitar, but he couldn't find a frontman so he became his own. Every incarnation of the band picks cool riffs and songs from his hours of tape recordings and they make an album. It's not rocket science, they play stuff they thought was cool and Dave's lyrics range from standard escapist magic/sorcery stuff, to coherent political and social topics, to examinations of specific psychological perspectives. One thing is consistent though, he doesn't like war. He believes that governments start wars, not the people they represent.

Imagine his surprise at misunderstanding the half-assed explanation of the IRA and The Troubles of Ireland he was given, the riot that ensued when he dedicated Anarchy in the UK to "The Cause," and the bulletproof vehicles they got to ride in for the short, short version of rest of that tour. That's Holy Wars...The Punishment Due. Nick Menza thought a song about Hangar 18 would be cool. Lucretia is about a ghost in Dave's attic. Nuclear war, human made environmental pollution, you get the idea.

The cool thing is that he doesn't make any commentary about any of this stuff. Rather, he takes on the persona of "this is what I see when I walk out into the world. We just take all this weird, horrible stuff at face value. I'm just describing all of you."

Oh yeah, the music is amazing and their producer was making Use Your Illusions I and II at the same time in the same studio, so he didn't actually do much with this album at all. Dave and the engineer did most everything themselves.

Like I said, it's kind of a coin toss between this and Peace Sells, but if I had to choose one it would be Rust In Peace. Thankfully, I don't. I get to keep all 7.

340) Countdown To Extinction (in context)

Countdown to Extinction might be the perfect album in every respect. That is to say that every aspect of the band, the business, the zeitgeist, everything just synced up and out popped an amazing album.

Everybody wrote a song on this album. Dave never wanted to be a one man show, he just couldn't convince anyone to get professional treatment for their addictions (he tried because that's what he wished James and Lars would have done). Now he had a stable lineup! They practiced, they tweaked and reworked songs to fit everybody's different playing styles, they played basketball in between takes (the whole thing was complicated by the 6pm curfew during the Rodney King riots, but that didn't hamper the inspiration too much). Their chosen producer actually participated in the process this time, contributing ideas on how to make it even better. Whaaaa?

In many ways it's the obvious Megadeth response to the Black Album. "Oh, you're going for mass appeal by doing an awesome job? Hold my beer. Emotions? I've got a few."

On the surface it looks like more random stuff: comic books, shadow governments, Saddam Hussein, the tragic reality of farming being too expensive, skydiving, trophy hunting, psychosis. But what do you get when you add it all up? You get a stained-glass portrait of humanity's adrenaline-junkie death wish. Kill kill kill for fun and profit. How's that taste? Like ashes in your mouth.

341) Youthanasia

You're going to look at me weird, but Youthanasia is the most beautiful sounding album I can think of. It's also the actual act of dying. Or rather, it's the end of the transformation from child to Vic Rattlehead, the not at all subtle doppelganger of Uncle Sam.

Whether he intended to or not, he was writing a story through Megadeth albums, and Youthanasia was the end of the story. It had to be absolutely perfect, completely democratic, and actually be the metaphorical death of Megadeth. It manifested itself as a kind of tug of war in the studio. Dave was meticulously anal retentive about the technical/musical stuff, but he demanded that the other three guys be equal and fight with him. It confused the hell out of everybody, because they didn't really get it.

Dave didn't want to be the egomaniacal owner of the band, but that's what the world turned him into. It's time for that character to die and be another useless corporate drone for our war machine of a country. We kill our youth and call it "winning."

He concludes that story, by the way, with a "life flashing before your eyes" moment constructed from Megadeth song titles. Then, they publish their soundtrack and tribute songs as an epitaph (Metallica was famous for refusing to let any of their music be used in movies or commercials, except for 1 documentary about Damian Echols). What's the bad guy supposed to do? Sell out. Such a good story. Go read it again, it's awesome.

342) Hidden Treasures

And let's not forget the covers and soundtrack songs they made along the way. Rest in peace, Megadeth's ascension from gutter rats to manicured gutter rats with keys to the executive washroom.

343) Grease

And the winner of the most insane thing to listen to after 7 Megadeth albums in two days goes to.....the soundtrack to Grease!

I'm partial to the theory that the whole thing is the death dream Sandy has as she's drowning in the ocean, but I'm nothing if not morbid for the sake of humor. If I were a character from Grease, I'd be Rizzo.

Hello, Frankie Valli. Grease is the word? Sure, it does have a meaning, but I though the bird was the word. Did Barry Gibb write this? Yes, yes he did. What are we doing here? Throwing away conventionality by listening to the Grease soundtrack after Megadeth. I already explained that.

Nearly drowned? It's a good theory.

As far as movie musicals go it's pretty darned popular. I'm still not known for agreeing with Roger Ebert, so I find it incredibly confusing why he gave it a 3 out of 4 but called it average and plastic. I don't share Gene Shallot's dude crush on John Travolta either. If brain tumors could actually help you learn Portugese maybe, but Face Off. He peaked as Vinnie Barbarino. Yeah, don't act like I didn't watch Welcome Back Kotter reruns, 'cause I totally did. Gabe Kaplan for life.

Guess which soundtrack it was second to in sales figures, go ahead guess. It rhymes with Latterday Blight Beaver.

The original version of "Look at me..." refers to Sal Mineo, but somehow Elvis' heart attack was less unnerving than Sal's death by being stabbed in a random mugging for the movie version. Brandon Lee got killed during the actual filming of his character's death in The Crow because the propmaster was lazy, so maybe I'm a little too jaded to care?

Grease: it's what the 70s thought the 50s were like. Cute. The songs are catchy (Beauty School Dropout is a freakin' classic in the Frankie Avalon catalog), and it's better than an actual Olivia Newton John album, so I really don't have much to actually complain about. Except Travolta, he flunked Shampoo.

344) Never On Sunday

Ha! Frankie Avalon said "hooker," so I guess it's time for another round of "soundtrack for a movie that sounds like an hour and a half of my brain I'm glad isn't filled with scenes from..." Never On Sunday.

Lots of academy award nominations and stuff. Pygmalion but from a hooker with a heart of gold perspective? No thanks. Quick wikinopsis: american guy falls for greek prostitute, convinces her to not be a prostitute. She finds out it was a ploy by Noface the pimp 'cause she's a bad example for all the other prostitutes, what with her independence and personal rather than subservient choices, and goes back to being the role model for all those young entrepreneurial prostitutes who don't need a pimp, and Homer says I guess I was wrong, yay Greek prostitutes. I'm sure I'm missing some subtleties or nuance or something, but still no thanks.

I'm gonna just pretend like it's an enthnomusicological survey of Greek popular music written by Manos Hadjidakis. He's your standard orchestral type composer, but he legitimately wanted to write modern music for a traditional folk instrument. The theme song won its Best Song Academy Award, and Melina Mercouri for Best Actress at Cannes in 1960. Still, no thanks.

The music is great though. Bouzouki is a long-necked fretted lute, flat top/rounded bottom. For you guitar players out there, imagine Ovation made a mandolin with a fretted broom handle.

Hide the jacket when you throw it on at your next dinner party and trick your friends into thinking you're just real keen on 60s Greek experimental pop. I don't throw dinner parties, but you might. Ya mas (that's Greek for cheers).

345) Movie time: Elektra (the opera, not the Avengers character)

... and then I thought of that phrase "it's all Greek to me." Let's watch my favorite movie version of a German expressionist take on the classic Sophocles work, Electra. German expressionism, so spell it with a k: Elektra. Hello, Fischer-Diskau!

I happen to like Richard Strauss, especially his operas. Strauss had a lot of stress for an apolitical composer/conductor. Musically speaking, he was considered a successor to Wagner, and Wagner was you know who's favorite composer (not Voldemort). Conducting wise, he was offered the position Toscanini quit in protest. Strauss' daughter-in-law was Jewish, he intentionally performed works by "banned" composers, hired a Jewish Librettist, wrote pieces that derided the Nazis, and gladly got fired. He used his influence to legally keep his daughter-in-law under house arrest during the War. Sadly, he wasn't powerful enough to do much for her extended family, but he tried. So much so, that he was specifically pardoned by name right before he died. Cool dude.

Now, the world of opera is just as bad about idolotry as commercial pop. Fischer-Diskau is great, so he performed everything, and people just got sick of only ever hearing his version of everything. Kronos Quartet is the same way. They are great, but that doesn't mean everybody else should just be understudies. I have his version of Winterreise hiding in here somewhere; way better than Sting's. I'm serious, Sting did a version of Winterreise. Anywho, I just really like the cinemetography of this particular version of Elektra.

Greek mythology is great because you've got thousand of characters all related and associated in detailed ways. Plus, everybody is morally ambiguous, they do good stuff and bad stuff and other characters react however you want them to react. Hofmannsthal's take is cool because he follows Sophocles, but limits the perspective to the actual first person view of Elektra. He downplays parts of the story that she wouldn't care much about personally, while emphasizing her particular psychological perspective during the conversations she has. Strauss himself would eventually move away from modernism, but this is right in the middle of his really dissonant, often bitonal gruesomness. Remember, Schoenberg abandons tonality and his umlaut 'cause Nazis, Webern is morally conflicted with his own political opinions, Picasso is painting people as deformed, fractured monsters, Switzerland is trying really hard to not reject all the gold and cultural artifacts being smuggled in, Churchill is all giddy 'cause he gets to order people to kill other people while he drinks watered down Johnny Walker Red 24 hours a day, and how anybody can feel like they won a prize for any of it is an enigma. Lots of NOS vacuum tubes for stereo and guitar amps are kind of a prize, I guess, but we've used most of them at this point (I only bring up the enigma machine because the encryption on this particular dvd is weird and it took forver to find a device in our house that could decode it. I finally cracked it using a Drogan's decoder wheel (Spies Like Us reference, yay!) What I'm trying to say is real ordinary everyday people didn't like living through WWII. Real people don't hate each other. Real people try to solve problems rather than beat up other people. Real people accept "no" for an answer and try something else. Having a world war at all is kind of a big flashing neon sign that centralized federal governments with despotic figureheads aren't particularly good for humanity at large, but what do I know, I'm a dumb musician. People like to kill each other, I guess.

The opening scene sums that up pretty well: the servants say they taunt Elektra 'cause it's fun to make her mad, and the one maid who's nice to her gets taken away to be tortured. Not to spoil it for you, but Orest avenge kills his mom and her lover, and Elektra does her version of the Flashdance/Footloose montage until she herself falls down dead. Nobody wins, everybody loses something, mostly their waking up tomorrow. Maynard wrote a song about Orestes, maybe we should listen to A Perfect Circle next... Shhh! The movie's starting.

346) A Perfect Circle - Mer de Noms

Billy Howerdel was Tool's guitar tech (among many other bands). You know, the guy who changed strings, and tuned guitars, made sure they were plugged in, and stuff. Maynard said he'd write lyrics if Billy formed his own band, and thus A Perfect Circle was born (Billy originally imagined a female singer, and now it's a duet). It's more fiddly than that obviously (like signing to Virgin Records so no one mistook it as a silly side project), but that's how Maynard works. Let him know when you've got the music written and he'll make up word things about stuff for it. He writes whatever he can hear himself singing for that particular track, and in general he's really good at it. Did I ever mention he did a duet version of Disco King with Bowie? Now I did.

The original lineup was kind of slapdash, too. Whomever they knew that wasn't doing anything else at that moment. It's like a secret sideman supergroup. Mer de Noms (literally "waterfall of first names" in their invented symbology) is their first album. Not surprisingly, most of the song titles are names. It's objectively awesome. You got your fairy tales, mythology (Orestes, remember), dead moms, sleazy girlfriends, Mexican deserts, und keine Eier! That's a Tool joke, but I couldn't resist.

Yes, it's rather dark, but it's a really pretty sounding album. Everything shimmers, and Maynard's particular brand of melismatic singing is on full display. It doesn't have the snark of Tool, he really gives this band a sensitive quality in spite of the morosity.

Interesting fact, Howerdel worked on one of the incarnations of Chinese Democracy. Uninteresting fact, I've lost my copy of Failure's Fantastic Planet (Failure toured with Tool and Troy Van Leeuwen's on this album).

Musically, this lives in a strange netherworld between alternative rock and alternative metal. "Alternative" to everything, there's not really anything else like this. You kind of just have to call it intelligent dark rock and enjoy.

347) John Zorn's Calculus

John Zorn's Calculus is tonight's album. These are 2 long-form pieces for piano trio. If you aren't familiar with Zorn then you're in for 40+ minutes of complete ADD. If you're a little familiar with Zorn's work then you'll at least know that he's primarily concerned with the way that a piece unfolds. Everything is fair game, but he's controlling how long, what mood, who plays when, how it progresses from one state to another, what kind of stuff is happening in any particular window of the gigantic architectural facade. This time it's piano/bass/drums and they are longtime, well practiced Zorn collaborators.

Don't get hung up on technical stuff, just listen to how each instrument sounds in relation to the others and how they all work together to give the sense of musical action. I can't tell you what that action is because it's your own personal response that matters. How you hear it matters, and no one has words to actually explain it.

348) TMBG - Apollo 18 and John Henry

I was going to write about how TMBG's John Henry is a great album simply because it informs you that there is a famous Belgian painter named James Ensor. How cool is it that they can actually inspire you to pick up the googlemaphone and look up a turn of the century artist? Then I remembered we're having the idiotic statue fight again, and that's from Apollo 18. "The statue got me high" is pretty apropos. Maybe I can squash both of them into some sort of box (or possibly bag) of beef.

Believe it or not, the ridiculous string of short musical ideas called "Fingertips" from Apollo 18 is probably the first ever attempt at misusing the "shuffle" function on a cd player. Even more hilarious, they play the whole thing for their Tiny Desk concert (they do, go find it, it's awesome). TMBG are one of those bands that everyone is allowed to like. They are silly, they are thought provoking, and they have no interest in messing with anybody.

Flood, Apollo 18, and John Henry are their 3rd, 4th, and 5th, albums respectively. The Apollo 18 mission was aborted, so TMBG wrote an album called that and became the official musical ambassadors of NASA. That's true. Even weirder, fans were actually pissed off that they hired real musicians to back them up on tour instead of just drum machines and tape recordings.

Not to waste that opportunity, they thought "that reminds me of a man vs. machine story" and made their first album with an actual band. Heads up kids, using a trademarked brand name in the name of your song is not, I repeat, not free speech. That'll cost you money. You can sing it, but you can't print it on the cover or copyright the title. As John and John learned, they have to sue you, they are required to sue you or the trademark defaults to public domain. Yes, even if they don't particularly care about your specific song. "Why must I be sad?" Is constructed from Alice Cooper song titles.

Why is 1994's John Henry so goddamned long? Because vinyl and cassette tapes are gone. CDs have always been able to hold more than an hour of audio data and any space you don't actually use is waste. Part of the reason I like vinyl and cassette is that those media match my ability to sit in a chair. I'm a get up and move around/need an intermission kind of guy. 1995 is my preferred cut off, but the major labels knew the technology cliff was rapidly approaching, and they didn't want to buy flux capacitors to save the train (Back to the Future 3 reference, I'm scraping the bottom of the barrel today).

My point is, yeah, tear those statues down, and pay a modern-day sculptor to replace them with something more relevant. Oh, proper sculpture isn't a relevant art form in the Age of Goriranda? Whose fault is that, Jeff Koonz and your stupid balloon dogs and suspended train installations?

Yeah, that's enough to chew on, please enjoy some erudite sillyness on our country's own national holiday.

349) Chubby Checker's Limbo Party

I don't even know where to start on this one. Trinidadian funeral practice turned American party dance? Chubby Checker being typecast as a dance song singer? That lawsuit he had with Hewlett-Packard over a penis guesstimate app for WebOS? The truly confusing Quantum Leap episode where Scott Bakula taught Chubby Checker how to do the limbo?

I'm really only qualified to talk about one of those things. I agree, he's a great all-purpose Rock & Roll singer, and I can't tell you how much I wish they let him sing other stuff. He's great. He got his start from an exec who liked him. The story is, Dudeguy McWhatshisface sent Chubby Checker's first song (a classroom skit concept that gave him the chance to do impressions of famous singers) to his friends and clients as a Christmas card. The response was so overwhelmingly positive that they gave Chubby Checker a career measuring shoe sizes, no wait that was the WebOS app, I meant singing dance songs. You know The Twist. Well, Limbo Party was a certified hit, so they turned it into a full album. It's R&B/R&R meets Calypso. Musically, it's great. I was never good at limbo, so don't bet the fate of your eternal soul on my leaning backward at your funeral. Let's not be slightly out of tune is all I'm saying.

You can make up your own mind, but I think it's pretty funny that the album ends with his version of La Bamba. La Bamba is a traditional wedding dance, on a funeral album. It's couples skate, grab your Corpse Bride, and try not to break your coccyx when you fall down on the second level and accidentally send Aunt Gladys to hell.

350) Prism - See Forever Eyes

Hello, Prism. It's good to see you again. Last time you're song was used to wake up some astronauts. What you got this time? Whole lotta synth, apparently.

    This album was pretty much mediocred by everyone, but I don't really understand why. Maybe I'm not as discerning as some, but this sounds like good Canadian 70s hard rock. Some great guitar solos and occasional horn sections and synth noise everywhere, like nobody could find the mop. I mean if you're just completely over keyboards and "space sounds," and you don't like being reminded of Styx or Europe (not subtle either, like there's an 8-year statute of limitations on stealing Canadian rock riffs or something) then hate on it, I guess. I don't think it's too far fetched to wonder if the "Final Countdown" was nothing more than rewriting "Crime Wave."

    Crime Wave is a great song, but everybody's like "pfffft, filler, next." Man, I can't name 'em all in the short time span of writing these reviews, but everybody and their mom's dog stole their famous riffs and songs from this album. Maybe Prism was copying everybody else, but everything I have looked up is definitely AFTER '77/'78 when they were writing this album. Or, maybe it was just something in the water; from what I've read it seems like a lot of this stuff came from studio jams, so ripping off the obscure, awesome Canadian guys seems pretty plausible.

    "Test tube babies pay the price," there's the weirdness I remember from their first album, like they were just right at the edge of being a full on scifi band, but didn't actually know they were allowed to do that.

    Maybe you guys have a different perspective, but this isn't mediocre at all. I won't disagree that there's room for improvement lyrically, but this doesn't sound like underachieving to me. It's not quite prog, not quite glam; maybe that's why nobody cares much. I care. It's good. Go check it out.

351) The Organ Symphony

Let's listen to the theme from Babe (both in and out of the city), I mean the thing they play at the French Pavilion at Epcot, I mean that Fitzgerald/Keeley song, I mean the Organ Symphony, I mean the Symphony (avec Organ), I mean Camille Saint-Saëns' 3rd and last (or 5th if you count the 2 he threw in the trash can) symphonic work that's technically four movements squashed into two, and features 6 hands and 2 feet worth of keyboard shenanigans that everybody uses in some project they worked on at some point. It might be the most famous work from the Romantic period you might vaguely recall hearing somewhere, sometime. That's pretty high praise for the barren wasteland of music that happened between Beethoven's 5th and Strauss' Also Spracht Zarathustra in the minds of 20th century pop culture. Ugh, that lame old emotionally chromatic sap is so passé. Except John Williams. Total innovator, that guy. Give me the musical Xanax of Lorde or Billie Eilish any day, am I right? (Oh sarcasm, how I adore thee. I like Lorde and Eilish, but you have to admit they are $500 worth of amphetamines away from exciting).

Saint-Saëns dedicated it to his friend who happened to have the same name as Franz Liszt, because he was Franz Liszt, but he died. It's a very Lisztian piece that continually transforms and reuses its thematic material, in this case plainsong themes from liturgical masses, many also spracht by Liszt himself.

Sadly, I don't think Earl Grant ever did a recording of it, so I guess we'll have to settle for Ormandy and E. Power Biggs.

I don't want to spoil the classic cinema for you, but they don't turn the porcine shepherd turned Spuds McKenzie savior into breakfast, lunch, or dinner.

352) The Sleeping Beauty - Tchaikovsky's version

You can have Swan Lake, the 1812 Overture, and The Nutcracker, but let me have The Sleeping Beauty. It's my favorite Tchaikovsky ballet, musically speaking. It's a battle between good and evil leitmotifs, but eventually Tchaikovsky says "screw it, everybody gets a theme." Obviously, you don't get the full two-hour ballet on one record, just the condensed orchestral suite.

They wanted him to write it, and he was quite willing, but mentioned that nobody really cared about Swan Lake, so don't get your hopes up too high. He died before it got really popular. I actually have the full Swan Lake on vinyl, but that's not my favorite, so Ballet-centric Orchestra conducted by child prodigy turned youngest faculty member of the Curtis Institute, Joseph Levine. Not to be confused with the famous Russian pianist Josef Lhévinne who was much older and a classmate of Rachmaninoff and Scriabin.

Interesting American legal douchebaggery. Disney owns the trademark to "Princess Aurora," so you know they might take a vested interest in trying to steal any money you might make by performing a 140-year-old ballet. Makes total sense if you're a goon, I guess. Screw those dancers, musicians, and set designers, we've got a media empire to exploit. I'm sure the newly appointed dynamic duo of Chapek and Iger will do awesome things with the interest on last year's $11 billion. Trading today at $116/share, but a $175 + $1 minimum investment? No wonder everybody says "good god no, don't buy stock direct from Disney." In case you don't understand, you shouldn't be paying Disney for the convenience of giving Disney working capital on a depreciated investment.

Any serious broker will eat that dollar and sell tomorrow without you even needing to ask. That's like handing the donut guy a 5-er, saying keep the change, and forgetting to take your donut. Yeah, I mean why wouldn't they try to skim royalties off a 19th century ballet when they don't even have to instill confidence in the market to make a profit?

Where was I? Oh yeah, Leningrad Cowboys' version of Sweet Home Alabama is far superior to the original (like every song they cover), even though they are from Finland. They use official Russian Army choir the Alexandrov Ensemble for backup, and claim to be from a little Serbian town called Mexico.

No, that's not it. Something about Tchaikovsky, maybe? I dunno, I'm too far out there to try to ice skate back. We'll try again tomorrow, after I've had a good long nap.

353) The Best of Sam Cooke

Shhhhhh. The King of Soul is singing. We aren't going to go into any of the circumstances of his death, because Bertha Franklin very much did shoot and kill him, just like Claudine Longet. The sticking point in this case is that the question boiled down to whether or not she was afraid for her life, and there was no plausible evidence to the contrary, unreliable witnesses with questionable occupations and subsequently damning circumstantial evidence or no.

Ok, I like conspiracies as much as anyone, so my theory is that he was indeed flashing cash at the restaurant, and that Carr and Boyer had the typical hotel owner/call girl arrangement. Franklin didn't really know anything, and night shift motel work is pretty sketchy on the best day in the history of motels. I don't believe it was premeditated, so we just have to say yeah, I guess I believe she was scared shitless. She only shot him thrice (probably 'cause the first shot rendered her deaf and even more scared, unless it was a Derringer, Nelson Muntz assures me those bullets are powerful weak, even though they aren't) and the mop handle beating afterward is completely undocumented in terms of severity. I can't really fault her for leaving LA afterward either (nobody likes LA), so there we are. Not nice, but legally probably the appropriate judgement. That's just a theory, but she hasn't killed anybody since then, so again there we are.

Man, he really was an extraordinary singer, and as far as best of albums go this is exactly what they were designed to be. Great songs from across his entire short career, brought to you by Hugo and Luigi on behalf of RCA Victor. If I have any criticism, it's that creating your stage name by just adding an "e" at the end is pretty lazy and uncreative. Luckily, he's awesome, so that's completely irrelevant. I love the late 50s/early 60s, especially this crossover period of Cooke, Ray Charles, Clyde McPhatter, and Etta James. James Brown is the Godfather of Soul, but Cooke is King in my book.

354) Hendrix and Redding at Monterrey

And then you say "blah blah blah, of course Jimi Hendrix and Otis Redding are awesome, why are their appearances at the 1967 Monterrey Pop Festival so historic? Well, this is the first American performance by The Experience. They walk out, play 40 minutes of kick-ass rock, and then he introduces Wild Thing by telling the crowd he's about to do something crazy, does it, then lights his guitar on fire.

Otis Redding crossed over from his small but loyal audience to mainstream stardom, playing well past the agreed curfew, because the crowd rushed the stage and no one dared stop the magic. I bet you didn't know Otis Redding wrote "Respect." The best part about that song is that it takes on completely different meanings when Otis or Aretha sings it. 6 months later he died in a plane crash, so this is generally considered his high point.

Both sets are great, and the recording quality is just ludicrously good for a live festival recording. Like most everybody, I wish it were longer. Oh well, snag it if you come across a copy.

355) Sweeny Todd

Originally, I was thinking I would make this post 366 to complete the project (a full year of album reviews), but as Cartman so rightly pointed out, I do what I want!

Contrary to what I may have led you to believe, Sweeny Todd is my second favorite musical. My absolute favorite musical in the entire universe is Cannibal, The Musical, but I don't have it any more. I somehow managed to hang onto the weird Germano-Spanish erotic cinema I found at Barnes and Noble one day two lifetimes ago (Vampiros Lesbos, and She Killed in Ecstacy), but I think I let someone borrow the greatest thing Trey Parker and Matt Stone ever created, and I'll never see it again. Such is life.

Luckily, Soylent Green isn't the only thing made of people. The real question is, which is better; the original cast audio or the partial original-cast stage performance?

Now, I'm not gonna stand here and lie to you: any Angela Lansbury is great Angela Lansbury, she's amazing. Who doesn't like Angela Lansbury? Seriously, who? She's literally Angela Lansbury. Hating Angela Lansbury is like A) hating your own grandmother, and Bngela Lansbury) complaining that your sushi is undercooked.

What I don't like is that everybody cuts the "pulling teeth" and "god, deliver me" scenes. Pay them their extra 20 minutes at union scale! That's why we're in all of this mess to begin with, right? Wheeler and Sondheim didn't write those scenes because they were bored, they're important to the overall aesthetic arch. You know run time is about money, about not having to pay the actors and musicians any more money than absolutely necessary, right? Pay them already you greedy-bastard nickel-pinching Scrooge McDouchebags! You can depreciate a half-a-million dollar speaker system over three years, but you can't fork over an extra 3 grand to watch Judge Turpin ironically flagellate himself for two minutes? No wonder we're all eating cat or kangaroo or whatever non-cattle beef substitute McDonalds found in the Bornean Rainforest. There're 2,000 head of cattle 2 miles that way, I can go pet them before I pick which one's for dinner, but I can't afford to buy it and have it butchered because Papa John is worried about losing his Disneyland resort of a personal residence? So sorry for demanding a raise for lifting your new air conditioner into your pickup truck and two-wheeling your water heater warranty fraud to your door.

Sorry, that rant got a little out of control. The answer is I'd rather watch the actual stage performance, but Len Cariou is infinitely more better than George Hearn and I don't want to reboot into Windows just to enjoy a little Sondheim awesomeness. Original cast recording wins.

356) Fire From The Gods - American Sun

How can I relate to a world that I feel is broken? To the minds that I feel won't open? And how can I speak life when all I see is death?

I was gonna rag on the Grassroots, but then I heard "Right Now" by Fire From The Gods, and it's such a great song that I figured we should just listen to their album American Sun (like I did for Volbeat). That's what a radio single is supposed to do, and it happens so rarely these days that I feel like I should point it out.

I haven't listened to it yet, so here are some of my expectations. I get a variety of vibes from Right Now: Sevendust, early Faith No More, a twinge of Linkin Park-y Nu Metal, but also a kind of TV On the Radio feeling of new sincerity. I've been listening to David Foster Wallace interviews the last couple of days, so it's fresh in my mind. I don't think any of you are surprised that the lead singer is black. I've just listed all the musical nuances the single brings up in my mind, and the overriding sense is that this is a generic djent band who wanted powerful melodic vocals rather than growling or screaming. I don't know if you know this, but that's a continuous phenomenon in rock, that back and forth between "bringing back pretty singing" and "getting mad and yelling." That's what shapes the evolution of mainstream rock and metal.

Enough dilly-dally. As The Arm (aka the little man) in the Red Room says, kcoR s'teL.

1. Rap, not a surprise. This is the prelude to the album, so what are the themes? War, cannibalism, children speaking wisdom, personal responsibility, power structures being torn down. This all seems right up my alley.

2. Man what a great song. The more I listen to it the more I hear the best parts of a lot of early 2000s emo-ish bands like Chevelle and Breaking Benjamin and The Used. Musically, that is. Lyrically this is much better and not at all mopey or self centered.

3. It's not just the word "refugee," there was a hint of that Jamaican dub flavor on the first track. The one thing that doesn't work is that the soft chorus is too soft. The horns are great, but he just pulls back too far. Not a bad song, though.

4. It's rap djent. It's much more appealing to me than most rap metal, probably because it sounds authentic. By that I mean, this is what they want to play, and they're good at it. Their choruses are stellar, just banging emotional grooves and...

5. I'm not surprised there's a POD collab. Now, the Jamaican patois is really iffy territory (Snow, Shaggy, you know, iffy), but I'll reserve judgement until I actually look them up.

6. Meh. This is one of those tracks that will probably get better with repeat listening, but the initial impression is that it's just an intentional flip-flop back to the metal side of the equation.

7. It's fine, but we're halfway through the album and we've lost all momentum. We aren't developing the theme, just saying "I'm still fighting, I guess." We're just recycling the

first two tracks and I'm losing interest.

    8. I did feel it. I said so. Ok, do it. Break it down. Go ahead. Feel what?

    9. Trap? Really? Oh, you won already? 4 more tracks?

    10. What happened in Philly in 1985? Oh, police dropped a bomb from a helicopter on the communal house of MOVE and destroyed the surrounding 64 houses in the process. They fought to defend that in court for 20 years? Are you serious? 2005 is when the city finally lost all the lawsuits against them. We aren't going to go into any of it, but the City of Brotherly Love bombed its inhabitants for having smelly trash and radical political ideas. Either that's normal for 'merica, or that's really fucked up. You can't have it both ways, and you damned sure better not think the first one. Great song, but there's that patois again.

    Spoiler alert, they don't tie it all together in the last 3 tracks. Disappointing. Break the Cycle is a good epilogue, but we never got the actual guts of what the album wanted to be. It's 13 mostly good songs that merely identify and clarify an observation. Don't misunderstand me, it's an important point of view (the same one I've been working on every day for the last 5 years. But, we're already on the same page. You aren't giving me anything to work toward, and it ends up just being self affirming comfort music.

    Let's see if the intertubenetweb can at least tell me where your accent is from. Ok, parents from Jamaica, Bronx to West Africa back to the Bronx and finally Austin. That at least clears up the in and out accents.

    Just like I thought, it's a djent band of huge lineup changes that likes hip hop, and the overall attitude is: be truthful about this country again. Be accountable. I like that.

    I don't like this not actually an album stuff. That's not the band, it's a production problem. These guys are good, why can't they do something more than just write a bunch of potential radio anthems?

Sadly, that means it's not a good album. It's not fun to listen to, it has no arch or trajectory, it's just the same sentiment each time. I need more than that. Tell me what actual conflicts you have, give it some personal relevance. I know the question is "how" 'cause I led off with it. The implication was that you were going to at least try to answer it, but you didn't. Good stuff, it just goes in the "oh yeah, I remember those guys" folder. That's a shame.

357) Golden Grass

Do The Grassroots deserve a greatest hits album? More importantly, are The Grassroots even a band? I know that may seem like a weird question, but it's hard to distinguish the so-called band from every employee who had nothing better to do than show up to work at Dunhill Records in the 60s.

I mean, it's a producer/songwriter project, like Fever Tree, or the Monkees, or Steely Dan. Steve Barri and P.F Chang, sorry Sloan, aren't ever credited as part of the actual band (they play "various instruments"), it's just a revolving cast of touring musicians who didn't actually make the recordings you are hearing. Most of their records were actually played by the Wrecking Crew, and at some point, every Dunhill staffer got a songwriting credit.

More importantly, I've never heard any of these supposed hits on a radio anywhere, ever. I don't disbelieve that they had big hits and gold records, I just wonder how much the notion that it was a fake band played into their obvious loss to the oblivion of time. Quite a lot, I suspect.

Believe it or not, the weirdest thing in all of this is that it's freakin' awesome. I'd rather listen to this than The Byrds or the Turtles any day. I'd put them right up with The Association for pure enjoyment. Oooooooooohhh! Live For Today, that's their biggest hit. Yeah, they just graduated from freakin' to fucking awesome. Sing it with me: SHA LA LA LA LA LA LIVE FOR TODAY!

It sucks that they put that song at the end of Side B, in the crackly, nasty waste of vinyl near the center, but definitely go check them out. I'm glad I didn't write about it yesterday. I might have said crappy things about them.

358) Wasnatch - Front to Back

I don't have to be that guy, but since they are currently getting the full meme treatment, I think we should all give a little love to the Pioneers of the intense Utah Reggae scene.

359) Dionne Warwick - No Night So Long

I've always been intrigued by the notion that random crap that happened the year you were born is interesting. I told you I've been listening to David Foster Wallace talk about stuff, and he gave a graduation speech once where he said the real value of education is giving you the choice to break out of that self-centered view that existence is a tedious personal offense. It's practicing the ability to choose how you interpret a situation that leads to a meaningful life, and what you worship can have a profoundly negative impact if you're not careful. What would be the opposite?

Dionne Warwick's 1980 album, No Night So Long. Pretty impossible to pretend that isn't a dead animal coat, isn't it? I don't have any moral queeziness about fur, or leather, or feathers, or eating animals; it's mass production and consumerism I find deplorable. Statues don't do it for Dionne, falling in love gets her high. I mentioned she got her start as a replacement Shirelle, didn't I? The coat is from her closet (and the jewelery), she made sure they printed that info on the actual jacket like it's important.

I don't care about the Psychic Friends Network, or that she was Whitney Houston's cousin, or even that she's the Miller Light of Adult Contemporary R&B. She's good at it. I'm rarely in the mood to overlook how much it blows, but if you're going to put on some garbage early 80s sequined glamour love drivel, Dionne Warwick isn't even close to the worst thing you could pick, by miles.

No, what bugs me isn't Dionne Warwick at all. It's her wardrobe lady, Suzy Creamcheese. Yeah, Leslie Fearon straight up said I'm going to make Zappa's imaginary groupie my actual brand name, then did, and probably made more money picking out ugly dresses for celebrities than Zappa did. Puke.

Granted, I was like 4 months old when this thing came out, but by the time I was able to form coherent thoughts in the middle of the decade I found it very confusing that this stuff was considered romantic. Sade and En Vogue sound sexy, this just sounds like shoulder pads and the smell of baby powder. Still, it's better than Patti Labelle, or Anita Baker, or Stephanie Mills, or Shirley Murdock. That's personal preference, feel free to completely disagree. Sure, I'd rather listen to Aretha Franklin, or Tina Turner, or Sade, but you're asking a lot when you limit it to the first half of 1980. Diana Ross and Donna Summer were pretty much her only competition. Not a lot of black female singers releasing major label albums in the post-disco wilderness of mainstream pop for the first few years of the decade.

There, see, I said both nice and terrible things about it, and the best part is it's all honest. I don't have to love or hate it, it's really not hard to enjoy once you accept that it's coming from a shallow and materialistic perspective.

360) Otto Klemperer and the Philharmonia Orchestra - Mozart 40/41

I don't feel like trying today. Let's listen to Klemperer conduct Mozart's 40 and 41. It's hard to complain too much about Mozart's two best symphonies on one record, but the first movement of 40 is just slightly too slow. Articulation is obviously improved, but it's uncomfortable. Other than tempo, the playing, blend, and dynamic contours are really top notch. And it's just that first movement, the rest is great. Overall, quite a lovely recording of Mozart's last two symphonies.

361) Peter Frankl plays Debussy

I have 4 more albums to complete this project. Did I intentionally plan it out to end on Sunday? No. Is it going to end with a Paul? Yes. Do I know what I'm actually going to write? No. Did I pick them because the composers share their first names with the Beatles? Yes, of course I did. I've taken the liberty of substituting Claude for Richard (Ringo's real name), but only because I had already decided I wanted to listen to Debussy's solo piano music before I came up with the theme for these last essays. Calgon, I mean Peter Frankl, take me away....

Debussy did not consider himself an Impressionist composer. Rather, if he had the word, he would have called himself a Symbolist. Symbolism is a moderately complicated philosophical orientation, but to quote Mallarmé, it is "to depict not the thing but the effect it produces." He was not particularly interested in being serious, and he and Satie got along quite well. He wasn't particularly well regarded for focusing on silly new compositional ideas instead of playing serious piano, or writing serious music, or even really being an upright pillar of any particular community. He did whatever he wanted to do, and said sorry, not sorry a lot. He was a kid during the Franco-Prussian War, got pretty famous at 40 with his decidedly Symbolist opera Palléas et Mélisande, and died at 55 in the middle of WW I.

Really, the gist is that he thought experimenting with the musical ideas of the rest of the world was pretty interesting, and told everyone else to like it or leave him alone. 155 minutes of dreamy solo piano music, here we come. Enjoy it, 'cause tomorrow is gonna be a gruesome nightmare by comparison.

362) Kronos Quartet - Black Angels

You know how much I like coincidence. Well, it just so happens that I took the liberty of writing tonight's album review yesterday. I knew what it was going to be and what I wanted to say, so it's ready to paste here after I tell you that I came home to the coolest surprise ever. Sam sent me The Science of Discworld II and my favorite musical of all time! The book was mine, the DVD was his. Now, I don't actually believe that Karma is real, but I do think it's a handy little scorecard, so I have to retaliate, I mean reciprocate, in a comparable fashion. In the meantime, please enjoy tonight's trip into the tragedies of human history while I grill some hamburgers and watch the creators of South Park and friends be ridiculous...

It's easy to rag on Kronos Quartet. As far as chamber ensembles go, they are annoyingly omnipresent celebrities. They've done some really cool things, such as The Juliet Letters with Elvis Costello (no, that's the Brodsky Quartetet, dumbass), but like I've already mentioned you can get tired of their versions of stuff real quick. They are the Leonardo DiCaprio of string quartets.

Speaking of Inception, Kronos Quartet exists because David Harrington heard George Crumb's Black Angels and decided forming a string quartet to play radical Avant Garde stuff like that was his purpose in life. 10 albums later they finally recorded it.

I made an album called Album of Death, but it's a joke compared to this monstrosity of all the darkest terror humans can create for each other (it's a joke in its own right because all the pieces are those tacky euphamisms we like to use, but that's beside the point). What else should go on an album whose title track is a direct artistic statement about the then currently happening Vietnam don't call it a War, built around the numerological structures of 7 and 13?

The answer, of course, is other random pieces about war. Tallis's Spem In Allum is based on a text from the story of Judith beheading Holofernes during Nebuchadnezzar's siege of Bethulia. Marta used two songs from field recordings he made in an unincorporated village in Romania, whose inhabitants were subsequently rounded up and their village destroyed to supposedly build a power plant (like speed, ethnomusicology kills). They actually sent a letter to him saying never come back to Romania, thanks. Not surprisingly, the two songs are about death and war.

Ives wrote "They are There" about WWI in 1917, coincidentally the year before Debussy died. Then in 1942 we decided to do the sequel, so he changed a few lyrics and republished it. Yes, that's actually Ives singing with the quartet overdubbed to match.

And just when you thought it was safe to come out of the water in your itsy bitsy teeny weeny yellow polka dot bikini (it's 1960 after all) Shostokovich writes the Purple People Eater (1958) of string quartets and dedicates it to the victims of fascism and war. Don't believe me that Shostokovich's 8th and Itsy...Bikini were created within a month or two of each other? Go look it up. My question is, which one actually took conceptually longer to write? If it took Vance and Pockriss longer than 12 minutes, then I'd say Shosti's 3 days is the clear winner by comparison. His symphonies were tombstones, and the 8th String Quartet is for everyone who vanished without a trace under both Hitler and Stalin. It's by far my favorite string quartet of all time, followed pretty closely by the quartets of Irwin Schulhoff and Silvestre Revueltas.

Honesty time, I've heard about 7,000 performances of Shostokovich's 8th quartet, but my favorite by miles was from a random youtube video by some high school students. Kronos is somewhere in the top 200.

My point is that this is a heavy album. Like, Crowbar heavy. We start with calling UH-1 Hueys "electric insects" and we end up at the testimony of a man who lived in personal fear of Stalin disappearing him if he didn't "Happy Happy Joy Joy" the everloving crap out of everything (yay Ren and Stimpy, boo despotism). Volkov's book is about as authentic as Schindler's writings about Beethoven, but you learn really early on that biographies and memoires are more about how their subject and author wanted to be perceived rather than what they actually said or really felt. Remember, less about the thing, more about the effect it produces. This album gives me tingly nightmare goosebumps. I'm not entirely sure whether it was Mr. Dumb or Mr. Dumber who said "I like it a lot."

363) John Adams - The Chairman Dances

Who's the most maximal minimalist in the tiny universe of Pulitzer Prize winning composers who didn't like serialism? John Adams. He asks the question, what do you do after minimalism? I wanted to use the pun post-malonimalism, but it's too awkward to do it properly (and that's how you insert an unusable pun).

To answer that question, you obviously have to define minimalism and take it to its logical end. If the minimum requirement for a piece of music is a single process that logically unfolds and returns to its original state, then when you remove the process itself you are left with simply pulse. That pulse can be rapid or infinitely long, but the pulse is all that remains this side of nothingness (what are the chances we step across that line tomorrow?).

Adams assembles his music from little kernels of musical thought; highly repetitive gestures that wriggle and mutate and accumulate to form larger structures. Critics often call him the most interestingly boring composer of all time, and I of course disagree. His music is boringly interesting and there's a world of difference when you turn those two words around. Reich, Reilly, and Glass are to my mind the musical equivalent of conceptual art. Adams though, really takes Cage to heart: anything can be the foundation of a musical work, it simply requires making it. That's a much better perspective than the Inception of an idea which is pointlessly banal to actually implement. What conceptual art (in the broadest sense) lacks is the structural recognition of its own apparent stupidity. We call that delusion.

His own word for his music is "architectonic." Ooh, I like that word. Structural conglomerations that move and rub and crash against each other; a larger process without discernable teleology. That, to me, is the essence of life. His pieces are alive. You must slow down and let the fast machine perform its own internal ritual.

I watched Nixon in China in the library at OU a long time ago. Something about a ping-pong tounament. Adams frequently includes saxophones and synthesizers in his orchestras. I think his works should be performed more, but I imagine the cost of doing so is astronomically ridiculous.

I guess what I'm trying to say is that the sky is blue, and all the leaves are green. My heart's as full as a baked potato. I think I know precisely what I mean when I say it's a shpedoinkle day. Enjoy.

364) Paul Giger - Schattenwelt

How do I end this project? Well, in some ways it will never end. The idea was to pick up an album and interact with it; connect it to real life, try to figure out why it exists, what value it might have right now, what story it might tell.

A lot has happened since last September, but the overwhelming ethos is negative and horrible. As far as public discourse goes, we've reached the entitlement stage. By that I mean, everyone is turning to blame and shame in a desperate attempt to "return to normal." Surely by now you know that I think that's a ridiculously childish mentality.

By complete coincidence, I read a book called The Ethical Assassin by David Liss yesterday. It's a good book because the core sentiment is that we are inescapably ideological creatures. The hard to accept truth is that this country, and the American ethos in general is mean, lazy, and extremely unethical. The climax of the book is the realization that our society has a place for thieves and rapists and murderers, but it does not have a place for the sick, the timid, the marginalized, or the revolutionary. So, it takes any challenging idea and criminalizes it. We live in the all-encompassing spirit of Punishment, and we foolishly pretend that it is a natural and obvious way to live.

What have my themes been over this last most of a year? War, death, absurdity, unethical corporate logic, lawsuits, finding good in the atrocious, being skeptical of assumed excellence, and the exploitation and hobbification of life itself.

My dad was alive on Sunday, and died on Monday. That became a part of these essays without my even noticing. Vietnam, WWII, and Desert Storm were happening inside the minds of all this music and we've been publicly recycling all those troubled ideas for the last few months. All of the things you point to as great advancements and marvels of modern life were built and are still built under the mentality that slavery and class hierarchy are justifiable, and that it's acceptable to hide them from our vision and say "how dare you not appreciate all these marvelous toys!?" All these systems are failing, not because their product is without some value, but because the real cost of maintaining them is the freedom to live and the freedom to die. One cannot truly understand one without first accepting the other.

So, let us for 1 day step across that threshold into the shadow world with perhaps the most obscure album in my entire collection, Schattenwelt by Paul Giger.

Giger is a Swiss Avant Garde violinist. Quite amusingly, Schattenwelt is his 3rd album (you may or may not realize that I am the 3rd and last Paul Tompkins with no middle name. Built of extremes, tee hee). You won't find this album on youtube, and I seriously doubt that I could squeeze it past youtube's slapdash "make the problem of copyright disappear" deal with the major labels and performing rights unions, but you can go find lots of things from Giger's catalogue and get a sense of how out there it is.

The core of the album is the Seven Scenes from Labyrinthos, with two separate pieces as bookends. I think of this as less an album of music and more an exploration of the essence of what it means to play the violin. It is extreme. It lives in the shadows at the edge of existence, it is utterly beautiful in its unashamedly alien nature, and I can't think of a better way to end this Year in the Life of Bottle the Curmudgeon. So, until we meet again (there are no goodbyes, only pulses in the stream of existence), cheers and enjoy.

Epitaph, I mean Epilogue

Like Lucy, I've got some 'splaining to do. I'd like to thank the following people for their support, comments, and encouragement. I'm perfectly happy to vomit words out into the ether, but it's always nice to know that people find some value in it. So, in no particular order, my thanks and love to Steven Stark, Sam Mauer, Chris Isch, Kris Karr, James Hirschberg, Jason Reynolds, Brenda Sutterfield, Sarah Clark, Jana Evans, Rocky Kanaga, Sue Mauer, Andrea Maxwell, Patrick Balm, John Johnson, Tim Verville, and my mom Cherie Tompkins.

Lastly, this book is actually dedicated to two people: Paul Tompkins, my dad, whose record collection accounts for the bulk of the music in this book, and Frank Mauer, who I choose to think of as my bonus dad. Though they no longer walk with us on this adventure, their spirit (at least in my little peep hole to the universe) moves through all things. So, I make a toast to the heroes in our heads. Cheers.

For those die-hard fans of real-life chronology, my rag tag team of imaginary minions and I are finishing up the final editing during the second impeachment trial of Trump. May we all survive to hold it in our hands as a thing that now exists in the real world, and possibly even its sequels…

So sayeth Bottle, 02/10/2021

Artists Being Reviewed (with special mention of Marty Paitch)

3rd Bass, 280
5th Dimension, 11, 51
A Perfect Circle, 421
Aerosmith, 356
Aesop Rock, 362
Alexander Brailowsky, 349
Alice In Chains, 278
Alkaline Trio, 281
Andre Kostelanetz, 105
Andrew Lloyd Webber, 122
Anita Kerr, 370
Anthony Newley, 88
Arlo Guthrie, 89
Art Garfunkel, 25
Average White Band, 45
Bad Company, 191
Bad Religion, 364, 365
Baja Marimba Band, 336
Bangels, 278
Barbara Mandrell, 91
Barbra Streisand, 93, 151, 298
Beacon Street Union, 12
Beegees, 367
Bill Rieflin, 242
Billy Joel, 29, 177
Billy Vaughn, 148
Bjork, 109
Black Oak, 235
Blood, Sweat & Tears, 9, 59
Blue Mink, 283
Bob Dylan, 20, 337
Brian Auger, 13, 99
Brother Eye, 212
Brown Bird, 112
Buddy Miles, 25
Burl Ives, 157, 337
Burt Bacharach, 345
Bush, 194
Butterfield Blues Band, 32
C.P.E. Bach, 327
Cage The Elephant, 205
Camille Saint-Saëns, 426
Canned Heat, 9
Caroliner, 213
Carpenters, 135, 303
Cheap Trick, 198
Cher, 58
Chicago, 33, 136
Chopin, 349
Chubby Checker, 424
Classics IV, 49
Claudine, 120
Cream, 80, 81
Creedence Clearwater Revival, 19
Crosby, Stills, Nash, & Young, 42
Curt Cobain, 245
Cyndi Lauper, 239
Dan Vapid and the Cheats, 404

Dave Grusin, 156
David Bowie, 243, 244, 257
Dead Hot Workshop, 112
Death Cab for Cutie, 309
Debussy, 237, 437
Dionne Warwick, 55, 435
Don Ho, 324
Don Janse, 110
Donna Summer, 47, 239
E. Power Biggs, 427
Earl Grant, 346
Eddie Kendricks, 47
Edward Bland, 350
Emerson, Lake, & Palmer, 4, 83, 173
Emmylou Harris, 183
Eric Burdon, 46
Feliciano, 354, 355
Ferrante & Teicher, 297
Fever Tree, 5
Finger eleven, 146
Fire From The Gods, 431
Focus, 70
Fred Waring, 104
George Harrison, 24, 172
George Szell, 237
Gin Blossoms, 113, 310
Glass Ox, 48
Go Gos, 278
Godsmack, 160
Grassroots, 434
Green Day, 276, 285
Grimes, 323
Grofé, 115
Guess Who, 27
Guns N' Roses, 86
Hair, 14
Hapshash and the Colored Coat, 64
Harry Nilsson, 29
Head East, 375
Helmet, 308
Herbie Mann, 326
Herman's Hermits, 123
Iron Butterfly, 15, 87, 111, 116
Jack Jones, 152
Jan DeGaetanni, 347
Jeannie C. Riley, 65
Jefferson Airplane, 60, 95
Jefferson Starship, 15
Jimi Hendrix, 429
Jimmy Hendrix, 25
Joe Cocker, 46, 341
Joe Walsh, 301
John Adams, 440
John Mayall, 8, 196
John Zorn, 422
Joni Mitchell, 6
Judas Priest, 179, 180
Julian Lloyd Weber, 348
Julie Driscoll, 13
Julie Tippets, 99
Kansas, 220
Katon de Pena, 219
KMFDM, 354
Korn, 296
Kronos Quartet, 35, 438
K-tel, 343
Laura Nyro, 28
Less Than Jake, 369
Lighthouse, 13
Linda Ronstadt, 241
Live, 3, 77, 119
Lord Sutch, 32

Lords of Acid, 162
Machines of Loving Grace, 145
Mancini, 339
Manos Hadjidakis, 418
Mantovani, 339
Marianne Faithfull, 282
Marilyn Manson, 307
Marty Paich, 40, 93, 94, 149, 153, 190, 191, 331
Mastodon, 131
Maureen McGovern, 54
Maurice Larcange, 121
MC5, 328, 329
Meat Puppets, 18, 228
Megadeth, 360, 409, 414
Melanie, 67, 153
Men At Work, 11
Metallica, 79
Michael Brown, 22
Michael Jackson, 20
Ministry, 242
Modest Mouse, 229
Moody Blues, 142
Moon Hooch, 142
Mothers of Invention, 13, 52, 137, 332
My Chemical Romance, 61
My Life With The Thrill Kill Kult, 134
Neil Peart, 144
Neil Young, 41
Neutral Milk Hotel, 202, 210
Nine Inch Nails, 232
Nino Rota, 376
Nirvana, 157
Noonish Moon, 200

Oak Ridge Boys, 94, 98
Offspring, 267
Otis Redding, 429
Otto Klemperer, 437
Ozzy Osbourne, 176
Paul Giger, 442
Paul McCartney, 22, 38, 132, 138, 141, 294
Paul Simon, 25
Pearl Jam, 272
Peter Frankl, 437
Pharoah Sanders, 7, 114, 156
Phillip White Hawk, 326
Pink Floyd, 302, 305, 379, 384, 397
Plastic Ono Band, 3
Poe, 403
Point Blank, 225
Portishead, 149
Primus, 45, 283
Prism, 211, 212, 425
Procol Harum, 4
Psychic of Orange, 118
Queen, 185
R.E.M, 180
Rammstein, 102
Ramones, 208
Rare Earth, 71
Rascals, 170
Ravi Shankar, 36
Refreshments, 113, 379, 386
REO Speedwagon, 84
Republica, 321
Richard Strauss, 419
Robert Maxwell, 405
Rod McKuen, 330, 370

Roland Shaw, 375
Rolling Stones, 33, 168, 251
Rotary Connection, 14, 89
Rush, 144, 188
Sagittarius, 82
Sam Cooke, 428
Sandpipers, 335, 336
Santana, 48
Scritti Politti, 406
Seals & Crofts, 17, 68
Seether, 274, 277
Shirelles, 174
Shostakovich, 122
Simon & Garfunkel, 24, 117
Simon the Magpie, 43
Soak, 44
Social Distortion, 307
Solex, 222
Sonny Bono, 75, 333
Spirit, 3, 38, 39
SPK, 163
Stan Getz, 155
Starlight Mints, 264, 374
Steppenwolf, 6, 49, 99, 130, 236
Steve Miller Band, 37
Steven Stark, 25, 234, 295, 444
Stone Temple Pilots, 104, 270
Sublime, 314
Supertramp, 18, 23
Supremes, 29, 154
Syd Barrett, 305
System Of A Down, 358
Tchaikovsky, 427
Ten Years After, 55
The 4 Seasons, 72
The Band, 19
The Beatles, 10, 96, 100, 105, 107, 109, 141, 155
The Believers, 353
The Black Dahlia Murder, 276
The Bob Seger System, 30
The Boomtown Rats, 163, 165
The Cars, 194, 293
The Doors, 27, 201
The Flaming Lips, 203
The Incredible String Band, 35
The Kingston Trio, 90
The Moody Blues, 17
The Royal Guardsmen, 150
The Strokes, 143
The Wonder Years, 226
They Might Be Giants, 313
Thomas Dolby, 129, 166
Three Dog Night, 77, 187
Throbbing Gristle, 126
Tilt, 218
TMBG, 423
Tom Petty, 206
Tony Mattola, 125
Tool, 372, 422
Toto, 189, 199
Uriah Heep, 69
Van Halen, 95, 185
Vanilla Fudge, 16
Ventures, 321
Violent Femmes, 182
Volbeat, 208
Wasnatch, 435

Weezer, 268
Whitney Houston, 238, 239
Willy Nelson, 178
Woodhawk, 54
Zager & Evans, 68
ZZ Top, 127

www.ingramcontent.com/pod-product-compliance
Lightning Source LLC
Chambersburg PA
CBHW031228290426
44109CB00012B/200